Communications in Computer and Information Science 543

Commenced Publication in 2007
Founding and Former Series Editors:
Alfredo Cuzzocrea, Dominik Ślęzak, and Xiaokang Yang

Editorial Board

W0193239

More information about this series at http://www.springer.com/series/7899

Rory V. O'Connor · Mariye Umay Akkaya
Kerem Kemaneci · Murat Yilmaz
Alexander Poth · Richard Messnarz (Eds.)

Systems, Software and Services Process Improvement

22nd European Conference, EuroSPI 2015
Ankara, Turkey, September 30 – October 2, 2015
Proceedings

 Springer

Editors
Rory V. O'Connor
Dublin City University
Dublin 9
Ireland

Murat Yilmaz
Çankaya University
Ankara
Turkey

Mariye Umay Akkaya
Turkish Standards Institution
Ankara
Turkey

Alexander Poth
Volkswagen AG
Wolfsburg
Germany

Kerem Kemaneci
Turkish Standards Institution
Ankara
Turkey

Richard Messnarz
I.S.C.N. GesmbH
Graz
Austria

ISSN 1865-0929   ISSN 1865-0937   (electronic)
Communications in Computer and Information Science
ISBN 978-3-319-24646-8   ISBN 978-3-319-24647-5   (eBook)
DOI 10.1007/978-3-319-24647-5

Library of Congress Control Number: 2015949440

Springer Cham Heidelberg New York Dordrecht London

Printed on acid-free paper

Springer International Publishing AG Switzerland is part of Springer Science+Business Media
(www.springer.com)

Preface

This textbook comprises the proceedings of the 22nd EuroSPI Conference, held from September 30 to October 2, 2015, in Ankara, Turkey.

Since EuroSPI 2010, we have extended the scope of the conference from software process improvement to systems, software, and service-based process improvement. EMIRAcle is the institution for research in manufacturing and innovation, which came out as a result of the largest network of excellence for innovation in manufacturing in Europe. EMIRAcle key representatives joined the EuroSPI community, and papers as well as case studies for process improvement on systems and product level will be included in future.

Since 2008, EuroSPI partners packaged SPI knowledge in job role training and established a European certification association (www.ecqa.org) to transport this knowledge Europe-wide using standardized certification and examination processes.

Conferences were held in Dublin (Ireland) in 1994, in Vienna (Austria) in 1995, in Budapest (Hungary) in 1997, in Gothenburg (Sweden) in 1998, in Pori (Finland) in 1999, in Copenhagen (Denmark) in 2000, in Limerick (Ireland) in 2001, in Nuremberg (Germany) in 2002, in Graz (Austria) in 2003, in Trondheim (Norway) in 2004, in Budapest (Hungary) in 2005, in Joensuu (Finland) in 2006, in Potsdam (Germany) in 2007, in Dublin (Ireland) in 2008, in Alcala (Spain) in 2009, in Grenoble (France) in 2010, in Roskilde (Denmark) in 2011, in Vienna (Austria) in 2012, in Dundalk (Ireland) in 2013, and in Luxembourg in 2014.

EuroSPI is an initiative with the following major action lines http://www.eurospi.net:

- Establishing an annual EuroSPI conference supported by software process improvement networks from different EU countries.
- Establishing an Internet-based knowledge library, newsletters, and a set of proceedings and recommended books.
- Establishing an effective team of national representatives (from each EU country) growing step by step into more countries of Europe.
- Establishing a European Qualification Framework for a pool of professions related to SPI and management. This is supported by European certificates and examination systems.

EuroSPI has established a newsletter series (newsletter.eurospi.net), the SPI Manifesto (SPI = Systems, Software, and Services Process Improvement), an experience library (library.eurospi.net) that is continuously extended over the years and is made available to all attendees, and a Europe-wide certification for qualifications in the SPI area (www.ecqa.org, European Certification and Qualification Association).

A typical characterization of EuroSPI is reflected in a statement made by a company: "… the biggest value of EuroSPI lies in its function as a European knowledge and experience exchange mechanism for SPI and innovation."

Since its initiation in 1994 in Dublin, the EuroSPI initiative has outlined that there is not a single silver bullet with which to solve SPI issues, but that you need to understand a combination of different SPI methods and approaches to achieve concrete benefits. Therefore, each proceedings volume covers a variety of different topics, and at the conference we discuss potential synergies and the combined use of such methods and approaches. These proceedings contain selected research papers under seven headings:

- Section I: SPI-Themed Case Studies
- Section II: SPI Approaches in Safety-Critical Domains
- Section III: SPI in Social and Organizational Issues
- Section IV: Software Process Improvement Best Practices
- Section V: Models and Optimization Approaches in SPI
- Section VI: SPI and Process Assessment
- Section VII: Selected Keynotes and Workshop Papers

Section I presents three SPI case study papers with the Osborne O'Hagan case study of Game Software Development Processes, while the second paper from Saarelainen and Jantti concentrates on the Incident Investigation Process, and finally in the third paper Ruiz et al. discuss cross-domain assurance projects.

Section II presents three papers under the umbrella topic of "SPI Approaches in Safety-Critical Domains." Firstly, Sporer examines Lean approaches in an automotive context. Macher et al. discuss the integration of tools to an automotive context. The final paper of this section by Ruiz et al. describes an avionics perspective on assurance cases.

Section III explores the theme of "SPI in Social and Organizational Issues." In the first of three papers, Yilmaz et al. present a study on personality profiling of software developers. Mayer et al. continue this theme by exploring governance, risk management, and compliance. In the final paper, Clarke and O'Connor investigate the challenge that situational context poses to software developers.

Section IV presents three papers dealing with associated issues surrounding the topic of "SPI Best Practices." In the first paper, Gasca-Hurtado et al. focus on design techniques for implementing software development best practices. In the second paper, Herranz et al. examine the relationship between gamification and SPI. In the final paper, Munoz et al. attempt to provide a starting point for SMEs in implementing SPI.

Section V discusses issues surrounding "Models and Optimization Approaches in SPI." In the first paper Natschlager et al. look at resource utilization in processes, while Picard et al. in the second paper present the TIPA approach for ITIL processes assessment. Finally, Karaffy and Balla examine data mining to support SPI approaches.

Section VI discusses issues surrounding "SPI and Process Assessment." In the first paper Mesquida et al. look at ISO/IEC 15504 (SPICE) and project management. In the second paper Ribaud and O'Connor present blended approaches for SPI assessment. Finally, in the third paper Varkoi and Nevalainen discuss safety and systems engineering process assessment.

Section VII presents selected keynotes from EuroSPI workshops concerning the future of SPI. From 2010 on EuroSPI invites recognized key researchers to publish on new future directions of SPI. These key messages are discussed in interactive workshops and help create SPI communities based on new topics.

In 2015, ECQA (www.ecqa.org) and EuroSPI created a vision of innovation in Europe discussing four key questions: (1) How to create a VISION and a dynamic network, (2) How to create a GLOBAL Community of TRUST, (3) How to be prepared for constant change and be able to (UN)LEARN, and (4) How to provide TRANSPARENCY of rules and business. The idea is create a space where SPI researchers and industry can network and grow. G. Sauberer, Aliyou Mana Hamadou, Jolanta Maj, and Valery Senichev present 10 key criteria to support global innovation and networking. Tomislav Rozman, Anca Draghici, and Andreas Riel present core competencies needed to include leading sustainability concepts in business management processes (EU project LEADSUS). János Ivanyos, Éva Sándor-Kriszt, and Richard Messnarz describe a capability and competency model to increase business capability, transparency, and trust in Europe and world-wide. Christian Reimann, Elena Vitkauskaite, Thiemo Kastel, and Michael Reiner describe how in a university network young people learn to work in networked projects and get prepared for a future networked innovative project environment.

Social Aspects of SPI: A workshop on conflicts, games, gamification, and other social approaches is organized in conjunction with the EuroAsiaSPI^2 conference, which provides an opportunity for academic and industry practitioners to discuss application of games, gamification, and social approaches in the field of SPI. The goal of this workshop is to provide a complete coverage of the areas outlined and to bring together researchers from academia and industry as well as practitioners to share ideas, challenges, and solutions that are related to SPI. The workshop covers topics such as the practical and industrial implications of games and game-like approaches especially for improving the software development process. In this section Jovanovic et al. present a set of games that are designed to improve the agile software development and management processes. Ribaud and Saliou investigate the relationship between personality types and competencies of information and communication technology professionals. Kosa and Yilmaz review the literature for digital and non-digital games that aim to improve the software development process, and highlight the pros and cons of such approaches. Since 2010, EuroSPI has been organizing functional safety-related workshops. In the workshop, different best practices and model-based design patterns to implement functional safety are exchanged. Masao Ito describes an approach to model the driver inside the functional safety flow and to analyze the controllability of the situation by the driver. Matthieu Aubron describes a practical experience from a leading automotive manufacturer of bikes who created a model-based framework to analyze hazards and safety goals and derive functional safety requirements.

October 2015

Rory V. O'Connor
Mariye Umay Akkaya
Kerem Kemaneci
Murat Yilmaz
Alexander Poth
Richard Messnarz

Recommended Further Reading

In [1], the proceedings of three EuroSPI conferences were integrated into one book, which was edited by 30 experts in Europe. The proceedings of EuroSPI 2005 to 2013 inclusive have been published by Springer in [2], [3], [4], [5], [6] [7] [8] [9] and [10], respectively.

References

1. Messnarz, R., Tully, C. (eds.): Better Software Practice for Business Benefit – Principles and Experience, 409 p. IEEE Computer Society Press, Los Alamitos (1999)
2. Richardson, I., Abrahamsson, P., Messnarz, R. (eds.): Software Process Improvement. LNCS, vol. 3792, p. 213. Springer, Heidelberg (2005)
3. Richardson, I., Runeson, P., Messnarz, R. (eds.): Software Process Improvement. LNCS, vol. 4257, pp. 11–13. Springer, Heidelberg (2006)
4. Abrahamsson, P., Baddoo, N., Margaria, T., Messnarz, R. (eds.): Software Process Improvement. LNCS, vol. 4764, pp. 1–6. Springer, Heidelberg (2007)
5. O'Connor, R.V., Baddoo, N., Smolander, K., Messnarz, R. (eds): Software Process Improvement. CCIS, vol. 16, Springer, Heidelberg (2008)
6. O'Connor, R.V., Baddoo, N., Gallego, C., Rejas Muslera, R., Smolander, K., Messnarz, R. (eds): Software Process Improvement. CCIS, vol. 42, Springer, Heidelberg (2009)
7. Riel, A., O'Connor, R.V., Tichkiewitch, S., Messnarz, R. (eds): Software, System, and Service Process Improvement. CCIS, vol. 99, Springer, Heidelberg (2010)
8. O'Connor, R., Pries-Heje, J., Messnarz, R.: Systems, Software and Services Process Improvement. CCIS, vol. 172. Springer, Heidelberg (2011)
9. Winkler, D., O'Connor, R.V., Messnarz, R. (eds.): Systems, Software and Services Process Improvement. CCIS, vol. 301. Springer, Heidelberg (2012)
10. McCaffery, F., O'Connor, R.V., Messnarz, R. (eds.): Systems, Software and Services Process Improvement. CCIS, vol. 364. Springer, Heidelberg (2013)
11. Barafort, B., O'Connor, R.V., Messnarz, R. (eds.): Systems, Software and Services Process Improvement. CCIS, vol. 425. Springer, Heidelberg (2014)

Organization

Board Members

EuroSPI Board Members represent centers or networks of SPI excellence having extensive experience with SPI. The board members collaborate with different European SPINS (Software Process Improvement Networks). The following six organizations have been members of the conference board for the last 13 years:

- ASQ, http://www.asq.org
- ASQF, http://www.asqf.de
- DELTA, http://www.delta.dk
- ISCN, http://www.iscn.com
- SINTEF, http://www.sintef.no
- STTF, http://www.sttf.fi

EuroSPI Scientific Program Committee

EuroSPI established an international committee of selected well-known experts in SPI who are willing to be mentioned in the program and to review a set of papers each year. The list below represents the Research Program Committee members. EuroSPI also has a separate Industrial Program Committee responsible for the industry/experience contributions.

Alberto Sillitti	Free University of Bolzano, Italy
Alok Mishra	Atilim University, Turkey
Anca Draghici	Universitatea Politehnica din Timisoara, Romania
Andreas Riel	Grenoble Institute of Technology, France
Antonia Mas Pichaco	Universitat de les Illes Balears, Spain
Antonio De Amescua	Carlos III University of Madrid, Spain
Bee Bee Chua	University of Technology Sydney, Australia
Christian Kreiner	Graz University of Technology, Austria
Christiane Gresse von Wangenheim	Federal University of Santa Catarina, Brazil
Dietmar Winkler	Vienna University of Technology, Austria
Fergal McCaffery	Dundalk Institute of Technology, Ireland
Jan Pries-Heje	Roskilde University, Denmark
Javier Gar'ca-Guzman	Carlos III University of Madrid, Spain
Jose Antonio Calvo-Manzano	Universidad Politecnica de Madrid, Spain
Keith Phalp	Bournemouth University, UK
Kerstin Siakas	Alexander Technological Educational Institute of Thessaloniki, Greece
Luigi Buglione	Engineering Ingegneria Informatica, Italy

Marion Lepmets	Dundalk Institute of Technology, Ireland
Markku Oivo	University of Oulu, Finland
Michael Reiner	IMC Fachhochschule Krems, Austria
Murat Yilmaz	Çankaya University, Turkey
Patricia McQuaid	CalPoly, USA
Paul Clarke	Dundalk Institute of Technology, Ireland
Paula Ventura Martins	FCT-University of Algarve, Portugal
Ricardo Colomo Palacios	Ostfold University College, Norway
Rory V. O'Connor	Dublin City University, Ireland
Taz Daughtrey	James Madison University
Timo Makinen	Tampere University of Technology, Finland
Timo Varkoi	Tampere University of Technology, Finland
Torgeir Dingsoyr	SINTEF ICT, Norway

General Chair

Richard Messnarz

Scientific Co-chairs

Rory V. O'Connor
Murat Yilmaz
Alexander Poth

Organization Co-chairs

Mariye Umay Akkaya
Kerem Kemaneci

Acknowledgments

Some contributions published in this book have been funded with support from the European Commission. European projects (supporting ECQA and EuroSPI) contributed to this Springer book including I2E (Idea to Enterprise), AQUA (Knowledge Alliance for Training Quality and Excellence in Automotive), LEADSUS (Leading Sustainability), and LSSH (Lean Six Sigma for Health Care).

In this case the publications reflect the views only of the author(s), and the Commission cannot be held responsible for any use which may be made of the information contained therein.

Education and Culture DG
Lifelong Learning Programme

Contents

Software Process Improvement Best Practices

Models and Optimization Approaches in SPI

SPI and Process Assessment

Selected Key Notes and Workshop Papers

Creating Environments Supporting Innovation and Improvement

Social Aspects of SPI: Conflicts, Games, Gamification and Other Social Approaches

Risk Management and Functional Safety Management

SPI Themed Case Studies

Towards an Understanding of Game Software Development Processes: A Case Study

Ann Osborne O'Hagan[1] and Rory V. O'Connor[2(✉)]

[1] Dundalk Institute of Technology, Dundalk, Ireland
ann.osborneohagan@dkit.ie
[2] Dublin City University, Dublin, Ireland
roconnor@computing.dcu.ie

Abstract. This paper aims to fill the gap that exists about software development processes in game development in the research literature, and address the gap in the research literature by investigating and reporting information about the software development processes used in game development. To investigate the role of the software development process in relation to the game development process, and to better understand the processes and practices used in game software development, a single industrial based case study was undertaken and reported to investigate in a real world context the software development processes and practices used in game development. This research contributes to our knowledge of the field of game development and potentially forms the foundation for further research in the area.

Keywords: Game development · Software process · Software Process Improvement (SPI)

1 Introduction

Creating computer games is a complicated task that involves the expertise of many skilled professionals from many disciplines including computer science, art and media design and business. Mcshaffry et al. [1] state that game software development differs from classical software development in many aspects. Games are products that have much more limited life cycle than conventional software products. According to [2] games are usually developed in a shorter timescale and all phases of the life cycle need to be minimised. The main maintenance activity for most computer games is corrective such as bug fixing as the average lifespan is 6 months before a new version of a game is released. As successful games may lead to one or more sequels this could involve some perfective maintenance based on user feedback. The pressure on game development companies to get a product to market as quickly as possible means that there are often schedule over runs and poor time estimation is a problem. For these reasons game project management differs significantly from traditional software project management.

The games development process remains relatively unchanged from inception to consumption despite the fluidity of the industry. The main activities are

© Springer International Publishing Switzerland 2015
R.V. O'Connor et al. (Eds.): EuroSPI 2015, CCIS 543, pp. 3–16, 2015.
DOI: 10.1007/978-3-319-24647-5_1

development/production, publishing / commercialisation, distribution and customer engagement. The publishing role is constantly increasing and changing as the market is getting increasingly more crowded. Traditional distribution is increasingly being bypassed by developers and publishers and there are many intermediates that act as virtual shop windows for online and mobile games. The role of customer engagement is moving beyond that of technical support and involves assisting users with game play and strategy. The Development/production activity is at the core of the game industry, all other activities emanate from this. The game development process will be explored further.

There are various challenges in the game development process. A survey of actual problems in computer games development from analysing post-mortems by [3] affirms that both the traditional software industry and games industry have mainly management problems rather than technology problems, some examples are:

- An important problem specific to the game industry is the communication among the team members. In the electronic games industry, a multidisciplinary team includes people with distinct roles, such as artists, musicians, scriptwriters and software engineers. This mix of roles although being positive in terms of having a more creative work environment, causes a division, dividing it in to "the artists" and "the programmers". This division can be a source for communication problems;
- Within the game development process the game requirements elaboration is complex, subjective elements such as "fun" do not have sufficient/efficient techniques for its determination. It is necessary to extend the traditional techniques of requirement engineering to support the creative process of the electronic game development. A method currently used is to create an early prototype of the game and start people playing it. This helps establish the fun gameplay and once there is a prototype in place there can be an evolutionary approach to development [4]. To develop great games means that you have to design the software to accommodate nearly constant change;
- Transitioning from design to development where there are many defined and undefined requirements can be problematic; it can be hard to project manage unstable and volatile requirements. There can be legacy problems from the pre-production stage. A lot of the game play elements may not have been established and these can cause a much bigger workload in production. It is vital that there is constant user feedback so that the fun elements of the game are developed and that features that are not used or are not delivering user satisfaction are removed or changed.

The subjective nature of game development and the tendency for problems to be related to managerial challenges is making the software development process used in game development worthy of consideration.

1.1   Software Development Processes in Game Development

The over-arching phases of game development according to [5] are preproduction, production, and testing (often referred to in the literature as post production).

Preproduction involves the conception of a game, and the construction of a Game Design Document (GDD). By the end of preproduction, the game design document GDD should be finished and will be updated during other phases. In the preproduction phase the game designers and developers do some game prototyping in order to establish the fun or innovative element of a game. This influences the next phase of production as actions in preproduction determine requirements and affect the production phase. Production is where the majority of assets are created, which includes software code. This is a challenging time in the life cycle of the game as a poorly managed production phase results in delays, missed milestones, errors, and defects. In the production phase, the developers can create prototypes, iterations and/or increments of the game. These changes in prototypes or iterations of the game can cause drastic changes to the GDD, with poorly managed changes causing widespread problems affecting functionality, scheduling, resources, and more. The testing phase is usually the last phase and involves stressing the game under play conditions. The testers, not only look for defects, but push the game to the limits for example the number of players could be set to the maximum and can be labelled stress testing (or load testing). These phases are more complicated than the overview given.

Current game development literature suggests that the traditional software development model, exemplified by the Waterfall Model that requires explicit requirement assessment followed by orderly and precise problem solving procedures is inadequate for the innovative and creative process of the videogame industry [6]. Agile development methodologies are less focused on documenting the pre-production phase and more focused on quickly getting a workable version of the game, by using iterative design and dynamic problem solving techniques that are facilitated through frequent and co located meetings. This goes some way towards easing the transition from pre-production to production. Shell [7] describes an iterative process that he calls looping, which essentially consists of an iterative cycle of design and test. Agile development methods are increasingly becoming the industry norm and according to [21] more agile practices should be incorporated into game development.

From an examination of the literature, most of the works relating to game software development focus on the design phase and design challenges, and on the problems associated with transitioning from preproduction to production. This is reiterated in [7] who state that the game development process literature mostly has design and design problems as a primary concern, as opposed to production and the issues that relate to production. A case study on a game development company reports on the organisational enablers for agile adoption [8]. Successful agile adoption requires project stakeholders to have common project objectives, employees having the ability to make decisions at relevant levels of abstraction, effective project management and a supportive learning environment.

The focus of this research is on the software development processes in game development and as such it would be beneficial to explore the SDLC used in the development phase of the game development process. The SDLC does not include all elements needed to create a game; it basically describes the steps and iterations needed to develop software. Overall there is a lack of published studies relating to the software development processes/methodologies used in game development and this gives supporting evidence for the proposition about the lack of research in the literature on the software development processes/methodologies used in game development.

In this research it was found that there is a lack of categorisation in the literature relating to game development processes and to lay a foundation it would be helpful to categorise and systematically analyse the literature in relation to game development processes in a scientific way. It is proposed that a Systematic Literature Review (SLR) would be a suitable method to do this and would also help establish a gap in the literature relating to the use of agile methods in the game development process.

A Systematic Literature Review of the software processes used in game development was conducted [9] where a total of 404 papers were analyzed as part of the review and the various process models that are used in industry and academia/research are presented. Software Process Improvement initiatives for game development are dis cussed. The factors that promote or deter the adoption of process models, and implementing SPI in practice are highlighted. Our findings indicate that there is no single model that serves as a best practice process model for game development and it is a matter of deciding which model is best suited for a particular game. Agile models such as Scrum and XP are suited to the knowledge intensive domain of game development where innovation and speed to market are vital. Hybrid approaches such as reuse can also be suitable for game development where the risk of the upfront investment in terms of time and cost is mitigated with a game that has stable requirements and a longer lifespan.

Given the above a set of four research questions were formulated as follows:

- What software processes are game development companies using and how are these software processes established?
- What phases/steps are involved in the software processes used in game development?
- How do the software processes, that game development companies are using, change and what causes these software processes to change?
- How do the operational and contextual factors, present in game development companies, influence the content of software processes?

2   Case Study Research Approach

It is proposed to conduct a single industrial case study using grounded theory data coding methods [10] to help with data analysis to develop theory about game development processes and to capture the best practices of a game development company.

An interview guide was developed as an instrument to help guide the interviewer in gathering specific data during an interview session, and to help the researcher collect data in a consistent and predefined manner. The interview guide included closed and open-ended questions and some related notes about ranges and samples of possible information appropriate to the research. Closed questions looked for specific information and open ended questions allowed scope for the participant to add contextual information that may be of importance to the research. The sample responses were included to help guide the interviewer and act as examples should they be required, these examples also helped keep the interviewer on the right track due to the fact that some of the terminology could have more than one meaning and therefore there could be misinterpretation.

The data analysis methods based on grounded theory coding were selected for use in this study as they were deemed to be more robust and traceable than qualitative data analysis and more explicit and systematic than content analysis. Coding can be described as the key process in grounded theory [11] and the three coding techniques proposed by Grounded Theory methodology are: open coding; axial coding; and selective coding[12]. The 4 main stages used in applying the grounded theory method that helped with data analysis are described:

- **Open Coding** - This involved identifying categories, properties, and dimensions.
- **Axial Coding** - This involved examining conditions, strategies, and consequences.
- **Selective Coding** - This involved coding around an emerging storyline.
- **The Conditional Matrix** – This involved reporting the resulting framework as a narrative framework or as a set of propositions.

The researcher investigated various tools which are used for data management in qualitative research and selected Atlas Ti [13] a tool designed specifically for using with grounded theory. This tool enabled the researcher to: store and keep track of interview scripts; to code and, manage codes and related memos; to generate families of related codes; and to create graphical representation for codes, concepts and categories. Atlas TI provided support for axial and selective coding used in this study. Overall Atlas TI supported data storage, analysis and reporting.

2.1   Case Study Company

The game development company was chosen based on the fact that it was in close proximity to the researcher and is representative of a typical case for game software development in a small start-up company which is representative of many indigenous Irish game companies. The researcher proactively studied the game development project during the production/implementation phase of development. The case study research was initiated in June 2014 and was executed over a three month period.

The game development company was founded in September 2012 with the goal of developing a Massively Multi-Player Online (MMO) game for the seven to twelve year old demographic with an educational aspect. The company is developing games for the mobile and online platforms. The company can be described as a VSE with an official employee count of 5. At the time of the case study the company had no games published and can be described as a start-up company. That company had one game development project in the production phase that had commenced in September 2013

2.2   Data Collection

Data collection involved the use of semi-structured interviews. To support the semi-structured interviewing process the researcher developed an interview guide with a formal question set. The interview guide contained 24 questions and these were divided into the following 7 sections: (i) General company and job description (ii) Process Establishment [14] (iii) How the process works [15] (iv) Software Process Improvement [16] (v) Project Success factors [17] (vi) Operational and contextual Factors [18] that affect the process [19] (vii) Ending. The use of an interview guided allowed the researcher collect data in a consistent and unbiased fashion. The questions were based on the researcher's prior knowledge and were proof read by someone external to the case study that had an expertise in software process. When conducting interviews it is desirable to have different viewpoints that can be analysed and compared and that are complimentary to each other. The researcher proposed to have two viewpoints: managers; and developers. Therefore interviews were conducted on company employees from both management and development roles in the game development company and as such allowed a complimentary analysis based on both viewpoints. The subject sampling strategy was to interview all employees currently employed at the game development company. The animator who was a member of the software development team was not available at the time of the study. Each participant was given an information sheet describing the research project and was asked to sign a consent form regarding the recording of the interview. All participants attended the interview voluntarily and data collected was treated in strict confidence. The three interviewees were from various roles within the game development company: (i) The general manager, (ii) a member of the development team and (iii) a senior technical member of the company.

The interviews varied between 20 minutes and 60 minute duration. The reason for the variation in the interview times was that the CEO who was the first interview only wanted to partake in the first section of the interview. This interviewee maintained that she had no knowledge of process and did not want to answer the remaining questions. The CEO had valuable information pertaining to the general company and was the main access to the company for carrying out further interviews. Some notes were taken by the researcher during the interviews. All interviews were audio recorded for later transcription and analysis. A session summary sheet was completed after each interview. This described who was involved, the issues covered, their relevance to the research questions, and any implications for subsequent data collection.

Data collection and analysis were conducted concurrently. Each interview was transcribed by the researcher. The transcribed files and any additional collected data were stored in the qualitative analysis tool Atlas Ti.

2.3 Data Analysis

The grounded theory coding analysis method was used to inductively generate theory about game development processes. The researcher used Glaser's[20] non-linear method of theory generation as guidance for the data analysis as illustrated in figure 1.

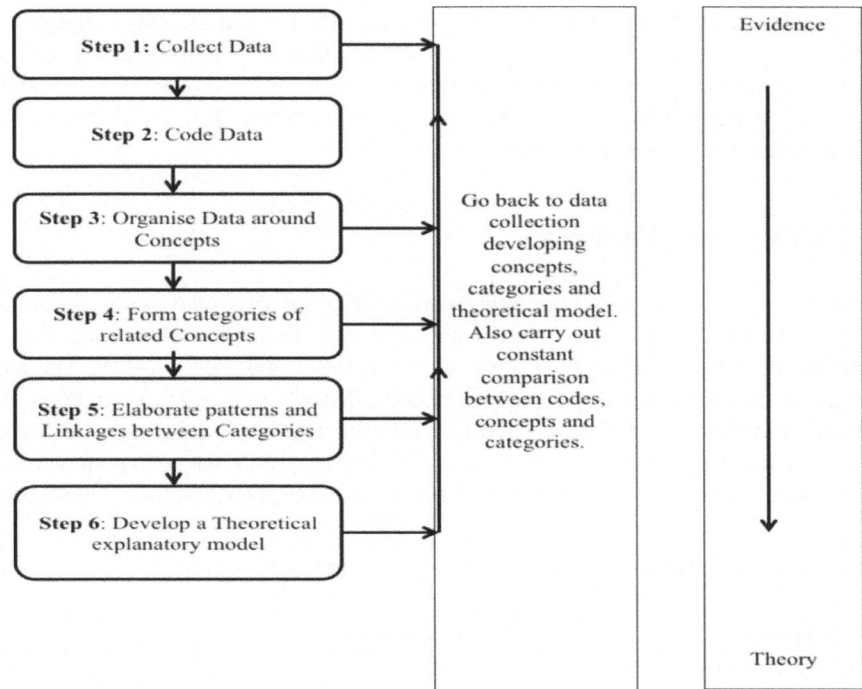

Fig. 1. Grounded Theory Data Analysis Steps

All interviews were recorded and transcribed, and the analysis was conducted with rigour using open coding, axial coding and selective coding techniques. The open coding technique: involved the following 2 steps: Step 1- The researcher assigned codes to various quotes in the transcript to classify or categorise it. A code can represent a certain theme. One code can be assigned to many quotes, and onequote can be assigned to more than one code. Codes can contain sub-codes. There was an initial code approach using gerunds and in vitro coding approaches. Each statement of interest in the transcribed material was coded and the next step (step 2) involved sorting the codes into categories based on how the codes are related and linked. The emerging categories were used to organise and group the initial codes into meaningful clusters. This involved breaking the interview data into discrete parts based on similarities and differences; the researcher went through the material to identify any phrases that are similar in different parts of the material, patterns in the data or variances of any kind. These code categories were then used in subsequent data collection. The open codes that were conceptually similar were grouped into more abstract categories based on their ability to explain the sub units of analysis.

The researchers analysed the three interviews and during this iterative process a small set of generalizations were formulated. Diagrams in the form of flow charts were produced to help focus what was emerging from the data and network charts of codes were generated to help link concepts to categories. The transcripts were re-read and re-coded in a different order to see if any new themes emerged and when no new themes emerged this suggested that the major themes had been identified. From the data collected, the key points were marked with a series of 220 codes, which were extracted from the text. The codes were grouped into similar concepts in order to make the data more workable, this grouping was facilitated using Atlas Ti. From these concepts, 25 categories were formed, which were the basis for the creation of a theory.

3   Case Study Findings

The theory is based on two conceptual themes, *Process of Game Development* and Game Software Development Process, and four core theoretical categories, *Project Management*, *Contextual Factors*, *Operational Factors* and *End Product*. The axial coding role identified the categories into which the discovered codes and concepts could be placed and selective coding was used to explain the relationships between the categories to provide the overall theoretical picture. The objective of selective coding was to identify a key category or theme that could be used as the fulcrum of the study results.

Table 1. Themes, Core Category and Main Categories

Theme	Main Categories
Process of Game Development	Company Profile Market Sector Business Drivers Company Formation
Game Software Development Process	As-is Process Drivers for Change Process improvement Process problems Process Strength Ideal process
Project management	Planning / Prioritise Tools
Contextual Factors	Team Size/Experience/Motivation Subjectivity Technology/Resources
Operational Factors	Up-capturing the intention Create the Right Working Environment Injection of Confidence Adequate Resources Capacity to Get a Good Review Vendor Requirements
End Product	Re-Use End-User Schedule Revenue

In this research, the analysis showed that there was one central category to support and link the two theoretical themes. The final list of themes, the core categories and the main categories identified by the study are shown in Table 1. Each category and code can be linked to quotations within the interviews and these are used to provide support and rich explanation for the results. The saturated categories and the various relationships were then combined to form the theoretical framework.

3.1   The Theoretical Framework

The emergent grounded theory was summarised in terms of themes, core categories and main categories. This summary is shown as a network diagram in Figure 2 which identifies the relationships between the major themes, core category, linked categories, and associated attributes. Within the theoretical framework, each node is linked by a precedence operator with the node attached to the arrowhead denoting the successor. All of the relational types within the framework are precedence and the network is read from left to right.

The root node of the framework, *Process of Game Development*, is a conceptual theme and is a predecessor of its four categories, *Company Profile, Market Sector, Company Formation* and *Business Drivers*.

The *Business Drivers* and the *Role and Experience of Employees* contribute to the *Process Origin* used as the basis for the company's software development activity and the *Process Model in use*. The *Role and Experience of the Employees* coupled with the *Background of Founder* of the company creates an associated *Management Style* and this, in conjunction with the adapted process model, creates the company's initial *As-is Software Development Process*.

The *Game Software Development Process* can be described as follows. The *Drivers for Change* to the *As-is Software Development Process* can *lead to Process Improvement*. *Process Improvement* along with *Process Problems* and *Process Strengths* can contribute to creating an *Ideal Process*. The *As-is Software Development Process* is influenced by *Project Management, Contextual Factors, Operational Factors* and *End Product* requirements.

End Product is affected by an *Ideal Process* and *Project Management*. *End Product* can itself then impact the organisation's ability to *Reuse*, meet *End Users* needs, provide *Revenue* and the ability to deliver a product on *Schedule*.

Project Management impacts the organisations ability *for Planning/Prioritise* what gets done and *Tool* usage.

Contextual Factors affecting the as-is game software development process include *Team Size/Motivation/Experience*, the *Subjective* nature of games and is impacted by the *Technology/Resources* available.

Operational Factors affecting the as-is game software development process include '*Up Capturing*' the *Intention Correctly, Creating the Right Working Environment*, having an *Injection of Confidence*, having *Adequate Resources*, having the *Capacity to get a Review* and meeting *Vendor Requirements*.

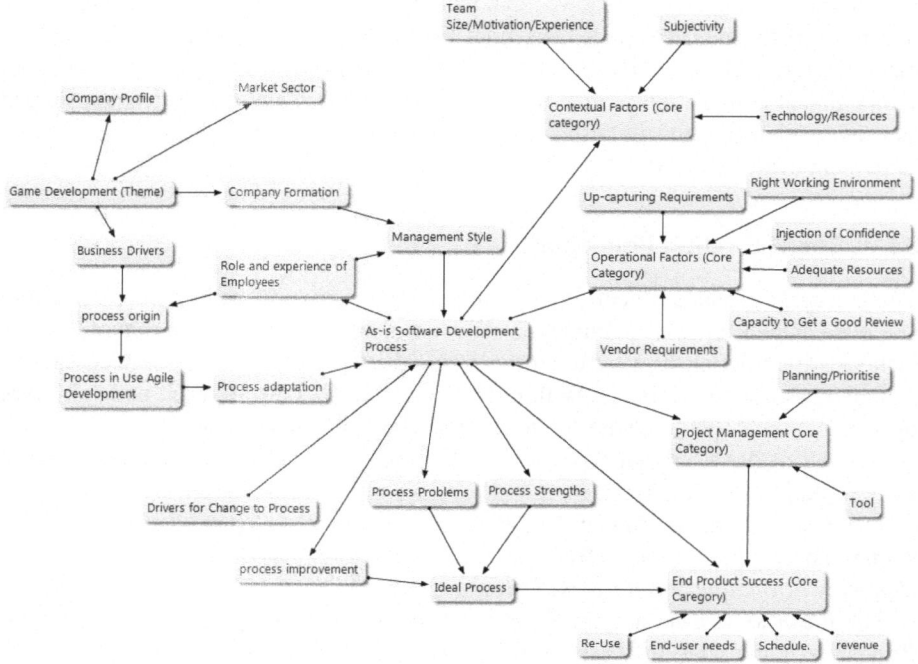

Fig. 2. Theoretical Framework

In creating the theoretical framework, several of the Atlas TI features were utilised. The Code Family option allows codes, created from both the open and axial coding phases to be grouped together under a family heading, for example, *End Product*. This facility allowed the various interviews to be searched for passages where references to codes, which were classified as members of the *End Product* family, had been raised by the practitioners. Another feature of Atlas TI that was used in developing the framework was the Code Frequency Table. This option shows how often codes occurred within a particular interview, and across the entire suite of interviews, thus providing support for developing the more widespread categories. In addition to employing the code family and frequency table aids, Atlas's query tool also provided major assistance with data analysis. The query tool contains Boolean and proximity operators which test for the co-occurrence of codes in the data. For example, a Boolean query can search for occurrences of Code A and/or Code B, whilst proximity can test the distance between, or closeness of, code occurrences in the text. An example of a proximity query included examining the distance between developer references to end user and a subsequent reference to a code in the *End Product* category.

4   Discussion

The focus of this research was on the software development processes in game development. Based on the proposed gap in the literature identified in this paper, the aims of this research was to explore the gap that exists about software development processes in game development in the research literature, and address the gap in the research literature by investigating and reporting information about the software development processes used in game development; and to Investigate the role of the software development process in relation to the game development process, and to better understand the processes and practices used in game software development. A set of four research questions were formulated. These research questions are revisited below and an analysis of the findings is reported.

Research Question 1 relates to identifying the software processes used by the game development company and finding out how the software processes was established. The software process in use is agile development using the Scrum methodology. The process in use has been established from the previous work experience of the CEO, CTO and the Developer. The previous experience of the CEO in managing previous companies led to a management style (umbrella) that in conjunction with the previous software development experience of the CTO and the Developer in Agile Development using the Scrum methodology contributed to process establishment. In this instance the CEO had little technology experience and was relying on the software development team for expertise in process for game software development. This could indicate that it is not a pre requisite for the CEO of a game development company to have technical expertise.

Research Question 2 relates to identifying the phases/steps that are involved in the software processes used in game development. It is interesting to note that the CTO describes all phases/steps of the game development process. He does not see a distinction between the game development process and the software processes used in game software development. The CTO has more experience of game development and is more aware of all that is involved in a full game development process. The developer is only aware of the current and preceding phase of game development. By contrast to the CTO perspective the game software development process as described by the developer is a subset of the game development process and is described as a design/development phase. The developer is describing the as-is software development process that is the design/development phase. There is a difference in the process described by both the CTO and Developer and the reason why is because the company is a start up game development company and the process is not fully enacted or established. It could be that the ideal game software development process involves a hybrid of process described by both the CTO and Developer and could consist of a design, develop and test steps within a development phase.

Research Question 3 relates to how the software process that the game development company is using change and to identify what causes the software process to change. There were variations between the CTO and the Developer as to how the software process changed. The CTO was aware of changes to do with tools such as the software repository tool: The software repository system was left at times because it was unreliable and was done in an alternative fashion. The Developer was aware of changes to some of the steps in the software development process such as: the Sprint cycle time was reduced from 2 weeks to 1 week. The Developer is best positioned to describe the actual software development process because he is the one doing the development work. The CTO carries overall responsibility for security in terms of version control, backup and security codes. Some of the above changes to the process caused an improvement to the process. An example of this was introducing the tool Illustrator to the process. This helped speed up the process. Any tool that helps speed up the process in terms of creating graphics is very worthwhile in game software development. The process in game software development is inextricably linked to satisfying the needs of end-users.

Research Question 4 relates to how the Contextual and Operational factors, present in game development companies influence the content of software processes. Contextual Factors cited by both the CTO and the Developer related to team attributes and resources. While these are common to both traditional and game software development there are variations in emphasis. The subjective nature of the game software development process alluded to by the CTO is critical in game software development. The following contextual factors can influence the game software development process: The team size affects the volume of work than can get done. A small, co-located team allows for a fluid process where creativity can flow and eliminates the need for a change management process. The small team size means that the workers need to be flexible and may need to share roles and tasks. The game is a moving target at all times and can require that the workers are highly enthusiastic and well motivated, also there needs to be a clear vision about the goal being undertaken. Some of the roles within the team are part time which means that workers must have the discipline and motivation to work on their own without too much overseeing. Often there is a lack of experience which means there is a very high learning curve. There can be a lot of experimentation needed and ideally the majority of this will have been worked out prior to the development phase. Games are played for pleasure, emotional challenge and not for functional reasons. The appeal of a game is an emotional contract formulated between the designer, developer and the end-user. The best way to counterbalance the deeply subjective nature of games is to engage with end-users as much as possible during the software development process. It is possible here to see what appeals to the end-user and cut out the functions that are not used or not appealing to the end-users.

4.1   Future Work

This research potentially forms the foundation for further research and as a follow on to the research the researcher would like to outline three areas with potential for future research: Firstly a multiple case study to investigate game software development processes would be of benefit. An advantage of a multiple case study would be its increased scope for replication and generalisation. This research made certain propositions and a multiple case study could build on these propositions and makes the results more generalisable.

Second, this research showed various gaps in research relating specifically to the game software development process. There is no 'best practice model for game software development'. A best practice model for game software development could be beneficial for the games industry and as such could reduce development time which could reduce time to market; it could also help improve the quality of game software. This is a gap here for this research to be done. Such a best practice model could be based on existing standards, such as ISO/IEC 29110 [22] if the were accepted [23] by organizations.

Finally there is no easy method to capture the likes and dislikes of computer game end-users. A tool that could easily capture these requirements of these end-users could greatly improve the game software development process. It was shown during this study that the interaction with the end-user is of paramount importance, but a tool to do this could effectively save time and money in terms of creating art assets.

References

1. McShaffery, M.: Game Coding Complete. Paraglyph Press (2005)
2. Ampatzoglou, A., Stamelos, I.: Software engineering research for computer games: A systematic review. Information and Software Technology **52**, 888–901 (2010)
3. Petrillo, B., Pimenta, M., Trindade, F., Dietrich, C.: Houston, we have a problem: a survey of actual problems in computer games development. In: Proceedings of the 2008 ACM Symposium on Applied Computing. ACM, Fortaleza (2008)
4. Shull, F.: Managing Montezuma: Handling All the Usual Challenges of Software Development, and Making It Fun: An Interview with Ed Beach. IEEE Software **28**, 4–7 (2011)
5. Kanode, C.M., Haddad, H.M.: Software Engineering Challenges in Game Development. In: Sixth International Conference on Information Technology: New Generations, ITNG 2009, April 27–29, pp. 260–265 (2009)
6. Winget, M.A., Sampson, W.W.: Game development documentation and institutional collection development policy. In: Proceedings of the 11th Annual International ACM/IEEE Joint Conference on Digital libraries. ACM, Ottawa (2011)
7. Schell, J.: The art of game design – A book of lenses. Morgan Kaufman Publishers, Burlington (2008)
8. Srinivasan, J., Lundqvist, K.: Organizational enablers for agile adoption: learning from GameDevCo. In: Abrahamsson, P., Marchesi, M., Maurer, F. (eds.) Agile Processes in Software Engineering and Extreme Programming. LNBIP, vol. 31, pp. 63–72. Springer, Heidelberg (2009)
9. Osborne O'Hagan, A., Coleman, G., O'Connor, R.V.: Software development processes for games: a systematic literature review. In: Barafort, B., O'Connor, R.V., Poth, A., Messnarz, R. (eds.) EuroSPI 2014. CCIS, vol. 425, pp. 182–193. Springer, Heidelberg (2014)
10. O'Connor, R.: Using grounded theory coding mechanisms to analyze case study and focus group data in the context of software process research. In: Mora, M., Gelman, O., Steenkamp, A., Raisinghani, M. (eds.) Research Methodologies, Innovations and Philosophies in Software Systems Engineering and Information Systems, Chapter 13. IGI Global, pp. 1627–1645 (2012)
11. Strauss, A., Corbin, J.: Basics of qualitative research: Grounded theory procedures and techniques. Sage, Newbury Park (1990)
12. Coleman, G., O'Connor, R.: Using grounded theory to understand software process improvement: A study of Irish software product companies. Journal of Information and Software Technology **49**(6), 531–694 (2007)
13. Coleman, G., O'Connor, R.: Investigating software process in practice: A grounded theory perspective. Journal of Systems and Software **81**, 772–784 (2008)

14. Coleman, G., O'Connor, R.: An Investigation into Software Development Process Formation in Software Start-ups. Journal of Enterprise Information Management **21**(6), 633–648 (2008)
15. O'Connor, R.V., Coleman, G.: An investigation of barriers to the adoption of software process best practice models. In: Proceedings of the ACIS 2007, p. 35 (2007)
16. Clarke, P., O'Connor, R.V.: An empirical examination of the extent of software process improvement in software SMEs. Journal of Software: Evolution and Process **25**(9), 981–998 (2013)
17. Clarke, P., O'Connor, R.V.: Business success in software SMEs: recommendations for future SPI studies. In: Winkler, D., O'Connor, R.V., Messnarz, R. (eds.) EuroSPI 2012. CCIS, vol. 301, pp. 1–12. Springer, Heidelberg (2012)
18. Clarke, P., O'Connor, R.V.: The situational factors that affect the software development process: Towards a comprehensive reference framework. Journal of Information and Software Technology **54**, 433–447 (2012)
19. Jeners, S., Clarke, P., O'Connor, R.V., Buglione, L., Lepmets, M.: Harmonizing software development processes with software development settings – a systematic approach. In: McCaffery, F., O'Connor, R.V., Messnarz, R. (eds.) EuroSPI 2013. CCIS, vol. 364, pp. 167–178. Springer, Heidelberg (2013)
20. Glaser, B.G.: Theoretical Sensitivity: Advances in the Methodology of Grounded Theory, Mill Valley. Sociology Press, CA (1978)
21. Petrillo, F., Pimenta, M.: Is agility out there?: agile practices in game development. In: Proceedings of the 28th ACM International Conference on Design of Communication. ACM, Brazil (2010)
22. Mora, M., Gelman, O., O'Connor, R., Alvarez, F., Macias-Luevano, J.: An overview of models and standards of processes in the SE, SwE, and IS Disciplines. In: Cater-Steel, A. (ed.) Information technology governance and service management: Frameworks and adaptations, pp. 371–387. IGI Global, Hershey (2009)
23. Sanchez-Gordon, M.-L., O'Connor, R.V., Colomo-Palacios, R.: Evaluating VSEs viewpoint and sentiment towards the ISO/IEC 29110 standard: a two country grounded theory study. In: Rout, T., O'Connor, R.V., Dorling, A. (eds.) SPICE 2015. CCIS, vol. 526, pp. 114–127. Springer, Heidelberg (2015)

A Case Study on Improvement
of Incident Investigation Process

Kari Saarelainen[1(⊠)] and Marko Jäntti[2]

[1] KPMG Finland, IT Advisory, Helsinki, Finland
kari.saarelainen@kpmg.fi
[2] School of Computing, University of Eastern Finland, Kuopio, Finland
marko.jantti@uef.fi

Abstract. IT service trending of root causes of service incidents and problems is an important part of proactive problem management and service improvement. This exploratory case study focuses on exploring human errors as root causes in IT service incidents. In the case study, we applied Human Factors Analysis and Classification System (HFACS) analyzing 65 incidents to related IT services, like servers, network, storage, and applications.

Based on the analysis, several improvement suggestions were identified in IT service management processes of case organizations, including improvements in incident investigation process, coupling incident investigation to continual service improvement, and need for an HFACS taxonomy adapted to IT service management (ITSM), which helps in identifying trends in incidents.

Keywords: ISO 20000 · ITIL · Incident management · Continual service improvement · Human error · HFACS

1 Introduction

Accidents, incidents, near hits, near misses, production breaks and reductions of services quality are all from the operator's point of view different levels of unplanned and unwanted events. In this research, the term incident covers all of these aforementioned terms. Incident management and problem management are key processes (category Resolution processes) in the service management system defined in the ISO/IEC 20000:1 standard [1].

While incident management aims at processing service-related incidents and restoring the service for customers and users to the normal state as soon as possible, the goal of problem management is to prevent incidents recurring by identifying their root cause and initiating preventive actions. This study addresses root causes of incidents related to human factors and the taxonomy used in categorization of those root causes. Root causes are identified and sometimes also categorized as a result of root cause analysis (RCA), which is part of ITIL problem management process [2]. Incidents themselves are categorized initially, when they are logged. This categorization of

© Springer International Publishing Switzerland 2015
R.V. O'Connor et al. (Eds.): EuroSPI 2015, CCIS 543, pp. 17–28, 2015.
DOI: 10.1007/978-3-319-24647-5_2

incidents is made usually according to CI (configurable item), reflecting e.g. device, system, service, etc. affected by the incident.

Incident trending refers to analysis of historical incident records with their incident categories and possible root causes categories in order to prevent the recurrence of these incidents [2]. Thus, incident trending can be seen as part of continual service improvement process [3], [4]. The recommended place to store this historical incident data is the SKMS (Service Knowledge Management System). It is a set of tools and databases that is used to manage knowledge, information and data. In place and properly updated SKMS is a fundamental organizational asset [3].

Understanding how incidents emerge and what the root causes behind them are, lays the basis for proactive measures to prevent incidents from occurring and recurring. Human factors play major role in all industries as root cause in incidents. Contemporary view is that human error investigation to be effective and efficient should be extended beyond the immediate harmful act to personal, teamwork, supervisory and organizational factors [5].

1.1   Related Research

Swiss Cheese Model in Incident Management

The most common model to explain the role of human factors in incidents is Reason's Swiss Cheese Model (SCM) [5]. In this Reason's Swiss Cheese Model the accident is seen as a result of long standing conditions, latent failures contributing the unsafe act. The model is often described as a sequence of planes, cheese slices, which describe organizational levels, defenses and barriers. Failures (holes in cheese slices) can emerge at anyone of these levels. When the holes are at the same time in the same trajectory, the incident is likely to occur. Reason's approach was psychological and originally related only to human factors.

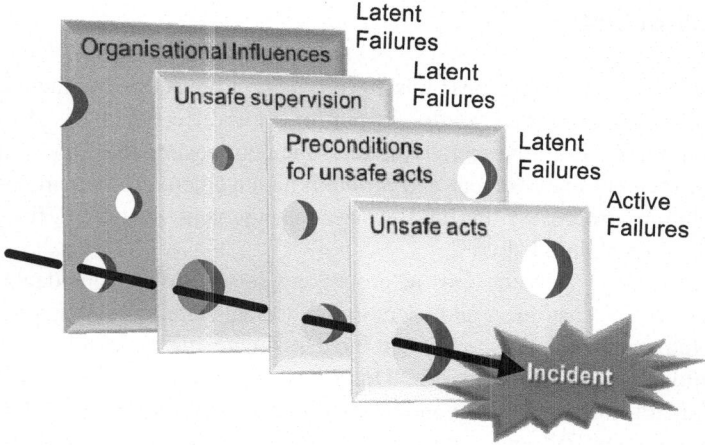

Fig. 1. Swiss Cheese Model (SCM) of incident causation with HFACS taxonomy

The Human Factors Analysis and Classification System (HFACS)
The most common application of the Swiss Cheese Model is HFACS) [6, 7]. It has multilevel taxonomy for active and latent human errors (Fig. 2).

HFACS has its origin in aviation, but has adaptations also in other industries [8] including military (DoD HFACS, HFACS-ADF) [9], [10], maritime (HFACS-M) [11], shipboard machinery (HFACS-MSS) [12], mining (HFACS-MI) [13], air traffic control (HFACS-ATC) [14], maintenance audit (HFACS-MA) [15], surgery [16], aviation maintenance (HFACS-ME) [17], biopharmaceutics (HFACS-bio) [18], railroads (HFACS-RR) [19], containerized dangerous cargoes (HFACS-CDG), etc. The level of modifications of these HFACS adaptations varies from minor terminological refinements to defining a new structure to root cause taxonomy.

HFACS splits various human errors into four main failure levels, slices of Swiss cheese: unsafe acts, preconditions for unsafe acts, unsafe supervision and organizational influences. These four levels are in turn divided in root cause categories.

Unsafe act presents here the active failure and the other levels present latent failure conditions, contributing factors to this act. In incident investigation the root cause(s) of incident is/are identified and is/are allocated to one or more of HFACS categories.

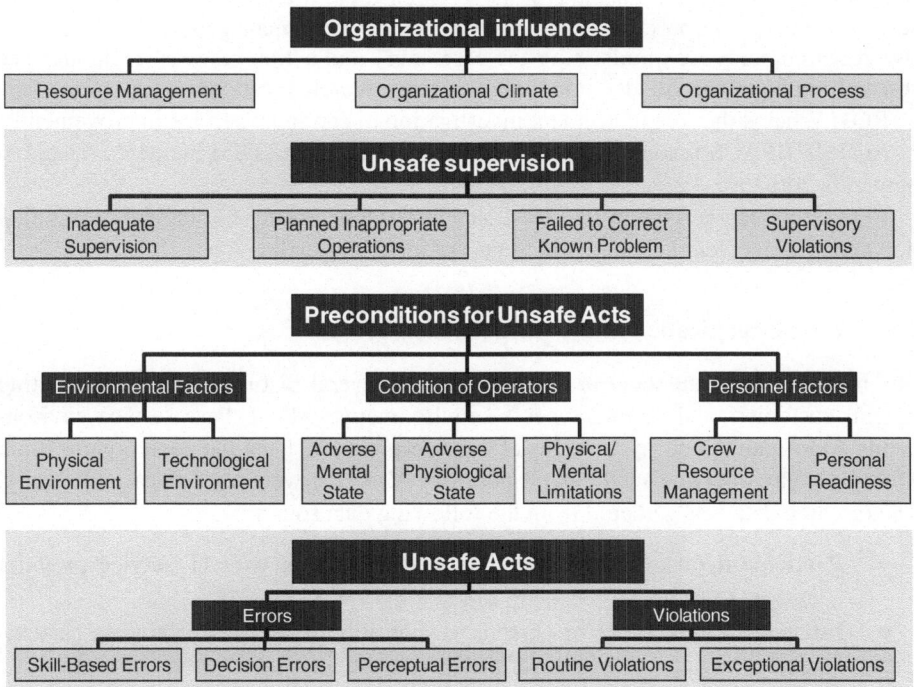

Fig. 2. Hierarchical HFACS taxonomy of human factor contribution on incidents and accidents.

1.2   Our Contribution

The main contribution of this paper is introducing the idea from just a "human error" or "configuration error" to real contributing factors behind this harmful act. This, in fact makes possible, to mitigate the probability of recurrence of incident by acting upon these latent causes. We also pointed out some deficiencies and flaws in general practices to execute in incident investigation and trending and made improvement proposals to them.

The remainder of the paper is organized as follows: In Section 2, the research methods of this study are described. In Section 3, the results of the study are presented. The discussion and the conclusions are given in Section 4.

2   Research Methods

The research problem in this study is: How human errors as root causes could be processed as part of service improvement efforts. The research problem was selected based on business needs of IT service provider companies. Root cause categorization of incidents is an actual and important research topic affecting the quality of other service management processes such as change and release management. This qualitative research study was built using the case study and action research methods. The research problem was divided into the following research questions:

RQ1: What is the role of accident investigation in continual service improvement?

RQ2: Is HFACS taxonomy suitable in categorization of ITSM incidents related to human factors?

RQ3: How categorization of ITSM should be done during the incident investigation and after incident investigation as part of incident trending?

2.1   Case Organization and Data Collection Methods

The research was conducted in 2012 – 2014 on several distinct occasions reflecting several customers and several types of environments. All of these service environments were maintained by a single IT service provider, later the case organization. Multiple data collection methods proposed by Yin [20] were used during the study. The research data was gathered from the following data sources:

- **Participant observation:** Meetings and discussion with IT service provider company's managers.
- **Interviews:** Interviews of persons, responsible of services offered to customers and interviews of experts of the service provider involved in the incident
- **Documents:** Incident reports, process descriptions (change, incident and prolem management), work guides and guidelines
- **Records and archives:** Change, incident and problem records.
- **Physical artifacts:** ITSM tool.

The case study method was used to identify the current state of incident categorization as well as study the incident types and HFACS categories. While our aim was also to improve working practices of the case organization by identifying weak areas in ITSM processes, we decided to use action research cycle inside the case study. According to Yin [20], triangulation of methods, data sources, researchers and theories increases the quality of a case study. The research followed the action research cycle as proposed by Baskerville [21]. Roots of action research are in the theory of organizational change such as in Lewin's change theory. Thus, action research can be utilized as a roadmap of an organizational change. In this study, the change refers to service management process improvement and introduction of improvements in contrast to organizational change [22]. The five phases of this cycle are presented in Fig. 3: A. Diagnosis, B. Action Planning, C. Action Taking, D. Evaluation, E. Specifying Learning.

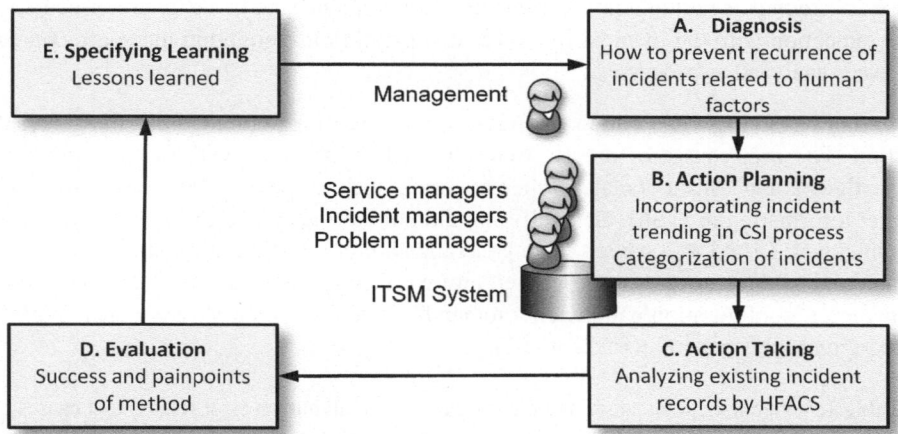

Fig. 3. The Action Research Cycle in this research

3 Results

As main results, we document the action research cycle that focused on developing methods to human factor related IT service incidents. The action research resulted in several improvements in incident investigation process and proposals to the HFACS categorization model of incident root causes, both in its structure and how to use it.

A. Diagnosis. The diagnosis phase aims at identifying the primary problem, which needs to be solved through action research. This phase started by organizing a meeting with the case organization's management. The objective of the management was to check the current state of IT service delivery and identify improvement areas. Root cause analysis of incidents revealed excessive amount of human errors. The management wanted to seek an approach to systemically process human error related incidents in order to improve IT service quality.

B. Action Planning. The action planning phase specifies actions of the organization to solve and investigate the problem identified in diagnosis phase.

We had 65 incidents with human error contribution with access to IT service production organizations service managers, and managers as well to the documentation and ITSM tools. These incidents presented 10 customer environments. The incident reports were written by 24 different authors. The planned action phases were

1. **Analysis of the incident reports:** The action planning phase started with analyzing the human error related incident reports, interviewing related persons and reviewing relevant facts from other sources. The root causes of incidents were reviewed against HFACS framework and its root cause categories. The root causes falling in HFACS categories were analyzed.
2. **Analysis of incident investigation processes:** The incident investigation processes were studied as part of continual service improvement. The investigation process in connection with the incident itself was compared to investigation made afterwards were analyzed as processes.

C. Action Taking. The action taking phase focuses on implementing the planned action. The root causes of reports were checked in interview with original incident investigator and also associated other material, such as process documentation and ticket information in ITSM. Generally, we did not have access to the persons acting in the incident. Listed root causes were generalized, e.g. "configuration error", "error in command", "error in start-up script", etc. were collected under the same general cause "Incorrect configuration/parameter/command". The root causes were then sorted according to this general term (Table 1).

Table 1. Generalized root causes and their occurences of all human error related root causes.

Generalized root cause	Occurrences
Incorrect configuration/parameter/command	42 %
Inadequate testing	9 %
Omitted instructions	6 %
Wrong port/tube/fiber/device/connector	6 %
Communication problem	5 %
Wrong information	4 %
Inadequate plan	4 %
Poor process design	4 %
Cooling was deactivated by accident	2 %
Error in instructions/documentation	2 %
Fail to estimate consequences	2 %
Poor system design	2 %
Violation of process	2 %
Other root causes	9 %

Then, we allocated the root causes using original incident report revised some times by other information sources to HFACS categories. We found that only 42% of reports had enough information to be allocated in certain HFACS category. E.g. the most common root cause "Incorrect configuration/parameter/command" as such cannot be allocated reliably anywhere without additional information. In order to allocate it in the HFACS first tier ("Unsafe act) the analyst should know, whether it was typing error (HFACS category "Unsafe act - skill-based error"), lack of competence ("decision error"), did not see the text on the screen properly ("perceptual error") or was it a intentional workaround against user guide made often ("routine violation") or only this time ("exceptional violation"). The key idea of HFACS is also to recognize the latent conditions behind the act. If the reason was typing error, was the latent condition behind this haste ("Preconditions of unsafe acts - adverse mental states"), illness ("Preconditions of unsafe acts - Adverse physiological states"), testing was not required by the process ("Organizational influences – organizational process") or there were no redundant back-up designed in the system ("Organizational influences – resource management").

D. Evaluation. 58% of incident reports in our study did not have enough information to fit in any HFACS category. Locating the root causes in right categories is very important since the chosen root cause category leads to improvement actions. The possible improvement actions to "Incorrect configuration/parameter/command" may be e.g. training, better change plans, testing after change, automation, fault tolerant design, proper allocation of persons to tasks, peer review, better instructions/documentation, etc. With the studied setup, existing incident reports and existing HFACS did not meet in a useful and practical way. However, the idea of latent conditions behind the harmful act, provides tools to improve service quality and is worth of preserving. If HFACS taxonomy will be used in incident analysis, the HFACS taxonomy should be used already in root causes analysis phase (RCA) (fig. 4) and the incident reports should be made more "HFACS compatible".

Making HFACS more IT Compliant. Although HFACS is used across different industries, its roots are in aviation. Many categories are still strange in IT service management. E.g. "Skill based errors" is relevant, when skill of handling stick and rudder is important. In ITSM the skill constitutes mainly on knowledge that is located in "Decision based errors" in the original HFACS. One option is to clarify the situation by replacing "Skill-Based errors" by "Attention/memory" and "Decision Errors" by "Competence". Expression "Crew resource management" is not often used in ITSM, "team work" is a more familiar term in ITSM. "Perception error" is useful in an airplane, when you may face fog, rain and snow, but it seldom is a problem in air-conditioned and well lighted premises of an IT service provider. On the other side, common categories in ITSM, like "Communication error" and "Wrong information" could have perhaps a joint category. HFACS with its categories should be adapted to ITSM environment as it is done in many other industries. Developing an adaptation to ITSM is an obvious next step.

Making IT Incident Reports more HFACS Compliant. HFACS is used as a tool for classification of incident root causes related to human factors. This, in turn is performed in order to improve service quality or safety in order to mitigate risk for incidents or accidents. There is no universal process for incident investigations. All the studied processes [23], [24], [25] contain at least the phases data collection, analysis and findings/reporting phases. Some of the process descriptions contained also planning phase in the beginning or corrective actions phase in the end of the accident investigation. The approach presented by European Safety Reliability and Data Association (ESReDA) with its iterative approach was used here (Fig. 4) [23]. ESReDA splits incident investigation into five phases: I. Collecting data, II hypothesis generation, III analysis, IV findings and V recommendations. Phases I, II, III and IV together are often called root cause analysis (RCA). RCA is part of ITIL problem management process. RCA is usually started in reaction to one or more incidents in order to find to the root cause and prevent the recurrence of the incident [2].

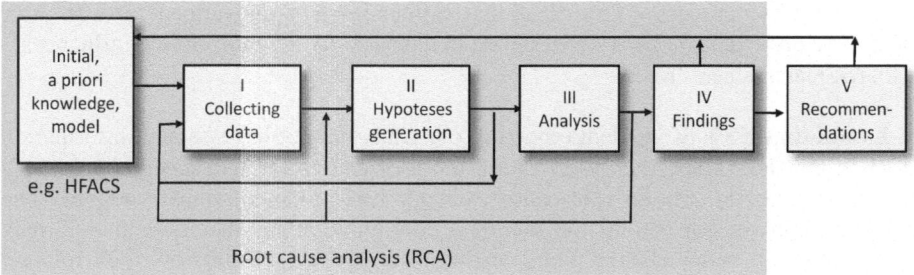

Fig. 4. Initial knowledge and incident/accident investigation [23]. In our study HFACS serves as a reference model in investigation.

Incident trending is analyzing historical incident records to identify one or more underlying causes that, if removed, can prevent their recurrence [2]. This is usually done either based on statistics from IT service management (ITSM) tools or reviewing stored written incident reports. In previous academic studies related to HFACS, it is also used or studied with existing incident reports. A typical way to apply HFACS in incident investigation process is presented in fig. 5.

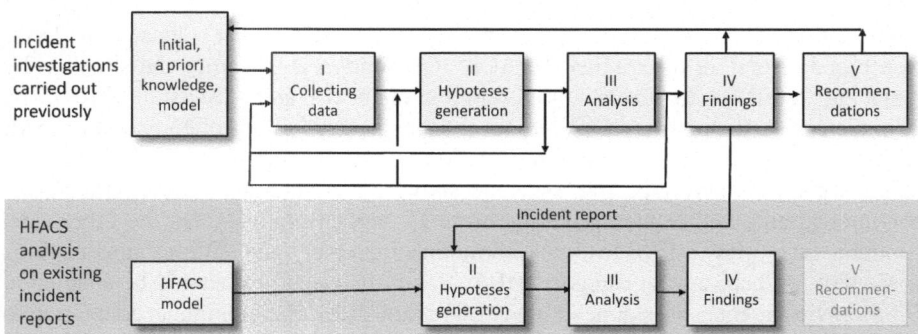

Fig. 5. Coding of HFACS categories afterwards by existing incident reports skips many parts of a investigation process and lacks iterative part for testing the hypothesis and gradual refinement of the findings.

Using HFACS (or any other incident model) in this way isolated from the original incident investigation process has certain drawbacks. The iterative part of process is missing between existing report and HFACS analysis, which causes difficulties in categorization. E.g. suppose that the root cause in the report is "configuration error". Was it because the employee did not know how to configure, made a typo or was the error based on false information? Was testing routinely or exceptionally skipped, which would have prevented discovery of the error before transfer to production?

This challenge leads us to conclusion, that in order to get more accurate results, HFACS taxonomy should be taken into account already in the data collection phase of the original incident report. In this way it is possible to get more accurate recommendations. Finding the right root cause is crucial, in order to find right remedy to it. If no further information is available, one should to be able to express this uncertainty in categorization. E.g. instead to be forced to set a category "Act – error – skill based error" there should also be available also the higher level category: "Act – error"

E. Specify Learning. In this study, we specified learning in the form of lessons learned. In the Specify learning phase organization identifies and creates knowledge gained during the action research. Both successful and unsuccessful actions enable learning. The following lessons learnt were derived.

Lesson 1: In order to identify service improvement opportunities one should go beyond the ordinary level of root cause "configuration error" and seek contributing factors behind this harmful act. Guidance (training, instructions, mentoring, etc.) to incident investigators is needed in order to get better incident reports. Our experience from other IT service providers suggest also, that the low quality of incident investigation and incident reports is also in general the biggest problem related to human error related incident management.

Lesson 2: HFACS taxonomy is not suitable as such for ITSM incident root cause categorization. An ITSM adaptation of HFACS is needed.

Lesson 3: To get more accurate results, HFACS framework and categories should be used already in the original incident investigation.

Lesson 4: HFACS and incident investigations in general should be seen as part of continual service improvement [26] rather than as an isolated exercise. In fig. 6 incident investigation is seen in PDCA (Plan-Do-Check-Act) service improvement cycle [1] and in a more detailed seven step improvement process [3]. PDCA and seven step improvement process both suggest binding the phases presented in incident investigation to planning and implementation/act phases. Since human factor related incidents present only approx. 20% of the total number of ICT incidents [8], human factor based incident trending is seldom a separated service improvement effort. Usually, it is part of a more comprehensive improvement project with common planning and improvement implementation, where human error related investigation is applied only to a subset of incidents. Therefore, it is highly advisable that human error related investigations are carried out in connection with the same process as incidents with other types of root causes.

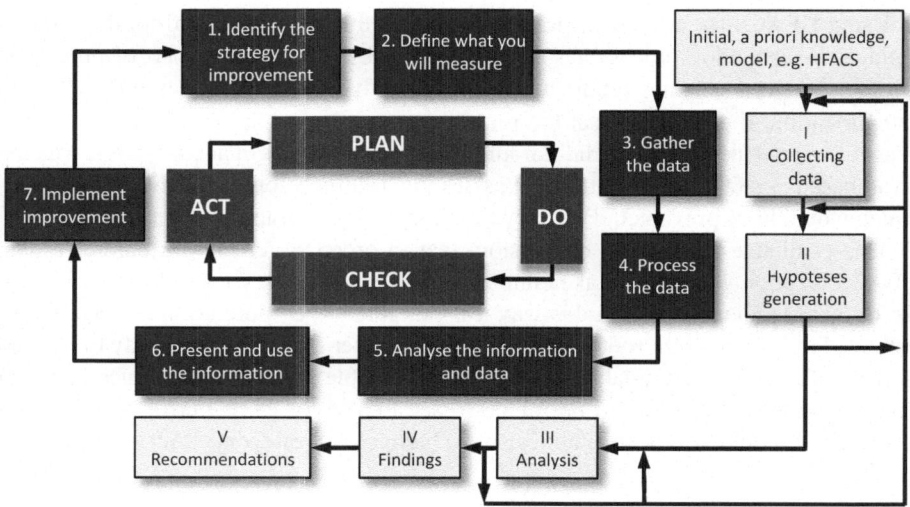

Fig. 6. HFACS and incident investigation process presented in context of ISO/IEC 20000:1 PDCA cycle and ITILv3 seven step improvement process.

4   Conclusions and Future Work

The research problem in this study is: How human errors as root causes could be processed as part of service improvement efforts. The unit of the study was a Finnish IT service provider company and its incident management process.

The research was conducted according to the phases of the action research cycle. The main contribution of the study was to describe how human factors should be taken into account in incident investigation process, in incident trending and in continual service improvement. Improvement proposal to HFACS were also identified.

Regarding RQ1 (What is the role of accident investigation in continual service improvement cycle) we present a fairly direct mapping between incident investigation, ISO/IEC 20000:1 PDCA cycle and ITILv3 seven step improvement processes.

Regarding RQ2 (Is HFACS taxonomy suitable in categorization of ITSM incidents related to human factors) we found that HFACS is not suitable as such for ITSM incident root cause categorization, and an ITSM adaptation of HFACS is needed.

Regarding RQ3 (How is categorization of ITSM should be done during the incident investigation and after incident investigation as part of incident trending) we propose, that the taxonomy and related framework should be applied already in the incident investigation and RCA phase to be useful in incident trending phase.

This publication is among the first ones together with [8] from the same authors that applies HFACS in IT services and among the few, that altogether discusses human errors in ITSM.

There are certain limitations related to this study. First, action research typically includes several iterative research cycles. However, in this paper, we focused on describing only one improvement cycle that focused on improving the analysis of IT service incidents and providing preliminary results on incident categorization. Second, action research benefits from a collaborative effort. Although we used multiple data sources, more effort could have been put on collaborative actions instead of a consultancy style problem solving. Third, the case study research method does not allow statistical generalization of results. However, case study results can be used to extend the theory. In this study we focused on contributing to incident investigation theory.

Future research could aim at design of an IT adaptation of HFACS model, which could be useful in actual service improvement work. The new taxonomy should also be validated. The validation itself should include at least measurement the inter-rater reliability of the model. This means measuring the consistency of results between different users at a specific time (inter-rater reliability).

Acknowledgment. We would like to thank the case organization's representatives for valuable feedback and responses that helped us to perform this study.

References

1. ISO/IEC 20000-1:2011, Information technology – Service management – Part 1: Service management system requirements (2013)
2. Office, C.: ITIL Service Operation. The Stationary Office, UK (2011)
3. Office, C.: ITIL Continual Service Improvement. The Stationary Office, UK (2011)
4. ISO/IEC TC JTC1/ SC7 WG10: Information technology — Process assessment — Part 8: An exemplar process assessment model for IT service management, s.29 Geneva, Switzerland (2012)
5. Reason, J.: Human Error. Cambridge University Press, New York (1990)
6. Harris, D., Li, W.C.: An extension of the human factors analysis and classification system for use in open systems. Theoretical Issues in Ergonomics Science **12**(2), 108–128 (2011)
7. Shappell, S., Wiegmann, D.: The Human Factors Analysis and Classification System—HFACS. US Department of Transportation (2000)
8. Saarelainen, K., Jäntti, M.: Human errors in IT services - HFACS model in root cause categorization. In: CIMT 2015: International Conference on Information and Multimedia Technology, Venice, Italy (2015)
9. Department of Defense Human Factors Analysis and Classification System - A mishap investigation and data analysis tool (2005)
10. Olsen, N.S., Shorrock, S.T.: Evaluation of the HFACS-ADF safety classification system: inter-coder consensus and intra-coder consistency. Accident Analysis and Prevention **42**(2), 437–444 (2010)
11. Bilbro, J.: An inter-rater comparison of DoD human factors analysis and classification system (HFACS) and human factors analysis and classification system—maritime (HFACS-M) classification system. Naval Postgraduate School, Monterey (2013)
12. Schroder-Hinrichs, J.U., Baldauf, M., Ghirxi, K.: Accident investigation reporting deficiencies related to organizational factors in machinery space fires and explosions. Accident Analysis and Prevention **43**(3), 1187–1196 (2011)

13. Patterson, J.M., Shappell, S.A.: Operator error and system deficiencies: Analysis of 508 mining incidents and accidents from Queensland. Australia using HFACS. Accident Analysis and Prevention **42**, 1379–1385 (2010)
14. Pounds, J., Scarborough, A., Shappell, S.: A human factors analysis of air traffic control operational errors. Aviation Space and Environmental Medicine **71**, 329–332 (2000)
15. Hsiao, Y., Drury, C., Wu, C., Paquet, V.: Predictive models of safety based on audit findings: Part 1: Model development and reliability. Applied Ergonomics **44**, 261–273 (2013)
16. ElBardissi, A.W., Wiegmann, D.A., Dearani, J.A., Daly, R.C., Sundt, T.M.: Application of the human factors analysis and classification system methodology to the cardiovascular surgery operating room. Annals of Thoracic Surgery **83**(4), 1412–1419 (2007)
17. Krulak, D.C.: Human factors in maintenance: impact on aircraft mishap frequency and severity. Aviation Space and Environmental Medicine **75**(5), 429–432 (2004)
18. Cintron, R.: Human Factors Analysis and Classification System Interrater Reliability for Biopharmaceutical Manufacturing Investigations. Ph.D. Dissertation, Walden University (2015)
19. Reinach, S., Viale, A.: Application of a human error framework to conduct train accident/incident investigations. Accident Analysis and Prevention **38**(2), 396–406 (2006)
20. Yin, R.: Case Study Research: Design and Methods. Sage Publishing, Beverly Hills (1994)
21. Baskerville, R.: Investigating Information Systems with Action Research. Communications of the Association for Information Systems **2**, Article 19 (1999)
22. Helms Mills, J., Dye, K., Mills, A.J.: Understanding Organizational Change. Routledge, London (2009)
23. Dechy, N., et al.: Guidelines for Safety Investigations of Accidents. ESReDA - European Safety Reliability and Data Association, p. 12 (June 2009)
24. Risktec: Six Steps for Successful Incident Investigation. RISKworld issue 14 autumn 2008 pg 6, Warrington, United Kingdom (2008)
25. Serious Accident Investigation Chief Investigator's Handbook Blm Manual H-1112-3. Bureau of Land Management, USA (2003)
26. ISO/IEC ISO/IEC TS 15504-8:2012(E): Software Engineering - Process Assessment - Part 8: An Exemplar Process Assessment Model for IT Service Management (2012)

An Industrial Experience in Cross Domain Assurance Projects

Alejandra Ruiz[1(✉)], Xabier Larrucea[1], Huascar Espinoza[1],
Franck Aime[2], and Cyril Marchand[2]

[1] ICT – European Software Institute Division, Tecnalia, Derio, Spain
{alejandra.ruiz,xabier.larrucea,huascar.espinoza}@tecnalia.com
[2] Airworthiness & Certification Directorate, Thales Avionics, Toulouse, France
{franck.aime,cyril.marchand}@fr.thalesgroup.com

Abstract. Companies related to safety critical systems developments invest efforts and resources to assure that their systems are safe enough. Traditionally reuse strategies have been proposed to reduce these efforts in several domains which criticality is not a key aspect. However reusing software artefacts across different domains establishes new challenges especially between safety critical systems. In fact we need to take into account different domain specific standards requirements at the same time. In this paper we present our experience on cross domain assurance involving a reuse of a software component developed for the railway domain, and to be used for the avionics domain.

Keywords: Compliance · Cross domain · Reuse · DO-178 · EN 50128

1 Introduction

Some challenges for safety assurance and (re)certification approaches are identified in [1]. Authors mention that one of the difficulties for a cross domain reuse is the need to comply with multiple standards and to provide a seamless certification process. This process needs to take into account different domains when developing a new product in a safety critical context. The main purpose when reusing one artefact from one domain into another is basically to reduce efforts and resources, and to increase the return on investment of this kind of products.

Cross-domain requires a common understanding of both domains, and to consider different processes and requirements from different sources at the same time. This understanding should include all stakeholders from these domains, and to define consistently a set of structured arguments to be used during the assessment process. In order to be able to reuse assessment data of already approved components we need to define some reuse criteria. It is important to gather this information in order to build a predictive performance model and to manage assessments in order to meet the certification objectives.

This paper is structured as follows. First a background is provided. Second our use case is described and our approach is described in detail. Third some results are presented. And a final section ends this paper.

© Springer International Publishing Switzerland 2015
R.V. O'Connor et al. (Eds.): EuroSPI 2015, CCIS 543, pp. 29–38, 2015.
DOI: 10.1007/978-3-319-24647-5_3

2   Background

Safety standard guidelines on how to manage safety design so as to mitigate the possible risk as a direct impact on cost. [3] Machrouh also mentioned that "Defining the commonalities between safety standards in various domains allows one to reduce the development cost of the critical embedded systems by mutualising the developments by reuse of components".

Reusing a project is difficult and even more when the context changes for example reusing across domain. Very few attempts have been made in order to harmonized the different domain approached in order to proposed a cross-domain reuse [3], [4], [5] have analysed the similarities and divergences of the different standards. Blanquart makes an analysis from the critical categories and highlight that all standard share the same fundamental concepts where critical categories are linked to the risk and effects of potential failures. The main divergence comes from acceptance frontier.

Papadopoulos and McDermid [6] defined a reference structure for the comparative review of standards. The structure is based on five principal dimensions of the certification problem: (1) Requirements for system development and safety processes, (2) Method for establishing the system Safety Requirements, (3) Definition, treatment and allocation of development assurance levels, (4) Requirements on techniques for component specification, development and verification and (5) Requirements on the content and structure of the safety case.

Zeller [7] proposed cross-domain assurance process in conjunction with any development methodology for safety-relevant software. The objective was to reduce the effort for safety assessment by reusing safety analysis techniques and tools for the product development in different domains.

As a result of these previous analyses the following similarities between the examined standards have be identified:

- Common notion of safety and certification
- Linear progressing safety process with dedicated phases
- Combined hazard assessment and risk analysis to derive safety requirements
- Criticality levels as means to allocation safety (integrity) requirements to system elements
- Verification activities are driven by the safety requirements
- Safety case provides evidence that safety requirements are fulfilled which is needed for certification

SAFECER project [8] proposed some cross domain case studies, the focus of the reuse across domain on these studies were on the tool qualification. On tool qualification there is a large overlap between standard. The main targets on these case studies were the DO -178 [9], IEC 61508 [10] and ISO 26262 [11]

3   Use case

3.1   Business Case

General context of the Avionics Use Case is a situation of product reuse from one domain (Railways) to another domain (Avionic). The goal is to build the Qualification Dossier, based on elements provided with the reused parts. The Qualification Dossier is then presented for certification. The reused product is the Execution Platform (Computing Unit and Operating System) which was developed for a given domain (Railways) and it will be installed in another domain (Avionic). The execution platform is considered as an independent item for which a qualification dossier will be built. This qualification dossier consists of plans, technical documents, and certification documents. Technical documents are specifications, validation and verification life cycle data. The certification documents are configuration index documents and accomplishment summaries. The initial execution platform and the associated documentation issued from the railway domain comply with railway standards (CENELEC EN50128 [12]). The final execution platform and the elaborated qualification documentation to be used in avionics domain must comply with avionics standards (ED-12c/DO-178).

One of the first challenges was to establish a mapping between standards from different application domains. When reusing from one domain to another the compliance evidence used for one standard need to find their equivalence of the new standard. Some standards are process oriented while others are product oriented. Therefore equivalences between standards require a detailed description of items. In addition we need not only to set up these equivalences, but also to define how assurance information is going to be reused on the new domain. We defined a cross domain reuse based on 3 criteria:

- Associated Process / Design Assurance: Process domain shall be reusable from source domain to target domain
- Technical Solution: Design details shall be available from source domain to target domain
- Intended function boundary: Intended function shall be reusable from source domain to target domain

3.2   Our Approach

Our approach is designed in four steps which are illustrated in the following Fig. 1.

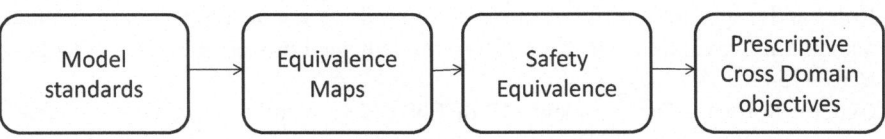

Fig. 1. The main steps in our approach

The first step in our approach is to model railway and avionics standards and we used the same metamodel [2]. In our case we will be focused on DO-178C and the EN 50128. This metamodel [2] is domain agnostic, and we can specify some requirements from standards. We developed an Eclipse based tool according to this metamodel, and we model these standards. Fig. 2 provides an overview of the main sections of the DO178C and a snapshot of our tool.

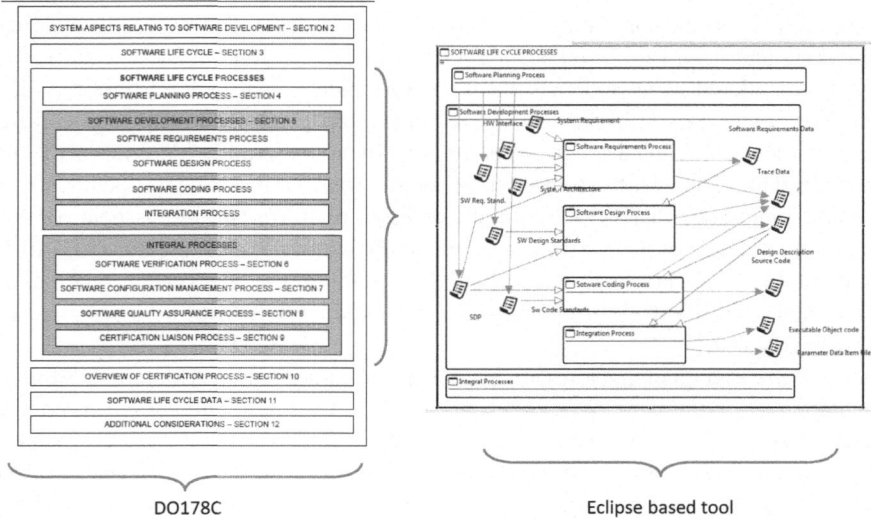

DO178C   Eclipse based tool

Fig. 2. DO178c standard and its representation in our Eclipse based tool

A second step is to compare each standard concept from railway domain to avionic domain. This mapping is called "equivalence map". In fact this mapping is not just focused on activities but also on generated work products. For example on the one hand EN50128 is a product based standard, and it prescribes product based features to ensure safety. On the other hand DO-178 prescribes processes to ensure safety. This equivalence map is graphically represented in Fig. 3. Both standards contain traceable activities and work products between them which represent 27,75% of the items. However there are other situations where there is no such relationship (19,23%) or even we can identify a partial relationship between items (53%). There are some orphan sections where standards requirements do not apply in our case study. Therefore there is no possible equivalence map. Fig. 3 illustrates these relationships and our findings can be summarized as follows:

- Roles and responsibility (§5 of EN50128) in railway are no equivalent in avionic,
- Validation in avionic is an Aircraft/System dedicated process and a part of ED79A /ARP4754A,
- Generic Software Development (§7 of EN50128) in railway are no equivalent in avionic at DO-178 level. Therefore, at system level, the Technical Standard Order (TSO) may be viewed as a generic development regarding the targeted aircraft but with the intended function well specified,

- Software deployment and maintenance (§9 of EN50128) in railway are no equivalent in avionic at DO-178 level. Therefore, at system level, the means of compliance of Certification Specification 25.1529 "Continued Airworthiness" may be viewed as an equivalent objective.
- Safety function in railway is the equivalent of avionic safety-related * functions at A/C definition level.
- Validation in avionic is an Aircraft/System dedicated process and a part of ED79A /ARP4754A.
- Transition criteria are an important asset for avionic domain, based on process control demonstration.
- Derived Requirement is an important asset for avionic domain, based on intended function demonstration (Certification Specification 25.1301).

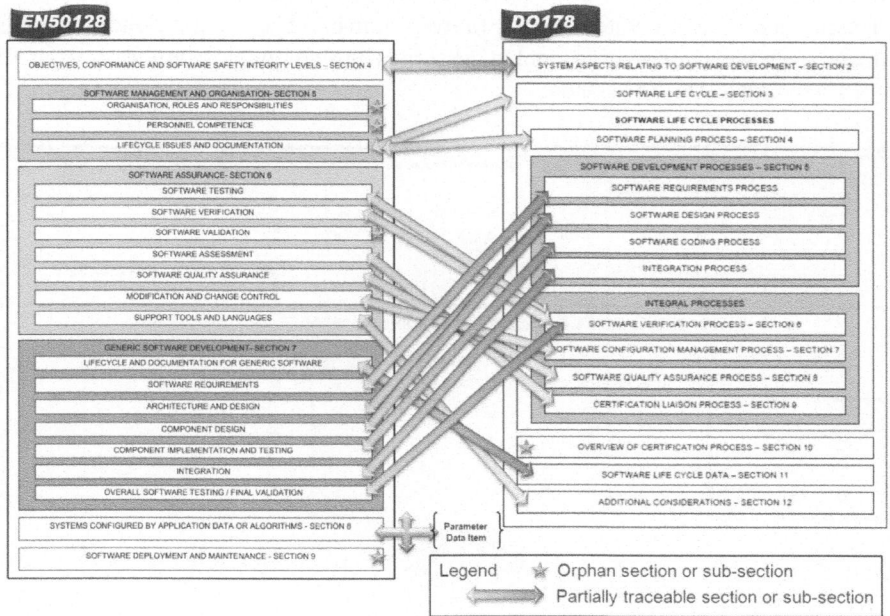

Fig. 3. Safety Standards Documents framework

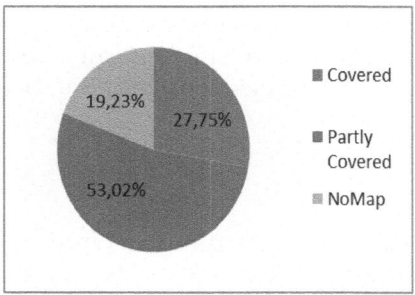

Fig. 4. Coverage between DO178C and EN50128

The third step for our analysis is focused on providing a mean to claim equivalence levels of safety from one domain to another. In this sense we need to identify Prescriptive Product Based objectives and Prescriptive Process Based objectives. All requirements are traced and evaluated. In addition we trace each objective from the railway process based standard to the objectives on the avionics base standard. These traces represent our prescriptive cross domain standard (PxB) including all requirements, and which represent safety equivalences.

The final step is the function analysis based on this Prescriptive Cross Domain Based standard. We need to identify additional or missing activities from source to target safety standard represented as post- conditions. These activities are carried out to meet objectives which are partially mapped or there is no map at all. All these elements are required to make the Execution platform ready to show compliance with certification requirements. Once equivalence mappings are created we apply them to our assurance project created for the railway domain. These equivalence mappings contain assurance information, and it generates the compliance artefacts from EN 50128 standard to Do178c standard.

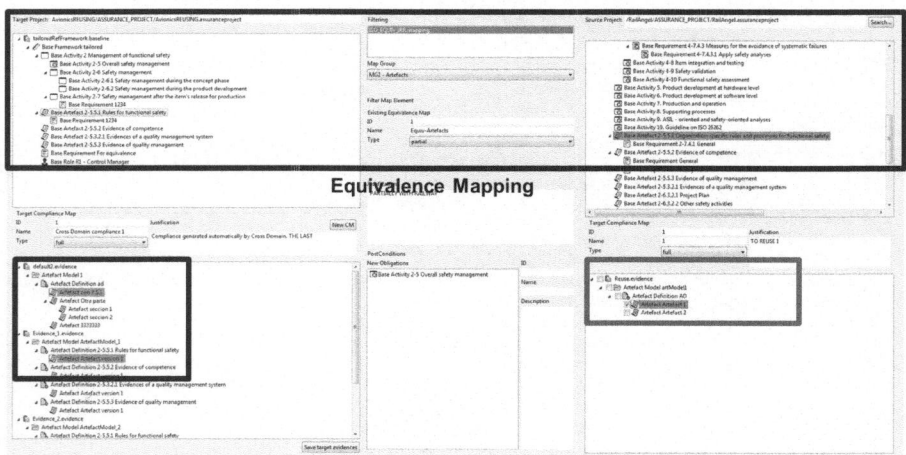

Fig. 5. Equivalence mapping application

Fig. 5 shows a wizard which supports our equivalence mapping between EN50128 and D0-178c. On the upper side equivalences between standards are identified. On the lower part the information about the specific standard is described. If we apply these equivalence maps we get the information complying with DO 178c standard.

4   Results

In order to measure the results of our cross domain experience we defined a set of metrics, and we gathered some values. Fig. 6 shows these metrics and values. We identified 4 aspects to be measured which can be seen on the question column on Fig. 6:

- Cost effectiveness of the assurance process across systems: This industrial experience focuses on the reuse of the execution platform from the railway domain to the avionics domain. The objective is to eliminate or limit additional activities to the original certification activity in the railway domain. Traditionally this activity leads to directly build qualification documents (configuration management and accomplishment summaries) according to avionics standards. Traditionally we manually perform an equivalence using existing documents from railway domain and then to build a qualification documents according to avionics standards.

  o Assurance asset reuse focusses on requirements defined in the standards. In this metric, we measure the total number of requirements which can be accomplished in the avionics domain as result of validating equivalent requirements in the railway domain.

  o Baseline elements that do not need a new compliance map, takes into consideration the expected detection of standards' elements in the avionics assurance project whose compliance with can be fully validated from the requirements already accomplished in the railway assurance project.

  o Assurable elements with applicable equivalence maps, metric refers to the equivalence maps between avionics and railway reference assurance frameworks, with focus on reference requirements. Making explicit the equivalence between standards from different application domains facilitate the assurance tasks.

Question	Metric	Value	Comments
Cost-Effectiveness of the Safety Assurance Process across Systems and Markets	Assurance asset reuse	0,74	Focused on Baseline Requirements
	Reused Assurance Assets	155	Reused Compliance Requirements
	Total Assurance Assets	210	Total Set of Avionics Baseline Requirements
	Baseline elements that do not need a new compliance map	0,19	Focused on Baseline Requirements
	Baseline elements that do not need a new compliance map	40	Number of assets reused whose compliance map is Full
	Total Baseline Elements	210	Total Set of Avionics Compliance Requirements
	Assurable elements with applicable equivalence maps	0,67	Focused on Reference Requirements
	Assurable elements with applicable equivalence maps	210	Number of Ref Requirements with Equivalence maps
	Total Assruable Elements	315	Total set of Ref Requirements
Automation of the Safety Assurance Process	Automated compliance map creation	0,74	Focused on automated compliance maps for base requirements
	Compliance maps automatically created	155	
	Total compliance maps	210	
	Automated impact analysis	0	None
	Automatically detected Impacted Elements	0	
	Total impacted elements	210	
Safety Assurance Reuse across Domains	Assurable elements equivalence	0,67	Focused on Reference Requirements
	MASE1+MASE2	210	Number of Ref Requirements with Equivalence maps
	ASE1+ASE2	315	Total set of Ref Requirements
	Assurance asset reuse across application domains	0,74	Focused on Baseline Requirements
	Reused across domains Assurance Assets	155	Reused Compliance Requirements
	Total Assurance Assets	210	Total Set of Avionics Baseline Requirements
Awareness of Reuse Consequences	Assurance assets whose reuse is possible	0	None
	Estimated Reusable Argumentation Elemnts	0	
	Total predicted Argumentation Elements	100	
	Baseline elements whose compliance with has to be shown	0,81	Focused on Baseline Requirements
	Baseline elements that need a new compliance map on the new domain	170	Number of assets that need a compliance map, Full or Partial, in the new domain
	Total Baseline Elements	210	Total Set of Avionics Compliance Requirements

Fig. 6. Metric Measurement Results for Reduction of Recurring Costs

- Automation of the Safety Assurance Process: Our platform provides automated support for generating avionics artefacts.

  o Automated compliance map creation, this can occur in an avionics assurance project regarding cross-domain reuse if equivalence maps have been specified between railway and avionics reference assurance frameworks. Our tool suite creates compliance maps automatically, so that all the possible baseline requirements in the avionics project, with full and partial equivalence in the railway project, are created automatically with the Cross-Domain reuse tool.

- Assurance Reuse across Domains: The problem of cross-domain transfers is that certification objectives may be specific to a domain, or differently expressed. The objective of the metrics is not to measure the level of commonality between domains, but its ability to help translation of artefacts between domains when correspondence can be established.

  o Assurable elements equivalence. This metric refers to the cross-domain equivalence maps between avionics and railway reference assurance frameworks, with focus on reference requirements.Making explicit the equivalence between standards from different application domains facilitate the assurance tasks.

  o Assurance asset reuse across application domains. In this metric, we measure the total number of requirements which can be accomplished in the avionics domain as result of validating equivalent requirements in the railway domain.Rationale for improvement: Having available the equivalence between requirements to be accomplished in different domains help reduce re-assurance costs.

- Awareness of Reuse Consequences: Our approach provides models for safety certification; it should be possible to improve the determination of reuse consequences.

  o Baseline elements whose compliance with has to be shown. When reusing information from the railway assurance project, out tool platform is expected to detect the baseline elements in the avionics assurance project whose compliance must be revised.

Fig. 7 summarizes the main numbers for this cross domain experience. "Traditional approach" header represents the effort and cost of activities which are under our approach influence. For instance, Standard interpretation for cross-domain reuse sub-activities called "Specification of cross-domain equivalences", "Compliance traceability", and "Specification of compliance requirements in relation to reused projects" can be improved by using out tool suite. These sub-activities represent the 45% of effort of the whole evidence collection activities. We can see that the 41,5% of the effort in global assurance and certification activities are susceptible of improvement by using our approach. The numbers showing on the figure were extracted from the reuse metrics described for the previous figure. The effort savings is approximately 26.95% based on our experience. However when we are using our approach, the effort savings is 54.4%.

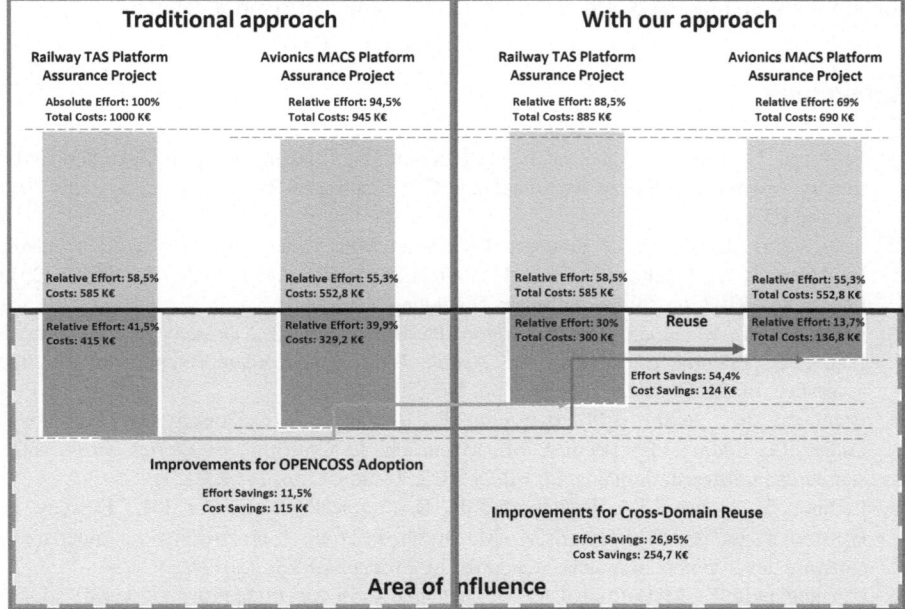

Fig. 7. Railway to Avionics Case Study

5   Conclusions and Future Work

From this industrial experience we can conclude that safety engineering activities in one domain have similarities to safety activities in other domain. Even safety related techniques have several commonalities. Our approach is based on a common meta-model for describing safety standards requirements in order to provide a common understanding between domains. In a near future this common understanding is going to be shared between stakeholders from different domains.

Criteria of cross domain reuse are identified in this paper. Innovative aspects based on cross-over effects between application domains are carried out in a real situation. We are able to reuse assessment data of already approved components from one domain into another. In addition our approach helps to identify gaps between standards. An improved version of this paper provides a deeper analysis of this case study, and it provides a better view on verification and validation data, and traceability.

The presented approach provides an agile assessment process for identifying and it increases understandability of standards requirements from different domains. In addition it enables a preliminary assessment of targeted certification objectives.

It also allows the development of a consistent set of structured arguments from different domains. We have proved a reduction of recurring costs for this case study mainly relate to costs for cross-domain assurance and certification.

From this experience Thales considers to implement a product family strategy to reduce costs, especially in recertification activities. These strategies may use cross domain reuse and model based engineering including certification language.

References

1. Espinoza, H., Ruiz, A., Sabetzadeh, M., Panaroni, P.: Challenges for an Open and Evolutionary Approach to Safety Assurance and Certification of Safety-Critical Systems 2011, pp. 1–6 (2011)
2. de la Vara, J.L., Panesar-Walawege, R.K.: SafetyMet: a metamodel for safety standards. In: Moreira, A., Schätz, B., Gray, J., Vallecillo, A., Clarke, P. (eds.) MODELS 2013. LNCS, vol. 8107, pp. 69–86. Springer, Heidelberg (2013)
3. Machrouh, J., Blanquart, J.P., Baufreton, P., Boulanger, J.L., Delseny, H., Gassino, J., Ladier, G., Ledinot, E., Leeman, M., Astruc, J.M.: Cross domain comparison of system assurance. In: ERTS 2012, Toulouse, pp. 1–3 (2012)
4. Blanquart, J.P., Astruc, J.M., Baufreton, P., Boulanger, J.L., Delseny, H., Gassino, J., Ladier, G., Ledinot, E., Leeman, M., Machrouh, J.: Criticality categories across safety standards in different domains. In: ERTS 2012, Toulouse, pp. 1–3 (2012)
5. Ledinot, E., Astruc, J.-M., Blanquart, J.-P., Baufreton, P., Boulanger, J.-L., Delseny, H., Gassino, J., Ladier, G., Leeman, M., Machrouh, J., et al.: A cross-domain comparison of software development assurance standards. In: Proc. of ERTS2 (2012)
6. Papadopoulos, Y., McDermid, J.A.: The potential for a generic approach to certification of safety critical systems in the transportation sector. Reliability Engineering & System Safety **63**(1), 47–66 (1999)
7. Zeller, M., Höfig, K., Rothfelder, M.: Towards a cross-domain software safety assurance process for embedded systems. In: Bondavalli, A., Ceccarelli, A., Ortmeier, F. (eds.) SAFECOMP 2014. LNCS, vol. 8696, pp. 396–400. Springer, Heidelberg (2014)
8. Safecer Project Safety Certification of Software-Intensive Systems with Reusable Components Web: http://www.safecer.eu
9. RTCA DO-178/EUROCAE ED-12, Software Considerations in Airborne Systems and Equipment Certification (2011)
10. IEC 61508 IEC61508, 61508 - Functional Safety of Electrical/Electronic/Programmable Electronic Safety-Related Systems. International Electrotechnical Commission (2011)
11. International Organization for Standardization (ISO), ISO26262 Road vehicles – Functional safety, ISO (November 2011)
12. CENELEC EN 50128 - Railway applications — Communication, signalling and processing systems — Software for railway control and protection systems (2011)

SPI Approaches
in Safety-Critical Domains

A Lean Automotive E/E-System Design Approach with Open Toolbox Access

Harald Sporer[✉]

Institute of Technical Informatics,
Graz University of Technology, Inffeldgasse 16/1, 8010 Graz, Austria
sporer@tugraz.at
http://www.iti.tugraz.at/

Abstract. Replacing former pure mechanical functionalities by mechatronics-based solutions, introducing new propulsion technologies, and connecting cars to their environment are only a few reasons for the still growing electrical and electronic systems (E/E-Systems) complexity at modern passenger cars. Smart methodologies and processes are necessary during the development life cycle to master the related challenges successfully. One of the key issues is to have an adequate environment for creating architectural system designs, and linking them to other development artifacts. In this paper, a novel model-based domain-specific language for embedded mechatronics-based systems, with focus on the support of different automotive sub-domains, is presented. With the described methodology, the domain-specific modeling (DSM) approach can be adapted to the needs of the respective company or project easily. Though, the model-based language definition can be implemented using various platforms (e.g. Eclipse Modeling Framework), also a custom-made open source editor supporting the DSM technique, is presented.

Keywords: System architectural design · Domain-specific modeling · Automotive embedded systems · E/E-Systems

1 Introduction

The electrical and/or electronic systems (E/E-Systems) in the automotive domain have been getting more and more complex over the past decades. New functionality, mainly realized through embedded E/E-Systems, as well as the growing connectivity (*Car2X-Communication*), will keep this trend alive in the upcoming years. Well-defined development processes are crucial to manage this complexity and to achieve high quality products. Wide-spread standards and regulations, like *Automotive SPICE®* and *ISO 26262*, give a guidance through the development life cycle.

Best practice for the E/E-System development process is still to refer to some kind of the V-Model. Starting with an initialization and analyzing phase, via the subdivided system elements, down to the implementation, and back up by integration and test phases towards the completed system, a multitude of

© Springer International Publishing Switzerland 2015
R.V. O'Connor et al. (Eds.): EuroSPI 2015, CCIS 543, pp. 41–50, 2015.
DOI: 10.1007/978-3-319-24647-5_4

work products arises and have to be managed properly. Trying to keep all of the artifacts consistent manually, is an error-prone and tedious task. Therefore, a lot of effort has been made through the last years to increase the quality by an adequate and highly automated tool support.

To create the system design, most of the existing approaches utilize some kind of UML profile (e.g. SysML[1]). Though these techniques have a lot of advantages, in some scenarios they are not best choice. On the one hand, the possibility to include mechanical parts or the flow of fluids and forces is missing, and on the other hand, a possible lack of UML skills, especially in small project teams, which wants to carry out a lean development, makes the UML-based design to an awkward task.

The main goal of this work is to contribute to the improvement of the existing system architectural design methods. The herein presented approach has been created for the development of embedded mechatronics-based E/E-Systems in the automotive field mainly. However, the techniques are also suitable for other domains. The mentioned improvement is accomplished by extending the widespread and common UML-based methods by domain-specific modeling (DSM) techniques. It's crucial to state that the existing design techniques shall not be replaced by the presented work.

Similar to the previous mentioned de facto standard *Automotive SPICE*, full traceability and consistency between the development artifacts are also one of the main objectives of this work. Various types of requirements are linked to the system architectural design elements, and in the case of requirement changes the affected system parts can be determined easily. Moreover, supported by the DSM definition, a software architectural design can be either created within the same environment as the system design, or a established seamless tool chain can be facilitated after a domain-specific model to UML-based model transformation. In both cases, a Simulink®[2] software framework model can be generated from the software architectural design.

In this contribution the highlighted aspect of the novel DSM approach is the methodology of creating new modeling toolboxes for a particular project or company. The definition of the domain-specific language in combination with the support from the newly developed designer tool, allows a straight forward and intuitive procedure for customizing the DSM to the specific needs. A big advantage of this solution is that the customization can be conducted by the user easily and without coding.

In the course of this document, Section 2 presents an overview of the related approaches, as well as of domain-specific modeling. In Section 3, a detailed description of the proposed modeling approach with a focus on the tailoring for specific (sub-)domains is provided. An application of the described methodology is presented in Section 4. Finally, this paper is concluded with an overview of the presented work in Section 5.

---

[1] http://www.omgsysml.org/
[2] http://www.mathworks.com/products/simulink/

2   Related Work

In recent years, a lot of effort has been made to improve the model-based automotive E/E-System design methods and techniques. Nowadays, the advantages of a model-based approach are clear and without controversy. Meseguer [12] grants much more reliability, reusability, automatisation, and cost effectiveness to software that is developed with modeling languages. However, model transformation within or also across different languages is crucial to achieve all these benefits.

Traceability, as well as consistency, between the development artifacts has always been an important topic. However, due to the increasing number of electronic- and electric-based functionality, these properties have become vital. If it comes to safety-critical functionalities, according to the 2011 released international standard ISO 26262 [8], traceability between the relevant artifacts is mandatory. A description of the common deliverables along an automotive E/E-System development, and a corresponding process reference model is presented by the de facto standard Automotive SPICE [2]. Neither the functional safety standard nor the process reference model enforces a specific methodology, how the development artifacts have to be created or linked to each other. However, connecting the various work products manually is a tedious and error-prone task.

One of the early work products along the engineering process, is the architectural system design. In the field of automotive E/E-System development, a wide-spread and common approach is to utilize a UML-based technique for this design, like the UML2 profile SysML. Andrianarison and Piques [1], Boldt [3], and many other publications (e.g. [6], [9], [13]) present their SysML methodologies for the system design.

To agree with Broy et al. [4], the drawbacks of the UML-based design are still the low degree of formalization, and the lack of technical agreement regarding the proprietary model formats and interfaces. The numerous possibilities of how to customize the UML diagrams, to get a language for embedded system design, drive these drawbacks. On the one hand, the meta model can be extended, and on the other hand, a profile can be defined [13]. Even if there is a agreement to utilize a common UML profile like SysML, a plenty of design artifact variations are feasible. This scenario doesn't provide an optimal base for the engineer who has to design the embedded automotive system from a mechatronics point of view. Ideally, the tool should be intuitive and easily operated also without specific UML knowledge. These findings led the author to the idea to create a more tailored model-based language for the stated domain. The definition and other details of this language can be found at [16].

Mernik et al. [11] describe a domain-specific language as a language that is tailored to the specific application domain. Enhanced by this tailoring, substantial gains in expressiveness and ease of use, compared to general-purpose languages, should be given. Even if a gain regarding the expressiveness is achieved by the utilization of SysML-based modeling techniques, the ease of use regarding an embedded automotive mechatronics system design is out of sight.

Preschern et al. [14] claim that DSLs help to decrease system development costs by providing developers with an effective way to construct systems for a specific domain. The benefit in terms of a more effective development has to be higher than the investment for creating or establishing a DSL at a company or department. Supplementary, the authors argue that in the next years the mentioned DSL development cost will decrease significantly, due to new tools supporting the language creation like the Eclipse-based *Sirius*[3].

Vujović et al. [17] present a model-driven engineering approach to create a domain-specific modeling (DSM). Sirius is the framework for developing a new DSM, respectively the DSM graphical modeling workbench. The big advantage of this tool is that the workbench for the DSM is developed graphically. Therefore, knowledge about software development with Java, the graphical editor framework (GEF) or the graphical modeling framework (GMF) is not needed.

According to Hudak [7], programs written in a DSL are more concise, can be written more quickly, are easier to maintain and reason about. In the authors opinion, this list of advantages is also valid for domain-specific modeling. Furthermore, Hudak determines the basic steps for developing a own domain-specific language as

- Definition of the domain
- Design of the DSL capturing the domain semantics
- Provide support through software tools
- Create use-cases for the new DSL infrastructure

The approach described in this paper is presented according to theses steps in Section 3 and 4.

3   Approach

In this section, the domain specific modeling methodology for automotive mechatronics-based system development, with a focus on the open toolbox strategy, is presented. As mentioned in Section 2, details on the definition of the domain specific modeling can be found in [16]. Therefore, just a brief description is given in the following subsection.

3.1   Domain-Specific Modeling Language

The established SysML-based design method from [10] is extended by the newly developed *Embedded Mechatronics System Domain-Specific Modeling (EMS-DSM)* for the automotive embedded system design. The main goal of this methodology is to provide a lean approach for engineers to facilitate an embedded automotive mechatronics system modeling on a high abstraction level. The focus of the approach is on the model-based structural description of the E/E-System under development. Additionally, the signals and interfaces are an essential part of the modeling.

---

[3] https://eclipse.org/sirius/

The definition of the newly developed model-based domain specific language is shown in Figure 1. The top node *EMS-DSM Component* is the origin of all other classes at the language definition. Therefore, each of the derived classes inherits the five properties (*ID*, *Name*, *Requirement*, *Verification Criteria*, and *Specification*) from the base class.

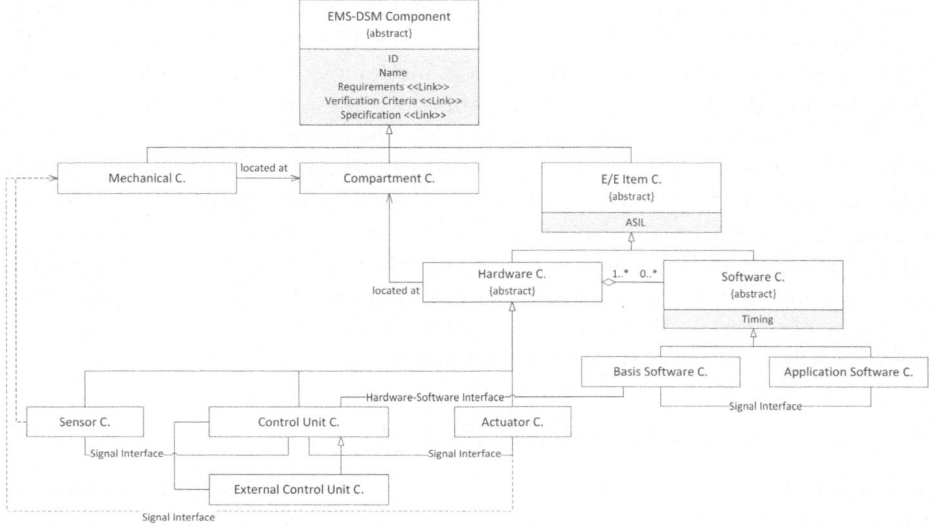

Fig. 1. *EMS-DSM* Definition (UML)

The language definition in Figure 1 represents the meta-domain of the model-based language. Subsequently, the EMS-DSM is tailored to the needs of the domain at the particular project or company. That is, design elements of possible types *Mechnical*, *Compartment*, *Sensor*, *Control Unit*, *Actuator*, *External Control Unit*, *Basis Software*, and *Application Software* are specified for the particular field of application. E.g. the domain of the presented application in Section 4 is *Embedded Mechatronics E/E-System Design for Compressed Natural Gas (CNG) Fuel Tank Systems*.

The EMS-DSM can be supported by a various number of tools, but at the time when the research project was initiated, a highest possible flexibility, as well as full access to the tools source code was desired. To achieve this, an own model editor (***E**mbedded **A**utomotive **Sy**stem Design*) has been developed, based on the open source project *WPF Diagram Designer* [5].

3.2   Traceability Between the Design and Other Artifacts

To achieve a lean development environment for automotive E/E-Systems, the whole engineering life cycle has to be supported. Therefore, not only the system architectural design, but also other artifacts, like requirements and test case specification, are in the scope of this work. For topics like project management and requirements management, the web-based open source application *Redmine*[4] is used in this project. The de facto standard Automotive SPICE [2] defines three different types of requirements at the engineering process group: *Customer Requirements*, *System Requirements*, and *Software Requirements*. Out of the embedded E/E-System view, at least the hardware focus is missing. Additionally, requirements and design items regarding the mechanical components, have been introduced for the design of an embedded mechatronics-based E/E-System. Similar to the Automotive SPICE methodology on system and software level, engineering processes has been defined for these missing artifacts.

Section 3.1 contains the description of how the different types of designs (system level, software level, etc.) are created corresponding to the novel domain specific modeling. To achieve full traceability, these designs, respectively the various components at the designs, have to be linked to the corresponding requirements. This is accomplished by the *Requirements Linker* at EASy Design, which establishes a connection to the MySQL database, and therefore has full access to the requirements data at Redmine. More details about the requirements management capability of the presented project can be found at [15].

3.3   Open Toolbox Approach at the DSM

The main objective of the open toolbox strategy is to provide a possibility for the user to tailor the modeling item set to their particular needs. Every non-abstract EMS-DSM class from Figure 1 can be instantiated and utilized as type for a new toolbox item. By selecting one of the provided types, the behaviour of the new toolbox item is defined. E.g. if a new *Application Software Component* is created at the toolbox, the aggregation "*1..* 0..*"* between *Hardware* and *Software Components* guarantees that the item can be used at the model within a *Hardware Component* only. These constraints contributes to the easy and intuitive handling of the modeling language. As mentioned previously, the defined modeling language and all presented features can be implemented on various modeling framework platforms, but at this project a self-made C# implementation has been preferred to achieve a highest possible grade of independence from third-party platforms.

To support the open toolbox methodology, additional functionality has been added to the custom-made software tool *EASy Design*. By selecting the command *Open Library Editor* at the menu bar, a new window (see Figure 2 in Section 4) is opened, offering toolbox modification options. At the window area *Create New Toolbox Item* the properties of the new toolbox item can be set. The drop down menu *Type* provides all non-abstract classes from the language definition. *Name* is a freely selectable identifier for the item, and *Mask* prompts the user to enter the path of a Portable Network Graphic (PNG), which determines the graphical representation of the toolbox item and its later appearance at the model. At the

---

[4] http://www.redmine.org/

window area *Delete Existing Toolbox Item* the no longer required item can be removed by choosing the respective name.

All library items are stored in an Extensible Markup Language (XML) file, corresponding to the following structure:

```
<EASyDesignLib>
  <LibItem>
    <Type></Type>
    <Name></Name>
    <Mask></Mask>
  </LibItem>
</EASyDesignLib>
```

4 Application

In this section the EMS-DSM approach with an open toolbox strategy is applied to the development of an automotive fuel tank system for compressed natural gas (CNG). For an appropriate scale of the use-case, only a small part of the real-world system is utilized. The application should be recognized as an illustrative material, reduced for internal training purpose for students. Therefore, the disclosed and commercially non-sensitivity use-case is not intended to be exhaustive or representing leading-edge technology.

To model the CNG fuel tank system, several mechanical, hardware, and software components are needed. As the main mechanical components, the following items being assumed to exist in the EMS-DSM library: *Tank Cylinder*, *Mechanical Pressure Regulator*, *Filter*, *Engine Rail*, and some *Tubing*. Moreover, four hardware components have already been added to the library: *In-Tank Temperature Sensor*, *CNG High Pressure Sensor*, *On-Tank Valve* (Actuator), and *Tank ECU* (Control Unit). So far, there are no software components at the library.

For a first draft of the system architectural design, an external control unit component *Engine ECU*, and a basis software component *CAN Driver* is needed. Therefore, the steps described in Subsection 3.3 are carried out for these new library items. The corresponding *Library Editor* windows are shown in Figure 2. The new library items are added at the EASy Design *Library Browser*, and the library file *EMS-DSM-Lib.xml* is extended by the following entries:

```
<LibItem>
  <Type>External Control Unit Component</Type>
  <Name>Engine ECU</Name>
  <Mask>"..\images\EASyLibExtEngECU.png"</Mask>
</LibItem> <LibItem>
  <Type>Basis Software Component</Type>
  <Name>CAN Driver</Name>
  <Mask>"..\images\EASyLibCANDriver.png"</Mask>
</LibItem>
```

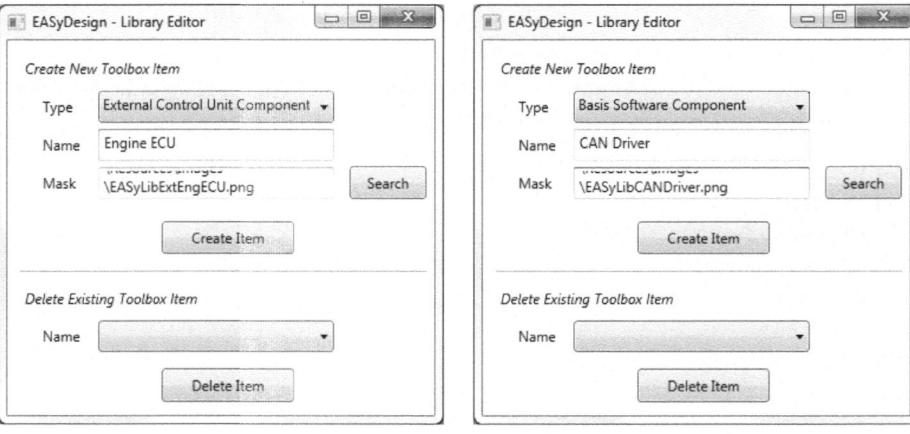

Fig. 2. Library Editor Windows for New Modeling Items

By adding these model items to the library, the system architectural design of the presented use-case can be created as shown in Figure 3. The CNG fuel tank system consists of seven mechanical components, which are blue coloured (Tank Cylinder, Filter, etc.) The medium flow between mechanical components, which is CNG in this use case, is displayed by blue lines with an arrow at the end. Furthermore, five hardware components are placed at the *System Architectural Design Model* level, which are yellow coloured (In-Tank Temperature Sensor,

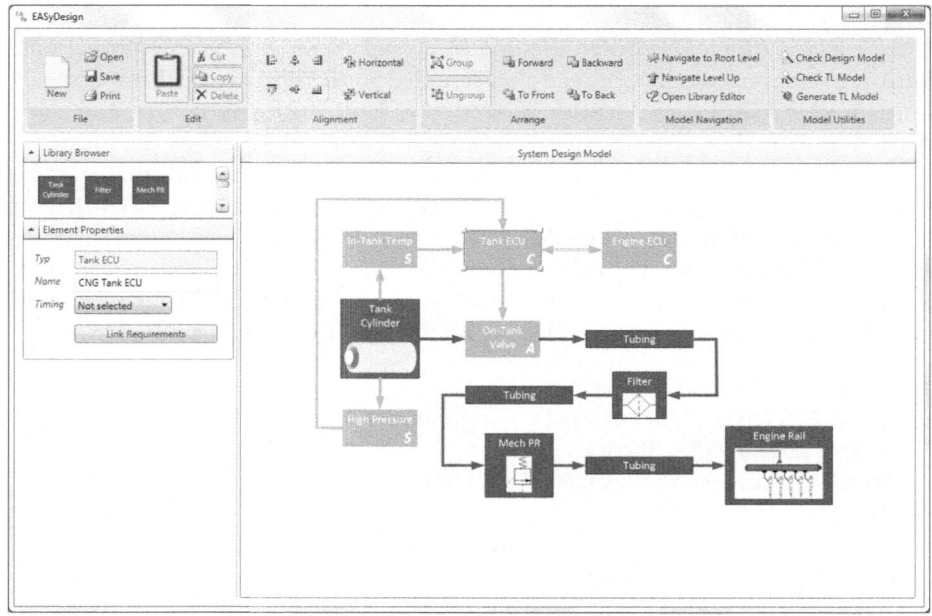

Fig. 3. CNG Tank System Architectural Design

Tank ECU, etc.) The signal flow between the components is displayed by yellow lines, ending with an arrow. Between the Control Unit and the External Control Unit component, a communication bus is inserted, characterized by the double compound line type and arrows on both ends.

As previously mentioned, the EMS-DSM definition requires at least one hardware component at the model to implement a software component. In this use-case the created basis software component *CAN Driver* shall be integrated at the *CNG Tank ECU*. With a double-click on the hardware component, the next modeling level is opened (named *E/E Item Design Level*), and the *CAN Driver* can be put in place.

5   Conclusions

In the previous sections, a lean method for the design of embedded automotive mechatronics-based E/E-Systems, with a focus on the open toolbox strategy, was presented. This approach has the potential to bring together the different engineering disciplines along the E/E-System development. Many artifacts like requirements, verification criteria, and various specifications can be linked to the models, created with the novel domain-specific modeling language. Supported by the linking of the artifacts, the vital traceability can be established. Depending on the respective tool chain and the organizations process landscape, the EMS-DSM models can also facilitate a single point of truth strategy.

By the model-to-model transformation mentioned in Section 2, a decision between the established SysML design techniques and the presented approach is not necessary. Instead, the EMS-DSM methodology can be utilized as an extension for mechatronics-based system designs to the existing tool chain. However, the possibility of modeling not only the system level, but also the software architectural level enables the presented work to be a standalone solution as well.

First use case implementations show promising results. However, there are several features on the open issue list, which have to be implemented in a next step. On the one hand, the options for describing the systems behavior, like e.g. some kind of task scheduling definition, shall be introduced. On the other hand, an advanced methodology for managing, as well as importing/exporting the signal interfaces has to be developed.

References

1. Andrianarison, E., Piques, J.-D.: SysML for embedded automotive Systems: a practical approach. In: Conference on Embedded Real Time Software and Systems. IEEE (2010)
2. Automotive SIG. Automotive SPICEProcess Assessment Model. Technical report, The SPICE User Group, Version 2.5 (May 2010)
3. Boldt, R.: Modeling AUTOSAR systems with a UML/SysML profile. Technical report, IBM Software Group (July 2009)

4. Broy, M., Feilkas, M., Herrmannsdoerfer, M., Merenda, S., Ratiu, D.: Seamless Model-Based Development: From Isolated Tools to Integrated Model Engineering Environments. Proceedings of the IEEE **98**(4), 526–545 (2010)
5. Code Project. WPF Diagram Designer - Part 4. Online Resource (March 2008). http://www.codeproject.com/Articles/24681/WPF-Diagram-Designer-Part (accessed March 2015)
6. Giese, H., Hildebrandt, S., Neumann, S.: Model Synchronization at Work: Keeping SysML and AUTOSAR Models Consistent. In: Engels, G., Lewerentz, C., Schäfer, W., Schürr, A., Westfechtel, B. (eds.) Graph Transformations and Model-Driven Engineering. LNCS, vol. 5765, pp. 555–579. Springer, Heidelberg (2010)
7. Hudak, P.: Domain-specific languages. Handbook of Programming Languages **3**, 39–60 (1997)
8. ISO 26262, Road vehicles - Functional safety. International standard, International Organization for Standardization, Geneva, CH (November 2011)
9. Kawahara, R., Nakamura, H., Dotan, D., Kirshin, A., Sakairi, T., Hirose, S., Ono, K., Ishikawa, H.: Verification of embedded system's specification using collaborative simulation of SysML and simulink models. In International Conference on Model Based Systems Engineering (MBSE 2009), pp. 21–28. IEEE (2009)
10. Macher, G., Armengaud, E., Kreiner, C.: Bridging Automotive Systems, Safety and Software Engineering by a Seamless Tool Chain. In: 7th European Congress Embedded Real Time Software and Systems Proceedings, pp. 256–263 (2014)
11. Mernik, M., Heering, J., Sloane, A.M.: When and how to develop domain-specific languages. ACM Computing Surveys (CSUR) **37**(4), 316–344 (2005)
12. Meseguer, J.: Why Formal Modeling Language Semantics Matters. In: Dingel, J., Schulte, W., Ramos, I., Abrahao, S., Insfran, E. (eds.) International Conference on Model-Driven Engineering Languages and Systems, MODELS 2014, Valencia, Spain. LNCS. Springer International Publishing Switzerland (2014)
13. Meyer, J.: Eine durchgängige modellbasierte Entwicklungsmethodik für die automobile Steuergeräteentwicklung unter Einbeziehung des AUTOSAR Standards. PhD thesis, Universität Paderborn, Fakultät für Elektrotechnik, Informatik und Mathematik, Paderborn, Germany (July 2014)
14. Preschern, C., Kajtazovic, N., Kreiner, C.: Efficient development and reuse of domain-specific languages for automation systems. International Journal of Metadata, Semantics and Ontologies **9**(3), 215–226 (2014)
15. Sporer, H., Macher, G., Kreiner, C., Brenner, E.: A Lean Automotive E/E-System Design Approach with Integrated Requirements Management Capability. In: 9th European Conference on Software Architecture (ECSA 2015), Dubrovnik/Cavtat, Croatia (in press, 2015)
16. Sporer, H., Macher, G., Kreiner, C., Brenner, E.: A Model-Based Domain-Specific Language Approach for the Automotive E/E-System Design. In: International Conference on Research in Adaptive and Convergent Systems, RACS 2015, Prague, Czech Republic (2015) (under review)
17. Vujović, V., Maksimović, M., Perišić, B.: Sirius: A rapid development of DSM graphical editor. In: 18th International Conference on Intelligent Engineering Systems (INES), pp. 233–238. IEEE (2014)

Integration of Heterogeneous Tools to a Seamless Automotive Toolchain

Georg Macher[1,2]([✉]), Eric Armengaud[2], and Christian Kreiner[1]

[1] Institute for Technical Informatics, Graz University of Technology, Graz, Austria
{georg.macher,christian.kreiner}@tugraz.at
[2] AVL List GmbH, Graz, Austria
{georg.macher,eric.armengaud}@avl.com

Abstract. Modern embedded multi-core system platforms are key innovation drivers in the automotive domain.

The challenge, is to master the increased complexity of these systems and ensure consistency of the development along the entire product life cycle. Automotive standards, such as ISO 26262 and automotive SPICE require efficient and consistent product development and tool support. The existing solutions are still frequently insufficient when transforming system models with a higher level of abstraction to more concrete software engineering models.

The aim of this work is to improve the information interchange continuity of architectural designs from system development level to software development level (Automotive SPICE ENG.3 and ENG.5 respectively ISO 26262 4-7 System design and 6-7 SW architectural design). An approach for seamlessly combining the development tools involved is thus proposed. This approach merges the heterogeneous tools required for development of automotive safety-critical multi-core systems to support seamless information interchange across tool boundaries.

Keywords: ISO 26262 · Automotive SPICE · Automotive systems · Multi-core · Architectural design · Traceability

1 Introduction

Embedded systems are already integrated into our everyday life and play a central role in many vital sectors including automotive, aerospace, healthcare, industry, energy, or consumer electronics. Current premium cars implement more than 90 electronic control units (ECU) with close to 1 Gigabyte software code [9], are responsible for 25% of vehicle costs and an added value between 40% and 75% [27]. The trend of replacing traditional mechanical systems with modern embedded systems enables the deployment of more advanced control strategies providing additional benefits for the customer and the environment, but at the same time the higher degree of integration and criticality of the control application raise new challenges. Today's information society strongly supports

© Springer International Publishing Switzerland 2015
R.V. O'Connor et al. (Eds.): EuroSPI 2015, CCIS 543, pp. 51–62, 2015.
DOI: 10.1007/978-3-319-24647-5_5

inter-system communication (Car2X) also in the automotive domain. Consequently the boundaries of application domains are disappearing even faster than previously due to the replacement of traditional mechanical systems. At the same time, multi-core and many-core computing platforms are becoming available for safety-critical real-time applications. These factors cause multiple cross-domain collaborations and interactions in the face of the challenge to master the increased complexity and ensure consistency of the development along the entire product life cycle.

Consequently, this work focuses on improving the continuity of information interchange of architectural designs from system development level (Automotive SPICE [29] ENG.3 respectively ISO 26262 [16] 4-7 System design) to software development level (Automotive SPICE ENG.5 respectively ISO 26262 6-7 SW architectural design). We further make a special focus on safety-critical multi-core system development, due to the higher complexity of such systems and limited availability of supporting methods and tools.

The aim of this work is to merge the heterogeneous tools required for development of automotive safety-critical multi-core systems (especially during transition phase from system to SW development) and establish a single source of information concept to ease cross-domain consolidation.

The document is organized as follows: Section 2 presents an overview of related works. In Section 3 a description of the proposed approach and a detailed depiction of the contribution parts is provided. An implementation prototype and a brief evaluation of the approach is presented in Section 4. Finally, this work is concluded in Section 5 with an overview of the approach presented.

2   Related Works

Model-based development in general and the development of embedded automotive systems in particular are engineering domains and research topics aimed at moving the development process to a more automated work-flow, which improves in terms of consistency and tackles the complexity of the development process across expertise and domain boundaries. Recent publications are either related to AUTOSAR [2] methodology based approaches, focus ISO 26262 [16] related methods, model-based development, multi-core system development or deal with Automotive SPICE [29] concept.

2.1   Publications Related to Model-Based Development

In [18], the authors describe a framework for a seamless configuration process for the development of automotive embedded software. The framework is also based on AUTOSAR, which defines architecture, methodology, and application interfaces. The steps through this configuration process are established by a system configuration and ECU configuration.

An approach for a design of a vehicular code generator for distributed automotive systems is addressed by Jo et al. [17]. The authors mention the increasing complexity of the development of automotive embedded software and systems and the manual generation of software leading to more and more software defects and problems. Thus the authors integrated a run-time environment (RTE) module into the earlier development tool to design and evolve an automated embedded code generator with a predefined generation process.

An important topic to deal with in general terms is the gap between system architecture and software architecture. Broy et al. [6] claim model-based development to be the best approach to manage large complexity of modern embedded systems and provide an overview of basic concepts and theories. The work illustrates why seamless solutions have not been achieved so far, it mentions commonly used solutions and the problems arising from the use of an inadequate tool-chain (e.g. redundancy, inconsistency and lack of automation).

The work of Quadri and Sadovykh [23] presents a model-driven engineering approach aiming to develop novel model-driven techniques and new tools supporting design, validation, and simulation. These authors defined profiles using a subset of UML and SysML for their approach and mentioned the usage of effective design tools and methodologies as crucial to be capable of managing complex real-time embedded systems.

The work of Holtmann et al. [14] highlights process and tooling gaps between different modeling aspects of a model-based development process. Often, different specialized models for specific aspects are used at different development stages with varying abstraction levels and traceability between these different models is commonly established via manual linking.

Chen et. al. [7] present an approach that bridges the gap between model-based systems engineering and the safety process of automotive embedded systems. More recently also the MAENAD Project [1] is focusing on design methodologies for electric vehicles based on EAST-ADL2 language.

Giese et al. [13] address issues of correct bi-directional transfer between system design models and software engineering models. The authors propose a model synchronization approach consisting of tool adapters between SysML models and software engineering models in AUTOSAR representation.

Fabbrini et al. [10] provide an overview of software engineering in the European automotive industry and present tools, techniques, and countermeasures to prevent faults. The authors also highlight the importance of tool integration and model-based development approaches.

Recent projects which focus on model-based development environments for automotive multi-core systems are the AMALTHEA Project [2], SAFE Project [3], and MAENAD Project [4].

The work of Asplund et. al [1] focuses on tool integration in context of ISO 26262. The authors mention that tool integration is a complicated issue and that guidance regarding tool integration into tool chains is very limited.

---

[1] http://maenad.eu/
[2] http://www.amalthea-project.org/
[3] http://safe-project.eu/
[4] http://maenad.eu/

2.2 Publications Related to Safety-Critical Development

Safety standards, such as the road vehicles functional safety norm ISO 26262 [16] and its basic norm IEC 61508 [15] present requirements and guidance for safety-critical system development. A guide to the functional safety of automotive systems according to ISO 26262 can be found in [4,12] or in the SafEUr functional safety manager trainings [25]. The AUTOSAR development cooperation also focuses on safety in the technical safety concept report [3] produced by this group.

The work of Gashi et al. [11] focuses on redundancy and diversity and their effects on the safety and security of embedded systems. This work is part of SeSaMo (Security and Safety Modeling for Embedded Systems) project, which focuses on synergies and trade-offs between security and safety through concrete use-cases.

Born et al. [5] recommend a transition from a document-centric approach to a model-based approach. Their work mentions the problem that organizations already have their own safety processes in place and want to keep their existing document-centric processes and tool landscape, which mostly inherits fundamental flaws in terms of traceability, a key requirement in ISO 26262.

SysML and model-based development (MBD) as the backbone for development of complex safety critical systems is also seen as a key success factor by Lovric et. al [19]. The integration of SysML models for the development of the ECU safety concept ensures efficient design changes, and immediate awareness of functional safety needs. The paper evaluates key success factors of MBD in comparison to legacy development processes in the field of safety-critical automotive systems.

The work of Ebert [8] highlights three key components of sustainable safety engineering in automotive systems: (a) system-oriented development, (b) safety methods closely coupled to engineering, and (c) process maturity. Ebert further mentions functional safety needs and that these are be seen as a critical product liability issue with all the consequences this implies and also that engineers need to understand the safety needs at all levels of the development process.

In the issue of improving processes or workflows especially those which deal with cross-domains affairs (such as the traceability of architectural designs from system development level to software development level), however, a comprehensive understanding of related processes, methods, and tools is required.

The work of Sechser [28] describes experiences gained at combining two different process worlds in the automotive domain. The author mentions, among other points, the need for a common language and process architecture.

The work of Raschke et. al [24] is based on the concept that development of systems is a sequence of evolutions, interrupted by revolutions. The authors build up a catalog of patterns for software modeling to these terms. This pattern catalog focuses on the dependencies between software models and software code and their possible relations.

According to the work of Sechser, the works of Messnarz et. al [20,21] also showed that the combination of Automotive SPICE and ISO 26262 functional

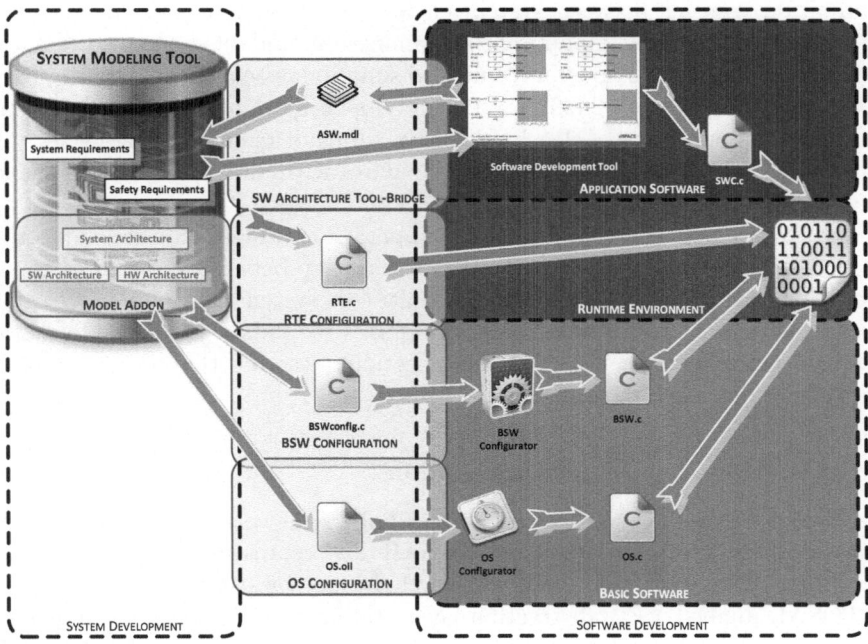

Fig. 1. presents an overview of the approach and highlights the key contribution parts.

safety processes is possible and worth the effort involved in developing generic best practices and process models.

3   Architectural Design Refinement Approach

While methods and tools for elicitation and definition of requirements along the different process steps (such as Automotive SPICE ENG.2 or ENG.4) are already settled, tool supported and well-known best-practices exist. The methodical support of system architectural design (ENG.3) and refinement of this design to software design (ENG.5), however, often fell short of the mark. To handle this situation the AUTOSAR methodology [2] provides standardized and clearly defined interfaces between different software components and development tools and also provides such tools for easing this process of architectural design refinement. Nevertheless, projects with limited resources in particular (as well as non-AUTOSAR projects) often struggle to achieve adequate quality in budget (such as time or manpower) with this approach. The approach presented in this work has thus emerged from full AUTOSAR based approaches and focuses forcefully on a central MBD database as a single-source of information concept.

The main benefit of this proposed approach contributes to closing the gap, also mentioned by Giese et al. [13], Holtmann et al. [14], and Sandmann and Seibt [26], between system-level development at abstract UML-like representations and software-level development. This bridging supports consistency of information transfer between system engineering tools and software engineering tools. Furthermore, the approach minimizes redundant manual information exchange between tools and contributes to simplifying seamless safety argumentation according to ISO 26262 for the developed system. The benefits of this development approach are clearly visible in terms of re-engineering cycles, tool changes, and reworking of development artifacts with alternating dependencies, as also mentioned by Broy et al. [6].

Figure 1 depicts the overview of the approach and highlights the key contribution parts. The approach bridges the existing gap between system design and software implementation tools (also for multi-core system development) to guarantee consistency of information and minimizes redundant manual information exchange between tools. The following sections describe the key contribution parts of the approach in more details.

3.1 SW Modeling Framework Addon

The first part of the approach is a modeling framework addon that enables software architecture design in AUTOSAR like representation. This enables the design of an automotive software architecture by taking advantage of an AUTOSAR aligned VFB abstraction layer and an explicit definition of components, component interfaces, and connections between interfaces. This provides the possibility to define software architecture (ENG5.BP1) and ensures proper definition of the communication between the architecture artifacts, including interface specifications (ENG5.BP3) and timing information (ENG5.BP4). In addition this SW architecture representation can be linked to system development artifacts and traces to requirements can be easily established (ENG5.BP2). This brings further benefits in terms of constraints checking, traceability of development decisions (e.g. for safety case generation), and reuse. Figure 2 shows the representation profile of software architecture artifacts.

3.2 HW Modeling Framework Addon

Special basic software (BSW) and hardware module representations are assigned to establish links to the underlying basic software and hardware layers. The AUTOSAR architectural approach ensures hardware-independent development of application software modules until a very late development phase and therefore enables application software developers and basic software developers to work in parallel. The hardware profile, depicted in Figure 3, allows representation of hardware resources (such as ADC, CAN), calculation engines (core), and connected peripherals which interact with the software (ENG5.BP5). This further enables the establishing of software and hardware dependencies and a hardware-software interface (HSI), as required by ISO 26262. Software signals of BSW modules can be linked to HW port pins via dedicated mappings. On the one hand this enables the modeling and mapping of HW specifics and SW signals. On the other hand, this mapping establishes traceable links to port pin configurations (ENG5.BP8).

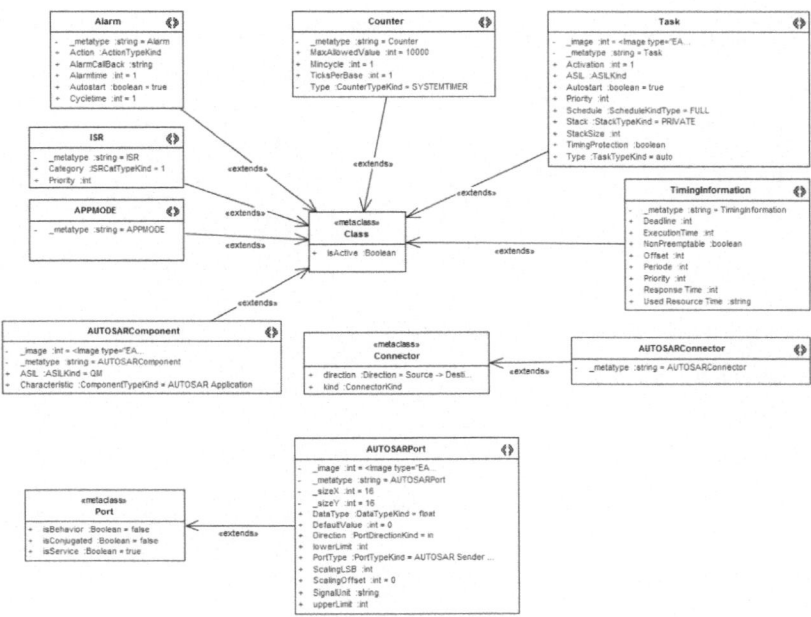

Fig. 2. shows the representation of SW architecture artifacts.

3.3 Software Architecture Toolbridge

The third part of the approach is an exporter, which is able to export the software architecture, component containers, and their interconnections designed in SysML to the software development tool Matlab/Simulink and thus, enabling the information handover to a special purpose tool (model-driven software engineering tools) for detailing of the SW architecture and SW modules (ENG5.BP6).

The import functionality, in combination with the export function, enables bidirectional update of software architecture representations. On the one hand, this ensures consistency between system development artifacts and changes done in the software development tool (related to ENG6.BP8 and ENG5.BP10). On the other hand, the import functionality enables reuse of available software modules, guarantees consistency of information across tool boundaries, and shares information more precisely and less ambiguously.

3.4 Runtime Environment Generator

The fourth part of the approach presented is the SW/SW interface generator (RTE generator). This dll- based tool generates *.c* and *.h* files defining SW/SW interfaces between application software signals and basic software signals from the modeled artifacts. The RTE generation eliminates the need of manual SW/SW interface generation without adequate syntax and semantic support and ensures reproducibility and traceability of these configurations (ENG5.BP3).

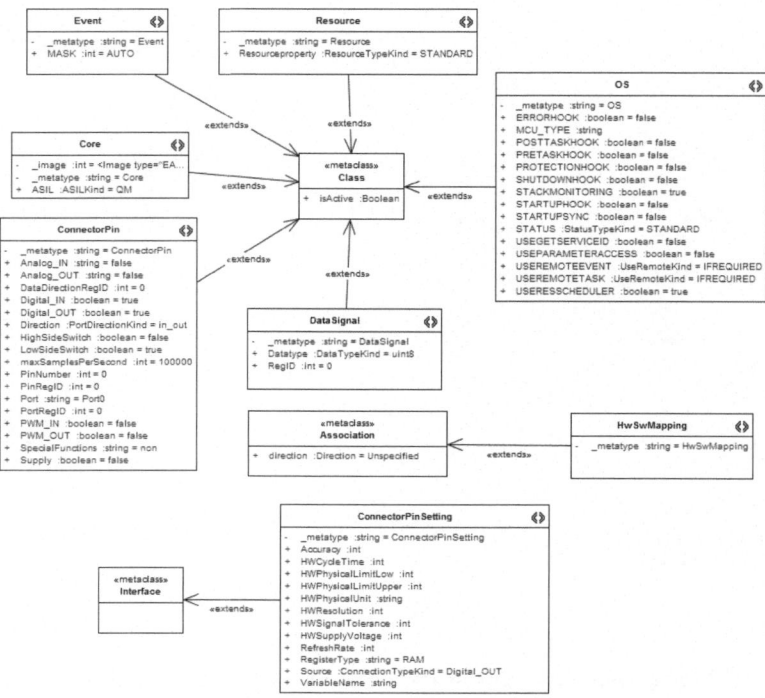

Fig. 3. shows the representation of HW architecture artifacts.

3.5   Basic Software Configuration Generator

The basic software configuration generator is also part of the dll- based tool, which generates BSW driver specific configuration files. These files configure the basic software driver of the HW device according to the HSI specifications and eliminates the need of manual information rework.

3.6   OS Configuration Generator

The last part of the approach is an exporter capable of exporting the RTOS configuration available from the model to an OIL file [22] and the corresponding import functionality. The exporter generates OIL files enriched with the available system and safety development artifact traces (such as required ASIL of task implementation). The import functionality enables bidirectional update of the information representation within the database. Most state-of-the-art software development frameworks are able to configure the RTOS according to the specifications within such an OIL file.

4   Prototypical Implementation and Application of the Proposed Approach

This section demonstrates the benefits of the presented approach for development of automotive embedded systems. For this evaluation a prototypical implementation of the approach has been made for Enterprise Architect [5]. An automotive use-case of a central control unit (CCU) of a battery management system (BMS) prototype for (hybrid) electric vehicle has been chosen for evaluation of the approach. This use-case is an illustrative material, reduced for internal training purpose and is not intended to be exhaustive or representing leading-edge technology.

Table 1. comprises an overview of the evaluation use-case SW architecture, element counts, and number of configurable attributes per element.

Object type	Element-count	Configurable Attributes per Element
ASW Modules	10	3
BSW Modules	7	3
ASW Module Inputs	54	10
ASW Module Outputs	32	10
ASW/ASW Module Interfaces	48	
ASW/BSW Module Interfaces	19	
HW/SW Interfaces	19	13

The definition of the software architecture is usually done by a software system architect within the software development tool (Matlab/Simulink). With our approach this work package is included in the system development tool Enterprise Architect. This does not hamper the work of the software system architect but enables the possibility to also link existing HSI mapping information to the SW architecture and offers a significant benefit in terms of traceability (ENG5.BP9 and ENG5.BP10), replicability of design decisions, and unambiguously visualizes dependencies.

The use-case consists of 10 ASW modules and 7 BSW modules with 19 interface definitions between ASW and BSW, which are transferred via the SW architecture tool-bridge and makes use of the 3 fundamental low level HW functions (digital input/output, analog input/outputs, and PWM outputs). A more complete overview of use-case is given in Table 1.

As can be seen in Table 1, 7 ASW/BSW input interfaces and 12 ASW/BSW output interfaces need to be defined. This definition sums up to more than 30 lines of code (LoC) which can be generated automatically with the runtime environment generator. The actual HW/SW interface, mapping of BSW signals to HW pins, also consist of 19 interfaces and 3 low level driver for this specific SW

---
[5] http://www.sparxsystems.com/

architecture. This mapping includes 23 settings per mapping and can be used to automatically generate basic software configurations with the help of the basic SW configuration generator and OS configuration generator. This ensures actuality of development artifacts and simplifies tracing of development decisions.

5 Conclusion

The challenge with modern embedded automotive systems is to master the increased complexity of these systems and ensure consistency of the development along the entire product life cycle. Automotive standards, such as ISO 26262 safety standard and automotive SPICE provide a process framework which requires efficient and consistent product development and tool support. Nevertheless, various heterogeneous development tools in use hamper the efficiency and consistency of information flows.

This work thus focuses on improving the continuity of information interchange of architectural designs from system development level (Automotive SPICE ENG.3 respectively ISO 26262 4-7 System design) to software development level (Automotive SPICE ENG.5 respectively ISO 26262 6-7 SW architectural design). For this purpose, an approach to seamlessly combine the development tools involved has been proposed and a prototypical tool-bridge implementation has been made. The approach presented merges the heterogeneous tools required for development of automotive systems to support seamless interchange of information across tool boundaries and helps to ease cross-domain consolidation via establishing a single source of information concept. The application of the approach presented has been demonstrated utilizing an automotive BMS use-case, which is intended for training purposes for students and engineers and does not represent either an exhaustive or a commercially sensitive project. The main benefits of this approach are: improved consistency and traceability from the initial design at the system level down to the software implementation, as well as, a reduction of cumbersome and error-prone manual work along the system development path. Further improvements of the approach include the progress in terms of reproducibility and traceability of design decisions.

Acknowledgments. This work is partially supported by the INCOBAT and the MEMCONS projects.

The research leading to these results has received funding from the European Unions Seventh Framework Programme (FP7/2007-2013) under grant agreement n 608988 and financial support of the "COMET K2 - Competence Centers for Excellent Technologies Programme" of the Austrian Federal Ministry for Transport, Innovation and Technology (BMVIT), the Austrian Federal Ministry of Economy, Family and Youth (BMWFJ), the Austrian Research Promotion Agency (FFG), the Province of Styria, and the Styrian Business Promotion Agency (SFG).

Furthermore, we would like to express our thanks to our supporting project partners, AVL List GmbH, Virtual Vehicle Research Center, and Graz University of Technology.

References

1. Asplund, F., Biehl, M., El-khoury, J., Frede, D., Trngren, M.: Tool Integration, from Tool to Tool Chain with ISO 26262. SAE Technical Paper. SAE International, April 2012
2. AUTOSAR development cooperation: AUTOSAR AUTomotive Open System ARchitecture (2009)
3. AUTOSAR Development Cooperation: Technical Safety Concept Status Report. Technical Report Document Version: 1.1.0, Revision 2, AUTOSAR development cooperation, October 2010
4. Boehringer, K., Kroh, M.: Funktionale Sicherheit in der Praxis, July 2013
5. Born, M., Favaro, J., Kath, O.: Application of ISO DIS 26262 in Practice. In: CARS 2010 (2010)
6. Broy, M., Feilkas, M., Herrmannsdoerfer, M., Merenda, S., Ratiu, D.: Seamless Model-based Development: from Isolated Tool to Integrated Model Engineering Environments. IEEE Magazin (2008)
7. Chen, D.J., Johansson, R., Lönn, H., Papadopoulos, Y., Sandberg, A., Törner, F., Törngren, M.: Modelling support for design of safety-critical automotive embedded systems. In: Harrison, M.D., Sujan, M.-A. (eds.) SAFECOMP 2008. LNCS, vol. 5219, pp. 72–85. Springer, Heidelberg (2008)
8. Ebert, C.: Functional Safety Industry Best Practices for Introducing and Using ISO 26262. SAE Technical Paper. SAE International, April 2013
9. Ebert, C., Jones, C.: Embedded Software: Facts, Figures, and Future. IEEE Computer Society **0018–9162**(09), 42–52 (2009)
10. Fabbrini, F., Fusani, M., Lami, G., Sivera, E.: Software engineering in the European automotive industry: achievements and challenges. In: COMPSAC, pp. 1039–1044. IEEE Computer Society (2008)
11. Gashi, I., Povyakalo, A., Strigini, L., Matschnig, M., Hinterstoisser, T., Fischer, B.: Diversity for safety and security in embedded systems. In: International Conference on Dependable Systems and Networks, vol. 26, June 2014
12. Gebhardt, V., Rieger, G., Mottok, J., Giesselbach, C.: Funktionale Sicherheit nach ISO 262626 - Ein Praxisleitfaden zur Umsetzung, vol. 1. Auflage, dpunkt.verlag (2013)
13. Giese, H., Hildebrandt, S., Neumann, S.: Model synchronization at work: keeping SysML and AUTOSAR models consistent. In: Engels, G., Lewerentz, C., Schäfer, W., Schürr, A., Westfechtel, B. (eds.) Nagl Festschrift. LNCS, vol. 5765, pp. 555–579. Springer, Heidelberg (2010)
14. Holtmann, J., Meyer, J., Meyer, M.: A Seamless Model-Based Development Process for Automotive Systems (2011)
15. ISO - International Organization for Standardization: IEC 61508 Functional safety of electrical/electronic/programmable electronic safety-related systems
16. ISO - International Organization for Standardization: ISO 26262 Road vehicles Functional Safety Part 1–10 (2011)
17. Jo, H.C., Piao, S., Jung, W.Y.: Design of a vehicular code generator for distributed automotive systems (DGIST). In: Seventh International Conference on Information Technology (2010)
18. Lee, J.-C., Han, T.-M.: ECU Configuration Framework based on AUTOSAR ECU Configuration Metamodel (2009)
19. Lovric, T., Schneider-Scheyer, M., Sarkic, S.: SysML as Backbone for Engineering and Safety - Practical Experience with TRW Braking ECU. SAE Technical Paper. SAE International, April04 2014

20. Messnarz, R., König, F., Bachmann, V.O.: Experiences with trial assessments combining automotive SPICE and functional safety standards. In: Winkler, D., O'Connor, R.V., Messnarz, R. (eds.) EuroSPI 2012. CCIS, vol. 301, pp. 266–275. Springer, Heidelberg (2012)
21. Messnarz, R., Sokic, I., Habel, S., König, F., Bachmann, O.: Extending automotive SPICE to cover functional safety requirements and a safety architecture. In: O'Connor, R.V., Pries-Heje, J., Messnarz, R. (eds.) EuroSPI 2011. CCIS, vol. 172, pp. 298–307. Springer, Heidelberg (2011)
22. OSEK/VDX Steering Committee: OSEK/VDX System Generation OIL: OSEK Implementation Language (2004). http://portal.osek-vdx.org/files/pdf/specs/oil25.pdf
23. Quadri, I.R., Sadovykh, A.: MADES: A SysML/MARTE high level methodology for real-time and embedded systems (2011)
24. Raschke, W., Zilli, M., Loinig, J., Weiss, R., Steger, C., Kreiner, C.: Patterns of software modeling. In: Meersman, R., et al. (eds.) On the Move to Meaningful Internet Systems: OTM 2014 Workshops. LNCS, vol. 8842, pp. 428–437. Springer, Heidelberg (2014)
25. SafEUr Training Material Committee: ECQA Certified Functional Safety Manager Training Material. Training dossier, April 2013
26. Sandmann, G., Seibt, M.: AUTOSAR-Compliant Development Workflows: From Architecture to Implementation - Tool Interoperability for Round-Trip Engineering and Verification & Validation. In: SAE World Congress & Exhibition 2012, (SAE 2012-01-0962) (2012)
27. Scuro, G.: Automotive industry: Innovation driven by electronics (2012). http://embedded-computing.com/articles/automotive-industry-innovation-driven-electronics/
28. Sechser, B.: The marriage of two process worlds. Software Process: Improvement and Practice 14(6), 349–354 (2009)
29. The SPICE User Group: Automotive SPICE Process Assessment Model. Technical report (2007)

A Tool Suite for Assurance Cases and Evidences: Avionics Experiences

Alejandra Ruiz(⊠), Xabier Larrucea, and Huascar Espinoza

ICT-European Software Institute Division, Tecnalia, Derio, Spain
{alejandra.ruiz,xabier.larrucea,huascar.espinoza}@tecnalia.com

Abstract. This paper describes a specification and an implementation of a flexible tool platform for assurance and certification of safety-critical systems. This tool platform is built upon a comprehensive conceptual assurance and certification framework. This conceptual framework is composed of a common information model called CCL (Common Certification Language) and a compositional assurance approach. Our tool platform allows an easy integration with existing solutions supporting interoperability with existing development and assurance tools. The ultimate goal of our platform is to provide an integrated approach for managing assurance cases and evidences resulting from a safety project.

Keywords: Tooling platform · Compliance · Standards · Argumentation · Evidence management

1   Introduction

Assurance [1] and safety certification[2] are among the most expensive and time-consuming tasks in the development of safety-critical embedded systems. Innovation and productivity in this market is curtailed by the lack of affordable certification and especially recertification approaches [3]. A common situation in safety-critical industrial domains is the fact that developers or manufacturers of a safety-critical system are required to demonstrate with evidences that their products are acceptably safe in a given context before it is formally approved for release into service. Conceptually, this means that all potential system hazards [4] – operational misbehaviour or conditions which might lead to an accident leading to injury or loss of human life or to damage to the environment – are either prevented or mitigated. The manufacturer is obliged to demonstrate the absence of risks and to increase the assessor's confidence with respect to the system's safety. In fact they must explicitly provide evidence of the system's conformance to relevant standards or reference models. This includes prescription that rigorous analysis, checking, and testing are carried out.

The identification of evidences [5] for the effectiveness of existing certification schemes is hard to come by. Typically a safety-critical application and its accompanying set of evidences are monolithic, based on the whole product, and a major problem arises when evolutions to the product came into play. Those evolutions become costly and time consuming because they entail regenerating the entire evidence-set.

© Springer International Publishing Switzerland 2015
R.V. O'Connor et al. (Eds.): EuroSPI 2015, CCIS 543, pp. 63–71, 2015.
DOI: 10.1007/978-3-319-24647-5_6

This paper is structured as follows; section 2 highlights current gaps in industrial environments. Section 3 presents the main concepts of our conceptual approach while on section 4 we discuss the principal functionalities over a particular example. Section 5 presents the benefits from using our tool suite and the main problems we try to give support to. Finally, section 6 indicates some main conclusions extracted from this work and the future work we are planning to deal with tool evolution.

2   Related Work

Practitioners face different situations during development and certification processes. One of them is to clearly define and maintain a chain of evidence adequate for safety certification. The identification and management of these evidences increase development time and costs. Different tools have been developed in order to support argumentation and evidence management efforts [12]. The arguments are usually packed into a safety case which can be defined as "*A structured argument, supported by a body of evidence, that provides a compelling, comprehensible and valid case that a system is safe for a given application in a given environment*" [6].. There are some graphical notations which include the main concepts for argumentation such as the GSN (Goal Structuring Notation) [10] or CAE (Claim Arguments and Evidence) [112]. Both graphical notations facilitate the understanding of argumentations performed by the reviewer or assessor during an assurance case assessment. One step forward is the Structured Assurance Case Metamodel (SACM) [7] which is a standard developed by the Object Management Group (OMG) to model the different concepts that come up while exposing an argument. It has a richer set of concepts than the ones made explicit in the GSN. In fact the notion of how a particular claim is used in an argument - e.g. as supporting or indirect, and umbrella types of element in the argument. In addition, it has some extra concepts such as counter-evidence or assumed claims. However, it also lacks of GSNs features such as modularity and some forms of patterning to provide argumentation templates. SACM does not prescribe a specific graphical notation but proposes the use of the existing ones are possible graphical notation for its concepts. Therefore GSN notation could be used for describing SACM models. Regarding argumentation tools, there has been some work from NASA working on Advocate tool which uses GSN notation for the argumentation [13]. D-CASE [14] is a tool created by DEOS project where argumentation pattern functionality is linked with the use of parameters. D-CASE and Advocate approaches do not present clear relations to standards requirements or evidence management. NOR-STA platform [16] also provides argumentation support based on TRUST-IT method but they do not provide an interface to describe standards based requirements, and to generate automatically a report on compliance with respect to these standards.

Some initiatives integrate information from different sources and tools. This is the case of ModelBus [15] which offers support for creating an integrated tool environment. Nevertheless, ModelBus is focused on data integration from different tools. This paper integrates in a consistent and meaningful way project safety information and standard compliance information.

3   Conceptual Platform

This paper is framed under a European project called OPENCOSS (Open Platform for EvolutioNary Certification Of Safety-critical Systems) which is a large-scale collaborative project of the EU's Seventh Framework Program. OPENCOSS focuses on the harmonization of safety assurance and certification management activities for the development cyber-physical systems in automotive, railway and aerospace industries. This paper presents a conceptual approach dealing with the aforementioned identified situations. This work is based on assurance cases and evidences approaches and we have identified the following challenges in safety critical systems [8]:

— **Unawareness of the certification process.** The lack of awareness on the certification aspects is a frequent problem in the current practice, in large part arising due to poor visibility into the architecture of systems, their design rationale, how components were verified and integrated, and finally how the system components and the system as a whole were certified.
— **Data exists in many places, with different formats, multiple copies and versions.** Usually, engineers submit paper-based reports and do not know where the reports go and are unable to follow up. Quality and safety managers assess and classify information. Excel and Word documents are often exchanged, of which multiple copies and versions exist.
— **Time-consuming to compile reports, artefacts and difficult to retrieve.** Often paper-based reports are filled, which are time-consuming to aggregate. It is painful to generate trend analysis reports because the organizations do not have easy access to data, reports and policies.
— **Difficulties in interpretations of argumentation.** Determining the degree of compliance with specified standards or practices for the different safety-critical market and technological domains is a challenging task. There are a variety of definitions of evidence, and how to evaluate it or derive it in regard the technology used, which makes cross-acceptance difficult.

System's safety is usually demonstrated by compliance to standards, processes, or generally accepted checklists [2]. In some industries, manufacturers are required to produce argumentation in the form of an explicit safety case, in order to demonstrate that all of the hazards have been prevented or mitigated and that the system is acceptably safe to operate in its intended context of use [9]. These argumentations are not just part of a set of requirements defined by standards. In fact a safety engineer must assure that all evidences are made explicit in order to have a confidence level enough to determine that a system is safe.

We have design a platform in order to give an answer and support a feasible approach to deal with all the mentioned issues. Fig 1 shows a general view of the functional decomposition of our conceptual platform. Our conceptual framework contains the following functionalities:

• **Prescriptive Knowledge Management:** Functionality related to the management of standards information as well as any other information derived from them, such as interpretations about intents, mapping between standards, etc. This functional group maintain a knowledge database about "standards & understandings".

- **Assurance Project Lifecycle Management:** This functionality factorizes aspects such as the creation of safety assurance projects. This module manages a "project repository", which can be accessed by the other modules.
- **Safety Argumentation Management:** This group manages argumentation information in a modular fashion. It also includes mechanisms to support compositional safety assurance, and assurance patterns management.
- **Evidence Management:** This module manages the full life-cycle of evidences and evidence chains. This includes evidence traceability management and impact analysis. In addition, this module is in charge of communicating with external engineering tools (requirements management, implementation, V&V, etc.)

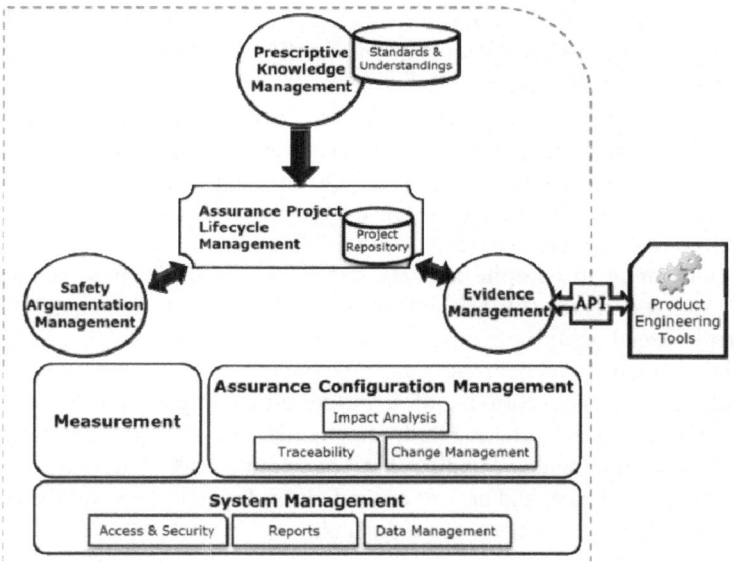

Fig. 1. Functional decomposition of our platform

- **Assurance Configuration Management:** This is an infrastructure functional module. This includes functionality for traceability management, change management, impact analysis.
- **System Management:** It includes generic functionality for security, permissions, reports, etc.
- **Measurement:** This module contains functionality related to safety indicators. Our first approach is based on basic indicators such as Mean Time Between Failures (MTBF).

4   Avionics Experience

It will be taken the example of Execution Platform (Computing Unit and Operating System) to build a scenario where complete Execution Platform will be installed in an IMA (Integrated Modular Avionics) platform using the aforementioned tool support. The execution platform is considered as an independent item for which a qualification dossier will be built. This qualification dossier consists of plans, technical documents, and certification documents. Technical documents are specifications, validation and verification life cycle data. The certification documents are configuration index documents and accomplishment summaries.

The execution needs to comply with DO178c [17] standard and ARP 4754 [18] guidelines. In addition the resulting software will be integrated into an IMA (Integrated Modular Avionics) platform [19].

Fig 2 depicts a process flow representing our tool platform. Each swim lane has its own editor and they support a predefined set of activities which has been tested for avionics software. The Standards editor, assurance projects editor, argumentations editor and evidences specification tool are closely integrated.

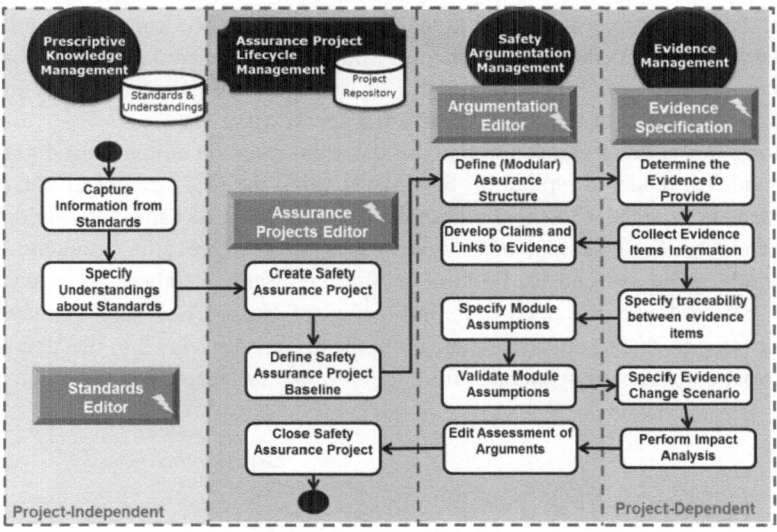

Fig. 2. Typical scenario for the tools

First we model our selected standards during the preliminary phase. The standard's editor offers services to retrieve, to digitalize and to store standards, recommendations, compliance means, intents and interpretations. All these standards are part of the so-called "reference framework". This reference framework is created just once, when the tools are deployed into the company. The reference framework of our case study includes the DO178c standard and the ARP 4754 guidelines.

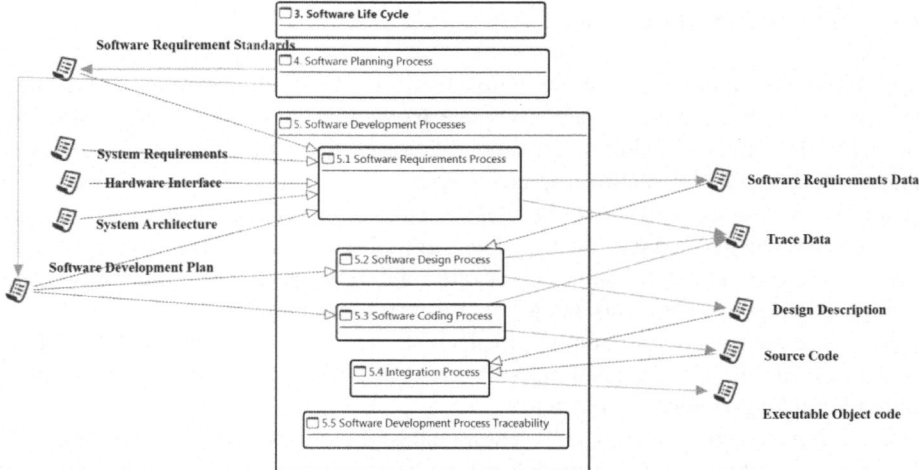

Fig. 3. Excerpt of the standard DO178C modelled with our tool

Once we have defined our reference framework, we need to define an assurance project. The new project is linked to the mentioned reference framework and it can be tailored to specific project requirements. One of the changes that can be done at this phase is defining which specific tools will be used on a defined activity just in the scope of this project or the role involved of a specific activity.

During the safety argumentation phase the argumentation editor is used to define an argumentation model compliant to SACM [7] using the GSN graphical notation [10]. Argumentation deals with (a) direct technical arguments of safety, required behavior from components, (b) compliance arguments about how prevailing standard has been sufficiently addressed and (c) backing confidence arguments about adequacy of arguments and evidence presented (e.g. sufficiency of Hazard and Risk Assessment). In order to support the argumentation creation, the arguments related to the standard compliance are automatically generated from the information selected on the baseline.

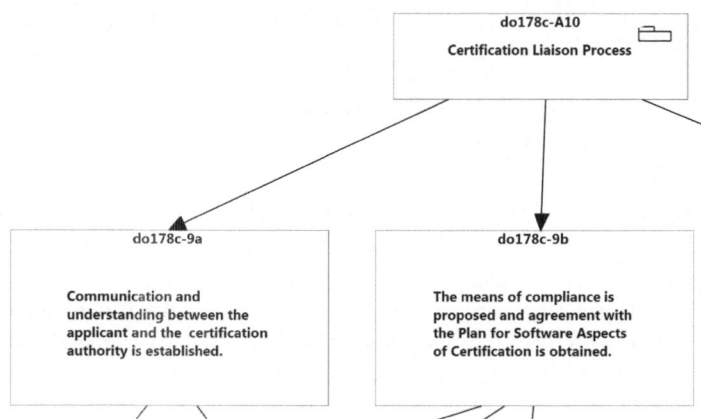

Fig. 4. Excerpt of the compliance argumentation

On the argumentation editor, we offer the possibility to take advantage of best practices by using argumentation patterns. The argumentation editor is able to re-use predefined patterns just by "drag and drop" the pattern into the working area. The use of the SACM model provides a semi-formal way for structuring.

In our avionics use case, our assurance case refers to required data such the PSAC (Plan for Software Aspects of Certification) or SAS (Software accomplishment summary) which are used as evidence for a certification process. However we do not only link these documents with the pieces of argumentation that they support but also to trace their evolution and evaluate our confidence on their safety. In addition we have implemented the following functionalities:

- Evidence storage: it provides a mean to determine, specify, and structure evidence. Evidence can be stored either locally on the system or on any revision management system as Subversion.
- Evidence traceability: it offers the possibility to specify and maintain the evidence relationships, like the relation between a specific document used as evidence and all the versions of that document that evolution thought the project lifecycle, of the relation between evidence and how it is used to support a specific claim. We are able to trace the evidence(s) used to comply with a specific requirement on one standard
- Evidence evaluation: we keep track of the evidence assessment for completeness and adequacy.

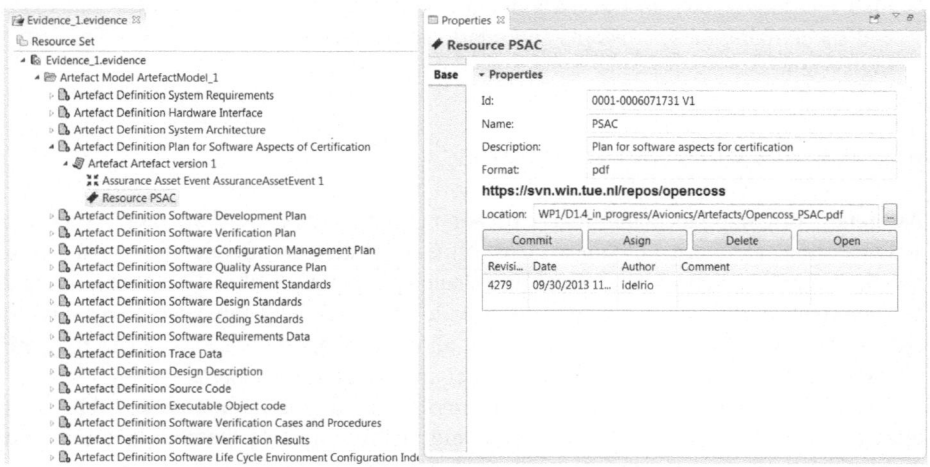

Fig. 5. View of the evidence model

We have also used the compliance maps functionality in order to define which and how all pieces of evidences stored do comply with the different aspects of the standard as it was capture on the reference framework. As a result of this we are able to show the compliance report.

5   Benefits from Using this Platform

We have used this platform for the implementation of differen case sutides along the Opencoss project. As result of users interviews we have identified the following set of benefits resulting from the use of this approach:

- **Centralized management of safety assurance assets.** Our tool infrastructure traces evidences with certification requirements
- **The Safety Case concept provides a comprehensible compilation of safety argumentation and evidence.** This approach promotes safety certification as a judgment based on a body of material that, explicitly, should consist of three elements: claims, evidence, and argument. To this end, we need to be able to propagate satisfaction from the fine-grained claims arrived at through decomposition to the higher-level claims. Supporting such propagation first and foremost requires elaborating the decomposition strategies to be used in different domains.
- **Harmonized and synchronized agreements in interpretations.** Without an upfront agreement between the system supplier/OEM and the certifier/assessor about the details of the arguments/evidences that need to be collected, there will invariably be important omissions, which need to be remedied after the fact and at significant costs. The presented tool suite support for negotiating detailed agreements about the required arguments/evidences to avoid unnecessary cost overheads during certification. This is achieved by exhaustively going through the concepts and their relations in the (abstract) arguments/evidences specifications for the standards and specializing these concepts and relations according to the needs of the underlying system.

6   Future work and Conclusions

Awareness of compliance and the certification process are some of the most expensive activities in a safety critical context. Cost-efficient system certification demands a continuous compliance-checking process by enhancing integration of certification goals and development workflow. The goal is to provide engineers with guidance about how to comply with standards and regulations and allow developers to assess where they are with respect to their duties to conform to safety practices and standards.

Our tool provides a centralized management of safety assurance assets. This tool infrastructure allow faster certification by automating most of the activities required for certification, so every change triggers a complete run of these activities, signaling those that need to be performed manually. This also includes facilitating integration with state-of-the-art engineering tools (e.g., DOORS, Simulink, safety analysis tools, etc.). In addition we provide a comprehensible compilation of safety argumentation and evidence. A key aspect of the certification language to be developed in a near future is to define the semantics of an argumentation language. We also need to support compositional certification by the use of a contract based approach and the possibility to validate the content of these contracts during runtime.

Acknowledgment. The research leading to these results has received funding from the FP7 programme under grant agreement n° 289011 (OPENCOSS) and n°608945 (Safe Adapt). We would also like to mention Angel López, Idoya del Río and Mª Carmen Palacios from Tecnalia for their effort developing some of the functionalities we have explained.

References

1. Hawkins, R., Habli, I., Kelly, T., McDermid, J.: Assurance cases and prescriptive software safety certification: A comparative study. Saf. Sci. **59**, 55–71 (2013)
2. Dodd, I., Habli, I.: Safety certification of airborne software: An empirical study. Reliab. Eng. Syst. Saf. **98**(1), 7–23 (2012)
3. Wilson, A., Preyssler, T.: Incremental certification and integrated modular avionics. In: 2008 IEEE/AIAA 27th Digital Avionics Systems Conference, pp. 1.E.3–1–1.E.3–8 (November 2008)
4. Vinodkumar, M.N., Bhasi, M.: A study on the impact of management system certification on safety management. Saf. Sci. **49**(3), 498–507 (2011)
5. Baumgart, S., Froberg, J., Punnekkat, S.: Towards efficient functional safety certification of construction machinery using a component-based approach. In: 2012 Third International Workshop on Product LinE Approaches in Software Engineering (PLEASE), pp. 1–4 (2012)
6. Defence Standard 00-56, Safety Management Requirements for Defence Systems, Issue 4, Part 1: Requirements, Ministry of Defence, Glasgow, UK (2007)
7. OMG, Structured Assurance Case Metamodel, (SACM) (2013)
8. Larrucea, X., Combelles, A., Favaro, J.: Safety-Critical Software [Guest editors' introduction]. IEEE Softw. **30**(3), 25–27 (2013)
9. Basir, N., Denney, E., Fischer, B.: Deriving Safety Cases for the Formal Safety Certification of Automatically Generated Code. Electron. Notes Theor. Comput. Sci. **238**(4), 19–26 (2009)
10. Goal Structuring Notation Working Group, GSN Community Standard (November 2011). Retrieved from http://www.goalstructuringnotation.info
11. Adelard, L.: (n.d.). Claims, Arguments and Evidence. Retrieved from http://www.adelard.com/asce/choosing-asce/cae.html
12. OPENCOSS project, D6.2_Detailed requirements for evidence management of the OPENCOSS platform_final (November 2012)
13. Denney, E., Pai, G., Pohl, J.: AdvoCATE: an assurance case automation toolset. In: Ortmeier, F., Daniel, P. (eds.) SAFECOMP Workshops 2012. LNCS, vol. 7613, pp. 8–21. Springer, Heidelberg (2012)
14. Matsuno, Y., Takamura, H., Ishikawa, Y.: A dependability case editor with pattern library. In: HASE, pp. 170–171 (2010)
15. Blanc, X., Gervais, M.-P., Sriplakich, P.: Model Bus: Towards the Interoperability of Modelling Tools. In: Aßmann, U., Akşit, M., Rensink, A. (eds.) MDAFA 2003. LNCS, vol. 3599, pp. 17–32. Springer, Heidelberg (2005)
16. Górski, J., Jarzębowicz, A., Miler, J., Witkowicz, M., Czyżnikiewicz, J., Jar, P.: Supporting assurance by evidence-based argument services. In: Ortmeier, F., Daniel, P. (eds.) SAFECOMP Workshops 2012. LNCS, vol. 7613, pp. 417–426. Springer, Heidelberg (2012)
17. RTCA DO-178/EUROCAE ED-12, Software Considerations in Airborne System and Equipment Certification
18. SAE ARP4754/EUROCAE ED-79, Certification Considerations for Highly Integrated or Complex Aircraft Systems
19. RTCA DO-297/EUROCAE ED-124 Integrated Modular Avionics (IMA) Development Guidance and Certification Considerations

SPI in Social and Organizational Issues

A Machine-Based Personality Oriented Team Recommender for Software Development Organizations

Murat Yilmaz[1], Ali Al-Taei[2], and Rory V. O'Connor[3]([envelope])

[1] Çankaya University, Ankara, Turkey
myilmaz@cankaya.edu.tr
[2] University of Baghdad, Baghdad, Iraq
alitaei@mtu.edu.iq
[3] Dublin City University, Dublin, Ireland
roconnor@computing.dcu.ie

Abstract. Hiring the right person for the right job is always a challenging task in software development landscapes. To bridge this gap, software firms start using psychometric instruments for investigating the personality types of software practitioners. In our previous research, we have developed an MBTI-like instrument to reveal the personality types of software practitioners. This study aims to develop a personality-based team recommender mechanism to improve the effectiveness of software teams. The mechanism is based on predicting the possible patterns of teams using a machine-based classifier. The classifier is trained with empirical data (e.g. personality types, job roles), which was collected from 52 software practitioners working on five different software teams. 12 software practitioners were selected for the testing process who were recommended by the classifier to work for these teams. The preliminary results suggest that a personality-based team recommender system may provide an effective approach as compared with ad-hoc methods of team formation in software development organizations. Ultimately, the overall performance of the proposed classifier was 83.3%. These findings seem acceptable especially for tasks of suggestion where individuals might be able to fit in more than one team.

Keywords: Organizational improvement · MBTI · Personality profiling · Personnel recommendation system · Neural networks · Multilayer perceptron

1 Introduction

Software development is concerned with the systematic production of quality software on a limited budget and time, which stills depend on complex human interactions to create an economic value. In more recent years, a significant number of researchers suggest that the major issues encountered in software development becomes are more sociological in their nature [1]. It is therefore

© Springer International Publishing Switzerland 2015
R.V. O'Connor et al. (Eds.): EuroSPI 2015, CCIS 543, pp. 75–86, 2015.
DOI: 10.1007/978-3-319-24647-5_7

becoming increasingly difficult to ignore the fact that *software development is a social activity* [2,3]. Software practitioners are usually work in collaborative groups in all stages of software development where working on such a team is an inherently social activity, which is important to sustain the software development organization's structure.

Social aspects of software development is an emerging field of interest which adds new kind of capabilities to software development organizations [4]. Consequently, the personality characteristics of software practitioners receive an increasing level of attention [5]. In fact, revealing the personality types of software practitioners allows us to understand the software organizations. It may help us to manage its development process and strengthen its evolution [6]. However, there has been few empirical endeavors that attempt to deal with the factors affecting software development efforts based on software practitioners behaviors and their personality types.

The process of personality typing has been used for nearly thousands of years dating back to Greek archetypes. Myers-Briggs Type Indicator (MBTI) is a personality typing assessment system. It was developed by psychologists Myers and Briggs as a self-report instrument. During our previous research [7], an MBTI compatible personality assessment tool was constructed to reveal the personality types of individuals who are working on software development organizations, which was developed particularly for software practitioners so as to build better software development teams. Ultimately, the goal of this study is to build a preliminary model for a personnel recommendation system for software development organizations from an industrial perspective.

This study seeks to address the following research questions: "*Is it possible to explore subjective characteristics such as personality types of software practitioners to classify participants to improve the social structure of software teams using a machine learning approach?*"

The working mechanism of such a recommendation system is planned on predicting a set of compatibility structures based on personality types of software practitioners of a software development organization, which could also offer recommendations regarding the most suitable members of a software team in terms of their personality preferences. The goal of this exploratory study is to investigate the possible combinations of software practitioners in software teams as regards to their job title. To this end, a neural network based personality classifier is employed. The classifier is trained with the real data which was collected from a software development organizations. Furthermore, proposed approach is tested by classifying a group of individuals based on this into teams using this information pattern.

Using a methodology based on the results of individual's personality test, the data collected from previous encounters in which the structure of current teams are analyzed. Furthermore, a set of compatibility options is predicted by the recommendation system approach. In light of these remarks, it has been thought that better results from previous studies are expected where the collected information will be a valuable asset for resolving multi-dimensional issues in the service of building more effective team structures.

The remainder of the paper is organized in the following manner. In section 2, we cover the background including brief details of the personality typing, the definitions of the proposed methods of machine learning (i.e. artificial neural networks), and their applications in the machine-based classification literature. Section 3 explains the details of the research methodology, which we use to conduct this study. In the next section, we discuss the results, which was used to classify software practitioners to the software development teams. In the final section, we draw some conclusions based on our preliminary results and detail the possible improvements for further research.

2   Background

Personality is considered as a set of relatively permanent traits (i.e. a set of patterns of behaviors) that can be found unique for a person. According to MBTI, this can be explained by four dichotomies namely E-I, S-N, T-F, J-P. Extroversion (E) versus introversion (I) shows how an individual regenerate his or her energy. Sensing (S) and intuition (N) is about how individuals make sense of their environment (i.e. process the information about the world). Sensing type of persons trusts more on their five senses while intuitive types are inclined to listen their subconscious and trusts their insights. Thinking (T) and feeling (F) preferences shows the decision-making style where an individual can be either objective thinker or a value oriented characteristics that focus on people and relationships. Lastly, Judging (J) and Perceiving (P) show the difference in individuals regarding their life style. Judging (J) persons prefer to see what lies ahead, organization and control while perceiving (P) individuals favor flexibility and keeping their options more open.

Typically, an MBTI assessment shows an individuals' inclination through one bipolar personality characteristic. Consequently, an MBTI type survey is usually conducted to collect the data where participants are asked to choose their highest preference (i.e. dominant function). To find an MBTI personality type, researcher should cross-reference the four dichotomies, which produces sixteen personality types.

Accordingly, a combination of these 16 personality types can be formed as shown in Table 1 [8].

Table 1. 16 MBTI personality types

ISTJ	ISFJ	INFJ	INTJ
ISTP	ISFP	INFP	INTP
ESTP	ESFP	ENFP	ENTP
ESTJ	ESFJ	ENFJ	ENTJ

In particular, MBTI has an important difference from other psychometric assessments: It does not suggest or recommend any preferred type. Instead, it reveals a person's place on four distinctive continuums of bipolar personality type scales. Such an approach is beneficial to software managers to understand the individual differences between software practitioners. It helps managers to avoid and resolve conflicts, identify gaps in software teams, improve team-based communication (i.e. encourage software team members to understand their teammates). It is therefore helpful to build better people skills, interactions as well as team configurations.

2.1   Neural Networks

A neural network (NN) can be similar to a network of parallel micro processing units, which are inspired from the model of a nerve cell in humans [9]. These units are based on a group of regression models which are chained to produce a combination of outputs by having a set of inputs embedded in a single mathematical approach [10]. Traditionally, after defining a particular problem a NN is trained to solve it. Most interestingly, however, the NN program does not know anything about the problem it addresses where the produced answers are usually emerged from the interaction between nodes by its evolutionary process [9].

The NN model consists of several neurons, i.e. island-like structures (or nodes) which are added such a way that only appropriate neighbors nested with them. Therefore, its algorithm is utilized to find the closest node that can fit by using the regression equations associated with it [10]. The collection of these nodes or neurons are called the neural net where these nodes have a number of inputs with associated weights, and a threshold value which determines either it is fired or not [9].

A neural net can be used to solve several kinds of problems such as classification, prediction, pattern recognition, etc. Multi layer perceptron (MLP) network is one of the most popular and commonly used neural network particularly for such processes [11]. MLP network consists of three distinctive kinds of layers: an input layer, one (or more) hidden layer(s), and an output layer. These layers are connected together by a set of weighted connections. The number of nodes in input layer is equal to the number of attributes in the input vector [10]. Hidden layer(s) and nodes in each layer are up to the designer's point of view as they can vary and should be managed carefully for better efficiency. And the final output from the output layer nodes represents the predicted outputs where each node in output layer represents a single output [11]. Figure 1 shows the typical MLP with one hidden layer.

Similar to a behavioral conditioning mechanism, an important approach used with MLP is the back propagation (BP) algorithm [10]. Basically, researcher starts with an input and propose a desired output. Consequently, the network is rewarded for close outputs to the desired input while the nodes are punished for an incorrect output. These activities are used to update the weights of the network so as to improve the results it produces. The MLP networks are frequently used with BP algorithm [11]. MLP initiates with small random weights, and

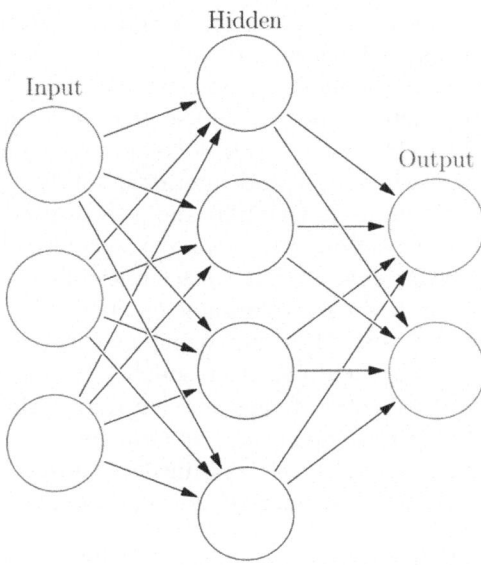

Fig. 1. Typical design of MLP artificial neural network [9]

a desired error rate. The learning process is achieved by using input: desired-output pair vectors to adjust the weights in order to minimize the error rate (i.e. calculate the difference between the real error and the desired error rates for all nodes in output layer). Next, the back propagation algorithm adjusts the weights [9].

2.2 Machine Learning in Personality Assessment Literature

The investigation of psychometric properties (e.g. traits, motivation, and personal preferences) of individuals have been studied in many different disciplines including but not limited to software engineering [7], game development [12], and economics courses [13]. In particular, several different methods (e.g. MBTI [8], Keirsey's Temperament Sorter [14], Big Five [15], etc.) have been utilized to assess personality types of participants. A search of the literature revealed a few studies which includes machine based classification of personality characteristics as follows.

Mairesse et al. [16] used linguistic cues for the purpose of predicting personality automatically from text and conversation. The suggested method was based on exploring Big Five personality traits depending on conversation and text of individuals, and the self and testers personality rating from observation. Accordingly, different methods were employed to test three the performance of different models. They used three approaches of machine learning methods: classification algorithms, regression, and ranking (e.g. Support Vector Machines (SVM), decision tree (DT), and nearest neighbor (NN)). Their results indicated that the performance of ranking models was the highest. Furthermore, performance of classification models trained using observed personality dataset was better than the models trained using self personality rating. In addition, it was observed that personality traits was the most important factor for extracting feature set.

Celli et al. [17] conducted experiments using six different machine learning methods (i.e SVM, NN, DT, naive Bayes, logistic regression, and rule learner) for the purpose of personality type and interaction style recognition based on profile pictures of Facebook users (N=100) and self-assessed personality test of Big Five traits. Feature extraction process was carried out by bag-of-visual-words (BoVW) technique. Results showed that the accuracy of each classifier depended on personality traits. The average performance was 66.5%.

Cowley et al. [18] claimed that employing machine learning methods to explore game-play experience and player personality type is still in early stages. In their study, they utilized two different decision tree methods (i.e. CART and C5.0) and used DGD player taxonomy on Pac-Man gamers to select appropriate rules for a classification. Training set contained 100 instances, while the testing set contained 37 instances. Ultimately, the validation testing performance of classifier was about 70%.

Aruan et al. [19] built a virtual tutor agent (VTA), which was developed for multiple users for the goal of problem-based learning in cooperative environments. It was inspired from massively multiplayer online games (MMOG). Both conceptual issues of learning using interface-supported cooperative environment and technological issues of deploying and dealing with massive users from MMOG perspective were combined together. In addition, some applications and coding have been used to achieve the goal, and the result was acceptable.

Golbeck et al. [20] proposed a model to predict personality of Twitter users. The model depended on information that publicly available in profiles of Twitter users and Big Five personality test. In particular, the Big Five test was administered to 279 of the users, and 2000 of their most common tweets were gathered. Next, feature was extracted through text analysis tools. Lastly, two regression methods (i.e Gaussian Process and ZeroR) were used to predict personality traits. Results showed that both of the methods performed similarly and the accuracy was reasonable.

To reduce the costs of monitoring and analyzing player personality, Kang et al. [21] proposed an automated system for the analysis of MMOG players' behaviors using trajectory (non-parametric) clustering algorithm with simple data. At first, they classified the data hierarchically, and then used trajectory clustering algorithm to analyze behaviors. The system was tested on world of warcraft (WoW) game environment and the results were good in both analyzing player's behavior and creating players' experience insights and profiles automatically.

Lotte et al. [22] reviewed a number of most common used classification methods (e.g. SVM, MLP, Hidden Markov Model (HMM)) and compared their performance to find the proper classification algorithm(s) for brain-computer interface (BCI) using *electro encephalo graphy* (EEG) dataset. The results and efficiency of each classifier were analyzed and compared among other classifiers to present a concrete base of knowledge that can be regarded when choosing the proper classifier for a specific task. In general, for the area of BCI using EEG dataset, it was found that SVM performs better than other classifiers. However, the performance of MLP was also acceptable for such a task. It is therefore likely to see the notion of neural networks, which are commonly used in BCI area of research.

This paper attempts to show that a machine-based personality classifier, which is planned as a recommendation system while selecting personnel for actual software teams. To date, studies investigating machine learning based personality classification have produced equivocal results. Most studies found in the literature in the field of personality based classification have mostly focused Big Five personality traits and SVM and DT as machine learning methods. However, this exploratory study aims to suggest software practitioners based on their MBTI personality types using a novel approach.

3   Method

Based on the data collected from 52 software practitioners, we aim to explore the patterns between personality types and roles of software practitioners who are working in teams. After revealing such relationships, the collected attributes were used to train a neural network (i.e. multi layer perceptron), and ultimately the goal is to create an initial version of a personality type-based team recommender. Authors believe that software managers could benefit from personality types or similar social aspects while searching for a suitable team for software practitioners.

In our previous study [7], we have already conducted an MBTI-like assessment for five teams of software practitioners from a software development organization. The personality types and roles of five software teams (total 52 people) were singled out. In addition, all selected teams were considered as productive teams, which consist of individuals with a minimum of five years of industrial experience. The software practitioners were also selected from the individuals who worked together for more than two years in software development projects.

After the data was transformed to binary values, the MLP was trained based on the patterns that were extracted from these team's roles and personality types. Accordingly, 10 input nodes were formed. 4 input nodes represents the personality types and 6 input nodes (e.g. role one is represented like 000001, and role two like 000010, etc.) to represent practitioners' job role. In the output layer, 5 output nodes represents 5 software teams which are based on the initial parameters, e.g. Team 1 represented as 00001, team 2 represented like 00010, etc.

Figure 2 illustrates the suggested MLP model where $\{I_1, I_2, I_3...I_{10}\}$, are the nodes (e.g. personality types and roles) that are shown in the input layer, and $\{T_1, ...T_n\}$, are the possible team formations.

To build a team classifier for software practitioners, we built a perceptron with three layers, which was equipped with back propagation algorithm. During the study, several outputs were examined to decide the best configuration parameters for classification. The findings were detailed through the next section.

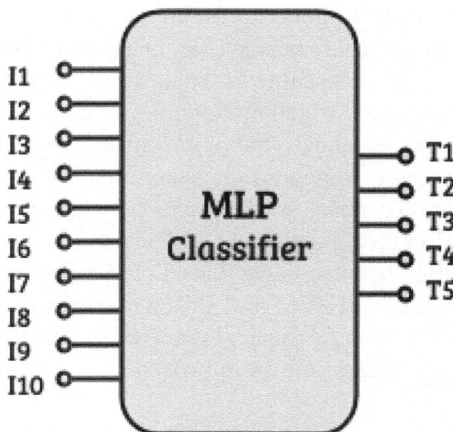

Fig. 2. The suggested model for MLP-based Team Recommnender.

4 Results

The vectors of input data (N=52) with their desired output were fed into the MLP model during the training process. The weights values were firstly created randomly between -1 and 1 and were iteratively updated until convergences toward the desired output, and decreasing the error rate until the minimum. Momentum parameter was used to increase the convergence [23]. The training mode continues until the number of epochs reaches 1 million or the error rate is equal or less than 0.01.

Leave one out cross validation (LOOCV) is one of the methods used in machine learning studies for validating model performance [24]. In this method data is splitted into N samples and perform N rounds of train/test processes (e.g. N-1 samples for training and 1 sample for testing). Then, the estimated performance is calculated as the average of testing samples [25].

To avoid over-fitting, LOOCV technique with 10-folds was used during the training process. Many configurations (e.g. error rate, learning rate) were investigated to explore the best performance within the predefined conditions. Accordingly, the optimal number of nodes in hidden layer was 15.

To test the classification performance of the proposed model, apart from the 52 software practitioners, 12 software practitioners were selected and fed into the classifier for seeking these practitioners a suitable place among the five software teams. The overall performance of the suggested model was 83.3%. The result seems acceptable especially for such tasks of suggestion considering the fact that some individuals might fit in more than one team. Table 2 shows the performance and error rate of the model for both training and testing processes (learning rate= 0.7, momentum= 0.69, number of epoch= 1396).

Table 2. Training-testing results for the classifier.

Training Process (N=52)		Testing Process (N=12)	
Correctly Classified	Incorrectly Classified	Correctly Classified	Incorrectly Classified
52 (100%)	0 (0%)	10 (83.3%)	2 (16.6%)
RMSE= 0.002		RMSE= 0.2	

To evaluate the face validity [26], all suggested personnel (N=12) for five selected teams were shared with the software management group. Next, we interviewed the research manager of the company in which we collected the empirical data (i.e. personality types and roles of software practitioners). The interviewee suggested that such an approach could be useful as a complementary tool for the personnel recruitment process. He also approved that (by following the classification results) three recommended software practitioners were suitable to assign to the team one (T1), while two other recommended practitioners were found acceptable for the team five (T5). Therefore, the preliminary results indicate that initial suggestions were helpful for selecting software practitioners. In light of this information, we have also found that there was a sense of agreement for the benefits of the classification model between interviewee (i.e. research manager) and the authors.

Interview quotation: "*I believe that building an effective software team is such a challenging task. It is also hard to do a manual reconfiguration especially after the initial declaration of software team members. Therefore, seeing more possibilities of team configuration is necessary. I found a tool that helps to predict a possible position for a team member is quite useful strategy. However, it would be more beneficial for us [the company] if you could suggest a team member who may fit for more than one team.*"

4.1 Limitations

Using personality assessments to investigate people's type of personality does not always yield very accurate results for many reasons, and therefore, they should be regarded as indicators for individuals' preferences and temperaments rather than solid evidence for their exact type [8]. Furthermore, artificial neural networks (ANN) and other similar methods of machine learning and pattern recognition have many parameters affecting model performance such as error rate, preparation process of datasets, actual size of data, and quality of training and testing sets. Therefore, they do not always provide the optimal results and they should be designed carefully [22].

The MLP team classifier was operationalized by using the empirical data that was collected from a single company. In fact, the personality types and the software practitioners' roles of the teams found in that company may not represent all possible software engineering team patterns or structures. Therefore, our results are limited in a (specific) software development company's identified patterns. To design a team recommender for another company, a new MLP should be trained accordingly.

5   Conclusions and Future Work

The main aim of this preliminary study is to explore the possibility of building a team recommender mechanism. It can be used to suggest a set of suitable software practitioners for the actual software teams regarding their possible roles and personality types. Based on a set of empirical data, we planned a suggestion mechanism for improving team management activities. Although the current study was based on a small sample of participants, the findings suggest that team-based personality patterns can be highlighted for improving team building activities or building a novel team configuration process.

Despite its exploratory nature, this study offers some insight into social aspects of software development. Firstly, software managers could likely to benefit from a machine-based team recommender approach. However, further experimental investigations are needed to estimate more team configurations. Secondly, we believe that the proposed method to achieve the actual results are reasonable as we aim to investigate the possibilities of a set of team formations in terms of their personality types of a selected population. Considerably, more work will need to be done to evaluate the effectiveness of a personality-based software team recommender.

Returning to the research question posed at the beginning of this study, authors confirm that personality types of software practitioners along with their team-based roles are useful information for observing (social) software team patterns. However, it would be interesting to assess the effects of personality types on software team formations on a more large scale. In light of these remarks, authors confirm that machine learning techniques can create a significant advantage for addressing problems of software engineering and process improvement research.

References

1. DeMarco, T., Lister, T.: Peopleware: productive projects and teams. Dorset House Publishing Company (1999)
2. Acuna, S.T., Juristo, N., Moreno, A.M., Mon, A.: A Software Process Model Handbook for Incorporating People's Capabilities. Springer-Verlag (2005)
3. Dittrich, Y., Floyd, C., Klischewski, R.: Social thinking-software practice. The MIT Press (2002)
4. Yilmaz, M., O'Connor, R.: An approach for improving the social aspects of the software development process by using a game theoretic perspective: towards a theory of social productivity of software development teams. In: 6th International Conference on Software and Data Technologies, vol. 1, pp. 35–40. SciTePress (2011)

5. Beecham, S., Baddoo, N., Hall, T., Robinson, H., Sharp, H.: Motivation in software engineering: A systematic literature review. Information and Software Technology **50**, 860–878 (2008)
6. Yilmaz, M., O'Connor, R.: Towards the understanding and classification of the personality traits of software development practitioners: Situational context cards approach. In: 2012 38th EUROMICRO Conference on Software Engineering and Advanced Applications (SEAA), pp. 400–405. IEEE (2012)
7. Yilmaz, M.: A software process engineering approach to understanding software productivity and team personality characteristics: an empirical investigation. PhD thesis, Dublin City University (2013)
8. Myers, I.B., McCaulley, M.H., Most, R.: Manual: A Guide to the Development and Use of the Myers-Briggs Type Indicator. Consulting Psychologists Press, Palo Alto (1985)
9. Kodicek, D.: Mathematics and physics for programmers. Cengage Learning (2005)
10. Garson, G.D.: Neural networks: An introductory guide for social scientists. Sage (1998)
11. Bishop, C.M.: Neural networks for pattern recognition. Clarendon press, Oxford (1995)
12. Bartle, R.A.: Designing virtual worlds. New Riders (2004)
13. Borg, M.O., Stranahan, H.A.: Personality type and student performance in upper-level economics courses: The importance of race and gender. The Journal of Economic Education **33**, 3–14 (2002)
14. Keirsey, D.: Please Understand Me II: Temperament, Character, Intelligence. Prometheus Nemesis Book Co. (1998)
15. John, O.P., Donahue, E.M., Kentle, R.L.: The big five inventoryversions 4a and 54. Institute of Personality and Social Research, University of California, Berkeley (1991)
16. Mairesse, F., Walker, M.A., Mehl, M.R., Moore, R.K.: Using linguistic cues for the automatic recognition of personality in conversation and text. Journal of Artificial Intelligence Research, 457–500 (2007)
17. Celli, F., Bruni, E., Lepri, B.: Automatic personality and interaction style recognition from facebook profile pictures. In: Proceedings of the ACM International Conference on Multimedia, pp. 1101–1104. ACM (2014)
18. Cowley, B., Charles, D., Black, M., Hickey, R.: Real-time rule-based classification of player types in computer games. User Modeling and User-Adapted Interaction **23**, 489–526 (2013)
19. Aruan, F., Prihatmanto, A., Hindersah, H., et al.: The designing and implementation of a problem based learning in collaborative virtual environments using mmog technology. In: 2012 International Conference on System Engineering and Technology (ICSET), pp. 1–7. IEEE (2012)
20. Golbeck, J., Robles, C., Edmondson, M., Turner, K.: Predicting personality from twitter. In: 2011 IEEE Third International Conference on Privacy, Security, Risk and Trust (PASSAT) and IEEE Third Inernational Conference on Social Computing (SocialCom), pp. 149–156. IEEE (2011)
21. Kang, S.J., Kim, Y.B., Park, T., Kim, C.H.: Automatic player behavior analysis system using trajectory data in a massive multiplayer online game. Multimedia Tools and Applications **66**, 383–404 (2013)
22. Lotte, F., Congedo, M., Lécuyer, A., Lamarche, F., Arnaldi, B., et al.: A review of classification algorithms for eeg-based brain-computer interfaces. Journal of neural engineering **4** (2007)

23. Hagan, M.T., Demuth, H.B., Beale, M.H., et al.: Neural network design, vol. 1. Pws Boston (1996)
24. Priddy, K.L., Keller, P.E.: Artificial neural networks: An introduction, vol. 68. SPIE Press (2005)
25. Cawley, G.C., Talbot, N.L.: Efficient leave-one-out cross-validation of kernel fisher discriminant classifiers. Pattern Recognition **36**, 2585–2592 (2003)
26. Lewis-Beck, M., Bryman, A.E., Liao, T.F.: The Sage Encyclopedia of Social Science Research Methods. Sage Publications (2003)

An ISO Compliant and Integrated Model for IT GRC (Governance, Risk Management and Compliance)

Nicolas Mayer[✉], Béatrix Barafort, Michel Picard, and Stéphane Cortina

Luxembourg Institute of Science and Technology,
5 Avenue des Hauts-Fourneaux, L-4362 Esch-sur-Alzette, Luxembourg
{nicolas.mayer,beatrix.barafort,michel.picard,
stephane.cortina}@list.lu

Abstract. GRC (Governance, Risk and Compliance) is an umbrella acronym covering the three disciplines of governance, risk management and compliance. The main challenge behind this concept is the integration of these three areas, generally dealt with in silos. At the IT level (IT GRC), some research works have been proposed towards integration. However, the sources used for the construction of the resulting models are generally mixing formal standards, *de facto* standards arising from industrial consortia, and research results. In this paper, we specifically focus on defining an ISO compliant IT GRC integrated model, ISO standards representing by nature an international consensus. To do so, we analyse the ISO standards related to the GRC field and propose a way of integration. The result of this paper is an ISO compliant integrated model for IT GRC, aiming at improving the efficiency when dealing with the three disciplines together.

Keywords: Governance · Risk management · Compliance · GRC · Standards

1 Introduction

Today, it is clearly acknowledged that Information Technology (IT) is no more only a technical issue. Indeed, IT organization has evolved from technology providers to service providers and, according to Peterson [1], "Whereas the domain of IT Management focuses on the efficient and effective supply of IT services and products, and the management of IT operations, IT Governance faces the dual demand of (1) contributing to present business operations and performance, and (2) transforming and positioning IT for meeting future business challenges". Thus, the complexity and importance of IT in companies involve a necessary governance layer. Such a governance layer generally encompasses risk management and compliance as steering tools. This evolution has implied the adoption of a new paradigm in IT, coming from the business world, usually referred to as "GRC". GRC is an umbrella acronym covering the three disciplines of governance, risk management and compliance.

The main challenge of GRC is to have an approach as integrated as possible to governance, risk management and compliance. The aim is to improve effectiveness and efficiency of the three disciplines, mainly compared to the traditional silo

© Springer International Publishing Switzerland 2015
R.V. O'Connor et al. (Eds.): EuroSPI 2015, CCIS 543, pp. 87–99, 2015.
DOI: 10.1007/978-3-319-24647-5_8

approach generally performed within organizations. Basically, according to Racz *et al.*, GRC can be defined as "an integrated, holistic approach to organization-wide governance, risk and compliance ensuring that an organization acts ethically correct and in accordance with its risk appetite, internal policies and external regulations through the alignment of strategy, processes, technology and people, thereby improving efficiency and effectiveness" [2].

It is usually acknowledged that GRC in general (i.e. corporate GRC), and more specifically IT GRC, has currently received very few attention from the scientific community [3]. However, some reference models for IT GRC have recently emerged [3, 4] and propose relevant processes towards an integrated approach of governance, risk management and compliance for IT. These integrated frameworks rely on various sources, such as formal standards, *de facto* standards, or scientific models, but it is difficult to select and adopt adequate underlying models, and even more difficult to justify their selection is sound [3].

However, at the International Organization for Standardization (ISO) level, the three individual domains of GRC have been considered as mature enough to be standardized at an international level (see Section 3). International standards have been developed for IT governance [5], risk management [6], and very recently for compliance [7]. Nevertheless, to the best of our knowledge, there is no published standard (or standard in progress) dealing with an integrated approach for IT GRC.

Our aim is to define an integrated IT GRC model with the widest range of adoption. Our main assumption is that such a model should be based on ISO standards, representing by nature an international consensus. The objective of the paper is thus to specifically focus on defining an ISO compliant IT GRC integrated model. To do so, we analyse in this paper the ISO standards related to the GRC field and propose a structured way of integration.

Section 2 describes the related work by surveying existing IT GRC models and approaches. Section 3 is an overview of the standards for IT governance, (IT) risk management and (IT) compliance at the ISO level. Section 4 is about the construction of an ISO compliant IT GRC model, comprising the analysis of the existing ISO standards and their integration in an integrated model. Finally, Section 5 draws conclusions about the results and proposes some future work.

2   Related Work

As stated in the introduction, our scope is focused on IT GRC that can be considered as a subset of corporate GRC [3]. Considering the lack of scientific references about IT GRC, we will also consider in this section some integrated approaches for corporate GRC, where IT GRC is contained.

Racz *et al.* have proposed a frame of reference for integrated GRC composed of three subjects (Governance, Risk Management and Compliance), four components (strategy, processes, technology and people), and rules associated to the subjects (respectively internal policies, risk appetite and external regulations) [2]. From this frame of reference, they have then defined a process model for integrated IT GRC management [3]. This process model is based on a mix between an ISO standard

(ISO/IEC 38500 [5]), an industrial standard (Enterprise Risk Management (ERM) — Integrated Framework [8] developed by COSO), and research results.

Based on the IT GRC process model of Racz *et al.*, Vicente and da Silva have proposed a business process viewpoint of IT GRC. Their research result is based on a merger between a conceptual model for GRC they defined [9] and the IT GRC process model of Racz *et al.* [3]. They have designed their business viewpoint for integrated IT GRC by modelling with ArchiMate [10], an enterprise architecture modelling language, the merger model and completing it with the business objects used between the business processes.

The Open Compliance and Ethics Group (OCEG), an industry-led non-profit organization, has published in 2012 the last release of the "GRC capability model (Red Book)" [11]. It is based on the so-called "Principled Performance" concept – a point of view and approach to business that helps organizations reliably achieve objectives while addressing uncertainty (both risk and reward) and acting with integrity (honouring both mandatory commitments and voluntary promises) – enabled by the GRC function in an organization. The scope of the GRC capability model is corporate GRC, and OCEG claims no compliance of their document to ISO standards or other references. COBIT 5 [12] is another governance framework owned by the Information Systems Audit and Control Association (ISACA), a non-profit organization. This framework for the governance and management of Enterprise IT helps enterprises to create optimal value from IT by maintaining a balance between realizing benefits and optimizing risk levels and resource use. This framework is consistent with the ISO/IEC 38500:2015 [5] standard and can be considered as a pragmatic way to implement its concepts and principles within the organizations.

Gericke *et al.* have developed and evaluated a situational method that supports the implementation of an integrated GRC solution [13]. However, they are more concerned by rollout aspects than by organizational and recurring processes of GRC. Asnar & Massacci have developed another method, entitled "SI*-GRC" [14], comprising a modelling framework, an analysis process, analytical techniques, and a supporting software tool. This method is dedicated to information security and the outcome is the analysis and design of suited security controls.

Finally, some high-level frameworks have been established for GRC. We can mention the RSA GRC Reference Architecture [15] providing a visual representation of GRC within an organization, its guiding principles and its final objectives. Frigo & Anderson have proposed a "Strategic Governance, Risk, and Compliance Framework" composed of three layers [16]. Paulus has proposed a "GRC Reference Architecture" [17] consisting in four steps to follow (requirements modelling, status investigation, situation improvement, and crisis and incident management). Last but not least, Krey *et al.* developed an "IT GRC Health Care Framework" [18], taking care of health specific characteristics.

As a conclusion, a set of references and/or models have been established for GRC (and sometimes for IT GRC), but none of them propose an integrated and ISO compliant approach. The sources used for the construction of these models are generally mixing formal standards (i.e. standards established by formal standards organizations such as ISO, IEC or ITU), *de facto* standards arising from industrial consortia, and research results.

3   Overview of the ISO Standards for IT Governance, (IT) Risk Management and (IT) Compliance

In this section, an overview of the ISO standards for IT governance, IT risk management and IT compliance (respectively ISO/IEC 38500:2015 [5], ISO 31000:2009 [6], and ISO 19600:2014 [7]) is performed. It is worth to note that ISO/IEC 38500:2015 is published by both ISO and IEC. IT being considered as an overlapping standardization domain between the respective scopes of ISO and IEC, they created in 1987 a Joint Technical Committee (JTC), known as ISO/IEC JTC1, to develop standards in the IT domain. In the next sections, each standard is presented first from an overall perspective, then from a structure perspective, and finally from a process perspective.

3.1   IT Governance

The reference document for IT governance at the ISO level is the ISO/IEC 38500:2015 standard [5] entitled "Information Technology — Governance of IT — for the organization". This International Standard is the flagship standard of the ISO/IEC 38500 series. The objective of ISO/IEC 38500:2015 is to provide guiding principles for governing bodies on the effective, efficient, and acceptable use of IT within their organizations. It also provides guidance to those advising, informing, or assisting governing bodies. The governance of IT is considered here as a subset of organizational governance (or corporate governance). ISO/IEC 38500:2015 is applicable to all types of organizations (i.e. public and private companies, government entities, not-for-profit organizations), whatever their size and regardless of the extent of their use of IT.

ISO/IEC TR 38502:2014 [19] provides guidance on the nature and mechanisms of governance and management together with the relationships between them, in the context of IT within an organization. The purpose of this Technical Report is to provide information on a framework and model that can be used to establish the boundaries and relationships between governance and management of an organization's current and future use of IT.

Structure: The IT governance framework developed by ISO/IEC lies on six principles (responsibility, strategy, acquisition, performance, conformance and human behaviour) and three main tasks (evaluate, direct and monitor). The main part of the standard is a guidance about the activities to perform for each of the six principles when passing through the "Evaluate – Direct – Monitor" process. Throughout the standard, ISO/IEC claims a clear distinction between the governing body, in charge of the IT governance, and managers, in charge of management systems for the use of IT, such as risk managers or compliance managers.

Process: The main tasks to be followed by IT governing bodies, represented in Fig. 1, are:

- **Evaluate** the current and future use of IT.
- **Direct** preparation and implementation of strategies and policies to ensure that use of IT meets business objectives.
- **Monitor** conformance to policies, and performance against the strategies.

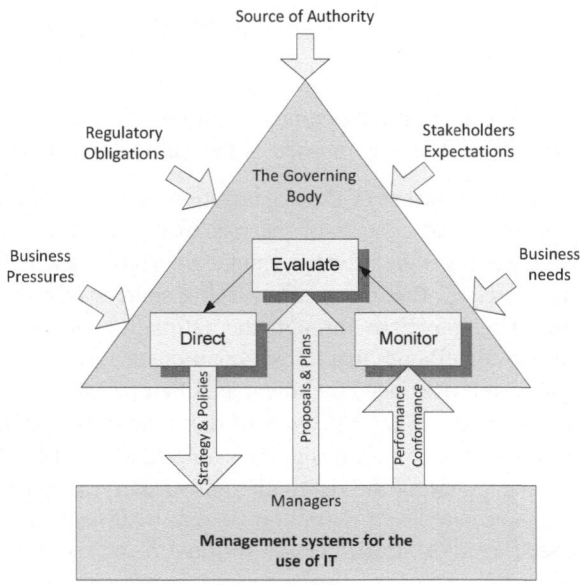

Fig. 1. Model for Governance of IT (as represented in [5])

3.2   IT Risk Management

There is no dedicated IT risk management standard at the ISO level. Thus, the reference document for IT risk management is the ISO 31000:2009 standard [6] entitled "Risk management — Principles and guidelines" that can be applied to any type of risk, whatever its nature. ISO 31000:2009 can be used by any public, private or community enterprise, association, group or individual and is thus not specific to any industry or sector. The scope of ISO 31000:2009 is not focused on IT risk management, but on risk management in general, whatever the application domain. ISO/IEC 27005:2013 [20] is another relevant risk management standard that has been considered, but that is focused on information security. Although IT risk management and information security risk management are broadly overlapping, it is important to be aware that their concerns are different. From one side, IT risk management will consider risks related to IT strategy or to IT investments in general (i.e. not directly related to information security) that are not considered in information security risk management. From the other side, information security risk management may consider non-IT (e.g., paper-based) processes and their associated risks, that would not be considered in IT risk management.

Structure: ISO 31000:2009 is structured in three main parts. The first one provides a set of eleven principles an organization should comply with for risk management to be effective. The second part is a high-level framework which main objective is to assist the organization to integrate risk management into its overall management system. This framework lies on a continual improvement cycle and suggest having such an approach for risk management. Finally, the last core part of the standard is the process to follow, embedded in the different phases of the general framework, and that is of main interest in this paper.

Process: The risk management process proposed in ISO 31000:2009 is represented in the next section within Fig. 2. It is composed of the following activities:

- **Establishing the context** of the organization, including the definition of the scope, objectives and context of the risk management process, and making clear what criteria will be used to evaluate the significance of risk.
- **Assessing the risks**, that means **identifying** sources of risk and areas of impacts, **analyzing** the risks through the estimation of the consequences of risks and the likelihood that those consequences can occur, and finally **evaluating** which risks need treatment and their priority level.
- **Treating the risks** via the selection of risk treatment options (e.g., modifying the risk with the help of design decisions leading to likelihood or consequences change, sharing the risk with another party, retaining the risk by informed decision, etc.) and definition of risk treatment plans. The risks are then assessed again to determine the residual risks: risk remaining after risk treatment.

In parallel of the preceding activities, it is also necessary to regularly monitor and review the risks and the underlying risk management process. Moreover, communication and consultation with the different stakeholders should take place during all stages of the risk management process.

3.3   IT Compliance

There is no dedicated IT compliance standard at the ISO level. Thus, the reference document for IT compliance is the ISO 19600:2014 standard [7] entitled "Compliance management systems — Guidelines". This standard provides guidance for establishing, developing, implementing, evaluating, maintaining and improving an effective and responsive compliance management system within an organization. Compliance is to be considered here as an outcome of an organization meeting its obligations, and is made sustainable by embedding it in the culture of the organization and in the behaviour and attitude of people working for it. The standard is based on the principles of good governance, proportionality, transparency and sustainability. The guidelines provided are applicable to all types of organizations.

Structure: The standard has adopted the so-called "high-level structure" developed by ISO to align the different management system standards. It consists of a fixed clause sequence, including common text and common terminology, which is completed with specific guidance on compliance management. The core of the standard is thus structured in seven main clauses (from Clause 4 to 10) that can be represented under the form of a flowchart described in more details in the next paragraph.

Process: The compliance management process proposed in ISO 19600:2014 is represented in Fig. 2 under the form of a flowchart. The main activities are the following:

- Establishment of the context of the organization, by **identifying external and internal issues**, and **interested parties and their requirements**. **Good governance principles** defined by the standard are also part of this context.
- **Determination of the scope of the compliance management system**, taking into account the context of the organization.
- **Establishment of a compliance policy** that is appropriate to the purpose of the organization, providing a framework for setting compliance objectives, and including a commitment to satisfy applicable requirements and to continual improvement.
- **Identification of compliance obligations** (including requirements the organization has to comply with and requirements it chooses to comply with) and **evaluation of related compliance risks**.
- **Planning on how to address compliance risks and how to achieve objectives.**
- Implementation of actions planned through **operational planning and control.**
- **Performance evaluation** through indicators development and application, audit, and management review.
- Improvement of the compliance management system by **managing non-compliances and continual improvement**.

4   An ISO Compliant IT GRC Model

In order to define an integrated IT GRC model, a bottom-up approach, based on the integration of the existing standards, has been followed. Our approach is composed of the following steps:

1. Identify common activities between risk management and compliance management
2. Extract in compliance management and risk management the tasks involving the governing body (at the opposite of what is under strict responsibility of managers) to encapsulate risk management and compliance management in a governance umbrella that integrates thus the three domains.

It is worth to note that the objective is not to exhaustively describe all of the activities to be performed in IT governance, IT compliance and IT risk management, but rather to focus on potential integration between activities that are redundant or interdependent in every single model. For example, the scope of IT governance is much broader than IT compliance and risk issues, and also encompasses topics such as generating business value from IT investments or optimizing the cost of IT services.

4.1   Common Activities Between Compliance Management and Risk Management

According to ISO 19600:2014, risk management is a key activity in a compliance management system. A compliance-related risk management process can clearly be drawn all along the different steps of the compliance management system establishment, as highlighted in Fig. 2.

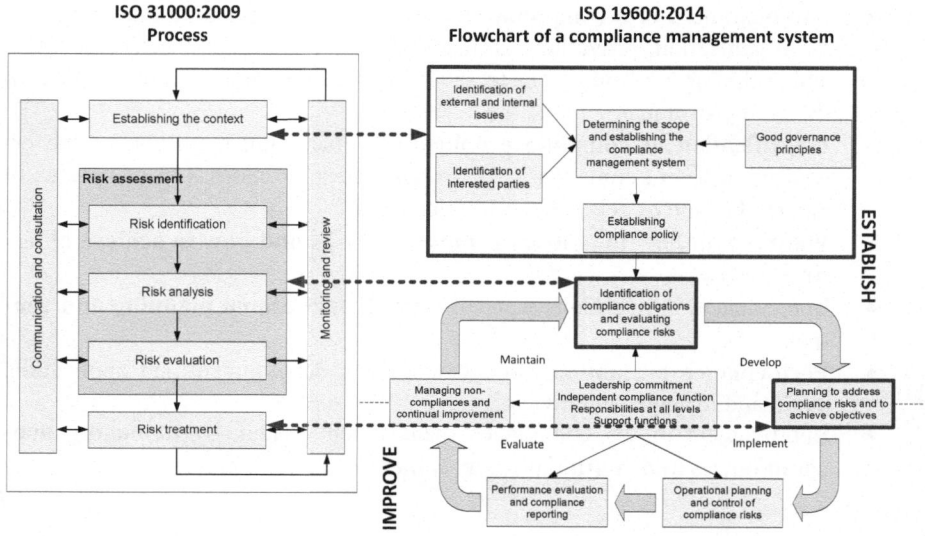

Fig. 2. Common activities between compliance management and risk management

Regarding ISO 31000:2009, the risk management process is part of the implementation step of the risk management framework, which is "intended […] to assist the organization to integrate risk management into its overall management system" [6]. In line with the preceding quote, we claim that to perform a compliance-related risk management process conforming with the ISO 31000:2009 process is fully aligned with ISO 19600:2014 requirements:

- By identifying external and internal issues, interested parties coming with their requirements, and following good governance principles, we are able to determine the scope and establish the compliance management system, then to establish the compliance policy (see Fig. 2). By doing this set of activities, we have especially established the context of the organization from a risk management perspective, including the definition of the risk-related scope, objectives and context.
- The next step about identification of compliance obligations (including requirements the organization has to comply with and requirements it chooses to comply with) and evaluation of related compliance risks consists in a risk assessment according to ISO 31000:2009.

- Finally, planning to address compliance risks and to achieve objectives includes a risk treatment process as described in ISO 31000:2009.

The other sets of requirements of ISO 19600:2014 that are related respectively to implementation of actions planned, performance evaluation, improvement of the compliance management system, and lastly compliance management system support activities (e.g., leadership commitment, roles and responsibilities, document management, etc.) are not directly related to the risk management process, but will provide the relevant and necessary inputs for the risk monitoring and review activity, as required by ISO 31000:2009. As a conclusion, when establishing a compliance management system, it is relevant to deal with risk-related activities through an ISO 31000:2009 process.

4.2 Governance Aspects of Compliance and Risk Management

Basically, our objective is to identify in compliance and risk management standards the tasks involving the governing body. Referring to Fig. 1, the compliance and risk management related activities the governing body performs are extracted from the studied standards and highlighted in the frame of the Direct – Evaluate – Monitor process. They are summarized in Table 1.

Table 1. Compliance and risk management activities related to the governing body

	Direct	*Evaluate*	*Monitor*
Compliance	Demonstrate leadership and commitment with respect to the compliance management system	Review and approve strategy based on regulatory demands	Review the reporting on the compliance management system performance
	Establish and endorse a compliance policy		Supervise the compliance management system
	Define roles and responsibilities		Escalation, where appropriate
	Active involvement in the compliance management system		
	Commit to the development of a compliance culture		
Risk Management	Define the risk appetite relating to the use of IT and specific control requirements	Review and approve strategy based on risks	Ensure that there is an adequate audit coverage of IT related risk management
		Approve key risk management practices such as those relating to security and business continuity	
		Evaluate what is an acceptable risk to the organization	

It is a straightforward process to identify in ISO 19600:2014 the activities that involve the governing body of the organisation from the other activities led and/or performed only by the managers of the organisation. The involvement of the governing body is indeed formally mentioned in the standard when applicable (references to the standard's clause are in square brackets):

- *[5.1] The governing body and top management should demonstrate leadership and commitment with respect to the compliance management system [...]*
- *[5.2.1] The governing body and top management, preferably in consultation with employees, should establish a compliance policy that:*
- *[...] and should be endorsed by the governing body*
- *[5.3.1] The governing body and top management should assign the responsibility and authority to the compliance function for [...]*
  b) reporting on the performance of the compliance management system to the governing body and top management
- *[5.3.2] The active involvement of, and supervision by, governing body and top management is an integral part of an effective compliance management system*
- *[5.3.3] The governing body and top management should: [...]*
  c) include compliance responsibilities in position statements of top managers
  d) appoint or nominate a compliance function [...]
- *[7.3.2.3] The development of a compliance culture requires the active, visible, consistent and sustained commitment of the governing body [...]*
- *[9.1.7] The governing body [...] should ensure that they are effectively informed on the performance of the organization's compliance management system and of its continuing adequacy [...]*
- *[10.1.2] Where appropriate, escalation should be to top management and the governing body, including relevant committees*

In ISO 31000:2009, there is no separation of responsibilities between the management and the governing body. The different activities to be performed are formulated in a general manner, stating that "the organisation should [...]". However, ISO/IEC TR 38502:2014, aiming at defining a framework and model about IT governance, provides further information about the role and responsibilities of the governing body, with regards, mainly, to risk management related to IT, but also some related to compliance:

- *[3.3] The strategies and policies for the use of IT set by the governing body and communicated to managers should provide the basis for the application of governance to the management systems of the organization. [...] They may include:*
  — Risk appetite relating to the use of IT and specific control requirements
- *[4.1.2] For example, the governing body should ensure that there is adequate audit coverage of IT related risk management, control, and governance processes as part of the audit approach*
- *[4.2.2] The governing body should approve the organization's business strategy for IT taking into account the implications of the strategy for achieving business objectives and any associated risks that might arise*

- *[4.3.2] In respect of IT, the governing body typically retains involvement in such things as:*
  - *— Approval of key risk management practices such as those relating to security and business continuity.*
- *[4.2.2] The governing body should ensure that the organization's external and internal environment are regularly monitored and analysed to determine if there is a need to review and, when appropriate, revise the strategy for IT and any associated policies.*
- *[4.5.2] The governing body should set policies on internal control taking into account what is an acceptable risk to the organization. This should include the risk appetite relating to the use of IT and specific control requirements.*

Moreover, ISO/IEC TR 38502:2014 recommends to have a compliance committee and a risk management committee respectively for compliance and risk management in order to deal with the activities listed in Table 1.

5   Conclusion and Future Work

In this paper, our objective is to propose an integrated model for IT GRC inspired by, and compliant with, related ISO standards. It lays on existing ISO standards targeting (IT) GRC and, respectively, individually focusing on governance of IT (ISO/IEC 38500 series of standards), risk management (ISO 31000:2009), and compliance management system (ISO 19600:2014). The resulting model has been split in two parts. First, a systematic bottom-up approach has been followed in order to identify common activities between risk management and compliance management. Both standards can be combined by establishing the compliance management system in alignment with risk-related activities of the risk management process. Then, the overall part of the model has been derived from the ISO/IEC 38500:2015 model for governance of IT, where the key elements under the responsibility of the governing body for integrated IT GRC have been identified, with respect to the management ones.

Our results can help to existing standards improvement. For example, a clear distinction in ISO 31000 between governing body activities and management ones can help to better understand and implement the standard. New standards such as an integrated IT GRC standard can also be proposed in order to tackle the issues coming from the business world.

The proposed ISO compliant and integrated model for IT GRC provides a twofold view with the IT governance layer and the IT risk management and compliance one, where strategy, processes, technology and people can be integrated. The alignment of processes is a particular vector of integration and interoperability between the three disciplines of GRC and will be developed further by the authors. More future works will consist in the experimentation of the implementation of our IT GRC process model in an organization and benchmark its efficiency compared to dealing with IT governance, IT risk management and IT compliance in silos, making our work evolve from a theoretical model to a practical way to apply these ISO standards in an integrated manner.

Acknowledgments. Supported by the National Research Fund, Luxembourg, and financed by the ENTRI project (C14/IS/8329158).

References

1. Peterson, R.R.: Integration strategies and tactics for information technology governance. In: Strategies for Information Technology Governance, pp. 37–80. Idea Group Publishing, Hershey (2004)
2. Racz, N., Weippl, E., Seufert, A.: A frame of reference for research of integrated governance, risk and compliance (GRC). In: De Decker, B., Schaumüller-Bichl, I. (eds.) CMS 2010. LNCS, vol. 6109, pp. 106–117. Springer, Heidelberg (2010)
3. Racz, N.: Governance, Risk and Compliance for Information Systems: Towards an Integrated Approach. Sudwestdeutscher Verlag Fur Hochschulschriften AG, Saarbrücken (2011)
4. Vicente, P., da Silva, M.M.: A business viewpoint for integrated IT governance, risk and compliance. In: 2011 IEEE World Congress on Services (SERVICES), pp. 422–428 (2011)
5. ISO/IEC 38500:2015: Information technology - Governance of IT for the organization. International Organization for Standardization, Geneva (2015)
6. ISO 31000:2009: Risk management – Principles and guidelines. International Organization for Standardization, Geneva (2009)
7. ISO 19600:2014: Compliance management systems — Guidelines. International Organization for Standardization, Geneva (2014)
8. Committee of Sponsoring Organizations of the Treadway Commission: Enterprise Risk Management – Integrated Framework (Executive Summary and Framework). Committee of Sponsoring Organizations of the Treadway Commission (2004)
9. Vicente, P., Mira da Silva, M.: A conceptual model for integrated governance, risk and compliance. In: Mouratidis, H., Rolland, C. (eds.) CAiSE 2011. LNCS, vol. 6741, pp. 199–213. Springer, Heidelberg (2011)
10. The Open Group: ArchiMate 2.0 Specification. Van Haren Publishing, The Netherlands (2012)
11. OCEG: GRC Capability Model (Red Book 2.1) (2012). http://goo.gl/7nrKku
12. ISACA: COBIT 5: A Business Framework for the Governance and Management of Enterprise IT (2012)
13. Gericke, A., Fill, H.-G., Karagiannis, D., Winter, R.: Situational method engineering for governance, risk and compliance information systems. In: Proceedings of the 4th International Conference on Design Science Research in Information Systems and Technology, pp. 24:1–24:12. ACM, New York (2009)
14. Asnar, Y., Massacci, F.: A method for security governance, risk, and compliance (GRC): a goal-process approach. In: Aldini, A., Gorrieri, R. (eds.) FOSAD 2011. LNCS, vol. 6858, pp. 152–184. Springer, Heidelberg (2011)
15. RSA: The RSA GRC Reference Architecture (2013)
16. Frigo, M.L., Anderson, R.J.: A strategic framework for governance, risk, and compliance. Strateg. Finance **90**, 20–61 (2009)
17. Paulus, S.: Overview Report: A GRC Reference Architecture (2009)

18. Krey, M., Furnell, S., Harriehausen, B., Knoll, M.: Approach to the Evaluation of a Method for the Adoption of Information Technology Governance, Risk Management and Compliance in the Swiss Hospital Environment. In: 2012 45th Hawaii International Conference on System Science (HICSS), pp. 2810–2819 (2012)
19. ISO/IEC TR 38502:2014: Information technology - Governance of IT - Framework and model. International Organization for Standardization, Geneva (2014)
20. ISO/IEC 27005:2011: Information technology – Security techniques – Information security risk management. International Organization for Standardization, Geneva (2011)

Changing Situational Contexts Present a Constant Challenge to Software Developers

Paul Clarke[1,2] and Rory V. O'Connor[1,2(✉)]

[1] Dublin City University, Dublin, Ireland
{pclarke,roconnor}@computing.dcu.ie
[2] Lero, the Irish Software Engineering Research Centre, Dublin, Ireland

Abstract. A software process can take many forms and its optimality demands that it should be harmonised with the needs of the given software development situational context. This theoretical proposition is reasonably clear. However, the finer details of the interaction between the software process and the factors of the situational context are much less obvious. In previously published research, the authors have elaborated a reference framework that identifies the factors of a situational context that affect the software process. In this paper, we report on the application of our reference framework in an examination of the changing nature of software development situational contexts. Our corresponding study of fifteen software development companies indicates that certain factors appear more subject to change than others. This finding is a potentially important insight that can help us with the recurring challenge of adapting the software process to changing circumstances.

Keywords: Software engineering · Situational context · Software development process · Software process adaptation

1   Introduction

Software development is a complex activity that is dependent on the performance of many individuals, in a multitude of different settings, and using a variety of development approaches. Recent decades have witnessed the emergence of many different software development approaches, some of which have met with widespread acceptance, including various agile methodologies [1-3] based upon the Agile Manifesto [4], CMMI [5], ISO/IEC 15504 [6] and ISO 9001 [7]. Despite this widespread acceptance of certain approaches, it is still believed that a degree of process adaptation, sometimes referred to as process tailoring, is required in order to address the needs of individual projects [8, 9]. Indeed, the impact of individual project characteristics has long been noted as a key consideration when designing a software process, leading to the claim that the most fundamental requirement of a software process is that it should "fit the needs of the project" [10].

The needs of software projects are dependent on the situational context wherein the project must operate and therefore, the most suitable process can be considered to be "contingent on the context" [11]. For this reason, software developers must "evaluate a

© Springer International Publishing Switzerland 2015
R.V. O'Connor et al. (Eds.): EuroSPI 2015, CCIS 543, pp. 100–111, 2015.
DOI: 10.1007/978-3-319-24647-5_9

wide range of contextual factors before deciding on the most appropriate process to adopt for any given project" [12], thus ensuring that the development approach should "best fit the conditions, product, talent, and goals of the markets and organisations" [13]. It is doubtful that experts in the software development field would argue about the importance of situational context, however, there is only limited published research into the morphology of software development contexts. Grounded in the accumulated knowledge of previous research into risk management, project cost estimation, software development standards, and software process tailoring (among other underlying research themes), the Situational Factors reference framework [14] is considered by the authors to be the most comprehensive source of information on software development contexts presently available. This framework organizes 44 factors of the context known to affect the software process under 8 classifications: Personnel, Technology, Requirements, Management, Application, Business, Organisation and Operations (refer to Figure 1).

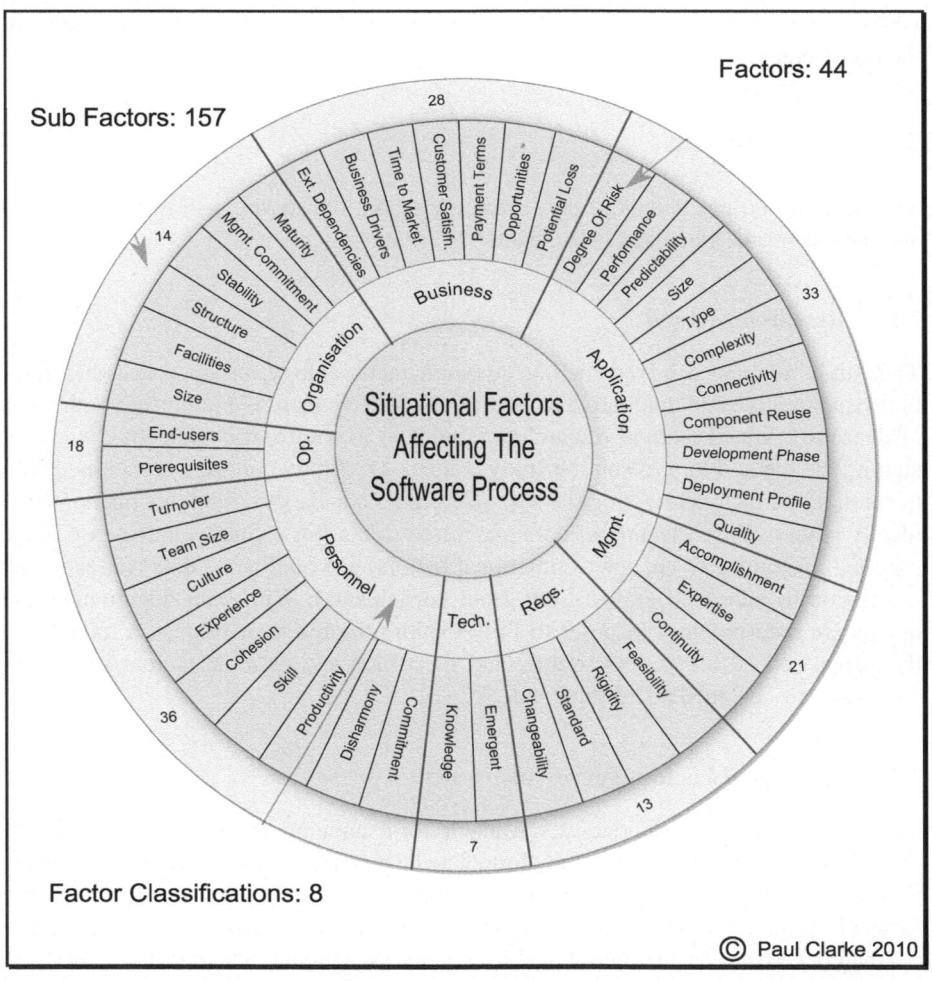

Fig. 1. Situational Factors Affecting the Software Development Process

If we look to the natural order of things in a general sense, we soon discover that change is a recurring challenge. Software developers are not immune to this challenge as they too must perceive changes in their environments and adapt to best address new realities. Of significance, it is recognised that this ability to adapt may be a critical capability for all types of businesses, that it is a key enabler of competitive advantage [15]. In the study presented in this paper, we have examined one aspect of this intriguing yet elusive capability: the nature of change in software development settings. Perhaps unsurprisingly, through the application of the Situational Factors reference framework [14] we have found that contextual change is ubiquitous in software development settings. However, we have also formed some insights into the characteristics of change, which we believe to be an important discovery that should be considered when developing and evolving software development approaches.

The remainder of this paper is structured as follows: Section 2 presents an overview of the study details. In Section 3, we provide an analysis of the data collected, while Section 4 offers a broader discussion on the implications of the data analysis. Section 5 contains the conclusion.

2   Study Details

This section outlines details of the research method, the survey instrument employed and the study timeframe and participants.

2.1   Research Method

This study adopted a mixed method research methodology, an approach that combines quantitative and qualitative techniques to collect, analyse and present both types of data [16]. Mixed method research is pragmatic in nature, it is concerned with designing the method to best suit the study context. Our study context is concerned with the situational factors affecting the software process, and examining this phenomenon ideally requires the collection of both quantitative data (for example, in the case of the reported magnitude of change to situational factors) and qualitative data (for example, in relation to enhanced explanations from participants). With both quantitative and qualitative data required in order to fully explore the research subject, a mixed method approach is therefore desirable, and for which a situational factors survey instrument was designed and discharged.

2.2   Situational Factors Survey Instrument

Since no pre-existing technique was available for examining situational change in software development settings, this study formulated a novel approach which involved transforming the situational factors reference framework [14] into a survey instrument. A key focus of the survey instrument was to provide a profile of the type of situational change that had occurred over the preceding 12 months to situational factors that are known to affect the software development process. The guiding principle was that all of the 44 individual factors in the reference framework should be addressed in individual questions in the survey, and where appropriate multiple questions should be developed for an individual factor (for example, where a large number of sub-factors exist).

Gradually, a series of questions were developed, taking the basic form of: *Have there been any modifications to [an aspect of the situation that can affect the software development process]?* By structuring the questions in this way, it was possible to get information on all changes – no matter how large or how small. This approach permits the elicitation of a comprehensive view of the extent and type of situational changes that have manifested in an organisation. In constructing the survey instrument, the basic classifications and factors of the situational factors framework were preserved. Therefore, the main body of the survey instrument has eight separate sections, one for each of the classifications in the situational factors framework. This step permitted the researchers to more easily guide participants through the survey and to provide updates on progress as the survey instrument was discharged.

Some of the sub-factors from the underlying situational factors framework were also included in the survey instrument for examining situational change. For example, in relation to the *Prerequisites* factor, the following question was developed: *Over the past year, has there been any modification to the operational prerequisites, including applicable standards and laws?* Through using the examples associated with the questions (for example: *applicable standards*), the finer detail regarding the sub-factors can also incorporated into a question. Using this technique, the fidelity of the underlying situational factors reference framework is significantly retained in the resulting survey instrument. This step was considered important as it ensured that the full scope of the situational factors framework was reflected in the survey instrument.

The survey instrument was subjected to a pilot with an industry partner. The purpose of the pilot was to check that the survey instrument was fit for purpose and that it could be discharged in a practical fashion. Moreover, the pilot was used to check that the participant could relate to and understand the various questions contained in the survey instrument. At the commencement of the pilot, the industry partner was informed that it was a pilot-run and they were encouraged to provide feedback on the content, flow and understandability of the survey. The primary item of feedback was a suggestion to reiterate throughout the survey discharge that the preceding year was the focus of the study, a recommendation which was adopted.

Regarding the content, flow and purpose of the survey instrument, the industry partner was positive concerning the general experience, and felt that the survey instrument provided an interesting mechanism for examining situational changes that affect the software development process. The pilot was the final phase in the survey instrument creation, which ultimately contained a total of 49 individual questions.

2.3   Study Timeframe and Participants

During the period of March to July 2011, the survey instrument was deployed to fifteen organisations, each of which satisfied the European Commission definition of an SME [17]. The majority of the participating organisations were primarily based in the Republic of Ireland, though a number of the companies were principally located elsewhere, including locations such as the USA and Chile. Three of the participating companies had fewer than 10 staff, with a further 4 companies having between 10 and 19 staff. The remainder of the participating organisations had between 20 and 129 staff. Each interview required approximately 1.25 hours to complete, giving a total of 18.75 hours interviewing time. The interviewee titles included Chief Technology Officer (CTO), Chief Executive Officer (CEO), Engineering Manager (EM), Managing Director (MD), Development Manager (DM), Director of Finance (DF), Director of Engineering (DE), and Chief Operating Officer (COO), with the scope of roles varying from company to company. The primary objective was the elicitation of a complete and accurate information set, and it was therefore sometimes necessary to interview more than one person in a single company.

A listing of the study participants (by role and company pseudonym) is provided in Table 1.[1]

Table 1. Participating organisations and interviewee job title

Company Pseudonym	Interviewee Job Title
Silverback	CTO
Grenoble	CEO, EM
Mega	MD
Cameron	MD, DM
Colleran	CEO
Lakes	MD, CTO
United	MD
Watch	DF, DE
BocaJ	MD
Tribal	DE
Dynamic	DE
Michelin	DE, DM
LordHenry	DE
When	COO
Oryx	COO, DM

Table 2. Modification rating scale for situational change

Modification Value	Modification Interpretation
0	No modification
1	Minor modification
2	Moderate modification
3	Significant modification

When eliciting the responses from interviewees, a modification rating for each reported change was agreed with the participant according to the details provided in

---

[1] In order to ensure the anonymity of the participating companies, pseudonyms (as opposed to actual company names) are utilised herein.

Table 2. This enabled the elicitation not just of the factors that were subject to change, but also of the extent of change to individual factors. Thus, a richer and more qualified data set was obtained.

3   Data Analysis

A basic analysis of the study data reveals that some aspects of the situational context are routinely reporting relatively large degrees of change while other aspects of the situation are subject to only minor change (or in some cases, no change at all). In this section, we present details of the most and least common areas for situational change. An overview of the hierarchy of situational change is presented in Figure 2.[2]

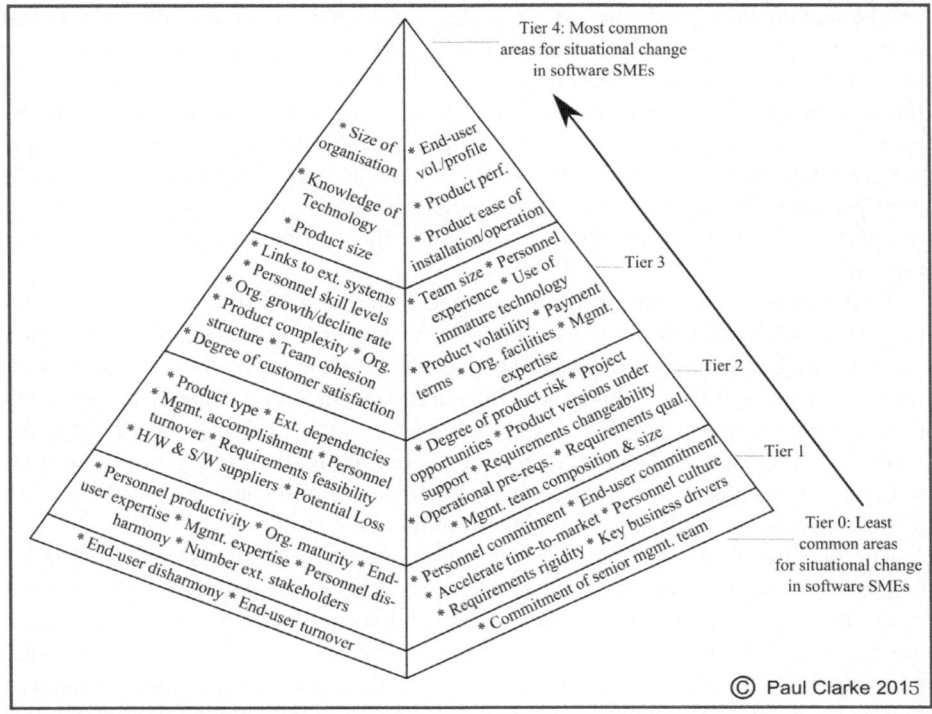

Fig. 2. Hierarchy of situational change for software SMEs

---

[2] The hierarchy presented in Figure 2 was constructed by analysing the responses from all participants to each question in the situational change survey instrument. Both the frequency and the amount of reported change in each situational aspect were jointly considered, with more frequent and/or more significant situational changes being placed higher on the pyramid.

3.1   Situational Factors Reporting Change

Staff headcount presented as the most common area for situational change across the study group. All fifteen participating companies reported changes to their headcount, with 11 of the companies reporting increases to headcount levels during the study timeframe. Nine of the participating companies witnessed headcount increases of 25% and greater over the year under investigation, while two of the organisations experienced headcount reductions of 40% or more during the same period. These reported changes to headcount figures represent significant fluctuations, indicating that headcount volatility is a major challenge in small and medium sized software companies. Such volatility is a major catalyst for process change, and may even suggest that small and medium sized software companies are more in need of regular process management than larger, more stable organisations.

The participating companies also reported considerable change in the volume and profile of end users of their software products, with 11 companies reporting increases to the net volume of transactions processed or to the volume of end users. In some of these cases the organisations reported a significant increase in the number of end users or volume of transactions that their products must support. Of note, not a single company reported a reduction in the number of end users or volume of transactions in their products. Furthermore, two of the participating companies reported changes to the profile of end users, resulting in a need for their products to cater for different types of end users.

Of the participating companies, 13 reported increases in the knowledge of technology. In some cases, this involved supporting new operating systems, such as Linux and emerging mobile device operating systems. In other cases, these changes were focused on the software development infrastructure, including changes to integrated development environments (IDEs) and changes to compilers. While the extent of the reported change in knowledge of technology varies across the study group, almost all of organisations reported an increase in their knowledge of technology mostly through the adoption and utilisation of emerging technologies.

The majority of the participating companies, twelve in total, also reported an increase in the required performance of their products. Those companies that did not report increases in performance requirements did not report decreases either, but rather that the performance requirements remain unchanged. In terms of the size of the products, 10 of the participating companies reported increases in one form or another. For some organisations, this increase took the form of increased data storage requirements while for other organisations, the reported change relates to the size of the code base. One of the companies reported a slight decrease in the code base as a result of an intensified refactoring effort.

A total of nine of the participating organisations reported that an increase in the required ease of installation and operation of their software products – emphasising the need to continually improve the installation procedures and to constantly strive to improve the end user experience of their product(s).

3.2 Situational Factors Reporting Little or No Change

Of all the situational factors examined in the study, just a single factor was reported as unchanged in all of the participating companies: *senior management team commitment to projects*. With respect to this finding, it should be noted that the personnel participating in the study were senior managers – who might be unlikely to report a decrease in their commitment to their project(s). Just two of the participating organisations reported a change to the number of external stakeholders over the period of investigation. In one case, this was the result of engaging external systems integrators on a more regular basis. In the case of the second organisation, the opposite effect was reported: systems integrators were no longer being used to deploy systems but rather the company had started to work more directly with its clients.

There was little reported change regarding the turnover of product end-users. For some companies, this was accounted for by the nature of their product(s). For example, several organisations developed middleware applications with little or no direct end-user interaction (but rather just a few specialised users would configure or interact with the product). The participating organisations also reported little or no change in the personnel culture, with disharmony levels (including interpersonal conflicts) remaining largely the same as in early periods. This finding is perhaps surprising when we consider the reported headcount volatility in the participating group – as the introduction of new people can be accompanied by friction within teams.

4   Discussion

There are a number of features of the data analysis that serve to highlight the challenges imposed on small and medium sized software companies as a result of changing situational contexts. Perhaps the most striking of these challenges is the rate of growth or decline in the *Organisational Size* situational factor (i.e. headcount). While it is to be expected that each of the companies might report some change to headcount, it was not anticipated that the rate of change would be so significant. Two of the participating companies witnessed a reduction in headcount of 40% or greater - losing 15 out of 35 employees in one case, and 8 out of 20 employees in the second case. A further 9 of the 15 participating companies experienced headcount growth of 25% or higher, with 6 of these organisations growing their headcount by 50% or more. In some cases, these percentage increases are partly accounted for by the fact that the organisations were very small at the start of the study. However, in other cases, a relatively large number of new personnel were introduced to the participating company. Large changes in headcount can have a significant effect on the process of work, and the data collected in this study suggests that this is not an uncommon phenomenon in small and medium sized software companies.

A further significant challenge potentially originates from changes reported in the *Operational End-users* situational factor, for example through increases in the volume of transactions that software products must process. Ten of the participating companies reported increases in the volume of transactions. Some of the organisations note that their *"traffic continues to grow"*, with others reporting the increase to be *"very significant"*. Further evidence of this challenge is evident in related responses that *"storage requirements are growing"* and that an increasing database size *"is one of the biggest challenges that we have now"*. Increased throughput and storage demands can place a heavy burden on software products, and increasing throughput and storage capacity in a system is an area that may require specialised and costly attention. However, small and medium sized software companies don't necessarily have a great deal of bandwidth or expertise in terms of addressing such challenges. Therefore, along with headcount challenges, increased demand for product throughput and storage may necessitate a change to the software process.

The issue of ever-increasing transaction volumes and storage issues may be further exacerbated by the reported demand for increases in the *Application Performance* situational factor and in this respect, it is possible that in fact, increases in *Operational* factors (such as the volume of transactions or end-users) are one of the primary drivers for change in the *Application Performance* situational factor. Twelve of the participating companies reported an increased required performance in their product(s) over the year under investigation. One of the organisations reported that the performance requirement had *"gone up by 20%"*, while a second company reported that performance had *"increased probably by 30%"*. Another organisation again reported that their product *"has to run twice as fast"*. Other companies reported that the increased performance requirement is *"significant"*, that it is *"always increasing"*, and that *"the customer is always demanding more fast and more reliable [products]"*. This increased demand for higher performance may present a significant challenge to the limited resources at the disposal of small and medium sized companies - as performance-related activities may detract from the development and evolution of product features designed to attract customers. Such activities may also affect the software process, for example, testing mechanisms and hardware selection processes may undergo change.

In addition to the challenges already noted, indications from the data are that the *Technology Knowledge* situational factor is also subject to significant change, and this suggests that the supporting technologies are themselves continually changing. Eight of the participating companies reported that they adopted new technologies over the year under investigation. Some of the organisations report changes to the programming related environment, including languages, compilers and associated tooling. Other companies report that they had to support additional operating systems, including traditional desktop operating systems and newer mobile device operating systems. The adoption of new technology requires effort, with one respondent stating: *"we've started using several different technologies over the past year and people have had to skill up on them and share their knowledge among the team"*. And such upskilling and knowledge sharing may require a change to the underlying software process. For example, it may be necessary to introduce a process – if only for a period of time – that enables knowledge sharing across the relevant parties.

5   Conclusion

In the broader business domain, it is acknowledged that the ability of an organisation to adapt their business processes in response to changing situational contexts may be a key source of competitive advantage [15]. For software development companies, the software process is a large and complex component of the overall business process, and therefore an area, which is a potential source of competitive advantage. However, there are very significant challenges when aligning changes in situational context with software process changes – as has been highlighted [18]: the essential observation being that the complexity in the relationship between the process and the corresponding context is too large to fully qualify. Our best route forward with this problem may therefore start with gaining a greater appreciation of software development situational contexts, and in particular in understanding which aspects of such contexts are witnessing more frequent or greater degrees of change. If the key concerns of context can be identified, then the problem may be reduced – and those tasked with developing and evolving software process approaches can consider incorporating mechanisms for process adaptation that are aligned with situational factors that witness more frequent or greater change – this is the essential importance of this work.

The research presented herein exhibits a number of limitations and weaknesses. It is limited to just fifteen companies, and these companies are either small or medium in size. Hence, the generalisability of findings requires further investigation. The data is collected from a small number of individuals within the participating companies and thus it exhibits the weakness that it may not be a complete view of the actuality of the context changes in the participating companies. Although difficult to realise from a practical perspective, broader focus group discussions may have helped to reduce the bias introduced by working with just one or two individuals from each of the companies. Nonetheless, the inquiries conducted required approximately 19 hours of interviewing time with participants, and considerable detail was obtained. Furthermore, a comprehensive situational factors reference framework [14] (itself a product of related research) was adopted, and this was carefully crafted into a survey instrument that was subject to an industrial pilot as part of its validation.

On the subject of the general nature of situational change in the participating companies, a number of our key findings from this exploratory research suggest that changing situational contexts present a constant and significant challenge to software developers. High levels of headcount volatility are consistently reported across the study group, which inevitably means that regular process adaptation is required. This may account for the finding in related published material that software process adaptation is a regular occurrence [19], and that greater levels of process adaptation are positively associated with increased business success [20]. It may also legitimise efforts to model the relationship between the software process and its corresponding situational context [21-23].

Of interest also is the revelation that there is some potential discordance with previously reported key areas for process improvement in smaller companies. For example, a number of previous studies highlight the importance of improvement to requirements capture in smaller companies [24, 25], whereas the findings from our inquiry suggest that requirements changeability and requirements quality are not witnessing relatively high levels of change. However, it should be stressed that these earlier studies were not looking to the broader business challenges but focused just on the core software development process (i.e. situational factors related to *Organisation* and *Operation* fell outside the scope of these earlier software process improvement studies). With these organisational and operational factors reporting relatively high levels of change within our study, it is perhaps the case that the role of such factors and their influence on the software process is not sufficiently well elaborated upon at the present time. If we take any of the presently popular software development approaches (e.g. agile methodologies [1-3], CMMI [5], ISO/IEC 15504 [6] and ISO 9001 [7]), there exists a software lifecycle centric focus that does not appear to offer direct provisions for dealing with significant fluctuations in headcount. This gap appears worthy of further investigation – as on the basis of the evidence collected in our study, there is constant and sometimes significant change to headcount.

Since software development contexts are continually changing, it would therefore be advantageous for researchers and practitioners to focus some of their energies on the objective of enhancing our understanding of the relationship between software contexts and software processes - and studies such as the one reported herein represent an important initial step along the journey to realising this objective.

Acknowledgments. This work is supported, in part, by Science Foundation Ireland grant 03/CE2/I303_1 to Lero, the Irish Software Research Centre (www.lero.ie).

References

1. Schwaber, K., Beedle, M.: Agile Software Development with SCRUM. Prentice Hall, Upper Saddle River (2002)
2. Beck, K.: Extreme Programming Explained: Embrace Change. Addison-Wesley, Reading (1999)
3. Poppendieck, M., Poppendieck, T.: Lean Software Development: An Agile Toolkit. Addison-Wesley, Upper Saddle River (2003)
4. Fowler, M., Highsmith, J.: The Agile Manifesto. Software Development, pp. 28–32 (2001)
5. SEI: CMMI for Development, Version 1.3. CMU/SEI-2006-TR-008. Software Engineering Institute, Pittsburgh, PA, USA (2010)
6. ISO/IEC: IS0/IEC 15504: Information Technology - Process Assessment, Part 1 to Part 5. International Organisation for Standardization, Geneva, Switzerland (2005)
7. ISO: ISO 9001:2000 - Quality Management Systems - Requirements. International Organisation for Standardization, Geneva, Switzerland (2000)
8. Coleman, G., O'Connor, R.V.: Investigating software process in practice: A grounded theory perspective. Journal of Systems and Software **81**(5), 772–784 (2008)
9. Kautz, K.: Software process improvement in very small enterprises: does it pay off? Software Process: Improvement and Practice 4(4), 209–226 (1998)
10. Feiler, P., Humphrey, W.: Software Process Development and Enactment: Concepts and Definitions. Software Engineering Institute, Carnegie Mellon University, CMU/SEI-92-TR-004. Pittsburgh, Pennsylvania, USA, (1992)

11. Benediktsson, O., Dalcher, D., Thorbergsson, H.: Comparison of software development life cycles: a multiproject experiment. IEE Proceedings - Software **153**(3), 87–101 (2006)
12. MacCormack, A., Verganti, R.: Managing the Sources of Uncertainty: Matching Process and Context in Software Development. Journal of Product Innovation Management **20**(3), 217–232 (2003)
13. Subramanian, G.H., Klein, G., Jiang, J.J., Chan, C.: Balancing four factors in system development projects. Communications of the ACM **52**(10), 118–121 (2009)
14. Clarke, P., O'Connor, R.V.: The situational factors that affect the software development process: Towards a comprehensive reference framework. Journal of Information and Software Technology **54**(5), 433–447 (2012)
15. Teece, D.J.: Explicating dynamic capabilities: the nature and microfoundations of (sustainable) enter-prise performance. Strategic Management Journal **28**(11), 1319–1350 (2007)
16. Petter, S.C., Gallivan, M.J.: Toward a framework for classifying and guiding mixed method research in information systems. In: Proceedings of the 37th Hawaii International Conference on System Sciences, January 5–8. IEEE Computer Society, Los Alamitos (2004)
17. Commission, European: Commission Recommendation of 6 May 2003 concerning the definition of micro, small and medium-sized enterprises. Official Journal of the European Union, L. 2003/361/EC **124**, 36–41 (2003)
18. Dyba, T.: Contextualizing empirical evidence. IEEE Software **30**(1), 81–83 (2013)
19. Clarke, P., O'Connor, R.V.: An empirical examination of the extent of software process improvement in software SMEs. Journal of Software: Evolution and Process **25**(9), 981–998 (2013)
20. Clarke, P., O'Connor, R.V.: The influence of SPI on business success in software SMEs: An empirical study. Journal of Systems and Software **85**(10), 2356–2367 (2012)
21. Jeners, S., O'Connor, R.V., Clarke, P., Lichter, H., Lepmets, M., Buglione, L.: Harnessing software development contexts to inform software process selection decisions. Software Quality Professional **16**(1), 35–36 (2013)
22. Jeners, Simona, Clarke, Paul, O'Connor, Rory V., Buglione, Luigi, Lepmets, Marion: Harmonizing software development processes with software development settings – a systematic approach. In: McCaffery, Fergal, O'Connor, Rory V., Messnarz, Richard (eds.) EuroSPI 2013. CCIS, vol. 364, pp. 167–178. Springer, Heidelberg (2013)
23. Clarke, Paul, O'Connor, Rory V.: An Approach to Evaluating Software Process Adaptation. In: O'Connor, Rory V., Rout, Terry, McCaffery, Fergal, Dorling, Alec (eds.) SPICE 2011. CCIS, vol. 155, pp. 28–41. Springer, Heidelberg (2011)
24. Keane, Brendan, Richardson, Ita: Quality: attitudes and experience within the irish software industry. In: Richardson, Ita, Abrahamsson, Pekka, Messnarz, Richard (eds.) EuroSPI 2005. LNCS, vol. 3792, pp. 49–58. Springer, Heidelberg (2005)
25. Sanders, M.: The SPIRE Handbook. Better, Faster, Cheaper Software Development in Small Organisations. Centre for Software Engineering Limited, DCU, Dublin, Ireland (1998)

Software Process Improvement
Best Practices

Protocol to Design Techniques for Implementing Software Development Best Practices

Gloria Piedad Gasca-Hurtado[1(⊠)], Vianca Vega-Zepeda[2],
Mirna Muñoz[3], and Jezreel Mejía[3]

[1] Maestría en Ingeniería de Software, Facultad de Ingeniería,
Universidad de Medellín, Carrera 87 no. 30-65, Medellín, Colombia
gpgasca@udem.edu.co
[2] Departamento de Ingeniería de Sistemas Y Computación,
Universidad Católica del Norte, Avenida Angamos 0610, Antofagasta, Chile
vvega@ucn.cl
[3] Centro de Investigación en Matemáticas, Av. Universidad no 222 98068, Zacatecas, México
{mirna.munoz,jmejia}@cimat.mx

Abstract. Software engineering best practices allow significantly improving the software development. However, the implementation of best practices requires skilled professionals, financial investment and technical support to facilitate implementation and achieve the respective improvement. In this paper we proposes a protocol to design techniques to implement best practices of software engineering. The protocol includes the identification and selection of process to improve, the study of standards and models, identification of best practices associated with the process and the possible implementation techniques. In addition, technical design activities are defined in order to create or adapt the techniques of implementing best practices for software development.

Keywords: Software process improvement · Standards · Models · Protocol · software engineering

1 Introduction

The implementation of best practices for software development projects contributes to its success only if there are techniques suitable for this implementation. Identifying and selecting best practices to implement improvements in the processes of software development, it should include assessment activities and verification in order to check the quality and quantity of the selected practices.

This paper is derived from the results of research projects development between the Universidad de Medellín (Colombia), the Universidad Católica del Norte (Chile) and the scientific contributions of Centro de Investigación en Matemáticas de México (CIMAT). The research projects have focused on the definition of techniques and mechanisms to improve the way you run the software development projects successfully.

© Springer International Publishing Switzerland 2015
R.V. O'Connor et al. (Eds.): EuroSPI 2015, CCIS 543, pp. 115–126, 2015.
DOI: 10.1007/978-3-319-24647-5_10

Each time a technique is proposed to implement a best practice for software development, iterative activities are generated. It allows design a new technique or adapt some existing techniques.

The purpose of this paper is to propose a guide to identify, select and design techniques that contribute to the implementation of best practices for software development.

The main reason why this guide is proposed is to establish a systematic and organized way to: identify, select, validate and propose techniques for implementing best practices in software development. This guide is called protocol because it includes the definition of a systematic and repeatable process. It is formalized and documented for use whenever it is required. This protocol can be used for any research project in software engineering that requires or includes the creation of techniques for implementing best practices.

Through the protocol, a methodical guide is proposed. It is composed of steps documented in detail. This proposal aims to optimize the results of the process, allowing quickly structuring any of the best practices that require one or more techniques needed for their implementation in a software development project.

For the construction of this protocol, different guide documents have been used that give sustenance to the proposal. Among these highlights:

1. "Procedures for Performing Systematic Reviews" [1] de B. Kitchenham
2. "Systematic Review in Software Engineering" [2] de J. Biolchini
3. "Models and Standards Similarity Study method" [3] de J. Calvo-Manzano, et al.
4. "Experimentation in Software Engineering. An Introduction" [4] de C. Wohlin.

The first two sources mentioned were used as a guide to identify the different components that make up the protocol. The third source has been adopted as the standard method for conducting Phase 2 of the protocol, while the Wohlin [4] proposal is the basis for the pilot phase included in the protocol.

Due to the team being geographically distributed in different countries, it became necessary to standardize the method of work to get consistent results in various selected areas. Additionally, the formalization and dissemination of procedures and methods applied, can serve as a guide for any researcher who wants to generate some methodology or strategy to enable the implementation of best practices.

The construction of the protocol was developed based on the experience of the researchers involved in the project, besides using as an example the definition of a protocol for the development of a systematic review [1].

The protocol has been adjusted keeping in view the results gotten in its application in different cases, of which one is described in detail in the present paper, as case study to validate the usefulness of this protocol.

The use of this protocol is recommended to all researchers who wish to propose a methodology, strategy or guide to help small and medium organizations to implement best practices suggested by international standards and models.

This paper is structured as follows: The second section provides a conceptual framework. The third section presents the protocol to design techniques for implementing of best practices, motivations and context of the work done. In the fourth part, the application of the protocol is shown for the creation of a technique to support the identification of the risks through a taxonomy, as a best practice aimed at achieving the success of software development projects. The paper ends with the conclusions drawn from the work done.

2   Overview

2.1   Process Improvement

The term *software process improvement* was originally proposed by WS Humphrey in 1988 [5]. The scope of process improvement considers to understand existing processes, evaluate and change them to improve the quality of the product that is being developed and / or reduce costs and development time [5].

It is important to note that in order to improve a process, adopting new methods or tools is not enough, organizational factors, procedures and standards that affect the process always exist.

Generally speaking, the improvement of a process is an iterative activity which considers three main stages: Measuring the current process, a step of analyzing where the process are valued and modeled and finally, the introduction of changes.

The cost of a process improvement project is a major barrier for small enterprise [6]. This has led researchers to propose "light" strategies for process improvement.

2.2   Best Practices for Software Development

Generally speaking, a practice is a method or technique used to conduct a part of a process and it describes how it is done. A *best practice* is some practice that has been incorporated on several projects and has been experimentally checked that contributes to the success of the objectives of these projects [6]. Given the above, software development best practices are recommended activities to replicate with a very high probability that the project will end successfully.

The capability to identify and transfer the best practices in an organization is a critical factor for to get a competitive advantage. This strategy has become one of the management techniques from the second half of the nineties.

These practices are published as success factors, lessons learned and observations [6].

Jacobson et.al [7] defines a practice as a guide for dealing with some dimension of software development. The authors suggest that this term despite of being commonly used in the software development industry has no single definition.

2.3   Techniques

According to the Real Academia de la Lengua Española [8], a technique is a "set of procedures and resources from which a science or an art is served" or "ability to run anything, or to get something."

In SWEBOK guide [9], various techniques are proposed to perform the tasks and processes associated with software development, it guide to practitioners on how to perform certain activities required for successful development projects. This is how you can find suggested techniques for requirements elicitation, or to measure software process, or techniques for the analysis and assessment quality, among many others [9].

Applying this concept to the work performed and described in this paper, it can be stated that the objective of an technique for implementation of software development best practices, is to establish the way (mechanisms, methods, tools) for organizations, especially in small setting, can adopt and adapt best practices for software development, proposed by the largest standards or international models recognized in business and academic area. This work is necessary, since these models and standards have been developed for large organizations or government entities, which causes that they are not directly applicable in small setting.

3   Protocol for Creation of Techniques to Implementation of Best Practices

The protocol to design techniques to implement best practices for software development has the following characteristics:

1. Repeatable process. It defines, describes and documents a protocol to systematically apply the procedure as many times as necessary to design techniques or adapt those that may be useful in a particular workspace.
2. Agility. The procedure is described and documented to generate results agile.
3. Process Optimization. Ability to optimize processes that rely on best practices, from a better selection of techniques.
4. Quality validation for selected techniques. The evaluation of quality of best practices selected and implemented in an organization, is facilitated when suitable techniques are used for each area process.
5. Ease of creating techniques. With the protocol, it is want to establish steps and examples that give ease of creation of techniques and effectiveness of the implementation of best practices.

The creation of protocol is based on the design science research cycles identified by Hevner [10]. This proposal involves three stages interconnected by research cycles: 1) Environment: aims to identify the application domain, 2) Design Science Research: include building processes of artifacts and its evaluation and, 3) Knowledge Base: includes the new foundations (theories and methods, experience, new products and processes) to the knowledge base of the organization. Stages one and two are connected by Relevance Cycle where research requirements are defined and field tests are conducted. During the second stage, the Design Cycle is develops, it is responsible for the creation and testing of new proposals. Stages two and three are joined by Rigor Cycle that is responsible for increasing the knowledge of an organization

3.1   Protocol Phases

The protocol is divided into 4 phases, each with a set of tasks to be developed. The phases and activities are:

Phase 1. Planning. Establish a plan of study of the process or area of susceptible process to improve for the software development.

Task 1.1. Identification of the process or process area.

Task 1.2. General description of the process or process area.

Task 1.3. General review of models and standards that may include the process or process area of interest.

Phase 2. Selection. Select and prioritize best practices that enable the achievement of the objectives to improve of a defined process.

Task 2.1. Selection of models and standards that incorporate the process area of interest.

Task 2.2. Comparative analysis of selected models and standards.

Task 2.3. Selection of best practices to be implemented

Phase 3. Standardization. Study and analysis of the implementation technique for the best practices selected.

Task 3.1. Description of the best practices selected

Task 3.2. Description of the recommended technique

Task 3.3. Creating process assets

Phase 4. Validation. It includes experimentation, evaluation and institutionalization of the process.

Task 4.1. Experimentation

Task 4.2. Quality assessment

Task 4.3. Recommendations for improvement

Task 4.4. Technique institutionalize and lessons learned

3.2   Protocol Description

The protocol to design techniques for implementing software development best practices consists of four consecutive phases, each one of them with a set of tasks to be performed. When the protocol application finalizes, results a new technique or the adaptation of an existing technique that allows software development organizations implement best practices in a particular process area, which contributes to improving development processes of organizations and software industry.

Next, phases and tasks that make up the protocol are detailed. In the explanation of each phase, will be detailed the relationship of each phase with the inputs and outputs, with the specific tasks that make up the corresponding phase. In the Fig. 1 the structure of the process to follow during each one of the phases are shown.

Phase 1. Study Plan of the Process or Process Area. The selection of the key process area is based on the experience and knowledge of the researchers involved in the project, besides the expert opinion and interest expressed by members of the companies that recognize which areas are most relevant to improve their software development processes. This phase is composed by these tasks:

Task 1. Select the process area. This selection is done based on the expert opinion of researchers and project managers.

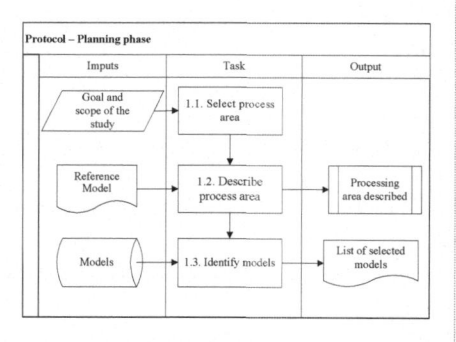

Phase 1. Planning. Establish a plan of study of the process or area of susceptible process to improve for the software development

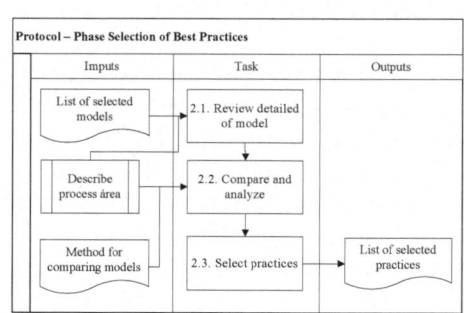

Phase 2. Selection. Select and prioritize best practices that enable the achievement of the objectives to improve of a defined process

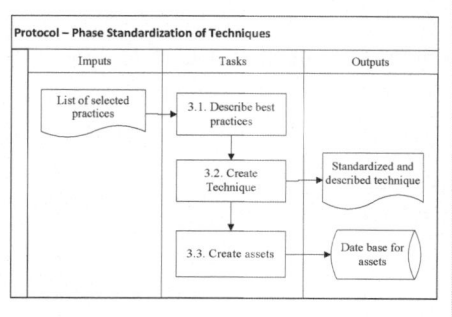

Phase 3. Standardization. Study and analysis of the technical implementation for the selected best practices

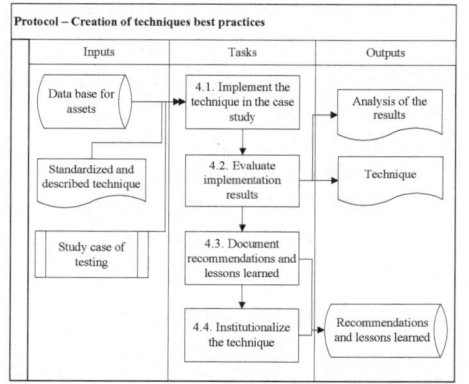

Phase 4. Validation. It includes experimentation, evaluation and institutionalization of the process

Fig. 1. Protocol Structure described by phase

Task 2. Describe the process area. It should develop a description of the process area selected, using as basis the reference model. The objective of this task is to fully understand the objectives and scope of the area to identify the presence of it in other models that could eventually be identified by a different name using it by said reference model.

The reference model is selected because of their relevance and prestige among the developer companies and academy.

Task 3. Identify models, policies and standards that incorporate the process area. The final task of this phase is a general review of models, policies and standards that also incorporate the process area of interest. The objective of this task is to select the most suitable models for comparison and selection of best practices.

In Figure 2, the tasks of Phase 1 are shown, with inputs and outputs for each task.

Phase 2. Selection and Prioritization of Best Practice. As input to the second phase of the protocol, you have the list of the models, policies and standards that according to the first overview also incorporate the process area of interest. Using the mentioned inputs, the tasks that make up this phase are:

Task 1. Detailed review of models, policies and standards. Standards and selected models are pre-screened for the selection of those that effectively incorporate best practices to the process area of interest. The criteria for selection or exclusion of some models should be discussed jointly by researchers and project participants.

Examples of criteria are:

- Those models developed by Institutions with recognized status are included, such as the Software Engineering Institute (SEI) from Carnegie Mellon University, International Organization for Standardization (ISO), Institute of Electrical and Electronics Engineers (IEEE), the Spanish Association for Standardization and Certification (AENOR), the Colombian Institute of Technical Standards (ICONTEC) and the National Institute for Standardization (INN) among others.
- Those policies or standards that are of interest from companies for certification are included.
- Proposals that include only a subset of best practices in some other way are excluded.

As a result of this task a more restricted list of models, policies and standard that incorporate the process area of interest is obtained.

Task 2. Comparative analysis of selected models. The objective of this analysis is to identify what are the most frequent best practices among the models and how practices that differ between them are complementary. It is suggested that this analysis is developed using as a basis the Method of Similarity Models and Standards (MESME) [3].

As result of this task you have the set of best practices that appear in the analyzed models, i.e. the practices that are repeated and the complementary.

Task 3. Selection of best practices to be implemented. The amount of practice and own practices selected depends on aspects such as available resources, the relationship between best practices, project restrictions, among other aspects to consider.

Phase 3. Formalization of Implementation Technique for the Selected Best Practices. The entrance to this third phase corresponds to the list of best practices that have been selected for implementation. The tasks to be developed in this phase are:

Task 1. Description of best practices selected. The aim is to characterize and understand in depth. It is very important to know what the inputs and expected results for each of the practices are, as well as traceability exists between best practices and techniques or tools for implementation.

Task 2. Creating implementation technique. This task refers to the creation of methods, methodologies, tools, frameworks or other mechanisms to implement and integrate, especially in small companies and best practices easily. With the creation of the implementation technique, it seeks to minimize the costs of incorporating best practices and achieving the objectives of improving the software development process that small organizations proposed.

This task must deliver as results a detailed description of the recommended technique, that is, identify and describe the steps and tasks to be performed, deliver an activity diagram or flow that allows to clearly understand what and how should be done.

Task 3. Create process assets. An active process is a collection of entities used in software process that aid in the development of activities thereof. They are useful in definition, maintaining and institutionalizing of the processes [11]. These assets allows to define standard processes of an organization [12].

Given the above definition, the objective of this task is to identify and design the assets and artifacts to facilitate the implementation and use of the proposed techniques. Between the process assets templates are considered, checklists, forms, among others.

This stage is very important, since for small enterprises, to have a process assets library is a key element that reduces training time and helps guide the approach in the organization [12].

Phase 4. Validation or experimentation. The fourth phase of the protocol corresponds to validation or experimentation of the proposal developed. This phase is composed by these tasks:

Task 1. Validation or experimentation. It corresponds to the implementation of a case study. It is important to highlight that this experimental method is empirical, so you can target both the qualitative and quantitative analysis [13].

There are three strategies for case studies [13]:
   a)   Comparison of results between a new proposal and a baseline.
   b)   Develop two projects in parallel ("brother projects") by choosing one of them as a base.
   c)   Apply the new proposal on selected components and compare these results versus those components which were not applied.

The selection of one of the above strategies must be analyzed taking into account the nature of the proposed technique, and the conditions and restrictions of the particular study.

Task 2. Quality assessment. After the application of the technique in the particular case, the quality of products obtained with the application of the new proposal must be evaluated, as well as the quality of the modified process. This quality assessment in post-mortem form will allow identifying lessons learned and adjustments needed to the proposal.

Task 3. Improvement recommendations. These improvements may be as in the applicability of the same, or the identification of activities/tasks necessary to include or adjust.

Task 4. Institutionalization of the technique. It corresponds to train staff of the organization that will adopt a new proposal and perform an accompaniment in the implementation of the new processes

Next, case study in which it has developed the validation protocol is described.

4   Case Study

The case study aims to identify mechanisms, techniques and methods for the implementation and adaptation of best practices for software development in a multi-model environment. The multi-model environment is a new approach to the process improvement that is characterized because it seeks the integration of multiple models for improving software development processes [14]. This approach seeks to harmonize and standardize best practices proposed by different models [14]. It has been found in this type of environment multi-model a good solution to reduce the complexity of process improvement in small and medium enterprises in Latin America, since it allows selecting and focusing on the best practices for small organizations, considering various models that allows a complement and strengthen of the identified practices.

This case study focuses on the application of each one of the phases of the protocol to identify a set of best practices that enables to improve the process of risk management in a medium sized enterprise.

Each one of the protocol phases, it was used and following results were obtained:

- Selection of a team of experts formed by: a) researchers and teachers involved in the study case, in order to have the academic vision, b) software professionals, to have the current view of the industry needs on process improvement and best practices, and c) a group of graduate students, which provide an updated vision through the constant search for information related to the area and the project context.
- Weighted average of a preliminary list of proposed areas of process such as: Traceability Requirements, Risk Management and Quality Management. This process results in an interest by creating a technique for Risk Management Process, particularly for identification and analysis risk
- Identification of best practices such as: risk classification as the basis of better identification [15], [16] through a taxonomy of risks [17].
- Incorporating fuzzy logic concepts to achieve a risk prioritization and subsequent analysis.
- The design of a method is defined to identify and analyze the risks comprising the following steps:

1. Examine each element of the structure proposed in the taxonomy.
2. Select the set of questions related for each element selected in the previous step, according to the proposal of the questionnaire made by the SEI [13].
3. Perform a plenary session involved in the software development project to identify risks in response to questions related to the selected items [18].
4. Review previous efforts risk management in similar projects, if any, and complement the questions with such review.
5. Examine documents lessons learned and complement the questions with such review.
6. Document identified risks, including the context, conditions and consequences of the risk occurring.
7. Select the items according to the structure proposed in the taxonomy.
8. Planning the next cycle of risk identification from the selected elements in the previous step.

The designed method is based on the following elements:

a) risk taxonomy based on questions proposed by the Software Engineering Institute [17] and,

b) risk analysis matrix based on fuzzy logic. These techniques help to decrease the sense of vagueness in defining the measures in the risk analysis when qualitative values are used.

The mentioned aspects are developed in a computer tool as a way to start the validation process and in order to expedite the identification of risks and the incorporation of fuzzy logic concepts for risk analysis.

Risk assessment is an "assessment" of something hypothetical defined as *risk*, which must then be interpreted as "high", or "low", or "tolerable" [19]. For our proposal we used the linguistic values of the fuzzy logic to risk analysis in a scale of values multiple, as show in the Table 1.

Table 1. Rating scale for risk analysis used fuzzy logic

Linguistic value	Very high	High	Medium	Low	Very Low
Numerical value	100	75	50	25	0

From the implementation of the method in a software tool a software prototype is achieved. It has been designed using the concepts of analysis, design and implementation of software engineering as part of the product development.

Using this functional prototype a pilot validation of the technique starts. The proposed pilot validation aims to evaluate the software tool in its first phase. From this assessment it is pretended to raise experimental project engineering software for validation of identifying and risks analyzing technique.

The results of the evaluation of software tool indicate that 67% of participants in validation previously identify it risks in their projects. The same proportion (67%) indicated that it was easy to identify risks to the applied technique making use of the tool, while 33% considers it was not easy to identify the risks.

In this case study the validation is considered such a limitation for our proposal, therefore, the next step in this research project in progress, is perform formal an experimentation in software engineering with the support of technological tools like the one validated so far.

5   Conclusions

The adoption and adaptation of best practices proposed on international models and standards, is not an easy task to perform, especially for small enterprises that do not have the financial resources or the time required to make a large investment in improving its processes. However, this improvement is a necessity to have organizations to improve product quality, increase productivity, and respond in the best way to the market [12].

With this reality in mind, the joint project arises between the Universidad de Medellin (Colombia), the Universidad Católica del Norte (Chile) and support from the Centro de Investigación en Matemáticas de México (CIMAT-Zacatecas). This project aims to facilitate small organizations, the instantiation of software development best practices in their own processes, thereby enabling increasing maturity and contributing in obtaining higher quality products.

The protocol presented in this paper corresponds to one of the outstanding results of this project. It arose from the need to standardize the labor from geographically distributed teams, and as a tool that is characterized by its ease for the orderly and consistent repetition in different scope or key process areas.

The strengths of the proposed protocol lie precisely in this feature, since the proposal achieves collect the knowledge gained during the execution of the research project on a method to define implementation techniques of best practices. Such techniques support small enterprises to incorporate a set of best practices related to a process area, in an agile way, reducing the effort and time to implement process improvement strategies.

In this paper the application of the protocol in the generation of a technique is presented to support risk management through a software tool that integrates: taxonomy based on questions of SEI [17], b) a method of implementation c) risk analysis based on fuzzy logic.

As future work, it is pretended to continue with the validation and testing of the case study through: a) the implementation of the technique in a computer tool and b) experimentation in software development projects of medium and small organizations. These two aspects will allow us to validate the technique and establish areas for improvement, in order to consolidate a useful asset for the implementation of best practices associated with risk management in software development projects process.

In addition, the consolidation of implementation of this protocol in other process areas will be searched for, such as: traceability requirements and practices for quality management in software development. These process areas have been identified as key to the development of software and are referred to in the research project of which this protocol is derived areas.

References

1. Kitchenham, B.: Procedures for Performing Systematic Reviews. Software Engineering Group Department of Computer Science Keele University (2004)
2. Biolchini, J., et al.: Systematic Review in Software Engineering (2005)
3. Calvo-Manzano, J., et al.: Estudio entre modelos y estándares de buenas prácticas enfocado a las prácticas de planificación de proyectos y utilizando CMMI-DEV v1.2 como referencia. In: 3ª Conferencia Ibérica de Sistemas y Tecnologías de la Información (CISTI 2008), Ourense, España (2008)
4. Wohlin, C., et al.: Experimentation in Software Engineering. An Introduction. Kluwer Academic Publishers (2000)
5. Sommerville, I.: Software Engineering, 9th edn. (2011)
6. Zarour, M., et al.: An investigation into the best practices for the successful design and implementation of lightweight software process assessment methods: A systematic literature review. Journal of Systems and Software **101**, 180–192 (2015)
7. Ng, P.-W., Jacobson, I., McMahon, P.E., Spence, I., Lidman, S.: The Essence of Software Engineering: Applying the SEMAT Kernel, 1st edn. (2013)
8. Real Academia Española de la Lengua (2015, Mayo). http://www.rae.es/consultas-linguisticas
9. Bourque, e.P., Fairley, R.E.: Guide to the Software Engineering Body of Knowledge, Version 3.0. IEEE Computer Society (2014). www.swebok.org
10. Hevner, A., Chatterjee, S.: Design science research in information systems. In: Design Research in Information Systems, vol. 22, pp. 9–22. Springer, US (2010)
11. Calvo-Manzano, J., et al.: A process asset library to support software process improvement in small setting. In: EuroSPI, Dublin, Ireland, pp. 25–35 (2008)
12. Albuquerque, A., Rocha, A.: An approach to evaluate and improve the organizational processes assets: the first experience of use. In: Sobh, T. (ed.) Innovations and Advances in Computer Sciences and Engineering, pp. 279–284. Springer, Netherlands (2010)
13. Wohlin, C., et al.: Empirical research methods in software engineering. In: ESERNET 2001–2003 (2001)
14. Mirna, M., Jezreel, M.: Establishing multi-model environments to improve organizational software processes. In: Rocha, Á., Correia, A.M., Wilson, T., Stroetmann, K.A. (eds.) Advances in Information Systems and Technologies. AISC, vol. 206, pp. 445–454. Springer, Heidelberg (2013)
15. The Standish Group International, "CHAOS Manifesto 2011". The Standish Group International, Inc. (2011)
16. Software Engineering Institute, "CMMI for Development, Version 1.3 CMMI-DEV 1.3" (2010)
17. Carr, M.J., et al.: Taxonomy-Based Risk Identification. Software Engineering Institute, June 1993
18. Kendall, R.P., et al.: A Proposed Taxonomy for Software Development Risks for High-Performance Computing (HPC) Scientific/Engineering Applications. Software Engineering Institute, Carnegie Mellon (2007)
19. Ingle, M.M., Atique, M., Dahad, S.O.: Risk Analysis Usign Fuzzy Logic. International Journal of Advanced Engineering Technology **2** (2011)

Gamiware: A Gamification Platform for Software Process Improvement

Eduardo Herranz[1], Ricardo Colomo-Palacios[2(✉)], and Antonio de Amescua Seco[1]

[1] Computer Science Department, Universidad Carlos III de Madrid,
Av. Universidad 30 28911, Leganés, Madrid, Spain
eduardo.herranz@uc3m.es, amescua@inf.uc3m.es
[2] Faculty of Computer Sciences, Østfold University College,
B R A Veien 4 1783, Halden, Norway
ricardo.colomo-palacios@hiof.no

Abstract. Motivation is one of the main obstacles for every organization. In software processes, where people are key, this aspect is even more critical. In this paper, authors present Gamiware, a gamification platform aimed to increase motivation in software projects. Grounded on both gamification roots and in software process improvement initiatives, it minimizes the cost of implementation of gamification initiatives and makes this discipline closer and more accessible for organizations aimed to improve their software process. Initial results on its implementation shows remarkable success.

Keywords: Gamification · Gamification frameworks · Gamification tools · Software development projects

1 Introduction

Monday morning. It is raining. A long week ahead of us and lots and lots of things to do: meetings, programming, documentation, quality tests, reporting, If only I had the motivation... Software practitioners often suffer lack of motivation finding their work boring, repetitive and, at the same time, demanding and stressful. Motivation is important for workers in general and, in the case of software workers, it is a one of the most frequently cited causes of software development project failures [1]. In the recent years, gamification and persuasive technologies have been pointed as powerful motivational tools in all aspects in life, including work environments. Focusing on the first concept, gamification can be defined as the use of game elements in non-game contexts to modify and influence the behavior of people [2]. One of the expected (and documented) consequences of gamification in people's behavior is the increase of motivation and engagement. Given that motivation is an important factor for software practitioners, gamification initiatives are beginning to be implemented in several software fields, being software process improvement (SPI) one of the most fertile areas [3].

The impact and attractiveness of gamification initiatives leaded to the development and commercialization of several gamification frameworks. These frameworks

© Springer International Publishing Switzerland 2015
R.V. O'Connor et al. (Eds.): EuroSPI 2015, CCIS 543, pp. 127–139, 2015.
DOI: 10.1007/978-3-319-24647-5_11

emerge both from software industry and academia and include both specific [4] and generic frameworks [5]. Focusing on the commercial solutions, the list of platforms includes players like Mozilla Open Badges, Gamify, Badgeville, Userinfuser, Bunchball, Leapfrog, CrowdTwist, Manumatix Bamboo, Big Door, Scvnr and Reputely, naming just some of the most relevant platforms. The list of software vendors is long enough to conduct efforts devoted to require a systematic decision making process for the selection of the most accurate one among these platforms. Thus, in the work of Kim [6], decision makers can find a decision support model for the selection of the most accurate gamification platform.

As stated before, gamification efforts for the software industry are not new but, to the best of authors' knowledge, there is not a specific gamification platform designed for software development projects. Given the specificities of software process and its undeniable human orientation, counting on a tool that could improve practitioners´ engagement and, at the same time, decrease project failure rates could be of great help for managers and software professional alike. In this paper, authors present Gamiware, a gamification platform that is intended to increase both motivation and employee engagement in software initiatives.

2   Gamiware: The Underlying Process

There is a popular interest in gamification that is also reflected in academic contexts and the number of works devoted to the topic are increasing [7]. In spite of the benefits of gamification as a discipline, gamified applications are not easy to implement and practitioners must take into account some aspects [8] in order to avoid a poor conceptualization of the environment that should lead to a failure. Apart from these aspects, elements like the high level of generalization (all organizations are dealt in the same way) and the divergences among current frameworks make gamification implementations even more difficult.

This leads to the definition of a methodological framework for gamification efforts in software environments. This framework should take into account particularities in terms of organizations, processes and personnel. This framework was presented in [3, 9] and is depicted in Figure 1. The framework presents seven phases. The first phase assesses the feasibility of implementing gamification in a given organization. In the second phase business objectives are established to determine whether gamification is feasible. The third phase explores all the professionals groups' motivations and profiles. Phase four is devoted to identify and discuss the activities towards gamification also, some of the essential aspects of the SPI proposal are considered.

The fifth phase is the core of the gamification framework. In this phase, the gamification proposal is developed. This proposal focuses on groups of software professionals. In addition, metrics and assessment techniques and feedback processes are established. In the next phase the implementation of the gamification proposal is issued. Final phase (7) is devoted to the analysis of outcomes and objectives achieved.

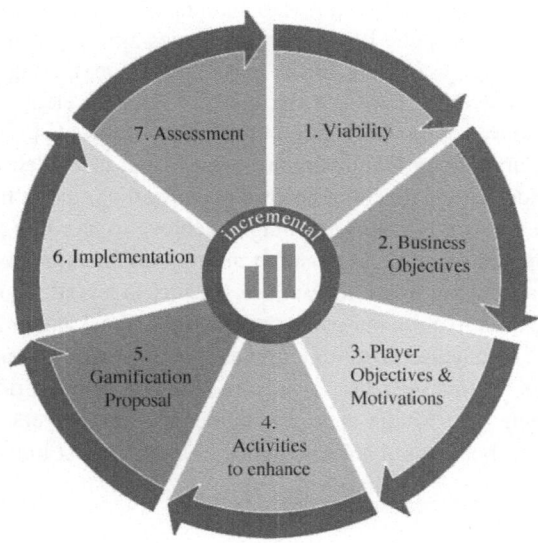

Fig. 1. Gamification Framework: Phases

3   Gamiware: Motivation

Framework presented in section 2 can be applied to any software organization. However, implementation costs can be big enough to impede implementation. This is the reason behind the development of Gamiware, a SaaS open source tool to support the process in an easy and affordable way. This tool is able to support the defined gamified iterative process making feasible gamification adoption softer.

Thus, Gamiware has been designed to be project and process independent. Gamiware is able to adapt to any context by means of a parametric customization in several organizational and gamification aspects. For instance, it is possible to code business objectives, software objectives or SPI objectives. Given the importance of personnel for software initiatives, it is also possible to identify software practitioners present in the gamification process, their tasks and associated KPIs. Moreover, in order to improve the alignment of business objectives and activities, it is possible to define the specific contribution of each task to the given business objective and by this mean check the fulfilment of these objectives.

4   Gamiware: Game Elements

Gamification is grounded on several psychological theories, namely, the Fogg Behavior Model, the self-determination theory and the flow theory. But apart from that, gamification is built on game elements: dynamics, mechanics and components of the game [2]. The dynamics of the game has to do with empowering the objectives and the potential effects on the people involved. The second element in gamification is mechanics can be considered as the basic actions that motivate and engage the user, and thus achieve the objectives specified by the game [2]. Game mechanics aim to govern the behaviour of people through incentive systems, feedback and competition, among others, with a reasonably predictable outcome [10]. The last element is game elements; these elements refer to specific instances of the dynamics and game mechanics [2].

Main dynamics underlying Gamiware are progression and relationships. While socialization is grounded in the essential need of socialization among human beings, progression means the sense of having something to achieve. According to [2], this is not to get isolated achievements but to demonstrate mastery and control in performing an activity within a consistent progression. Achieve mastery is a goal for many workers and this need should be used to align our goals with organizational and process [11].

With regards to mechanics within Gamiware, one can find competition, cooperation and challenges, encouraged by rewards and supported by various kinds of feedback. The components that shape these mechanics are very diverse including points, levels, badges, leader boards and achievements, citing the most important ones.

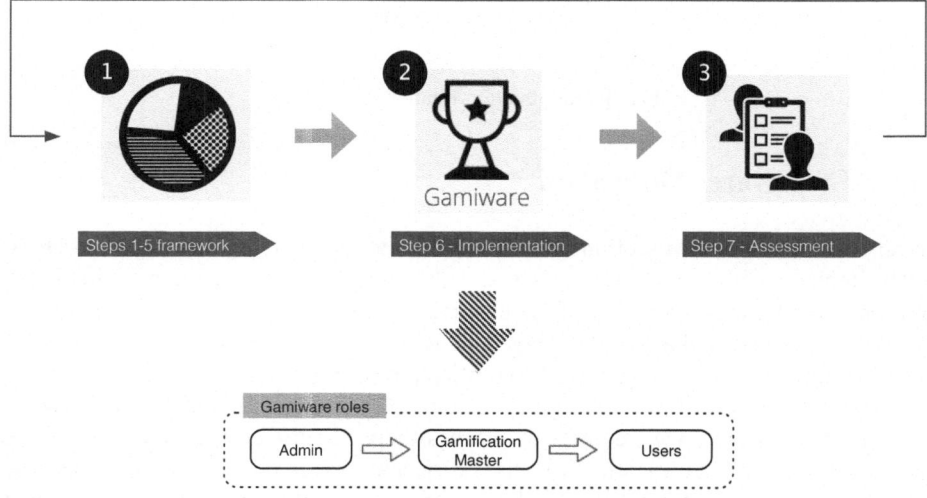

Fig. 2. Gamification Framework: Phases

As is shown in Figure 2 is necessary to have carried out the first 5 stages of the framework before considering the implementation of Gamiware. Without results of these initial phases, the expected benefits cannot be reached given that Gamiware will not be able to be customized in a proper way. Only after these phases Gamiware should be implemented in a given organization.

Successful Gamiware adoption is rooted on the progressive involvement of each of its defined roles. Thus, for instance Admin role will be responsible for registering the Gamification Master and preconfigure the system according to the software organization. Once in the system, the Gamification Master configures the entire system for a particular project and organization and registers all other participants.

5   Gamiware: Roles

Although literature has studied in deep roles in software engineering teams e.g. [12–16] , each organization presents its particularities. In order to guide implementers in the selection of roles and responsibilities, Table 1 presents a mapping among Gamiware roles and main software roles defined in [17] on the one hand and SPI roles defined by Johansen and Pries-Heje [18]. In any case, due to the configurable nature of Gamiware, the responsibilities can be modified by the Admin. In what follows, a description of the main responsibilities of the predefined roles are depicted.

Table 1. Criteria, sub-criteria and indicators

Gamiware roles	Baddoo & Hall practitioners	Johansen & Pries-Heje roles	Gamiware functionalities	
Admin			· Configure main context parameters: tasks, goals, roles, … · Add Gamification Masters	
Gamification Master			· Adjust context parameters · Create projects & add users · Establish gamification mechanics · Validate tool execution	
Executive	Senior manager	Sponsor	· Dashboards	
High Manager	Project manager	Project organizer (steering committee)	· Activity feed	· Create Teams · Verify tasks
		Expert	· Suggestions	
Low Manager		PI Project manager	· Profile	Update tasks: · Progression · Goals achieved · Metrics
		Process Owner		
Member	Developer	PI Developer		· Init a task · Gamification mechanics · Establich points and rewards
		User		

5.1   Admin Role

Admin is responsible for performing the first configuration of the execution context. Thus this role analyses previous projects and configures the tool with a set of parameters. Among these parameters are: business goals and their metrics, software goals and their metrics, main tasks and roles, among others.

5.2   Gamification Master Role

Is responsible for setting up the gamification project in the given organization and the given project. Once the project is created and configured, he or she will be able to assign people to the project.

At this point, gamification layer is added. Gamification Master must analyse results from Phase 5 and include them in a reliable way in Gamiware. Thus, main gamification techniques will be defined in terms of execution rules. Using this mean, Gamification Master will define which techniques will be employed in each task along with their contribution to the goals and points assigned to each of these techniques. Users will be assigned to tasks and a responsible to communicate their completion will be appointed. Gamification Master's work does not end here. During the execution of tasks, he or she will be responsible for ensuring the proper use of gamification techniques. For example, it will be necessary to check that challenges and rewards suggestions by users in each task are reasonable. This work validation aims, firstly, to ensure common sense in using different gamification techniques and, second, avoid cheats that jeopardize the viability of the entire system. An overall view on his or her responsibilities can be found in Figure 3.

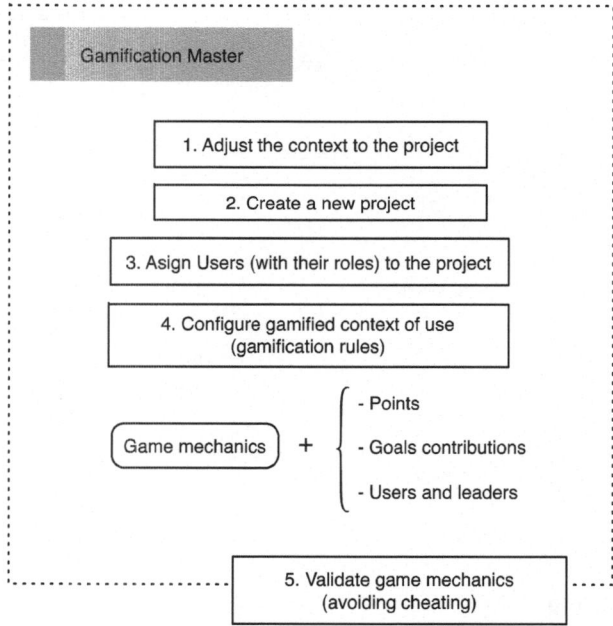

Fig. 3. Gamification Master Functionalities

5.3   User Role

Users will be personnel assigned to software tasks or SPI initiatives. Three kinds of users are available in Gamiware, namely, Executive, Manager and Member. Figure 4 depicts main features of these roles.

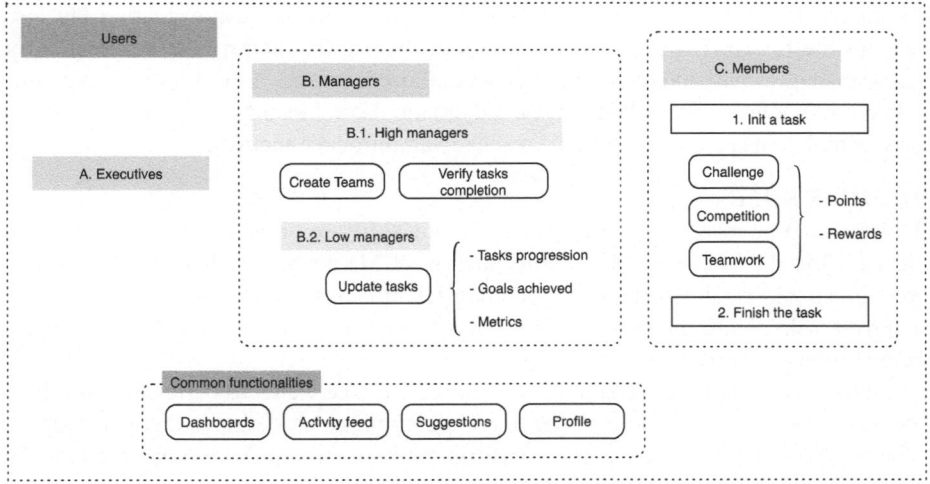

Fig. 4. Gamification User Functionalities

There is a set of features available for all kinds of users. Each user presents a formalized feedback mechanism and a customized dashboard to the needs of each role. Thus, for instance, the Executive dashboard displays information regarding business aspects, hiding details on software issues. On the other hand, the feedback presents a notification system that sends personalized messages to each type of role. In addition, all roles can access their Activity feed. This feed presents a record of all activities in which they are involved together with the results of the implementation of gamification techniques.

Furthermore, all roles are able to write and discuss ideas or suggestions. They are able also to comment and vote these ideas or suggestions. This participation is stimulated with gamification points. The goal is simply to enhance participation.

EXECUTIVE ROLE
Within Gamiware, as presented in Table 1, Executive role is an approach to Senior managers defined by Baddoo and Hall [17] and Sponsors as defined by Johansen and Pries-Heje [18]. In the tool, this role does not have specific functions except those discussed previously as common functionality.

MANAGER ROLE
In order to reflect certain peculiarities in SPI initiatives, this role has been subdivided into High and Low Manager. Thus, High Level Manager is similar to Expert or Steering Committee [18] while Low Level Manager represents Process Owner and PI Project Manager [18]. This taxonomy is not applicable for software projects where Project Manager [17] is applicable to both subgroups.

In any case, High Level Manager will reach his or her own functionalities along with the Low Level Manager ones. Thus, High Level Managers have a project dashboard where relevant data from the execution of the software or SPI tasks are displayed. In addition, he or she is able to create teams for task execution but also responsible for verifying the completeness of these tasks. During the verification of tasks, managers will add or subtract points to those involved, according to the rewards scheme previously established. On the other side, Low Level Manager may initiate a task or update its progress, set goals reached and introduce metrics.

MEMBER ROLE

This role can be mapped to Developer [17] on a software project or PI Developer and User [18] in the SPI arena. The main function of Members is to launch gamification techniques and establish the corresponding rewards associated with achievement of assigned tasks. Thus, the user has three gamification techniques available: Challenges, competition or cooperation.

Thus, a user can pose a challenge to whom he or she wants to perform a task. Furthermore, the user can choose to start a competition. In competitions there is always a winner and a loser, and all parties perform tasks on an equal footing. It should be noted it is possible to perform challenges and competitions among teams. Introducing collaborative and social components reduces the stress generated by highly competitive mechanisms [19]. The latest gamification technique available is cooperation, a team work devoted to achieve a common goal in a collaborative way.

6   Gamiware: A Pilot Study

The research objective of this pilot study is twofold. On the one hand, the aim is to measure the impact of the tool on software practitioners' motivation. On the second hand it is aimed to test the overall applicability of the tool in SPI initiatives. Thus, using Gamiware and the gamification framework presented in [3, 9] a pilot study was designed and conducted. The internals of this study are depicted in what follows.

6.1   The Study

Taking into account this research objective, a pilot study was launched. This study is described in what follows. It is worth to note that the study was focussed on User roles. This decision was rooted in the interest in obtaining a greater range of findings, and was based on the largest presence of this role. The role assigned to participants was the PI Developers [18].

SAMPLE

This study was conducted among students attending Software Development Projects Management and Distributed Software Development (Bachelor in Computer Science), Universidad Carlos III de Madrid. A total of 24 students (17 men and 7 women, ages 20-25 M = 21.3, SD = 0.8) accepted voluntarily participate in the study.

With regards to the courses, it was selected from a group of courses in the field of software engineering whose allow the execution of tasks related to SPI initiatives.

PREPARATION

Starting from a viable gamification deployment hypothesis, a set of software and business objectives were established. For business goals, a generic objectives were raised. It was supposed that this generic approach will not influence the study taking into account that the visibility of these kind of objectives is not considered as a motivator for PI Developers [17].

Once established the objectives motivations and profiles of participants were studied. To do so, first of all, the results of motivational studies by Baddoo & Hall [17] for similar roles to those involved (see correspondence roles in Table 1) were analysed. After this analysis, it delves into the specific profile of the participants in the study. In this line, participants were asked to complete the test Bartle[1] in order to determine his or her archetype of player so we can improve the fit of the game elements. Later, it was established what would be the tasks to be carried out by participants. In line with the SPI initiatives, the following tasks were defined:

1. Definition of a technical solution to the problem.
2. Traceability and dependency of software requirements.
3. Code inspection to estimate technical debt: bugs, bad practices, etc.

After that, materials were prepared and gamification proposal was defined. Based on the results of the previous phases, it was decided to use competitive game mechanics simultaneously with collaborative mechanics. That is, participants would perform the tasks in teams, and these teams will compete among them.

Finally, Gamiware was configured by researchers using gamification master role. Participants were randomly divided in teams of four members and each team selected its official. Then experiment and tool were explained to participants.

INSTRUMENTS AND DATA COLLECTION

Two questionnaires were circulated to participants: the first, as explained in the previous section, was provided before starting the test and its purpose was to determine the player profile of participants. This questionnaire consists in 30 questions (2 possible answers) and is based on Bartle test [20]. Data collection was done in a manual basis.

After the execution of tasks, a new questionnaire was circulated. The aim of this second instrument is to measure the motivation of participants in relation to the tasks. This questionnaire is based on task evaluation questionnaire from intrinsic motivation inventory [21]. This questionnaire was adapted to Gamiware context. Thus, this questionnaire is composed of 9 items assessed by means of a 5-point Likert scale. Items are present in Table 2.

6.2   Results

From the 24 participants, only 22 completed both questionnaires (91.6%). Regarding the first questionnaire, 10 participants were labelled as Achiever (45%), 4 as Killer (185), 3 as Explorer (14%) and finally, 5 more as Socializer (23%).

---

[1] http://www.gamerdna.com/quizzes/bartle-test-of-gamer-psychology

Regarding the second questionnaire, responses were coded using the Likert Scale (5 = strongly agree, 4 = agree, 3 = neutral, 2 = disagree, 1 = strongly disagree) and the mean was calculated. The frequencies of each of these responses, along with item means, for each question are reported in Table 2. Results show that 82% of the participants agreed that they were able to test their progression comparing their results with other participants. However, while 44% of the participants perceived tasks as fun, only 18% felt relaxed while doing these tasks. In spite of that, 73% of the participants are satisfied with their performance while only 45% of the sample felt skilled at these tasks. On the other hand, 27% of participants felt under pressure when performing these tasks and, after working on them for a while, felt very competent. Finally, and despite the tension experienced, 82% of participants felt that using Gamiware increased their motivation to perform tasks.

Table 2. Frequencies and mean ratings for Likert-scale evaluation items

Questions	Strongly agree	Agree	Neutral	Disagree	Strongly disagree	Mean
I noticed how well I did the tasks, compared to other participants	7	11	2	1	1	4
The use Gamiware made the tasks funnier	2	7	7	5	1	3.181
I felt relaxed while doing the tasks	0	4	13	4	1	2.909
I am satisfied with my performance at these tasks	6	10	5	2	0	4.045
I thought the tasks were very boring	1	2	5	10	4	2.363
I felt pretty skilled at these tasks	4	6	5	4	3	3.181
I felt pressured while doing the tasks	2	4	7	6	2	2.772
After working in these tasks for a while, I felt pretty competent	4	12	6	0	0	3.909
In general, Gamiware increased my motivation for doing the tasks	6	12	2	2	0	4

6.3   Discussion

Results of this pilot study suggest that, through the use of Gamiware, participants perceived that their motivation had been increased with regards to SPI tasks. In addition, most of the participants were aware of their good results compared to the other participants. Moreover, a significant majority was satisfied with his performance and competent in performing the tasks.

However, although these results can be considered positive, there are other weaker results to be analysed. Among these results, we find the lack of relaxation when performing the tasks, or even the lack of increase in the fun when performing tasks through Gamiware. The latter is challenging, given that the tasks themselves were not considered, mostly as boring. With regard to these results, it is likely that the introduction of competitive game mechanics leads to stress and to an impact on fun, as indicated in previous studies [22]. In spite of this, the impact on motivation is not revealed as one of consequences of the introduction of these game mechanics. This can be rooted in two different aspects: firstly, the alignment of gamification proposal with sample and secondly, on the introduction of teamwork mechanics along with the competitive game mechanics. These mechanics reduce stress and increase motivation, especially in academic environments [22]. Despite these remarkable results, there are several limitations that prevent the generalization of the results. It should be noted that the pilot study was conducted with a limited sample and in an academic environment. Thus, although participants were randomly selected, their demographics were quite linked to academic environments and not to industry. Also, as previously indicated in the literature [7], the effects of gamification are enormously dependent to the context of implementation and users, so some results obtained in education should not be generalizable to professionals. All these aspects should be considered in future empirical validations.

7   Conclusions and Future Work

To the best of author´s knowledge, Gamiware is the first tool of its kind in software environments. In its conception and design, Gamiware integrates gamification main elements with the aim of increasing motivation and engagement in software personnel. Gamiware leads to an increase in the implementation of gamification methods in a software organization. Using Gamiware these organizations will be able to implement gamification setups and benefit from this new discipline. Due to its customization features and flexibility Gamiware is able to adapt to a panoply of environments and organizations. Thus, Gamiware supports both software development activities but also leads way to SPI initiatives. In any case, and due to the inherent nature of gamification, this tool can be adopted in environments highly dependent on human capital.

An important limitation of Gamiware is its connection with the gamification framework defined. Thus, in spite of its customization features, Gamiware is not yet configurable as part of wider tools like Enterprise Architect, Jira or Redmine like some previous efforts in other fields like software process deployment and evaluation did [23]. Authors consider this extension as one of the future works.

Initial results on its implementation suggest that the deployment of such a tool could be both appropriate and feasible in SPI initiatives. However, these preliminary results cannot be generalized due to various constraints that should be taken into account in subsequent empirical validation. Other future developments include the evaluation of the tool comparing its results with other gamification frameworks or approaches without specific tool support. Finally, authors aim to analyze results of implementation in several kinds of organizations and countries in both SPI environments and software development initiatives.

References

1. DeMarco, T., Lister, T.: Peopleware: Productive Projects and Teams. Dorset House Publishing Company, Incorporated, New York (1999)
2. Werbach, K., Hunter, D.: For the Win: How Game Thinking Can Revolutionize Your Business. Wharton Digital Press, Philadelphia (2012)
3. Herranz, E., Colomo-Palacios, R., de Amescua Seco, A., Yilmaz, M.: Gamification as a Disruptive Factor in Software Process Improvement Initiatives. J-Ucs. **20**, 885–906 (2014)
4. Simões, J., Redondo, R.D., Vilas, A.F.: A Social Gamification Framework for a K-6 Learning Platform. Comput. Hum. Behav. **29**, 345–353 (2013)
5. Herzig, P., Ameling, M., Schill, A.: A generic platform for enterprise gamification. In: Joint Working IEEE/IFIP Conference on Software Architecture (WICSA) and European Conference on Software Architecture (ECSA), pp. 219–223 (2012)
6. Kim, S.: Decision Support Model for Introduction of Gamification Solution Using AHP. Sci. World J. **2014** (2014)
7. Hamari, J., Koivisto, J., Sarsa, H.: Does gamification work? – a literature review of empirical studies on gamification. In: 2014 47th Hawaii International Conference on System Sciences (HICSS), pp. 3025–3034 (2014)
8. Koivisto, J., Hamari, J.: Demographic Differences in Perceived Benefits from Gamification. Comput. Hum. Behav. **35**, 179–188 (2014)
9. Herranz, E., Colomo-Palacios, R., Amescua-Seco, A.: Towards a New Approach to Supporting Top Managers in SPI Organizational Change Management. Procedia Technol. **9**, 129–138 (2013)
10. Dorling, A., McCaffery, F.: The gamification of SPICE. In: Mas, A., Mesquida, A., Rout, T., O'Connor, R.V., Dorling, A. (eds.) SPICE 2012. CCIS, vol. 290, pp. 295–301. Springer, Heidelberg (2012)
11. Zichermann, G., Linder, J.: The Gamification Revolution: How Leaders Leverage Game Mechanics to Crush the Competition. McGraw Hill Professional (2013)
12. Cruz, S., da Silva, F.Q.B., Capretz, L.F.: Forty years of research on personality in software engineering: A mapping study. Comput. Hum. Behav. **46**, 94–113 (2015)
13. Kosti, M.V., Feldt, R., Angelis, L.: Personality, emotional intelligence and work preferences in software engineering: An empirical study. Inf. Softw. Technol. **56**, 973–990 (2014)
14. Colomo-Palacios, R., Casado-Lumbreras, C., Misra, S., Soto-Acosta, P.: Career Abandonment Intentions among Software Workers. Hum. Factors Ergon. Manuf. Serv. Ind. **24**, 641–655 (2014)
15. Colomo-Palacios, R., Casado-Lumbreras, C., Soto-Acosta, P., García-Peñalvo, F.J., Tovar-Caro, E.: Competence gaps in software personnel: A multi-organizational study. Comput. Hum. Behav. **29**, 456–461 (2013)
16. Colomo-Palacios, R., Tovar-Caro, E., García-Crespo, Á., Gómez-Berbís, J.M.: Identifying technical competences of IT Professionals: the case of software engineers. Int. J. Hum. Cap. Inf. Technol. Prof. **1**, 31–43 (2010)
17. Baddoo, N., Hall, T.: De-motivators for software process improvement: an analysis of practitioners' views. J. Syst. Softw. **66**, 23–33 (2003)
18. Johansen, J., Pries-Heje, J.: Success with improvement — requires the right roles to be enacted — in symbiosis. Softw. Process Improv. Pract. **12**, 529–539 (2007)

19. Paharia, R.: Loyalty 3.0: How to Revolutionize Customer and Employee Engagement with Big Data and Gamification. McGraw-Hill Professional, New York (2013)
20. Bartle, R.: Players Who Suit MUDs. J. Online Environ. **1**, 1–25 (1996)
21. Ryan, R.M., Koestner, R., Deci, E.L.: Ego-involved persistence: When free-choice behavior is not intrinsically motivated. Motiv. Emot. **15**, 185–205 (1991)
22. Hanus, M.D., Fox, J.: Assessing the effects of gamification in the classroom: A longitudinal study on intrinsic motivation, social comparison, satisfaction, effort, and academic performance. Comput. Educ. **80**, 152–161 (2015)
23. Ruiz-Rube, I., Dodero, J.M., Colomo-Palacios, R.: A framework for software process deployment and evaluation. Inf. Softw. Technol. **59**, 205–221 (2015)

Providing a Starting Point to Help SMEs in the Implementation of Software Process Improvements

Mirna Muñoz[1(✉)], Jezreel Mejía[1], Gloria P. Gasca-Hurtado[2], Vianca Vega-Zepeda[3], and Claudia Valtierra[1]

[1] Centro de Investigación en Matemáticas, Av. Universidad no 222 98068, Zacatecas, México
{mirna.munoz,jmejia,claudia.valtierra}@cimat.mx
[2] Facultad de Ingeniería, Universidad de Medellín, Medellín, Colombia
gpgasca@udem.edu.co
[3] Departamento de Ingeniería de Sistemas y Computación, Universidad Católica del Norte, Avenida Angamos 0610, Antofagasta, Chile
vvega@ucn.cl

Abstract. Nowadays software development organizations look for tools and methods that help them maintain their competitiveness. A key approach for organizations in order to achieve this competitiveness is a successful implementation of software process improvement. Unfortunately, most of the times, software process improvement involves a path full of obstacles almost impossible to achieve. The most common and critical problem consists of the selection and application of the right reference model for guiding this implementation. To provide a solution to this problem this paper shows a framework, which aims to set a starting point regarding the model, standard or agile methodology to be used as reference based on the SME actual needs, features and work culture.

Keywords: Software process improvement, Human factor, Small and medium enterprises · Process patterns · Improvement effort · SMEs · Improvement starting point

1 Introduction

Nowadays software development SMEs are considered a key element in the consolidation of software industry [1, 2, 3]. In México, software development SMEs represents the 87% of the total of the software development industry [4].

This fact highlights the importance of guaranteeing the quality of their software products. In this context, improving their software process provides a key opportunity for SMEs to have the skills to create strategic advantages with respect to its competitors [5-7], based on the affirmation that the quality of software products is directly related with the quality of the processes used for its development [8].

Unfortunately, even when many authors have recognized the importance of implementing SPI as mechanism to launch the competitiveness and efficiency in software industry, it has been path full of obstacles for most organizations [6] due to the lack of knowledge on how to address the improvement effort.

© Springer International Publishing Switzerland 2015
R.V. O'Connor et al. (Eds.): EuroSPI 2015, CCIS 543, pp. 140–151, 2015.
DOI: 10.1007/978-3-319-24647-5_12

In order to help SMEs addressing their improvement efforts, this paper aims to present a framework that sets a starting point, so that the improvement effort can be addressed based on the identification of the SME main problems.

This way allows providing a guidance to human factor, which it's a key aspect toward the implementation of a successful process improvement [9,10], on those problems with high priority that need to be focused on and how they can be reduced throughout the implementation software process improvements.

This paper is structured as follows: after the introduction section; section 2 presents the framework background; section 3 shows the framework development; section 4 describes how the framework was validated; and finally, section 5 presents the conclusions.

2   Framework Background

This research work arises focusing on two premises: (a) processes entirely depend on the organization work culture and the motivation of people to evolve processes and (b) human factor is the main source of commitment and responsibility to achieve effective, efficient and quality processes, then, they should be involved as key aspect to achieve successfully.

Those premises together with the problem mentioned in section one referring to the lack of knowledge on how to address the improvement effort, highlights the importance of this research work.

The framework presented in this research work arises from the idea presented in [11] named as *"proposal one: characterization of software development SMEs' according to their needs for implementing a software process improvement (SPI)"*

The proposal consisted on identifying and defining process improvements patterns, which enable an organization to identify its current scenario and to provide the best way to start a SPI according to its specific features.

Therefore, this proposal is focused on providing a set of process patterns as a solution to the problem that SMEs should face in selecting a right way to implement a SPI initiative.

According to [12] process patterns are reusable building blocks that organizations adapt or implement to achieve mature software process. Then, the proposal is composed of three key aspects: (a) patterns elements: elements that should be included in the definition of a pattern [13, 14]; (b) characterization: features that help to characterize an organization environment focused on characterizing software processes improvement needs in SME's [15]; and (c) contextual aspects: a selection of contextual aspects that are considered key aspect in the implementation of SPI [16].

It is important to highlight that the proposed framework should cover a set of needs that SMEs must face in the implementation of SPI and that most of the time represent an important barrier to implement SPI in SMEs. The focused needs are: 1) use a model or standard tailoring it to SMEs needs; 2) find a customizable guide that addresses the organization through the best way to implement SPI according to its specific needs and environment; 3) provide rules adapted to the SMEs size and level of maturity in the implementation of the SPI; 4) support the development of skills and abilities in the implementation of SPI; and 5) get tangible results in short period of time.

3   Framework

As mentioned before, this paper present a framework, which aims to provide a starting point to in order to help SMEs to focus its improvement effort base on actual problems and organizational actual situation regarding its working culture and experience in the use of model, stanadars or agile methodologies.

The framework is composed of three main elements: a) a set of process patterns; b) a method that allows to select a correct process pattern according the SME current situation and problems; and c) a software tool that automatizes the use of both of them. This way, allows focusing on real and current SME problems and set a "starting point" that helps SME to address its improvement effort and the process and model that can be implemented to reduce the problem.

3.1   Software Process Improvement Patterns

To define the set of process patterns, on one hand, a characterization previously made in [15] and [17] by the authors was taken as a base. On the other hand, the pattern elements defined by Coplien [13] and Appleton [14] were taken into account. Then, the set of process patterns were developed following the next steps:

1. *Identify context*: this step aims to establish a set of contexts most commonly detected in SMEs regarding the implementation of software process improvement. To achieve that from the characterization performed and showed in [15,17], those factors directly related to the human factor were focused and analyzed. As a result, three main contexts were identified: *do not have defined processes; do not have knowledge in the implementation of software process improvements and lack of personnel because they have few employees.*
2. *Identify patterns*: this step aims to identify the generic problems that SME can have associated to each identified context. Then, each generic problem is established as one pattern. To achieve it, the set of main features and limitations identified as part of the SME characterization performed in [15] and [17] were analyzed. Figure 1 shows the performed analysis.

    As result of perform these activities 11 processes patterns were identified, Then, each generic problem was classified and associated with the identified context. The result of this classification was:

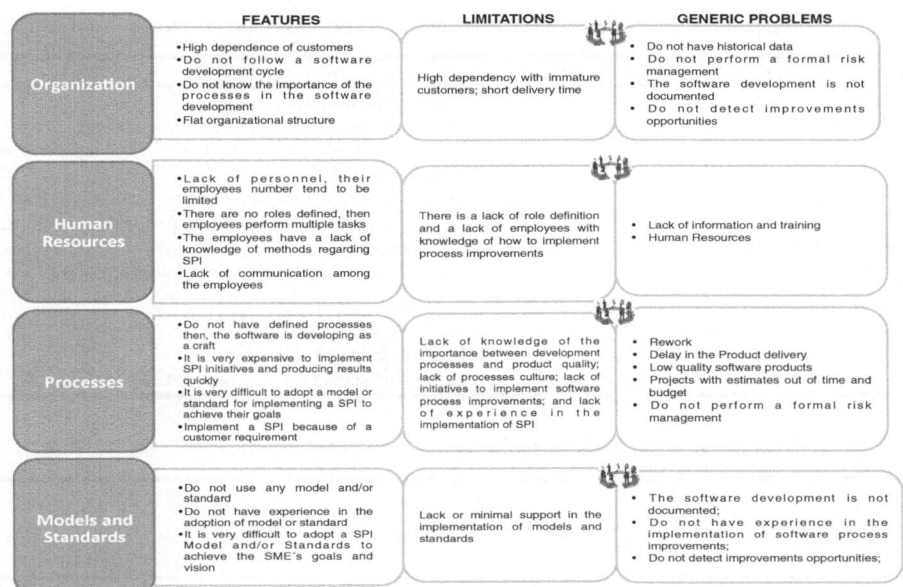

Fig. 1. Identifying the context

a) *Do not have defined processes:* (1) Rework; (2) Do not have historical data; (3) Delay in the Product delivery; (4) Low quality software products; (5) Do not perform a formal risk management; (6) Projects with estimates out of time and budget; and (7) The software development is not documented.

b) *Do not have knowledge in the implementation of software improvements:* (8) Lack of information and training; (9) Do not have experience in the implementation of software process improvements and; (10) Do not detect improvements opportunities

c) *Lack of personnel because they have few employees:* (11) Human resources

3. *Identify problems*: this step aims to identify specific problems derived from the generic problems. To achieve it, for each generic problem a list of most common problems were developed based on the author experience. Next, Table 1 shows an example of the specific problems and its related pattern. The table includes two problems for each context.

4. *Identify forces*: this step aims to establish a set of questions, which reflects actions, causes and consequences, and allow identifying SME actual problems. To achieve it, a questionnaire, which should reflect the process pattern forces, was developed. Next, Table 2 shows the number of forces associated to each pattern and an example of some questions.

Table 1. Example of specific problems derived from the patterns

Context	Pattern	Problems
Do not have defined processes	Rework	Tasks performed incorrectly
		New tasks resulting from continuous changes
		Duplicated tasks as result of a bad management or shared products
Do not have knowledge in the implementation of software improvements	Lack of information and training	Unproductivity or low productivity
		Lack of knowledge of processes performed within the organization
		Lack of an strategy to optimize project resources
Lack of personnel because they have few employees	Human Resources	Low quality personnel
		Lack of communication
		Lack of defined roles
		Lack of personnel responsibilities and commitments

Table 2. Example of set of forces associated to specific problems

Pattern	Problems	# of forces	Forces
Rework	Tasks performed incorrectly New tasks resulting from continuous changes	1	To determine the corrective actions, Are the problems analyzed?
		6	To determine the impact of correctives actions regarding work products, related work products, schedule and cost. Are the change request analyzed?
Lack of information and training	Lack of knowledge of processes performed within the organization	4	Are the mechanisms to provide required knowledge and abilities analyzed and selected?
	Lack of an strategy to optimize project resources	4	Are the requirements of facilities, equipment and components determined?
Human Resources	Low quality personnel	5	Are the abilities and knowledge available identified?
	Lack of communication	3	Is the state of assigned task and the obtained work products regularly communicated among stakeholders?

5. *Provide solutions*: this step aims to set a starting point regarding the model and process that the SME should focus in order to address its improvement effort to reduce a detected problem. To achieve it based on the results obtained in [15] and [17] regarding the models, standards and agile methodologies most used. Then, the starting point can be established using SCRUM [18]; Moprosoft [19]; ISO 15504 [20] and CMMI [21]. Next, an example of a solution provided is shown in Table 3. Finally an example of a complete pattern is showed in Table 4.

Table 3. Example of solutions

Problems	Forces	Solution
Tasks performed incorrectly	To determine the corrective actions, Are the problems analyzed?	CMMI: Project Monitoring and Control Moprosoft: Specific project management ISO15504: Project evaluation and control SCRUM: Dairy scrum
Lack of knowledge of processes performed within the organization	Are the mechanisms to provide required knowledge and abilities analyzed and selected?	CMMI: Configuration management Moprosoft: Resource management ISO15504: Configuration management SCRUM: Sprint review
Lack of knowledge regarding the best practices contained in the organizational processes	Are the activities of process and product quality assurance recorded in enough detail to know the status of quality results?	CMMI: Product and processes quality assurance Moprosoft: Specific project management ISO15504: Quality software assurance SCRUM: Sprint retrospective
Low quality personnel	Are the abilities and knowledge available identified?	CMMI: Project planning Moprosoft: Process management ISO15504: Project planning SCRUM:Sprint planning meeting

3.2   Selection Method

The method to select process patterns guides and supports SMEs in the identification of an adequate process pattern according to their actual problems throughout three steps as follows:

(*a*) *Identify*: this step aims to analyze the SME's actual environment and situation so that it can be characterized with the process patterns contexts and problems. This step performs two steps:

1. Collecting information about SME context: this step collects information such as number of employes and experience in the use of models, standards or methodologies.

2. Collecting information about SME actual problems: this step developing a questionaire based on formal software engineering practices related to four processes focused by SMEs in the implementation of improvements (project planning, project monitoring and control, configuration management and product and process quality assurance). This way allows organizations to cover the most common problems they have. Besides, the questions are related to the forces of the patterns.

(b) Select: this step aims to analyze the questionnaire answers and uses the process patterns, so that the actual SME problems are detected and prioritized.

Then, each question, which is related with the forces of the process patterns, has assigned a value in the range of 20% to 100% where: 20% means never occurs; 40% means rarely occurs, 60% means sometimes occurs; 80% means usually occurs; and 100% means always occurs.

Table 4. Example of complete pattern

Context: Do not have defined processes
Pattern: Do not perform a formal risk management
Related pattern: Do not have experience in the implementation of software process improvements

Problems	Forces	Solution
Not identified risks	Are the commitment not satisfied or at significant risk of not been satisfied identified? Is the documentation of the risk state periodically reviewed? If additional information is available. Is the risk documentation updated? Is the state of risks communicated to relevant stakeholders?	CMMI: Project monitoring and control Moprosoft: Specific project management ISO15504: Project evaluation and control SCRUM: Dairy scrum
Unforeseen errors	Are the problems obtained through processes reviews and performance? To determine corrective actions. Are the problems analyzed? To address identified problems; Are the corrective actions documented? Are the corrective actions reviewed and agreed with relevant stakeholders? Are the changes in external and external commitments treated?	CMMI: Project monitoring and control Moprosoft: Specific project management ISO15504: Project evaluation and control SCRUM: Dairy scrum
Bad risk management	Are project risks identified? Are project risk documented? Is the completeness and correctness of documented risks reviewed and agreed with relevant stakeholders? Are risks reviewed appropriately? Is the state of risks communicated to relevant stakeholders?	CMMI: Project planning Moprosoft: Process management ISO15504: Project planning SCRUM: Planning sprint meeting CMMI: Project monitoring and control Moprosoft: Specific project management ISO15504: Project evaluation and control SCRUM: Dairy scrum

After, the total percentage is calculated by adding all forces related with the same problem. In this way, it is possible to identify the prioritized problem, so that, an adequate pattern can be selected. The next scale is used: <30%: high, the problem lies in the SME representing a big problem; ≥ 30% < 70%: medium, the problem lies moderately in the SME and; ≥ 70%≤ 100%: low, the problem lies in the SME but it does not seriously affects it. Finally, the pattern with the lowest percentage is the one that best ties with the current situation and problems.

(c) Guide: this step aims to show the starting point set to guide SMEs to address their improvement effort toward the implementation of a software process improvements. The guide contains the next information: (1) the information of the process patterns regarding the problem; (2) the problems priority according to the analaysis performed in the selection phase and (3) the information of the process patterns regarding the list of models, standards and agile methodology as well as the processes and the set of practices that are recommended to implement to reduce or eliminate the detected problems.

3.3   Software Tool

This section shows the web tool developed to use the process patterns and the method to select the adequate pattern.

- *Actual organizational context*: this module automatize the phase "identify: collecting information about SME context" of the selected method. This module identifies the main features of the SME toward the implementation of a software process improvement, such as: number of employees, domain sector and its experience using any standard, model or agile methodology.

- *Actual organizational situation*: this module automatizes the phase "identify: collecting information about SME actual problems" of the selected method. The module provides the set of four questionnaires focused on identifying the specific problems in SME. Then, it automatizes the phase "select", because the tool analyzes the questionnaires answers, so that, an adequate process pattern, which best ties with the actual SME environment and situation, is selected. Figure 2 shows the software screen tool related to this phase.

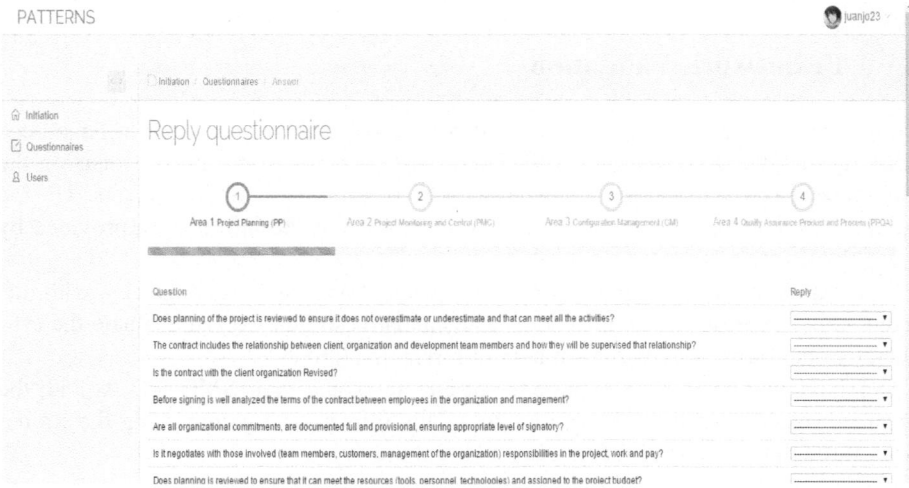

Fig. 2. Actual organizational situation screen

- *Guide*: this module automatizes the phase "guide" of the selected method. The module shows the information regarding the improvement "starting point", containing the following information: (a) it provides a list of the detected problems and their priority (it uses red, yellow or green colors depending on the impact of the problem in the SME); and (b) it includes the models (CMMI or Moprosoft), standard (ISO 15504) or agile methodology (SCRUM) and the processes to be focused on and the set of related best practices that will help the SME to reduce or eliminate the identified problems. Figure 3 shows the software screen tool related to this phase.

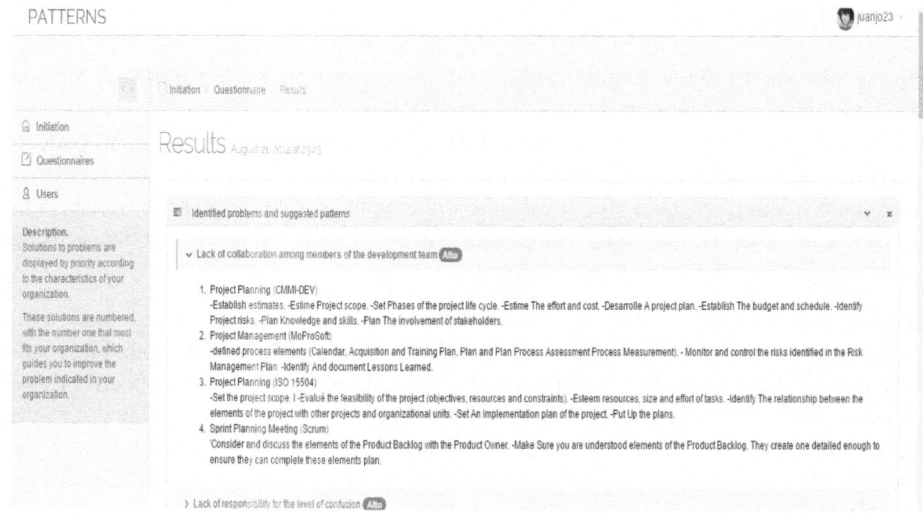

Fig. 3. Guide screen

4   Framework Validation

To evaluate the framework there were invited a set of professionals who have been working in software development SMEs, due to the framework aims to focus on the human perspective in the implementation of software process improvements. Then, a survey was developed to collect information to know if the information provided by using the software was useful for them.

It is important to highlight that the set of professional includes engineers with different experience in the use of models and standards so that we can evaluate the efficiency of the framework with people in different conditions.

Next, Table 5 shows the experience of engineers and their SME context and; the obtained results regarding the evaluation of the information gotten using the framework through the software tool is showed in Figure 4.

Table 5. Engineers experience and SME context

Engineer	No. of SME Employees	SPI Experience	Experience using models, standards or methodologies
1	4	Never	Often
2	5	Seldom	Seldom
3	8	Seldom	Seldom
4	10	Often	Often
5	12	Seldom	Seldom
6	20	Seldom	Seldom
7	15	Often	Often

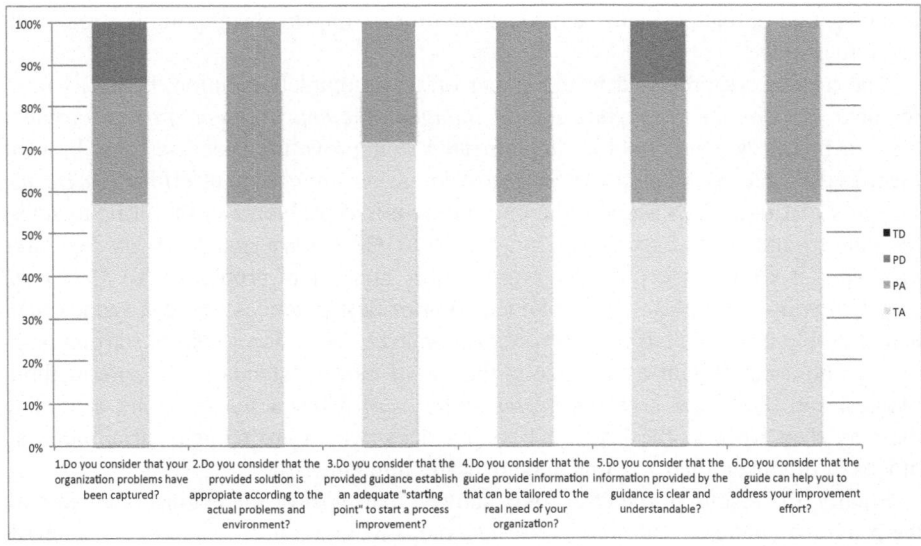

Fig. 4. Framework evaluation

As Figure 4 shows mots of the answers are in the range of total agree and partial agree, so that, there can be assumed that the framework has in general good results. Then we analyse the comments of the engineering's, to highlight the best and the worst comment which are: (a) the best comment was that according his experience the framework makes easy to identify important information which help him to address the improvement effort; (b) the worst comment were related to the questions, because since his point of view the question must be lightened for a better understanding.

5   Conclusions

Not all organizations obtain the same results when implementing improvements in their processes. Two main problems are associated with: 1) models and standards to be used as reference and 2) the lack of knowledge of where to start the process improvement. These problems are increased in SMEs because the limitations of time, budget and human resources they have regarding the implementation of process improvements.

As a solution, this paper presents a framework that is focused on the human perspective and aims to guide SMEs in the identification of their actual situation, environment and problems, so that, a starting point could be set and an adequate guide can be provided.

In this way, it is possible to provide the knowledge to start an implementation of software process improvements based on the identification of SME real problems and using those practices that will help them to reduce those identified problems, having early results and maximizing the limited resources because the improvement effort can be adequately addressed. Since the human perspective to provide support in the identification of real problems and a starting process improvement point is a real challenge to achieve.

The framework proposed in this paper offers a complete solution, being its main features: (a) *Manage the organizational change in the improvement effort*: it provides a set of practices that should be implemented to improve the processes based on the identified problems, helping the SME to address its improvement effort; (b) *Do not lose focus*: it takes into account the current identified problems in the SME to select the pattern and set the starting point; (c) *Know the culture and focus on identified problems*: it allows to capture the work culture and actual problems; (d) *Motive all people involved*: it guides the implementation of best practices that can reduce their actual problems; (e) *Focus the improvement on experience*: it provides a starting point taking into account their experience in the use of models, standards or agile methodologies; and (f) *Create learning organization*: it provides a starting point according the way they work at the level of best practices, which are recognized as building blocks of organizational learning and are easily implemented.

Finally, the results of the case study showed that most of the engineers agree with the provided guidance and think the results helps them to know where to start regarding their actual situation, environment and problems at a detail level so that it is possible to get information of the model, process and practices that should be implemented to reduce the problems.

As future work, the framework will be updated according to the comments and more engineers will be invited to use the tool, so that, the results can help to improve the framework and integrated it in a SPI platform which aims to provide a complete tool for implementing software process improvements.

Acknowledgements. This work is sponsored by Research Center of Mathematics (CIMAT).

References

1. Moreno, T.M.: Four Achilles Heel for SMEs, SME Observatory. Spanish papers (2008). http://www.observatoriopyme.org/index.php?option=com_content&view=article&id=74& Itemid=102 (accessed October 2013)
2. Ministry of Industry. More information about the new definition of SMEs in EU, vol. 2012 (2012)
3. Ministry of Economy. SMEs: fundamental Link to the growth of Mexico, vol. 2013 (2013)
4. AMITI. Outline of government support for Software Industry, Mexican Association of Information Technology Industry (2010)
5. Gupta J., Sharma, S., Hsu, J.: An overview of knowledge management, Idea Group Inc. chap. 1 (2004)
6. Molina, J.L., Marsal M.: La gestión del conocimiento en las organizaciones. Ch. VII Herramientas de la gestión del conocimiento; IX gestión del cambio, pp. 60–68 and 87–94 (2002)
7. Turban E., Aronson J.E., Liang T-P.: Knowledge Management, In: Decision Support Systems and Intelligent Systems. Pearson and Prentice Hall, Uppers Saddle River and NJ, Ch. 9, p. 487 (2005)

8. Williams, T.: How do organizations learn lessons from projects; and do they? IEEE Transactions on Engineering Management **55**(2), 248–266 (2008)
9. Korsaa, M., Johansen, J., Schweigert, T., Vohwinkel, D., Messnarz, R., Nevalainen, R., Biro, M.: The people aspects in modern process improvement management approaches. Journal of Software: Evolution and Process. J. Softw. Evol. Proc. **25**, 381–391 (2013)
10. O'Connor, R., Basri, S.: The Effect of Team Dynamics on Software Development Process Improvement. International Journal of Human Capital and Information Technology Professionals **3**, 13–26 (2012)
11. Muñoz, M., Mejia, J., Gasca-Hurtado, G.P., Valtierra, C., Duron, B.: Covering the human perspective in software process improvement. In: Barafort, B., O'Connor, R.V., Poth, A., Messnarz, R. (eds.) EuroSPI 2014. CCIS, vol. 425, pp. 123–134. Springer, Heidelberg (2014)
12. Ambler, S.W.: An Introduction to Process Patterns. An AmbySoft Inc. White Paper (1998)
13. Coplien J.O.: A development process generative pattern language. Pattern languages. In: Proceedings of PLoP/94, pp. 183–237 (1994)
14. Appleton, B.: Patterns for Conducting Process Improvement. In: conference PLoP 1997, pp. 1–19 (1997)
15. Valtierra, C., Muñoz, M., Mejia, J.: Characterization of Software Processes Improvement Needs in Sme's. In: International Conference on Mechatronics, Electronics and Automotive Engineering (ICMEAE 2013), pp. 223–228 (2013). ISBN 978-1-4799-2253-6
16. Petersen, K., Wohlin, C.: Context in Industrial Software Engineering Research. In: Third International Symposium on Empirical Software Engineering and Measurement, pp. 401–404 (2009)
17. Muñoz, M., Gasca-Hurtado, G.P., Valtierra, C.: Characterizing SME's needs for implementing a software process improvement: A comparative between the reality and the theory. Revista Ibérica de Sistemas y Tecnologías de Información **E1**, 1–15 (2014)
18. Kniberg, H.: Scrum-Xp from the trenches. InfoQ Enterprise Software Development Series, pp. 1–122 (2007)
19. Oktaba, H., Alquicira, C., Su Ramos, A., Martínez, A., Quintanilla, G., Ruvalcaba, M., López, F., Rivera, M., Orozco, M., Fernández, Y., Flores, M.: Modelo de procesos para la industria de software (MoProsoft), pp. 1–121 (2003)
20. AENOR. 2004. ISO/IEC 15504: 2004 Information technology – Process assessment, 1st edn. (2004)
21. Beynon Jr., D.R.: Interpreting Capability Maturity model Integration (CMMI) for business Development organizations in the Government and Industrial Business Sectors. Technical Note CMU/SEI-2007-NT-004 (2007)

Models and Optimization
Approaches in SPI

Optimizing Resource Utilization by Combining Activities Across Process Instances

Christine Natschläger[1]($\boxtimes$), Andreas Bögl[2], Verena Geist[1], and Miklós Biró[1]

[1] Software Competence Center Hagenberg GmbH, Hagenberg Im Mühlkreis, Austria
{christine.natschlaeger,miklos.biro,verena.geist}@scch.at
[2] Pascom Kommunikationssysteme GmbH, Arbing, Austria
andreas.boegl@pascom.at

Abstract. Resource-efficient business processes are a key asset of an organization in a competitive market environment. Current efforts address this issue either at the process schema level by specifying an optimal sequence of process activities or at the process instance level by optimizing resource utilization within a single running process instance.

In this paper, we present a novel approach for combining activities across process instances to optimize resource utilization. The proposed approach comprises the (i) definition of business processes and combinable activities, (ii) identification of possible combinations at runtime, (iii) determination of optimization potential, and (iv) actual combination of activities across process instances. The approach further supports partial activity combinations and dynamic resource selection for combined activities. The applicability of the approach is demonstrated by a case study.

1 Introduction

Efficient business processes are a key asset for a company's success and are addressed by the discipline *Business Process Management* (BPM), which comprises the definition, implementation, control, and improvement of business processes. In this paper, we present the *Combined-Instance Approach*, which improves resource utilization in business processes by combining activities across running processes instances. It thereby considers different resource types including physical, human, and financial resources. Optimization potential is given if the capacity of a resource is (or can be) higher than required by the actual process instance, so that activities from further process instances can be integrated, thereby saving their setup and/or execution costs. With the proposed approach, we address the goals of the Industry 4.0 project of the German government, which emphasizes the demand for adaptable processes and resource efficiency in

The research reported in this paper has been supported by the Austrian Ministry for Transport, Innovation and Technology, the Federal Ministry of Science, Research and Economy, and the Province of Upper Austria in the frame of the COMET center SCCH. This publication has been written within the project *AdaBPM* (number 842437), which is funded by the *Austrian Research Promotion Agency* (FFG).

© Springer International Publishing Switzerland 2015
R.V. O'Connor et al. (Eds.): EuroSPI 2015, CCIS 543, pp. 155–167, 2015.
DOI: 10.1007/978-3-319-24647-5_13

traditional industries. Some preliminary ideas were presented at a workshop on resource management in service-oriented computing (see [12]).

2   The Combined-Instance Approach

The *Combined-Instance Approach* combines activities of different process instances to optimize resource utilization and consists of the following four steps: (1) definition of business processes with data objects and constraints, (2) identification of candidates for process instance combinations, (3) determination of an optimization potential, and (4) actual combination of business process instances. An overview of the four steps applied to a running example is shown in Fig. 1. The running example relates to an order execution process of a sand and fertilizer producer in Upper Austria, called S&F company for short. The company produces and delivers several thousand tons of sand and fertilizer products to various destinations in Europe, where they are mainly used for cultivating sport fields, golf courses and for producing other final products in the cement industry.

2.1   Business Processes with Data Objects and Constraints

The first step of the combined-instance approach is to extend the business process with additional definitions required for possible instance combinations. The basis for all process instances is the *business process schema* ($\mathcal{S}$), which provides the process specification including data objects and resources. For the combined-instance approach, $\mathcal{S}$ is extended with (i) *meta-information* specifying possible resources and their capacities, (ii) *type-level constraints* defining general restrictions that apply to all instances either based on given data or being specified manually, and (iii) *combinable activities* ($\mathcal{C}$) comprising a *combinable condition* (*cc*) that defines the required matching of two activity instances for a possible combination and an *optimization function* (*of*) that determines the optimization potential of a combination. The *cc* and the *of* must be specified individually for every combinable activity and the combinable activity is then marked with a 'C' in the process diagram. All constraints must be formally specified (e.g., based on the *Object Constraint Language* (OCL)) to support business process execution.

In our running example shown in Fig. 1, $\mathcal{S}$ defines an order execution process comprising activities for order handling, production, delivery, and invoicing with corresponding data objects (e.g., order, product, and invoice) and resources (e.g., production and transportation means). Due to space limitations not all of them are shown in Fig. 1. $\mathcal{S}$ is then extended with (i) *meta-information* like possible transportation means and their capacity, (ii) *type-level constraints* like the capacity of a resource (based on data) or that a ship can only be used if both departure and destination point have a harbor and are connected by a river (manually specified constraint), and (iii) *combinable activities*. In our example, the production and delivery activity specify a *cc* and an *of* (see Section 2.3 for *of*), so these two activities are combinable ($\mathcal{C}$). The *cc* of the production activity specifies that two production activities are combinable, if the product types

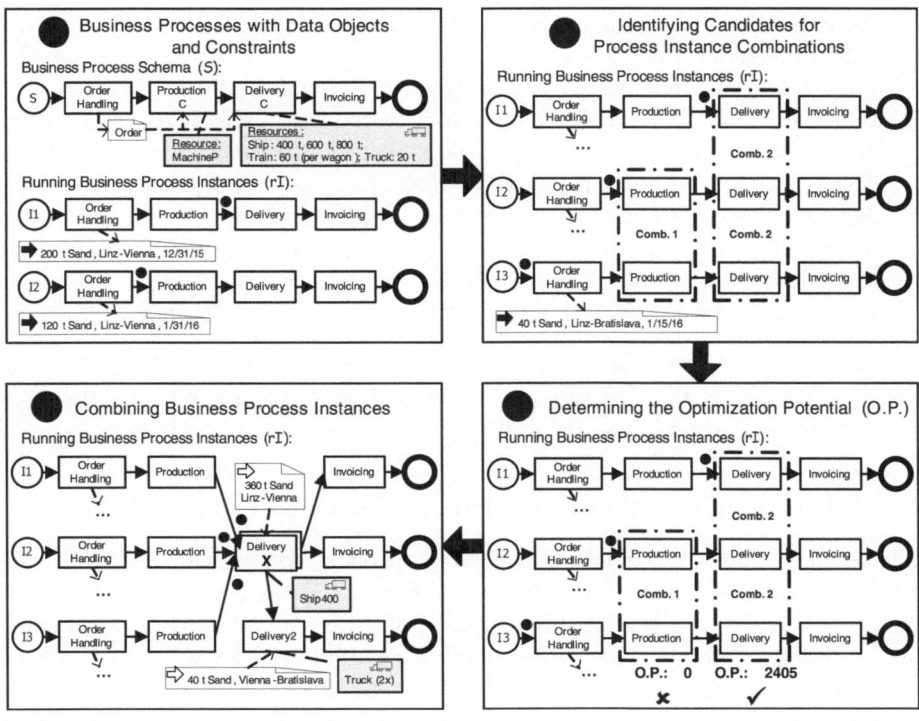

Fig. 1. Combined-Instance Approach

are the same (ProductType1 = ProductType2). The cc of the delivery activity defines that the routes must be overlapping or, more specifically, that it is shorter to go from the departure point (dep) to one destination (dest) and then to the other than starting twice from the departure point (min(distance(dep, dest1) + distance(dest1, dest2), distance(dep, dest2) + distance(dest2, dest1))   <   distance(dep, dest1) + distance(dep, dest2)).

An instantiation of $\mathcal{S}$ is called a business process instance $\mathcal{I}$. During execution of $\mathcal{I}$, data objects and corresponding constraints defined in $\mathcal{S}$ are instantiated and provide concrete instance-specific data and restrictions. No additional constraints are expected on the instance-level, since process execution must be kept simple for end-users. A running business process instance $r\mathcal{I}$ indicates that $\mathcal{I}$ is active and comprises one or more tokens that mark the current position(s) in the process flow (shown by a black-filled circle in Fig. 1).

In our running example, the order execution process is instantiated three times ($\mathcal{I}1$, $\mathcal{I}2$, and $\mathcal{I}3$). The first process instance comprises an order of 200 t of sand that must be sent from Linz to Vienna until 12/31/15. The order of $\mathcal{I}2$ has the same route but with 120 t of sand that must be delivered until 01/31/16. Finally, 40 t of sand are ordered in $\mathcal{I}3$ (see step 2) and must be sent to Bratislava until 01/15/16. All three instances are active, but the current positions differ.

We, thus, have the following special resource-constrained scheduling problem:

- Activities $\mathcal{I}i_{OrderHandling}$, $\mathcal{I}i_{Production}$, $\mathcal{I}i_{Delivery}$, $\mathcal{I}i_{Invoicing}$, $i = 1, 2, 3$ with processing times $pi_{Activity}$, earliest release times $ei_{Activity}$ given by the tokens, and deadlines $di_{Delivery}$ (only for delivery activities).
- Resources $k = 1, ..., n$ with R_k units of resource k available (capacity), in our case $k = MachineP, Ship400, Ship600, Ship800, TrainWagon, Truck$ with $R_{MachineP} = unlimited$, $R_{Ship400} = 400t$, $R_{Ship600} = 600t$, etc.
- Activity x occupies $r_{x,k}$ units of resource k (demand) for $k = 1, ..., n$ during processing, e.g., if x is $\mathcal{I}1_{Delivery}$ then x occupies $r_{x,Ship400} = 200t$.
- Precedence constraints $m \rightarrow n$ only between the activities $\mathcal{I}i_{OrderHandling}$, $\mathcal{I}i_{Production}$, $\mathcal{I}i_{Delivery}$, $\mathcal{I}i_{Invoicing}$ of the same process instance $\mathcal{I}i$.

Finally, we require some auxiliary functions that return all $r\mathcal{I}$, the current token position(s) of $r\mathcal{I}$, the state of $\mathcal{C}$ (open, active, or completed), whether $\mathcal{C}$ is still reachable, and the expected costs and execution time of activities.

2.2 Identifying Candidates for Process Instance Combinations

The second step of the combined-instance approach receives the extended business process schema $\mathcal{S}$ and all running process instances (set of $r\mathcal{I}$). The goal then is to identify two combinable instances of $\mathcal{C}$ that satisfy all constraints and can be called a candidate pair. The search for candidate pairs is initiated whenever a token reaches an instance of $\mathcal{C}$ and the triggering activity is compared with the corresponding activity of every other $r\mathcal{I}$. If the other activity is open and reachable and all constraints and the cc are satisfiable, then the two instances of $\mathcal{C}$ are a candidate pair. Several candidate pairs may be combined to sets of higher cardinality. In subsequent research, we intend to also consider future process instances, i.e. the current process instance waits for further combination possibilities for as long as possible while not violating any deadlines or until the maximum capacity of the resource is reached.

In our running example, the token of $\mathcal{I}2$ reaches the production activity and triggers a search. A combination with $\mathcal{I}1_{Production}$ is not possible, since the activity already completed. However, $\mathcal{I}3_{Production}$ is still open, reachable and all constraints are satisfiable. The cc is also fulfilled, since the product type (sand) is the same. Thus, $\mathcal{I}2_{Production}$ & $\mathcal{I}3_{Production}$ are a candidate pair. In addition, the token of $\mathcal{I}1$ reaches the delivery activity and triggers a further search. In this case, $\mathcal{I}2_{Delivery}$ and $\mathcal{I}3_{Delivery}$ are still open, reachable and all constraints are satisfiable. The cc of $\mathcal{I}1_{Delivery}$ and $\mathcal{I}2_{Delivery}$ is obviously fulfilled, since both activities have the same route. Furthermore, the cc of $\mathcal{I}1_{Delivery}$ and $\mathcal{I}3_{Delivery}$ is also satisfied, since the distance from Linz to Vienna to Bratislava (approx. 265 km) is shorter than the distance from Linz to Vienna (approx. 185 km) plus the distance from Linz to Bratislava (approx. 265 km). Thus, we identify two candidate pairs $\mathcal{I}1_{Delivery}$ & $\mathcal{I}2_{Delivery}$ and $\mathcal{I}1_{Delivery}$ & $\mathcal{I}3_{Delivery}$ which can, after re-evaluating the cc, be combined to $\mathcal{I}1_{Delivery}$ & $\mathcal{I}2_{Delivery}$ & $\mathcal{I}3_{Delivery}$.

Whether identified candidate pairs can actually be combined depends, however, on three further conditions:

1. if the other (not-triggering) activity ever receives a token (after a preceding split an alternative path may be taken).
2. if waiting for the other (not-triggering) activity does not violate a deadline.
3. if the combination achieves improvement (optimization potential). This condition is evaluated within the next step.

2.3   Determining the Optimization Potential

The third step of the combined-instance approach receives a set of combinable candidates. The goal then is to identify possible combinations and whether they are economically worthwhile by applying the *optimization function (of)* defined for every C. The *of* calculates a value for comparison (e.g., costs, time) with a predefined optimum (lowest/highest value). In some cases, possible candidates satisfy the *cc*, but concrete tasks differ, so that activities cannot be fully combined, e.g., due to routes being overlapping but not identical. To cope with this issue, the combined-instance approach provides the possibility to split activities so that part of it can be combined and the remaining part is executed individually (partial activity combination). The method for splitting activities can also be applied to optimally use resources with respect to their maximum capacity (i.e. activities are split to fill resources). If activities are split, the optimization function has to consider all sub-activities.

So the main goal of the third step is to compare the separate execution of activities with possible combined executions, in the following called separate and combined solutions. Considering the separate solution, all activities are defined by S and receive instance specific data and constraints. The *of* then calculates a value for comparison for the separate solution that reflects the main goal of the optimization, e.g., costs, time, or quality indicators. The calculation is based on a predefined formula and a list of given values.

Considering combined solutions, it is first necessary to determine all possible combinations of identified candidates (also taking activity splits into account). If predefined resources of the separate solution do not fit for a combination, then either a fitting resource is identified (dynamic resource selection) or the combination is disregarded. The next step is to apply the *of* and calculate a value for each combination, thereby using the same value type and calculation process as defined for the separate solution. The values of the combined solutions are then compared with that of the separate solution to identify all combined solutions with an optimization potential. The combination with the highest potential is ranked first; however, if several expected combinations initiated by different activities are overlapping, then an overall optimal solution must be identified.

In our running example, there is only one resource ($MachineP$) with no capacity limitation available for the production activity, which is taken by separate and combined solutions. To calculate a value for comparison, we define the formula: productionCosts = productAmount x costsPerUnit(productAmount) and a list of costs: producing 1 t sand costs €3; 20 t sand costs €2.9 (per t); 200 t sand costs €2.5 (per t); and 1000 t sand costs €2 (per t). So the calculated production costs for $I2_{Production}$ (120 t) are € 348 and for $\mathcal{I}3_{Production}$ (40 t) € 116 (sum: € 464). Considering possible combinations, both production activities can fully be combined so that 160 t of sand can be produced at once. However, the resulting production costs are again € 464, so no optimization potential is given by combining $\mathcal{I}2_{Production}$ & $\mathcal{I}3_{Production}$.

Considering transportation means, all possible resources are defined in $\mathcal{S}$ and shown in Fig. 1. Not explicitly given are the costs of a resource, but we assume that $Ship400$ costs € 10/km, $Ship600$ € 14/km, $Ship800$ € 17/km, $TrainWagon$ € 4.5/km, and $Truck$ € 2/km. The formula is then: `transportationCosts = resourceCosts x distance`. So for the separate solution, the optimal means of transportation for $\mathcal{I}1_{Delivery}$ is $Ship400$ (€ 10 x 185 km = € 1850), for $\mathcal{I}2_{Delivery}$ two $TrainWagon$ (2 x € 4.5 x 185 km = € 1665), and for $\mathcal{I}3_{Delivery}$ two $Truck$ (2 x € 2 x 265 km = € 1060) (sum: € 4575). For the combined solution, different combinations of candidates are possible:

1. $\mathcal{I}1_{Delivery}$ & $\mathcal{I}2_{Delivery}$ (resource for combination: $Ship400$, costs of combination: € 1850, optimization potential: € 1665),
2. $\mathcal{I}1_{Delivery}$ & part of $\mathcal{I}3_{Delivery}$ (from Linz-Vienna) (resource for combination: $Ship400$, costs of combination: € 1850 + € 320 (remaining part of $\mathcal{I}3_{Delivery}$: two $Truck$ from Vienna-Bratislava, 80 km), optimization potential: € 740),
3. $\mathcal{I}2_{Delivery}$ & part of $\mathcal{I}3_{Delivery}$ (from Linz-Vienna) (resource for combination: $Ship400$, costs of combination: € 1850 + € 320 (remaining part of $\mathcal{I}3_{Delivery}$), optimization potential: € 555), and
4. $\mathcal{I}1_{Delivery}$ & $\mathcal{I}2_{Delivery}$ & part of $\mathcal{I}3_{Delivery}$ (from Linz-Vienna) (resource for combination: $Ship400$, costs of combination: € 1850 + € 320 (remaining part of $\mathcal{I}3_{Delivery}$), optimization potential: € 2405).

So compared to the separate solution, all combined solutions provide an optimization potential, but the best solution is the fourth combination ($\mathcal{I}1_{Delivery}$ & $\mathcal{I}2_{Delivery}$ & part of $\mathcal{I}3_{Delivery}$) with an optimization potential of € 2405.

2.4   Combining Business Process Instances

The fourth step of the combined-instance approach receives a set of combinable candidates with optimization potential. The goal then is to actually combine activities to permit common use of resources. However, combining activities of different process instances requires a new process element, which we call *Combined Activity* ($\mathcal{X}$). The difference between a *Combinable Activity* ($\mathcal{C}$) and a *Combined Activity* ($\mathcal{X}$) is that $\mathcal{C}$ marks potentially combinable activities at the schema-level, whereas $\mathcal{X}$ represents actually combined activities at the instance-level. Syntactically, $\mathcal{X}$ is addressed by several incoming and outgoing flows from different process instances and receives the data objects and resources of all participating activities. The semantics is that $\mathcal{X}$ consumes a token from every participating process instance, executes the combined activity using the recommended resource(s) and, finally, produces the same amount of tokens and returns them to the process instances. So, $\mathcal{X}$ comprises two constructs that can merge and split tokens from different process instances. For the graphical representation in the process diagram, we recommend two overlapping activities where the front activity is marked with a bold 'X'. A similar element with the same semantics is not available in any other business process modeling language (BPMN, UML, EPC, or YAWL).

For the actual combination, we consider all activities from the set of combinable candidates with optimization potential. However, some candidates may not be reached at all (alternative path is taken) or not reached in time. Thus, we propose a deferred approach for the actual combination. The activity triggering the search for possible combinations has necessarily been activated by an incoming token. We then have to wait for further candidates to be activated. However, the waiting time must be restricted:

- by a predefined amount of time (e.g., 24 h),
- by not explicitly delaying the activity but considering the time before execution as implicit waiting (e.g., if delivery is planned for next Monday then the time in between is considered as implicit waiting), or
- by a given deadline of the activity minus the expected processing time.

In addition, it should be checked regularly whether reachable candidates still exist, since otherwise waiting can be stopped. When a second combinable activity is reached in time, $\mathcal{X}$ is created and replaces the two activities (if necessary an activity is thereby split). If a further candidate receives a token in time, it is also integrated in $\mathcal{X}$. When all possible activities are integrated or the waiting time expired, $\mathcal{X}$ is executed and separately written in the log-file of every process instance (together with further split activities).

In our running example, $\mathcal{I}1_{Delivery}$ is first activated by a token and then waiting for corresponding candidates in other $r\mathcal{I}$. The waiting time is limited by deadline $d1_{Delivery}$ (12/31/15) minus the expected processing time $p1_{Delivery}$ (approx. 1 day), so delivery must at latest be started by 12/30/15. We assume that all other delivery activities receive a token in time. The next delivery activity being activated is, presumably, $\mathcal{I}2_{Delivery}$. $\mathcal{I}1_{Delivery}$ and $\mathcal{I}2_{Delivery}$ are fully combined and replaced by an $\mathcal{X}$. Afterwards, also $\mathcal{I}3_{Delivery}$ receives a token. However, this activity must be split so that part of it (delivery from Linz to Vienna) can be integrated in $\mathcal{X}$ and the remaining part (delivery from Vienna to Bratislava) is executed individually (i.e. it is inserted as new activity "Delivery2" after $\mathcal{X}$ in process instance $\mathcal{I}3$).

3   Related Work

Related work is provided by different domains. In the mathematical domain, scheduling problems are investigated and algorithms are provided that calculate the optimal solution. Interesting for our research are dynamic optimization problems, constrained optimization problems, and resource-constrained scheduling problems [2,5,8,9]. If several objectives must be optimized simultaneously, then multi-objective optimizations [6] are applied.

In the business process domain, resource optimization is typically based on goals, constraints, or performance optimizations (e.g. [10]). However, presented approaches either focus on the schema level or on single active process instances sometimes in combination with completed process executions as suggested in [7].

The probably most relevant related research in the business process domain is provided by Pufahl and Weske in [13–15]. The authors synchronize multiple process instances by introducing the concept of batch activities in process modeling and execution. Commonalities with the combined-instance approach are the combination of activities across different processes instances, the goal to thereby save setup and execution costs, and the consideration of resources and their capacities. A difference, however, is the identification of possible instance combinations. The approach by Pufahl and Weske is data-based (i.e., a data view comprises relevant attributes for comparison and only instances with identical values are combinable), whereas the combined-instance approach is constraint-based (i.e., constraints specify how data values must correlate for a possible instance combination). The data-based approach provides better usability, since only relevant attributes must be selected, but the approach is restricted to equality of data attributes. The constraint-based approach is more complex but also supports extensive definitions, thereby enabling the concept of activity splits. Another difference is the synchronization method. Batch activities are not merged to retain single instance autonomy and only the execution of activities is delayed. In contrast, the combined-instance approach provides an actual combination of activities across process instances and therefore introduces the *Combined Activity* element. Advantages of the individual execution are instance autonomy, no additional process element, and the support of batch regions. The advantage of the combined-instance approach is the possibility to dynamically select a different resource for the combined activity. In addition, a further important benefit of the combined-instance approach is the consideration of optimization potential. So, summing up, although both approaches combine activities across different process instances, there are significant differences regarding the chosen methods.

Another similar approach supporting instance-level adaptation is provided by Browne et al. in [3]. The authors introduce the concept of activity crediting to eliminate redundant or overlapping activities at runtime. The paper provides a notion for partial crediting resembling our concept of activity splits, but the suggested approach is restricted to single workflow instances.

For further related research in the business process domain, we refer to the areas of service composition and dynamic resource allocation (e.g. [1]).

Finally, applications and methods have been developed that optimize resource utilization in specific domains like logistics or production (e.g., dynamic logistics process management problems [4,17]). However, our goal is to address resource optimization on a higher level of abstraction, i.e. business processes, so that resources from different domains can be considered within the same business process (e.g., optimization of production and transportation means).

4   Discussion and Case Study

In this section, we provide a detailed discussion of possible resource optimizations and validate the approach by a more comprehensive case study. First of all, we identify all resources with optimization potential. A classification of business resources is given in [16] and consists of the following seven groups:

- **Physical Resources** like machinery, equipment, raw material, or land.
- **Financial Resources** like internal/external funds or financial instruments.
- **Legal Resources** like patents, licenses, copyrights, or trademarks.
- **Relational Resources** including relationships within the company or towards suppliers/customers/competitors/external parties.
- **Human Resources** including their experience, education, and networks.
- **Organizational Resources** like routines, processes, and reputation.
- **Informational Resources** including information about the industry, customers, suppliers, internal processes, and products.

Obviously only the utilization of scarce resource types can be optimized by activity combination. If a resource type is not scarce, it means that the full amount remains available while using any amount of it. For example, combining activities that both use the same patent does not improve the utilization of the patent. So no optimization potential is given for legal, relational, organizational, and informational resources. The remaining resource groups (physical, financial, and human) provide the possibility for resource optimization for most types, e.g., an exception is the education of an employee which is not scarce. Nevertheless, these three resource groups are interesting for our approach and are considered in the following examples:

1. A company produces twelve types of ice-cream cones which are all baked with a distinct batter composition by one machine using different plates. Changing production to another type requires cleaning the machine, changing the plates, and mixing the required batter. Thus, combining orders with same ice-cream cone types improves the workload of the machine (physical resources) and saves cleaning and cooking time (human resources).
   cc: same ice-cream cone type
2. Every employee requiring office supplies forwards the demand to the administration which places the orders. A combination of (not urgent) order activities saves working time (human resources) and may provide the opportunity for a quantity discount (financial resources). *cc*: same office supplies
3. Starting a new project in a company frequently requires that project members install new software. In some cases the activity "Install Software" can be combined so that instead of forcing every project member to install the software locally, the software is once installed on a server and provided as virtual application. This saves all types of resources: working time of the project members (human resources), disk space on local computers (physical resources), and sometimes license fees (financial resources).
   cc: same software (available as virtual application)

The examples presented above show that human resources are often optimized by saving working time whereas financial resources are addressed by saving money. Only physical resources have a greater variation and reach from raw material to production means to disk space. Nevertheless, also physical and human resource optimizations finally result in a financial benefit. The financial benefit of activity combination can emerge from saving setup and/or execution costs, e.g. combining orders in the ice-cream cones example saves setup costs, whereas execution costs are saved by combining transportation in the running example in Section 2.

In addition, we used the combined-instance approach in an actual business environment to evaluate the practical utility of the suggested concepts. We therefore considered the support process of a hardware manufacturer, software developer and system solution provider for building security, service billing, alerting, multimedia and IT services in health care. The business process schema of the support process is shown in Fig. 2. An instance of the support process is created whenever the company receives a support request of a customer. A service ticket is then opened and the actual problem is analyzed. If the problem is already solved, the service ticket is closed. However, if the problem is not solved, then the ticket is forwarded to a technician who decides whether it is a software or hardware problem. If it is a hardware problem, then a replacement device is ordered or created and the firmware is installed. Afterwards, the replacement unit is delivered to the customer. However, if it is a software problem, then a software ticket is created followed by an error analysis and correction in the software component. After correcting the error, it is checked whether remote maintenance is possible. If this is the case, then the software is updated remotely, otherwise a technician visits the customer to update the firmware on-site.

The support process is instantiated several thousand times a year making activity combination and resource optimization an interesting improvement opportunity. In sum, we identified the following combinable activities:

- *Order or Create Replacement Device:* Replacement devices are, e.g., Media-Boxes, PT-Terminals, or Multimedia Telephones. Optimization potential is given by combining orders to external companies (lower delivery costs, quantity discount) and by combining internal production orders (saving working time and setup time of production means). cc: same external company (for external orders); same product (for internal orders)
- *Deliver Replacement Device to Customer:* Optimization potential is given by combining different deliveries to the same customer. cc: same customer
- *Error Analysis and Correction in Software Component:* Optimization potential is given by combing analysis and correction with other errors in the same software component. Similar errors can be assigned to the same software developer reducing familiarization effort and time for quality control. cc: same software component
- *Plan Visit at Customer:* Optimization potential is given by combining visits of nearby customers (similar to our running example in Section 2), thereby

saving traveling time of the technician and transportation resources. *cc*: see
cc of delivery activity in Section 2
– *Update Firmware at Customer:* Optimization potential is given by combining
  firmware updates (also of other products), e.g., updates to correct errors with
  planned updates comprising new features. *cc*: same customer

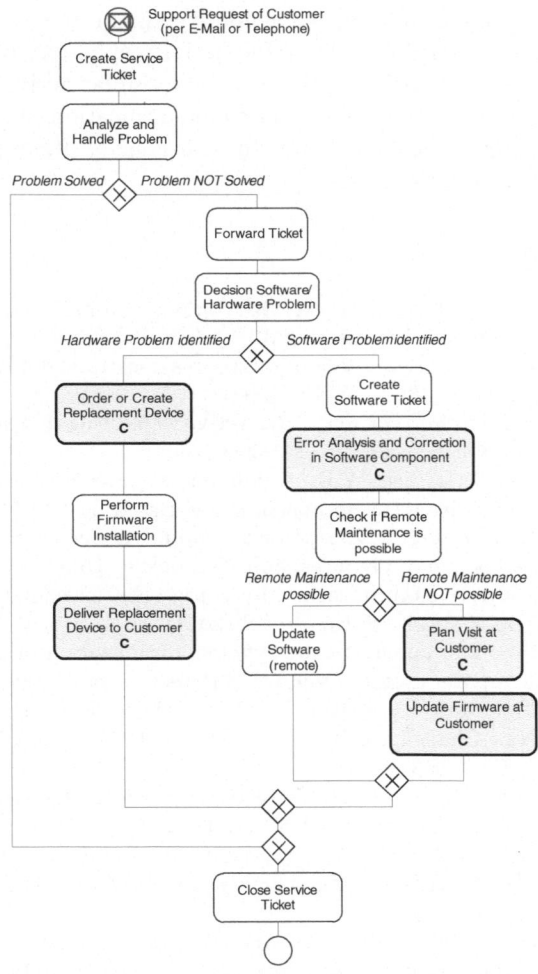

Fig. 2. Case Study: Support Process

5   Conclusion

In this paper, we suggest a novel approach for resource optimization. The key
idea of the proposed *Combined-Instance Approach* is to combine corresponding

activities of different process instances and to thereby improve resource utilization (e.g., by combining delivery activities of different orders). The approach consists of four steps and various concepts to increase resource efficiency, e.g., calculation of optimization potential, dynamic resource allocation for combined activities, and activity splitting to partly combine activities. The applicability of the combined-instance approach was demonstrated by applying it to a running example and by using it within a case study. We further expect that using this approach provides a financial benefit for many companies.

Our future goals are to formally define activity splits, to provide exception handling for combined activities, and to combine similar activities derived from different process schemas (e.g., based on the identification of similarities [11]). We will further extend the case study by considering other processes of the company as, e.g., an *order execution process*.

References

1. Ardagna, D., Pernici, B.: Adaptive service composition in flexible processes. IEEE Transactions on Software Engineering **33**(6), 369–384 (2007)
2. Biró, M.: Object-oriented interaction in resource constrained scheduling. Information Processing Letters **36**(2), 65–67 (1990)
3. Browne, E.D., Schrefl, M., Warren, J.R.: Activity crediting in distributed workflow environments. In: ICEIS, vol.3, pp. 245–253 (2004)
4. Chow, H.K., Choy, K.L., Lee, W.B.: A dynamic logistics process knowledge-based system - an RFID multi-agent approach. Know-Based Syst **20**(4), 357–372 (2007)
5. Cruz, C., González, J., Pelta, D.: Optimization in dynamic environments: a survey on problems, methods and measures. Soft Computing **15**(7), 1427–1448 (2011)
6. Deb, K.: Multi-objective optimization. In: Burke, E.K., Kendall, G. (eds.) Search Methodologies, pp. 403–449. Springer, US (2014)
7. Ernst, M.: Method and apparatus for dynamic optimization of business processes managed by a computer system (1999). US Patent Number 5890133
8. Golden, B., Raghavan, S., Wasil, E.: The Vehicle Routing Problem: Latest Advances and New Challenges. Operations Research/Computer Science Interfaces Series. Springer, US (2008)
9. Hartmann, S., Briskorn, D.: A survey of variants and extensions of the resource-constrained project scheduling problem. EJOR **207**(1), 1–14 (2010)
10. Huang, Z., van der Aalst, W., Lu, X., Duan, H.: Reinforcement learning based resource allocation in business process management. Data & Knowledge Engineering **70**(1), 127–145 (2011)
11. Leopold, H., Niepert, M., Weidlich, M., Mendling, J., Dijkman, R., Stuckenschmidt, H.: Probabilistic optimization of semantic process model matching. In: Barros, A., Gal, A., Kindler, E. (eds.) BPM 2012. LNCS, vol. 7481, pp. 319–334. Springer, Heidelberg (2012)
12. Natschläger, C., Bögl, A., Geist, V.: Optimizing resource utilization by combining running business process instances. In: Toumani, F., Pernici, B., Grigori, D.e.a. (eds.) ICSOC 2014 workshops and satellite events. LNCS, Springer (2014)
13. Pufahl, L., Herzberg, N., Meyer, A., Weske, M.: Flexible batch configuration in business processes based on events. In: Franch, X., Ghose, A.K., Lewis, G.A., Bhiri, S. (eds.) ICSOC 2014. LNCS, vol. 8831, pp. 63–78. Springer, Heidelberg (2014)

14. Pufahl, L., Meyer, A., Weske, M.: Batch regions: Process instance synchronization based on data. In: EDOC, pp. 150–159. IEEE (2014)
15. Pufahl, L., Weske, M.: Batch activities in process modeling and execution. In: Basu, S., Pautasso, C., Zhang, L., Fu, X. (eds.) ICSOC 2013. LNCS, vol. 8274, pp. 283–297. Springer, Heidelberg (2013)
16. Seppänen, M., Mäkinen, S.: Towards classification of resources for the business model concept. International Journal of Management Concepts and Philosophy **2**(4), 389–404 (2007)
17. Wang, Y., Caron, F., Vanthienen, J., Huang, L., Guo, Y.: Acquiring logistics process intelligence: Methodology and an application for a chinese bulk port. Expert Systems with Applications, pp. 195–209 (2014)

A Maturity Model for ISO/IEC 20000-1 Based on the TIPA for ITIL Process Capability Assessment Model

Michel Picard[✉], Alain Renault[✉], and Béatrix Barafort[✉]

Luxembourg Institute of Science and Technology,
5 Avenue Des Hauts-Fourneaux 4362, Esch-Sur-Alzette, Luxembourg
{michel.picard,alain.renault,beatrix.barafort}@list.lu

Abstract. The growing adoption of ISO/IEC 20000-1 raises the need for the IT service management community that has been applying the IT Infrastructure Library best practices for many years to position their organizations against the requirements of this standard. We have designed an ITIL-based maturity model that guides organizations on their way to an ISO/IEC 20000-1 certification while enabling them to understand their readiness to ISO/IEC 20000 certification. The model has been designed applying an extended transformation process for maturity and process assessment models design and engineering. It is compliant with the ISO/IEC 33000 series that defines the requirements for maturity model and is based on the TIPA for ITIL process model. The paper presents a detailed view on the maturity model and discusses its adequacy for evaluating the ISO/IEC 20000 certification readiness.

Keywords: IT service management · ITIL · TIPA for ITIL · Maturity model · Process assessment · ISO/IEC 20000 · ISO/IEC 33000 · ISO/IEC 15504

Introduction

There are lots of discussions within the IT Service Management (ITSM) community about the best path for implementing and improving ITSM processes [1,2,3] . This shows that no existing ITSM maturity model is globally accepted as the reference. Few of the existing maturity models are consistent with the IT Infrastructure Library (ITIL) [4], the most popular best practices set for managing IT services. Moreover no maturity model enables to determine the level of readiness of the organizations in regard to a potential ISO/IEC 20000 [5] certification. As the adoption of this ISO standard is growing everyday [6], the organizations' needs for positioning against this standard become increasingly critical.

More and more organizations engaged in an ITIL process improvement approach using Tudor's IT Process Assessment (TIPA) framework [7], came and asked the same following question: "what capability level should my ITIL processes reach to meet ISO/IEC 20000-1 requirements?"

As an answer to the above question we have developed an ITIL-based maturity model targeting compliance to the ISO/IEC 20000-1:2011. This ITIL-based maturity model has the specific feature to be compliant with the ISO/IEC 33000 requirements

© Springer International Publishing Switzerland 2015
R.V. O'Connor et al. (Eds.): EuroSPI 2015, CCIS 543, pp. 168–179, 2015.
DOI: 10.1007/978-3-319-24647-5_14

[8] for process reference, assessment and maturity models (formerly ISO/IEC 15504), and results from the application of our transformation process [9,10,11], which has been extended for supporting the design of organizational maturity models [12].

Besides describing the resulting ITIL-based maturity model in section 4, this paper makes clear the concepts surrounding the maturity matter (section 2) and presents related work (section 3) before discussing the limits of the maturity model (section 4) and concluding with the possible ways to improve it.

Terminology

In the context of capability and maturity models, the terminology is not very precise and there is confusion between process capability, process maturity and organizational maturity model. There is indeed a commonly accepted way of mentioning maturity models in the Software engineering field [13,14], mainly inherited from Capability Maturity Model Integrated (CMMI) product suite with the set phrase: Capability Maturity Model. CMMI [15,16] defines a Capability Maturity Model as: "A model that contains the essential elements of effective processes for one or more areas of interest and describes an evolutionary improvement path from ad hoc, immature processes to disciplined, mature processes with improved quality and effectiveness." It defines a capability level as the "Achievement of process improvement within an individual process area." and a maturity level as "Degree of process improvement across a predefined set of process areas in which all goals in the set are attained."

CMMI provides two approaches for improvement: a continuous representation and a staged representation. A continuous representation is *"A capability maturity model structure wherein capability levels provide a recommended order for approaching process improvement within each specified process area."* And a staged representation is *"A model structure wherein attaining the goals of a set of process areas establishes a maturity level; each level builds a foundation for subsequent levels."*

As this paper relates a maturity model based on the ISO/IEC 33000 series requirements, the terminology used is based on the process reference, process assessment and maturity models definition of ISO/IEC 33001 [17].

In ISO/IEC 33001, a **process reference model** is a: *"model comprising definitions of processes in a domain of application described in terms of process purpose and outcomes, together with an architecture describing the relationships between the processes"* while a **process assessment model** is a: *"model suitable for the purpose of assessing a specified process quality characteristic, based on one or more process reference models"*. As well a **maturity model** is a: *"model, derived from one or more specified process assessment model(s), that identifies the **process sets** associated with the levels in a specified scale of organizational process maturity"*. Organizational process maturity is *"the extent to which an organizational unit consistently implements processes within a defined scope that contributes to the achievement of its business needs (current or projected)"*.

The capability of a process is a property of a process and is considered in ISO/IEC 33000 series as a process quality characteristic which is defined as a: *"measurable aspect of process quality*". The process quality characteristics considered in our maturity model is the process capability.

Related Work

Many maturity models have been developed in the IT domain. The CMMI [15] and the ISO/IEC 15504 standard series for Process Assessment contributed to their spreading, particularly for Software Engineering in the 1990's and more widely for IT purposes in the 2000's. We can particularly mention the capability maturity models for IT service management purposes such as: IT Service Capability Maturity Model (ITSCMM) [19], Capability Maturity Model Integration for Services (CMMI-SVC) [16], Maturity Model for Implementing ITIL v3 [20,21].

Next to the ITSM maturity models, there are also a number of ITSM process models that are compliant to ISO/IEC 33000 such as: a Process Reference Model (ISO/IEC 20000-4) [22] and a Process Assessment Model (ISO/IEC 15504-8) [23] for IT Service Management, and the COBIT 5 Process Assessment Model [24]. These are not maturity models, but given the ISO/IEC 33001 definition of a maturity model, they can be considered as possible artifacts to build an ITSM maturity model.

Despite this wide range of models, only few of them can claim to be consistent with the ITIL framework and none enables to determine the organization's readiness for an ISO/IEC 20000 certification.

The technical report ISO/IEC TR 20000-5 [25] brings some contributions for this purpose as it is *an exemplar implementation plan providing guidance on how to implement a Service Management System (SMS) to fulfil the requirements of ISO/IEC 20000-1:2011*. However, this standard only covers process implementation, and even though it advocates the need for a gap analysis prior to plan process implementation, the standard does not provide any guidance on the way to proceed. The existing PAM from ISO/IEC 15504-8 [23] brings its own contribution, but it focuses on processes and does not provide an organizational maturity standpoint. Moreover both ISO/IEC TR 20000-5 and ISO/IEC 15504-8 only cover the ISO/IEC 20000-1 requirements and do not embrace all the processes from the ITIL 2011 framework. Last, ISO/IEC TR 20000-11 (still under development) [26] is the only document providing guidance on the relationship between ISO/IEC 20000–1:2011 and the ITIL framework. This technical report proposes a high-level correlation of ITIL to ISO/IEC 20000-1 clauses but does not recommend any implementation path nor propose a readiness assessment approach with a maturity scale to pave the way for certification.

The ITIL-Based Maturity Model for ISO/IEC 20000

It is commonly accepted that implementing ITIL within an organization is not easy [1], mainly because ITIL dictates "what" organizations should ideally do but not much on "how" they should do it. The use of an ITSM maturity model is often considered as (part of) the solution to determine the "how" but it is a misunderstanding of the maturity model concept as a maturity model only describes stable states (i.e. maturity levels) that an organization should achieve during its process implementation/improvement journey (see section 2). However the way to achieve these "maturity states" can be quite different from one organization to another.

Maturity models are powerful tools for organizations that want to demonstrate their excellence through a staged approach of (third-party) assessments. They can also be used to target the scope of these assessments and so define a structure for improvement initiatives as they are supposed to provide consistent sets of processes for each level of maturity. The maturity model described in this paper should be considered in that perspective. It shows how an organization can evolve from *reactive* (level 1) to *managed* (level 2), and *integrated* (level 3) where it covers most of the ISO/IEC 20000-1 requirements, including the ones covering the management system. The organization can even go further to level 4 (*governed*), and ultimately to level 5 (*optimizing*). The 36 processes coming from selected PAMs are spread over those 5 maturity levels such as illustrated in Fig. 1. An organization that does not demonstrate effective implementation of the processes that are fundamental for providing IT services (i.e. the process set from maturity level 1) does not reach level one and is I defined as *immature*.

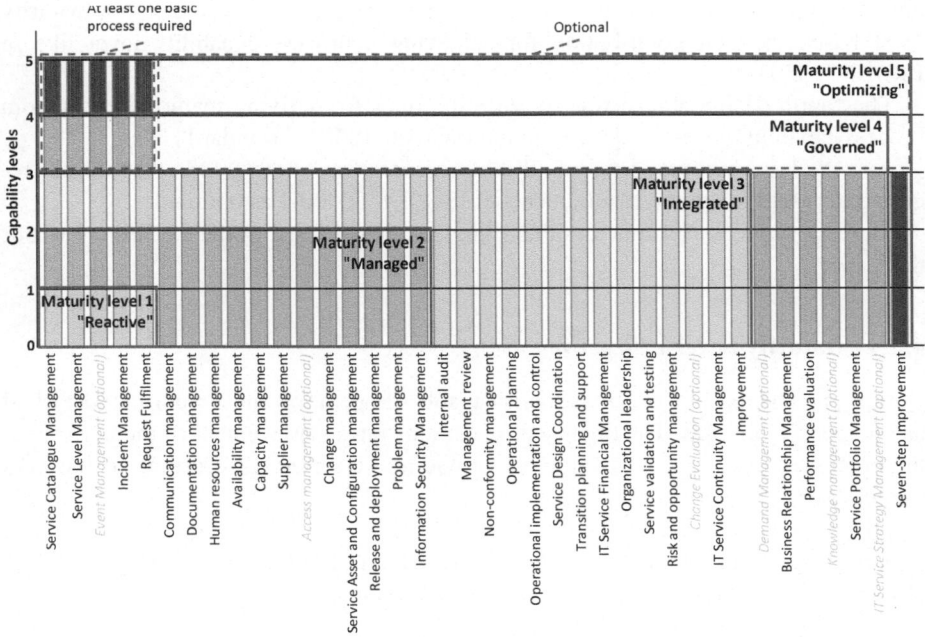

Fig. 1. Overview of the ITIL-based Maturity Model for ISO/IEC 20000

Each maturity level is described (sections 4.2 to 4.6) with its name, a general definition, the rule defining how to achieve it and the set of processes it contains.

4.1   Main Design Choices

The design of this maturity model has required making choices that were extensively described in [12]. Some of these design choices need however to be reminded.

The first one relates to the Process Assessment Models used as reference. Our maturity model is based on two existing PAMs:

- the TIPA PAM for ITIL which contains 26 ITSM processes and addresses the best practices described in ITIL 2011 [4];
- the draft ISO/IEC 33070-4 PAM for Information security management [27], which among others, embeds 12 processes covering the practices common to all management systems.

The second design choice was the structure of the maturity scale which *de facto* reflects a certain service delivery strategy for the target organization with states progressing from *reactive* (level 1) to *optimizing* (level 5).

The third design choice, related to the previous one, was to allocate processes to maturity levels to form consistent sets of processes based on their purpose and on the objective set for each maturity level (rather than allocate the processes to a maturity level based on their contribution for achieving a process capability level like in ISO/IEC 15504-7).

The fourth design choice was to reuse the rules for deriving maturity levels from process capability levels as defined in the ISO/IEC 15504-7 standard [18].

And the last choice was to tag all the processes from both PAMs that are not required to comply with the requirements of ISO/IEC 20000-1 as optional.

These design choices, among other things, are challenged in the discussion part of this paper.

4.2   Maturity Level 1: *Reactive*

Definition: The reactive organization is capable of operating and supporting identified and agreed IT services. The organization demonstrates achievement of the purpose of the processes that are fundamental for providing IT services, according to business expectations.

Rule to reach this level: To achieve Maturity Level 1, all processes assigned to level 1 shall achieve process capability level 1 or higher.

Table 1. Basic process set for Maturity Level 1

PAM	ID	Process Name	Comment
TIPA	SCM	Service catalogue management	
TIPA	SLM	Service level management	
TIPA	EVTM	Event management	optional
TIPA	INCM	Incident management	
TIPA	REQF	Request fulfilment	

4.3   Maturity Level 2: *Managed*

Definition: The managed organization is capable of proactively operating and supporting existing, new, or changed IT services. The organization demonstrates management of the resources and processes for providing and supporting existing, new, or changed IT services, according to business expectations.

Rule to reach this level: To achieve Maturity Level 2, all processes assigned to levels 1 and 2 shall achieve process capability level 2 or higher.

Table 2. Extended process set for Maturity Level 2

PAM	ID	Process Name	Comment
ISO	COM.01	Communication management	
ISO	COM.02	Documentation management	
ISO	COM.03	Human resources management	
TIPA	AM	Availability management	
TIPA	CAPM	Capacity management	
TIPA	SUPM	Supplier management	
TIPA	ACCM	Access management	optional
TIPA	CHGM	Change management	
TIPA	SACM	Service asset and configuration management	
TIPA	RDM	Release and deployment management	
TIPA	PRBM	Problem management	
TIPA	ISM	Information security management	

4.4   Maturity Level 3: *Integrated*

Definition: The organization is capable of providing consistent design, transition and operation of existing, new, or changed services with integrated processes. The organization demonstrates effective definition and deployment of the IT service management processes that are integrated in a controlled management system.

Rule to reach this level: To achieve Maturity Level 3, all processes assigned to levels 1, 2 and 3 shall achieve process capability level 3 or higher.

Table 3. Extended process set for Maturity Level 3

PAM	ID	Process Name	Comment
ISO	COM.05	Internal audit	
ISO	COM.06	Management review	
ISO	COM.07	Non-conformity management	
ISO	COM.08	Operational planning	

Table 3. (*Continued*)

ISO	COM.09	Operational implementation and control	
TIPA	SDC	Service design coordination	
TIPA	TPS	Transition planning and support	
TIPA	ITSFM	IT service financial management	
ISO	TOP.1	Organizational leadership	
TIPA	SVT	Service validation and testing	
ISO	COM.11	Risk and opportunity management	
TIPA	CHGE	Change evaluation	optional
TIPA	ITSCM	IT service continuity management	
ISO	COM.04	Improvement	

4.5   Maturity Level 4: *Governed*

Definition: The organization understands current and future market expectations and can guarantee its ability to meet them. The organization demonstrates objective control of its fundamental processes. The organization's strategy is translated in a portfolio of services that governs the performance and management of the processes and management system. It operates an effective influence on market demand accordingly.

Rule to reach this level: To achieve Maturity Level 4, all processes assigned to levels 1, 2, 3, and 4 shall achieve process capability level 3 or higher. One or more processes in the basic process set shall achieve process capability level 4 or higher.

Table 4. Extended process set for Maturity Level 4

PAM	ID	Process Name	Comment
TIPA	DEMM	Demand management	optional
TIPA	BRM	Business relationship management	
ISO	COM.10	Performance evaluation	
TIPA	KM	Knowledge management	optional
TIPA	SPM	Service portfolio management	
TIPA	ITSSM	IT service strategy management	optional

4.6   Maturity Level 5: *Optimizing*

Definition: The organization is continually improving its services according to its strategy. The organization demonstrates the ability to optimize its processes and its IT services.

Rule to reach this level: To achieve Maturity Level 5, all processes shall achieve process capability level 3 or higher. One or more of the processes in the basic process set shall achieve process capability level 5.

Table 5. Extended process set for Maturity Level 5

PAM	ID	Process Name	Comment
TIPA	SSI	Seven-step improvement	

Discussions

5.1   Appropriate PAMs as Input?

The original motivation for developing this maturity model was to be able to determine the readiness towards an ISO/IEC 20000-1 certification of organizations implementing ITIL and using TIPA for ITIL to measure their process capability. The use of the TIPA for ITIL PAM is thus obvious and cannot seriously be contested. However ISO/IEC 20000-1 contains a significant number of requirements that are not included in ITIL and so in the TIPA for ITIL PAM. These requirements target mainly the implementation of the management system (MS), for which ISO now requires a common structure in all Management System Standards (MSS) as stated in the Annex SL of the ISO directives [28].

Management system processes are defined in ISO/IEC 15504-8 but are not aligned with those from the Annex SL. So we took the option to use the most advanced PAM (still in draft) aligned with the requirements of the ISO Annex SL [28]: the information security management PAM for ISO/IEC 270001:2013 (ISO/IEC PDTS2 33070-4) [27] to cover this part of the standard.

The generic descriptions of the MS processes in this PAM make possible to use these process descriptions for building a maturity model targeting IT service management field. But on the down side, this genericity feature also means that the MS process descriptions does not embrace the specificities inherent to each domain, reduce the consistency with each individual MSS and finally reduce the ease of use of both the PAM and our ITSM maturity model.

Since our objective is to measure the coverage of ISO/IEC 20000-1 requirements based on a TIPA assessment, we are reconsidering the choice of ISO/IEC PDTS2 33070-4 as complement to TIPA for ITIL PAM since the ISO/IEC 27001 PAM does not take sufficiently account of the specificities of the ITSM domain. We are currently investigating the possibility to use an in-house PAM for the management system processes that will be fully aligned with the content of ISO/IEC 20000-1.

5.2   Structure of the Maturity Model

As explained in section 4, this maturity model enables to characterize an ITSM organization as *reactive* (level 1) up to *optimizing* (level 5). At maturity level 3 (*integrated*), *the organization demonstrates effective definition and deployment of the IT service management processes that are integrated in a controlled management system.* However, we can see that some processes have been allocated to the Maturity level 4 and 5 process sets. This situation can be considered as an inconsistency. It results from a combination of

two factors: first, the structure of the maturity scale has been mainly influenced by its meaningfulness for the users (i.e. the ITSM community); and second, having all processes distributed over 3 process sets only did not seem appropriate, meeting all the standards requirements being such a challenge.

Most maturity models use a 5-levels scale. Some processes do by nature reflect the purpose of maturity levels 4 and 5 and so were allocated to these levels even though related to lower levels if only based on the ISO/IEC 20000-1 requirements.

We are well aware that the context of each organization is unique and there are no "silver bullets" for taking the ITIL implementation challenge up. But we are convinced that defining five (or less) stable states that ITSM organizations can consider as milestones will bring added value to the ITSM community. The feedback from this community collected during the validation phase (just started) will be analyzed carefully and our maturity model improved accordingly.

5.3   Coverage of ISO/IEC 20000-1 Requirements

Despite the combination of both PAMs mentioned above to cover the content of ISO/IEC 20000-1, some 22 elementary requirements of this standard are not directly covered by any process of these two PAMs (through their base or generic practices). It means that even if you successfully assess all non-optional processes, you still must take care of 22 additional requirements. Most of these 22 requirements are about core ITSM processes such as Change Management, Release and Deployment Management and Configuration Management. Although these processes are included in the TIPA for ITIL PAM, the missing ISO/IEC 20000-1 requirements are not considered as key assessment indicators. This issue can be easily addressed by adapting the TIPA questionnaires of the concerned processes.

In contrast, an inherent limit of the maturity model (because compliant to ISO/IEC 33000) is that the granularity level is the process. It means that any process that is targeted by just a few (or even one) requirement(s) of ISO/IEC 20000-1 has to be fully performed to make visible the fulfillment of these requirements in the process profile and maturity profile resulting from an assessment.

5.4   Rules for Deriving the Maturity Levels

As mentioned in section 4, we have reused the rules for deriving maturity levels from process capability levels as defined in the ISO/IEC 15504-7 standard. Up to maturity level 3, these rules impose that all the processes from all current and previous maturity levels achieve the same capability level than the current maturity level (e.g. achieve process capability level 2 to reach maturity level 2). This can make sense in a maturity model where the maturity levels reflect the process capability. But the situation is different in our maturity model, as maturity levels are more related to the contribution of a set of processes to a target business objective for the organization. Similarly to some processes that only contribute to a few ISO/IEC 20000-1 requirements, the achievement of capability levels 2 and 3 are much more constraining that the ISO/IEC 20000-1 requirements.

Moreover, maturity levels 4 and 5 can currently be reached provided any process from the basic process set is achieving the same capability levels. Maybe should these specific processes be clearly identified (even if subject to contextualization).

In order to better align our maturity model to the ISO/IEC 20000-1 requirements, we are considering adapting the rules for deriving the maturity levels.

Conclusion

The Maturity Model for ISO/IEC 20000-1 based on the TIPA for ITIL Process Capability Assessment Model proposes a staged approach to support organizations that want to evolve following a structured path with defined states of organizational maturity. This maturity model offers several consistent sets of processes reflecting the growing ability of organizations to reach specific objectives. It shows how an organization can evolve from *reactive* (level 1) to *managed* (level 2), and *integrated* (level 3) where it covers most the ISO/IEC 20000-1 requirements, including the ones covering the management system. The organization can even go further to level 4 (*governed*), and ultimately to level 5 (*optimizing*). The maturity model is currently under review by the community of interest and while the first comments seem positive we will wait for more feedback before drawing final conclusions as some potential issues were pointed while writing this paper.

Though maturity models are powerful tools for organizations that want to demonstrate their excellence through a staged approach, they do not seem to be the best means to demonstrate an organization's readiness towards a requirements' standard such as ISO/IEC 20000-1 due to the difference of granularity that both approaches are offering. This difference in granularity is triggering an over investment to implement full processes to have them visible on the maturity profile whereas they are sometimes only targeted by a couple of requirements only.   This makes to draw the exact profile of an organization satisfying all the standards requirements.

Future works will analyze market feedback to improve the maturity model, while exploring alternatives to answer the original question, including using target profiles defined in ISO/IEC 15504-9 to help organizations using TIPA for ITIL measure their readiness to meet ISO/IEC 20000-1 requirements.

References

1. Nicewicz-Modrzewska, D., Stolarski, P.: ITIL implementation roadmap based on process governance. In: EUNIS 2008. Adam Mickiewicz University Computer Centre (2008)
2. Cater-Steel, A., Tan, W.G.: Implementation of it infrastructure library (ITIL) in Australia: progress and success factors. In: IT Governance International Conference on Australia: Progress and Success Factors, Auckland (2005)

3. Shang, S.S.C., Lin, S.-F.: Barriers to implementing ITIL – a multi-case study on the service-based industry. Contemporary Management Research **6**(1), 53–70 (2010)
4. The Cabinet Office. ITIL Lifecycle Publication Suite. The Stationery Office Edition (2011)
5. ISO/IEC TR 20000-1:2011. Information Technology — Service management — Service management system requirements. International Organization for Standardization, Geneva (2011)
6. Cots, S., Casadesús, M.: Exploring the service management standard ISO 20000. Total Quality Management & Business Excellence (2014). doi:10.1080/14783363.2013.856544
7. Public Research Center Henri Tudor. ITSM Process Assessment Supporting ITIL. Van Haren Publishing (2009). ISBN 9789087535643
8. ISO/IEC 33004. Information Technology — Process assessment — Requirements for process reference, process assessment and maturity models. International Organization for Standardization, Geneva (2015)
9. Barafort, B., Renault, A., Picard, M., Cortina, S.: A transformation process for building PRMs and PAMs based on a collection of requirements – example with ISO/IEC 20000. In: the International Conference SPICE 2008, Nuremberg, Germany (2008)
10. Cortina, S., Picard, M., Valdés, O., Renault, A.: A challenging process models development: the ITIL v3 lifecycle processes. In: The International Conference SPICE 2010, Pisa, Italy (2010)
11. Cortina, S., Mayer, N., Renault, A., Barafort, B.: Towards a process assessment model for management system standards. In: Mitasiunas, A., Rout, T., O'Connor, R.V., Dorling, A. (eds.) SPICE 2014. CCIS, vol. 477, pp. 36–47. Springer, Heidelberg (2014)
12. Renault, A., Cortina, S., Barafort, B.: Towards a maturity model for ISO/IEC 20000-1 based on the TIPA for ITIL process capability assessment model. In: Rout, T., O'Connor, R.V., Dorling, A. (eds.) SPICE 2015. CCIS, vol. 526, pp. 188–200. Springer, Heidelberg (2015)
13. Salviano, C.F., Figueiredo, A.M.C.M.: Unified basic concepts for process capability models. In: 20th Int Conf on Sw. Eng. and Knowledge Eng. SEKE (2008)
14. von Wangenheim, C.G., Hauck, J.C.R., Salviano, C., von Wangenheim, A.: Systematic literature review of software process capability/maturity models. In: The International Conference SPICE 2010, Pisa, Italy (2010)
15. CMMI for Development, Version 1.3 (PDF). CMMI-DEV (Version 1.3, November 2010). Carnegie Mellon University, Software Engineering Institute (2010)
16. CMMI for Services, Version 1.3 (PDF). CMMI-SVC (Version 1.3, November 2010). Carnegie Mellon University, Software Engineering Institute (2010)
17. ISO/IEC 33001. Information Technology — Process assessment — Concepts and terminology. International Organization for Standardization, Geneva (2015)
18. ISO/IEC TR 15504-7:2008. Information Technology — Process assessment — Assessment of organizational maturity. International Organization for Standardization, Geneva (2008)
19. Niessinka, F., Clerca, V., Tijdinka, T., van Vliet, H.: IT Service Capability Maturity Model. Vrije Universiteit (2005)
20. Pereira, R., da Silva, M.M.: ITIL maturity model. In: The 5th Iberian Conference on Information Systems and Technologies (CISTI) (2010)
21. Pereira, R., da Silva, M.M.: A maturity model for implementing ITIL v3. In: 6th World Congress on Services (SERVICES-1), USA (2010)
22. ISO/IEC TR 20000-4:2010. Information Technology — Service management — Process reference model. International Organization for Standardization, Geneva (2010)

23. ISO/IEC 15504-8:2012. Information Technology — Process assessment — An exemplar process assessment model for IT service management. International Organization for Standardization, Geneva (2012)
24. ISACA. COBIT 5: Process Assessment Model (PAM): using COBIT 5 (2013). ISBN 978-1-60420-264-9
25. ISO/IEC TR 20000-5:2013. Information Technology — Service management — Part 5 AN exemplar implementation plan for ISO/IEC 20000-1:2011. International Organization for Standardization, Geneva (2013)
26. ISO/IEC DTR 20000-11:2014. Information Technology — Service management — Guidance on the relationship between ISO/IEC 20000-1:2011 and service management frameworks. International Organization for Standardization, Geneva (2014)
27. ISO/IEC PDTS2 33070-4. Information Technology — Process assessment — Process capability assessment model for Information Security Management. International Organization for Standardization, Geneva
28. ISO/IEC Directives, Part1, Annex SL. International Organization for Standardization, Geneva (2014)

Applying Text Analyses and Data Mining to Support Process Oriented Multimodel Approaches

Zoltan Karaffy[1,2(✉)] and Katalin Balla[1,3]

[1] Budapest University of Technology and Economics, Budapest, Hungary
zoltan.karaffy@hu.bosch.com, balla@iit.bme.hu
[2] Robert Bosch Elektronika Ltd., Hatvan, Hungary
[3] SQI – Hungarian Software Quality Consulting Institute Ltd., Budapest, Hungary
balla.katalin@sqi.hu

Abstract. The target of this research is to develop an automatic and quantitative methodology and tool combination using text analyses, data mining and machine learning for the analyses of process oriented international quality approaches and documented quality systems of organizations in the field of software development. Such comparisons require at the moment lots of engineering work by experts thus resulting in inefficient human resource utilization. Our long-term goal is to have a tool that enables the auditors and other stakeholders in a software organization to perform quantitative and automatic pre-assessment about the conformance of the organizations' documented quality systems compared to international quality approach(es) with efficient human resource utilization. This article is presenting the results of searching for the optimal methodology via comparing CMMI-DEV 1.3 and HiS Scope of Automotive Spice 2.5 standards and creating similarity maps.

Keywords: Multimodel · Process oriented quality improvement · Text analyses · Data mining · Machine learning · CMMI-DEV · Automotive spice · Quantitative comparison · Automatic comparison · Similarity map

1 Introduction and Target Definition

Organizations developing software are frequently facing the challenge of having to implement or adapt their development process to be in conformance with several international process oriented standards, reference models and other process oriented approaches due to different requirements formulated by customers or other stakeholders ('multimodel' environment) [8,9,10], [12].

There are many different international standards, reference models and other process oriented approaches like CMMI-DEV [1], ASPICE [2], ISO/IEC 15504 [3],

---

[1] Capability Maturity Model® Integration for Development, Version 1.3, **further referred only as CMMI-DEV**.

[2] Automotive Software Process Improvement and Capability Determination, Process Assessment Model, Version 2.5 (10.05.2010), **further referred only as ASPICE**.

[3] Set of technical standards in information technology related to process assessment issued by International Organization for Standardization (ISO) and International Electrotechnical Commission (IEC).

© Springer International Publishing Switzerland 2015
R.V. O'Connor et al. (Eds.): EuroSPI 2015, CCIS 543, pp. 180–189, 2015.
DOI: 10.1007/978-3-319-24647-5_15

ITIL[4], Cobit[5], SoX[6] existing. From now on all of these international standards, reference models or other process oriented approaches will be generally referred only with the term 'international quality approach'.

Textual data is roughly 80% of all potentially useful data of businesses [3], thus it is a key factor of successful business operation to analyze this large information quantity. Text analyses, data mining combined with machine learning provides the possibility to eliminate or at least significantly reduce the need of expert human resources for manual analyses of textual information [1,2,3].

Based on literature research [6,7], [10,11,12], [19,20] and having own experience in the field[7], one can notice that in spite of having a huge variety of text analyses, data mining and machine learning methods and techniques available, they have not been applied to perform quantitative, automatic content level analyses in the field of process oriented approaches.

Considering the previously described problem, the **final target** of our PhD research is to develop a methodology and tool combination that enables auditors and other stakeholders to perform **automatic** and **quantitative analyses** of international quality approaches and documented quality systems **based on text analyses, data mining and machine learning** methods and techniques. Likewise, finally to create a **tool for automatic and quantitative pre-assessment** about the conformance level of the organizations' documented quality system compared to international quality approaches.

As the **first step** of this research activity, described in the present article, we have investigated the application of text analyses, data mining and machine learning methodologies for the quantitative analyses and comparison of international quality approaches. **An efficient combination of text analyses and data mining methodologies – i.e. a new methodology - was developed in order to quantitatively and automatically identify similarities between international quality approaches.**

To perform our first comparisons, which is described in this article, we have chosen the CMMI-DEV and HIS scope [8]of ASPICE at process capability level 1. The bases of our decision was that the amount of embedded software in automotive application is continuously growing, and therefore numerous comparisons are available performed in the past by experts manually. These comparisons (e.g. the study by VDA-QMC/Verband der Automobilindustrie/ [12]) can be the baseline of measuring the efficiency of our new methodology.

2   State of Art and Related Literature

Similarities and differences between the various international quality approaches have been investigated in several studies and articles.

---

[4]   Information Technology Infrastructure Library, Version 3.
[5]   Control Objectives for Information and Related Technology, Version 5.
[6]   Sarbanes-Oxley Act of 2002.
[7]   Authors worked for more than 10 years in software industry and used several standards and quality approaches in practice.
[8]   HIS scope: subset of 15 processes, called Hersteller Initiative Software (HIS) scope.

Manual comparison is the most typical type of comparison being performed either at the structural or at the content level of international quality approaches by experts of software development. A specific example of this structural comparison is to evaluate the correlation between different standard elements via counting cross references inside CMMI-DEV [6], or to study the relationship between CMMI-DEV and ISO/IEC 15504 maturity levels and processes capability profiles [7]. Some specific examples of content level analyses aimed at the comparison of CMMI-DEV to ASPICE [10,11,12], [19,20]. Another popular direction of research is to analyze and combine the different international standards manually into a 'metamodel' [5], [8,9], [19]. All of these comparisons result in detailed analyses, but as performed without pre-defined algorithms, a significant subjective portion will remain. This analyses by experts is also very expensive as requires many work hours. Further different research approach is to use natural language processing [13,14] or some basic text mining tools [15].

Summarizing the state of the art concerning multimodels and existing similarity evaluations, we can conclude that there is no appropriate automatic and quantitative algorithm and methodology existing which could be used for the analyses and comparison of international quality approaches, nor to create an automatic and quantitative pre-assessment methodology.

3   Approaches and Techniques

Text analyses incorporates many different fields of science having the target to turn unstructured textual information via predictive pattern recognition into evaluated, interpreted structured result [1,2,3,4], [16,18]. Text analyses always starts with Natural Language Processing (NLP) in order to transform the textual data into a structured database. Afterwards the analyses of this already structured database requires the usage of data mining or statistical methods and techniques.

3.1   Natural Language Processing (NLP)

The first step in text analyses is always the transformation of unstructured text including its semantic information and linguistic organization as input into a collection of useful terms (terms can be single words, word phrases or their combination). These techniques are the field of NLP.

This document processing using NLP in our research starts with the separation of international standards into smaller units according to the processes areas they are covering. The main steps of processing, as we understand them based on multiple descriptions [1,2,3,4], [16], and how they were used in this study are indicated in the figure below.

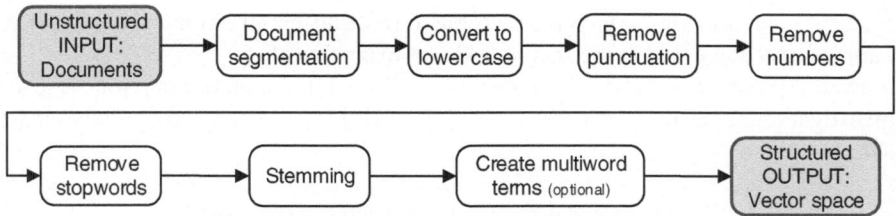

Fig. 1. Process steps of document processing based on NLP technics

At the end of natural language processing we create a vector space composed of a vectors, where each vector represents one process of CMMI-DEV or ASPICE:

$$\vec{d_j} = [tf_{1j}, ..., tf_{Tj}] \qquad (1)$$

where $\vec{d_j}$ is the vector of document j, T is the number of terms and tf_{ij} is the term i of document j [1].

To perform all of these natural language processing steps we selected and used the text mining module of the SPSS Modeler as it is the only software containing also a dictionary for the local Hungarian language which can be useful for the analyses of company level documents.

3.2   Data Mining Combined with Machine Learning

Machine learning algorithms relieve the burden of manual knowledge acquisition [1,2]. The most frequent algorithms use supervised pattern recognition. In supervised pattern recognition the aim is to detect general, but high accuracy classification patterns in the training set, that are highly predictable, to correctly classify new, previously unseen instances of a test set [16]. In our study – as we have chosen to compare CMMI-DEV and ASPICE - the software has to learn which CMMI-DEV process areas are describing which software development processes (e.g. project management, requirement engineering). Then the software has to be able to decide automatically - based on this previous knowledge - which ASPICE process description is most similar to a defined software development process. The main steps of our data mining algorithm are presented in Fig. 2. For all these processing steps the Matlab software package was used to support the evaluation process.

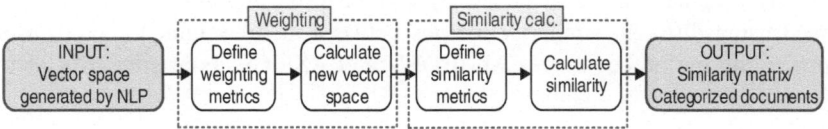

Fig. 2. Process steps of data mining in our research

The first step of data mining in our research is the application of weighting metrics, which has the target to differentiate between the terms in a way that the best terms for document c_i are the ones which are distributed most differently in the sets of positive examples of c_i compared to the sets of negative examples of c_i.

Seven different weighting techniques were selected based on our previous research / investigation about their efficiency [1], [4], [18], [21] and they are summarized in Table 1.

Table 1. Weighting methods used during our research[9]

Weighting metric	Mathematical formula	Remark
Tfidf (Term frequency-invers document frequency)	$\ln \dfrac{N}{df_i}$	One of the most frequent weighting method due to its simplicity [1]
Chi-square	$\dfrac{N[P(t_k, c_i)P(\overline{t_k}, \overline{c_i}) - P(t_k, \overline{c_i})P(\overline{t_k}, c_i)]^2}{P(t_k)P(\overline{t_k})P(c_i)P(\overline{c_i})}$	Calculates how the results of an observation differ (i.e. independent) from the results expected according to an initial hypothesis [18], [22]
NGL (Ng-Goh-Low)	$\dfrac{\sqrt{N}[P(t_k, c_i)P(\overline{t_k}, \overline{c_i}) - P(t_k, \overline{c_i})P(\overline{t_k}, c_i)]}{\sqrt{P(t_k)P(\overline{t_k})P(c_i)P(\overline{c_i})}}$	Similar to Chi-square, but it favours those words that are highly indicative of membership of class c_i and does not select those words which indicate non-membership to the class [18], [22]
IG (Information gain)	$-P(t_k, c_i)\, log_2 \frac{P(t_k, c_i)}{P(t_k)P(c_i)}$	Following the logic of information entropy via measuring the extent of information related to a certain term in a certain document [1]
Odds ratio	$\dfrac{P(t_k, c_i)\,(1 - P(t_k, \overline{c_i}))}{(1 - P(t_k, c_i))P(t_k, \overline{c_i})}$	Quantifies how strongly the presence or absence of term A is associated with the presence or absence of term B in a given document [1]
GSS coefficient	$P(t_k, c_i)P(\overline{t_k}, \overline{c_i}) - P(t_k, \overline{c_i})P(\overline{t_k}, c_i)$	A simplified Chi-squeare weigting metric [22]
Tf-rf (Relevance frequency)	$log_2 \left(2 + \dfrac{P(t_k, c_i)}{P(t_k, \overline{c_i})}\right)$	Calculats the relevance frequency of terms, in some appilcations outperformed many other approaches [21]

Table 2. Similarity and distance metrics applied in our research study[10]

Similarity / Distance metric	Mathematical formula	Remark
Cosine similarity	$\dfrac{\sum_{i=1}^{n} A_i \times B_i}{\sqrt{\sum_{i=1}^{n} A_i^2} \times \sqrt{\sum_{i=1}^{n} B_i^2}}$	Basically it is the cosine of the angle between vectors representing two chosen processes from international approaches, thus bounded between 0 and 1 [25]
Euclidean distance	$\sum_{i=1}^{n} \left(\dfrac{A_i}{\sqrt{\sum_{j=1}^{n} A_j}} - \dfrac{B_i}{\sqrt{\sum_{j=1}^{n} B_j}}\right)^2$	Based on the Euclidean distance from geometry (ordinary distance between two points) addionally extended with a weighting with the length of the document [25]
City block coefficient	$\sum_i \left|\dfrac{A_i}{\sum_j A_j} - \dfrac{B_i}{\sum_j B_j}\right|$	Absolute distance with addional weighting [24]
Jaccard coefficient	$\dfrac{\sum_i A_i B_i}{\sum_i A_i^2 + \sum_i B_i^2 - \sum_i A_i B_i}$	Compares the summarised weight of shared terms to the summarised weight of terms that are present in either of the two document but are not the shared terms [25]

When the weighted vector space has been created the similarity evaluation can be performed using different similarity metrics between these weighted vectors, which are representing the processes of CMMI-DEV and ASPICE. Four similarity metrics

---

[9]   Probabilities are interpreted on an event space of documents: e.g. $P(\overline{t_k}, c_i)$ indicates the probability that, for a random document x term t_k does not occur in x and x belongs to category c_i ; N is the number of documents.

[10] $\overline{A}$ and $\overline{B}$ vectors are the weighted document vectors of process A and process B, A_i and B_i denote the number of occurrence of term i in document A and B.

were chosen for this purpose after performing a research / analysis about their expected efficiency [1], [16], [22,23]. These similarity metrics are presented in Table 2.

4   Results

In the first part of presenting the results we compare different weighting metrics; in the second part we describe the application of different similarity metrics in order to optimize our statistical evaluation and in the third part we investigate the usage of multiword terms because it is always a major question in NLP to decide between the usage of single words or word combinations.

4.1   Comparing Different Weighting Methods

In this part of the research single words terms were taken as the output of language processing and different weighting calculation methods were applied. Finally the document similarity was compared using cosine similarity metric. The results were compared to a reference study created by VDA-QMC (Verband der Automobilindustrie) [12]. Four document (process) pairs of CMMI-DEV and ASPICE were chosen where a high level of similarity is expected based on this study performed by VDA-QMC.

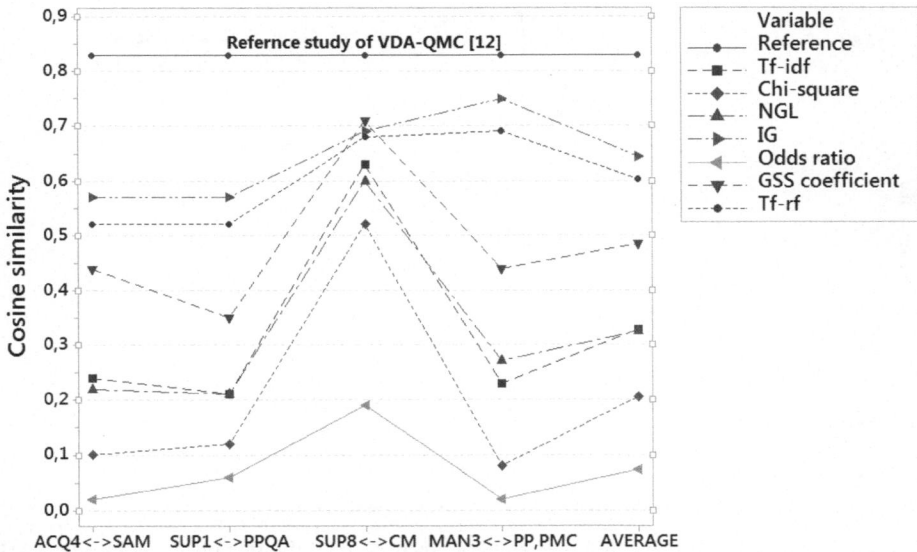

Fig. 3. Cosine similarity results using single words as input and different weighting metrics in a comparison to the VDA-QMC [12] result as reference

It can be seen that the application of **IG weighting metric** resulted in the best average performance. The only exception is the comparison of configuration management processes of CMMI-DEV and APICE, where the GSS coefficient slightly outperformed the IG coefficient.

4.2   Comparing Different Similarity and Distance Metrics

In this step the performance of different similarity and distance metrics were evaluated. As input single word terms were used in a combination with the best performing IG weighting metric. Based on the below results (see Fig.4) the best average performance in comparison to the VDA-QMC reference [12] was achieved using the
cosine similarity. This methodology not only had the best overall average efficiency,
but for each document pair resulted in a similarity value closest to the reference
VDA-QMC study [12].

4.3   Single Words versus Multi Words as Input for Data Mining

The target with using multi word terms was to check if the efficiency of similarity
evaluation can be increased in comparison to the used single word terms. Similarity
numbers calculated using IG weighing metric and cosine similarity in a combination
with multiword terms are presented in Fig.4. It is clearly visible, that the similarity
numbers have reduced significantly. It also fits to some of the previous experiences
found in the literature [1], [17], that for the text analyses in most applications the **single word** based evaluations have the best performance.

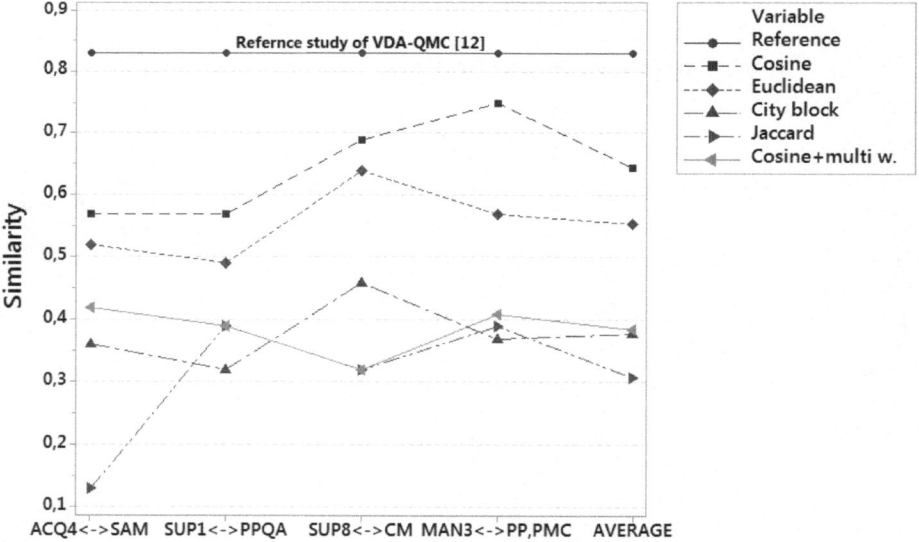

Fig. 4. Similarity results using different similarity metrics, IG weighting metric and single word
terms[11] and including the result achieved using multiword terms ('Cosine+multi w.').

---

[11] Distance metric results have been transformed into similarity numbers in order to be able to
compare to the similarity numbers. All in a comparison to the VDA-QMC [12] result as
reference.

4.4   Summary of Results

The best methodology is clearly the combination of single word terms with IG weighting metric and cosine similarity reaching an average efficiency of 78% (100% efficiency is assumed for the reference study performed by VDA-QMC [12]).

Fig. 5 presents the similarity results of using this optimal combination of methods in the form of contour line graph. The contour line graph highlights the isolines (constant similarity values) and similarity numbers. High level of similarity (>50%) has been calculated for the case of the following document/process pairs: configuration management (SUP8-CM), project management (MAN3-PP,PMC,IPM), quality assurance (SUP1-PPQA), supplier monitoring/management (ACQ4-SAM) and software requirements (ENG4-REQM).

In case of all of these document/process pairs except the last one the study of VDA-QMC [12] defines full coverage 'in all significant aspects' and for the software requirements (ENG4-REQM) VDA-QMC defines coverage for the 'majority of aspects'. Generally we can conclude that our automatically generated similarity maps fits at a very high level to this previous VDA-QMC result.

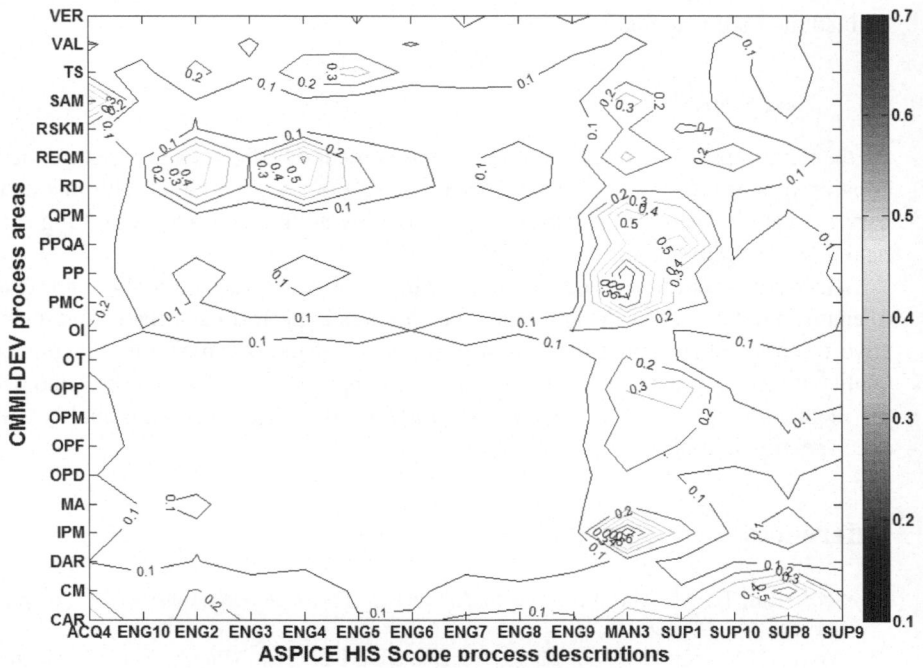

Fig. 5. Contour line graph of document cosine similarity at maturity level 1 using single words as input, IG weighting metric and cosine similarity metric

5   Conclusions and Next Steps

5.1   Conclusions

A new methodology based on text analyses and data mining has been successfully developed in order to quantitatively and automatically identify similarities between international quality approaches.

According to our research the most efficient methodology is the combination of using **single word terms** in natural language processing and applying **IG weighting metric** and **cosine similarity** during the statistical evaluation.

Using this new methodology a **similarity map** has been generated between CMMI-DEV 1.3 and HiS Scope of Automotive Spice 2.5 international quality approaches and the results are fitting to the previous study of VDA-QMC [12] with high accuracy. **Average efficiency** achieved with this newly developed methodology in relation to the reference study of VDA-QMC [12] is **78%**.

This already can be a useful tool to find the connected document/process elements of different international quality approaches or to identify connected documents/processes in the documented quality system of an organization in relation to a defined international quality approach.

5.2   Next Steps

As the next steps of the research further improvement of efficiency is expected via the creation of software quality assurance specific dictionary. The target with this dictionary is to apply 'knowledge based' term weighting additionally to the existing statistical based weighting metric.

Afterwards according to our long term target we will create a pre-assessment tool to enable auditors, assessors and other stakeholders to perform automatic and quantitative pre-assessment about the conformance level of the organization's documented quality system compared to international quality approaches. This will be done using the methodologies described in this article extended with the software quality assurance specific dictionary.

References

1. Sebastiani, F.: Machine Learning in Automated Text Categorization. ACM Computing Surveys **34**, 1–47 (2002)
2. Weiss, S.M., Indurkhya, N., Zhang, T., Damerau, F.J.: Text Mining, Predictive Methods for Analyzing Unstructured Information. Springer (2005)
3. Gharehchopogh, F.S., Khalifelu, Z.A.: Analysis and evaluation of unstructured data: text mining versus natural language processing. In: 5th International Conference on Application of Information and Communication Technologies (AICT) (2011)
4. Uchyigit, G.: Experimental evaluation of feature selection methods for text classification. In: 9th International Conference on Fuzzy Systems and Knowledge Discovery (2012)

5. Rahman, A.A., Sahibuddin, S., Ibrahim, S.: A Taxonomy Analysis for Multi-Model Process Improvement from the Context of Software Engineering Processes and Services. International Journal of Digital Content Technology and its Applications **6**(22) (2012)
6. Kelemen, Z.D., Kusters, R., Trienekens, J., Balla, K.: Towards Complexity Analysis of Software Process Improvement Frameworks. Technical report (2013)
7. Peldzius, S., Ragaisis, S.: Investigation Correspondence between CMMI-DEV and ISO/IEC 15504. International Journal of Education and information technologies **5**(4) (2011)
8. Peldzius, S., Ragaisis, S.: Framework for usage of multiple software process models. In: Mas, A., Mesquida, A., Rout, T., O'Connor, R.V., Dorling, A. (eds.) SPICE 2012. CCIS, vol. 290, pp. 210–221. Springer, Heidelberg (2012)
9. Kelemen, Z.D., Kusters, R., Trienekens, J., Balla, K.: A Data Model for Multimodel Process Improvement. Technical report (2013)
10. Bella, F., Hörmann, K., Vanamali, B.: From CMMI to SPICE – experiences on how to survive a spice assessment having already implemented CMMI. In: Jedlitschka, A., Salo, O. (eds.) PROFES 2008. LNCS, vol. 5089, pp. 133–142. Springer, Heidelberg (2008)
11. Baldassarre, M.T., Piattini, M., Pino, F.J., Visaggio, G.: Comparing ISO/IEC 12207 and CMMI-DEV: towards a mapping of ISO/IEC 15504-7. In: Proceedings of the Seventh ICSE Conference on Software Quality (2009)
12. VDA QMC: Automotive Spice Process Assessment Model, Process assessment using Automotive Spice in the development of software based system, 1st edn. (2008)
13. Jeners, S., Lichter, H.: Smart integration of process improvement reference models based on an automated comparison approach. In: McCaffery, F., O'Connor, R.V., Messnarz, R. (eds.) EuroSPI 2013. CCIS, vol. 364, pp. 143–154. Springer, Heidelberg (2013)
14. Jeners, S., Lichter, H., Pyatkova, E.: Automated comparison of process improvement reference models based on similarity metrics. In: 19th Asia-Pacific Software Engineering Conference (2012)
15. Kelemen, Z.D., Kusters, R., Trienekens, J., Balla, K.: Towards Applying Text Mining Techniques on Software Quality Standards and Models. Technical report (2013)
16. Moens, M.-F.: Information Extraction: Algorithms and Prospects in a Retrieval Context. Springer (2006)
17. Apte, C., Damerau, F.: Automated Learning of Decision Text Categorization. ACM Transactions on Information Systems **12**(3), 233–251 (1994)
18. Dave, K., Taghva, K.: Study of feature selection algorithms for text-categorization. UNLV Theses, University of Nevada (2011)
19. Peldzius, S., Ragaisis, S.: Usage of multiple process assessment models. In: Woronowicz, T., Rout, T., O'Connor, R.V., Dorling, A. (eds.) SPICE 2013. CCIS, vol. 349, pp. 223–234. Springer, Heidelberg (2013)
20. Ehsan, N., Perwaiz, A., Arif, J., Mirza, E., Ishaque, A.: CMMI / SPICE based Process Improvement. In: Proceedings of the 2010 IEEE ICMIT (2010)
21. Lan, M., Sun, S.-Y., Low, H.-B., Tan, C.-L.: A comparative study on term weighting schemes for text categorization neural networks. Proceedings of the IJCNN 2005 **1**, 546–551 (2005)
22. Cha, S.-H.: Comprehensive Survey on Distance/Similarity Measures between Probability Density Functions. International Journal of Mathematical Models and Methods in Applied Sciences **1**(4), 300 (2007)
23. Huang, A.: Similarity measures for text document clustering. In: New Zealand Computer Science Research Student Conference (2008)

SPI and Process Assessment

The Project Management SPICE (PMSPICE) Process Reference Model: Towards a Process Assessment Model

Antoni-Lluís Mesquida[1(✉)], Antònia Mas[1], and Béatrix Barafort[2]

[1] Department of Mathematics and Computer Science,
University of the Balearic Islands, Cra. De Valldemossa, km 7.5, Palma de Mallorca, Spain
{antoni.mesquida,antonia.mas}@uib.es
[2] Luxembourg Institute of Science and Technology,
5 Avenue des Hauts-Fourneaux L-4362, Esch-sur-Alzette, Luxembourg
beatrix.barafort@list.lu

Abstract. Since the publication of ISO 21500, companies can be aware of the processes that can be applied for effectively managing the projects they carry out. However, guidance for assessing and improving these project management processes is not provided. The Project Management SPICE (PMSPICE) Framework will provide a process assessment and improvement model in the project management domain. This paper details how the requirements of ISO 21500 were transformed to develop the PMSPICE Process Reference Model (PRM), which is compliant with the requirements of ISO/IEC 33004. Based upon the PMSPICE PRM, a process assessment model will be build.

Keywords: PMSPICE · Project management · Process reference model · ISO/IEC 21500 · Transformation process

1 Introduction

In a process-oriented organization it is feasible to organize work in projects and managing them efficiently. This fact provides greater control over both the work done and the performance of the employees and, as a result, improves the efficiency of the company. The standard ISO 21500 Guidance on project management [1] provides *"concepts and processes that are considered to form good practice in project management and can be used by any type of organization… and for any type of project, irrespective of complexity, size or duration."*

The maturity of an organization is associated with its capability to define, implement and improve in all the processes it uses to perform the work. A process-oriented organization can consider different process frameworks. On the one hand, it can implement production processes related to the activity performed in its business area. On the other hand, it can also consider specific processes related to the company's project management.

The international scientific community dedicated to process assessment and improvement has focused their research on developing Process Reference Models (PRMs) and Process Assessment Models (PAMs) for specific areas, resulting in the

© Springer International Publishing Switzerland 2015
R.V. O'Connor et al. (Eds.): EuroSPI 2015, CCIS 543, pp. 193–205, 2015.
DOI: 10.1007/978-3-319-24647-5_16

appearance of new process models in different domains. This is the case of MDevSPICE®, a software process assessment model for Medical Device Software Processes which is being developed to meet the specific safety-critical and regulatory requirements of the medical device domain [2, 3].

Another example is TIPA®, an IT Service Management framework [4] composed of a PRM and a PAM for ITIL (Information Technology Infrastructure Library), a documented assessment method (including a toolbox for TIPA Guidance), and lately a Maturity Model for ISO/IEC 20000-1 based on the TIPA for ITIL Process Capability Assessment Model [5] that uses the principles of the ISO/IEC 15504 and 33000 standard series for IT service management process assessment.

Related to the information security management domain based on the ISO/IEC 27001:2005 requirements, in [6] the authors propose a process model to describe processes involved in information security management by reusing a previous process model derived from the ISO/IEC 20000-1 standard for IT service management. In [7] the IT service management requirements of ISO/IEC 20000-1 are integrated in an organizational management system. In [8] the authors include information security controls in the ISO/IEC 12207 software lifecycle process model. Currently at ISO, there is a project in progress for developing a process reference model and a process capability process assessment model based on the ISO/IEC 27001:2013. In the field of software product management, the authors made in [9] a wide state of the art study related to the development of PRMs in the software product engineering domain.

Other proposals address the development of specific process models. Some examples of PAMs already published as standards are ISO/IEC 15504-5 [10] for software life cycle processes, ISO/IEC 15504-6 [11] for system life cycle processes or ISO/IEC TS 15504-8 [12] for IT service management processes.

Our research is focused on developing the Project Management SPICE Framework (PMSPICE) [13]. The PMSPICE Framework will define a PRM, a PAM and an Organizational Maturity Model (OMM) for project management. The PMSPICE PRM should be based on the project management processes described in ISO 21500. The PMSPICE PAM should be used to perform ISO/IEC 15504 conformant assessments of the project management process capability in accordance with the requirements of ISO/IEC 15504-2 [14]. The PMSPICE OMM should be conformant to the requirements established in ISO/IEC TR 15504-7 [15] for constructing an Organizational Maturity Model.

With the aim of developing the PRM and the PAM for the PMSPICE framework a literature review of the existing process reference and process assessment models that have been developed to assess against the ISO/IEC 15504 standard was performed. In [16] the authors describe the construction of the core content of a process assessment model for management system standards. In [17] the TIPA transformation process for building PRMs and PAMs is detailed and an example for transforming ISO/IEC 20000 requirements into a PRM and a PAM is illustrated. In [18] the authors examined how to develop a PAM to assess Medical IT networks against 80001-1 by applying the TIPA transformation process and in [19] an ISO/IEC 15504-2 compliant PRM and PAM for assessment against IEC 80001-1 is presented. In [20] the authors propose how to improve process models for better ISO/IEC 15504 process assessment and, in [21] they consider the use of both a transformative view and a coordination view of a process to support the design and validation of PRM processes based on a collection of requirements. The knowledge obtained from these experiences will be taken into account for the development of our specific PMSPICE Framework for project management.

This paper describes the application of the TIPA transformation process [17] to the ISO 21500 standard in order to obtain the PMSPICE PRM. It is structured as follows. Section 2 presents the ISO 21500 standard and outlines the three development stages for constructing the PMSPICE Framework. Section 3 considers the ISO requirements and the associated constraints for the design of process reference models. Section 4 details the application of the TIPA transformation process to develop the PMSPICE PRM and shows an example of process in the PRM. Finally, Section 5 opens discussion about the results obtained and Section 6 concludes with next steps to be carried out in the PMSPICE Framework development.

2   The Project Management SPICE (PMSPICE) Framework

ISO 21500 [1] *"identifies the recommended project management processes to be used during a project as a whole, for individual phases or both."* The processes in ISO 21500, defined in terms of purpose, description and primary inputs and outputs, are interdependent. Although they are presented as separate elements, in practice, they overlap and interact in ways that are not detailed in the standard. Moreover, in the interest of brevity, it does not indicate the source of all primary inputs or where primary outputs go.

The 39 ISO 21500 project management processes may be viewed from two different perspectives: as *process groups* for the management of the project; and as *subject groups* for collecting the processes by subject. The five process groups in ISO 21500 are: Initiating, Planning, Implementing, Controlling and Closing. The ten subject groups in ISO 21500 are: Integration, Stakeholder, Scope, Resource, Time, Cost, Risk, Quality, Procurement and Communication.

The processes described in the ISO 21500 standard have been considered as one of the key inputs when developing the PMSPICE Framework. This framework will be the result of a construction process divided into three sequential stages:

- **Development of the PMSPICE PRM.** It re-structures the descriptions of the project management processes in ISO 21500 to be compliant with ISO/IEC 15504-2 and be aligned to the standard ISO/IEC TR 24774 Guidelines for process description [22]. This standard provides rules for the formulation of process descriptive elements as a means to ensuring consistency in standard process reference models. This first stage has been completed and this paper presents the transformation process which has been followed to develop the PRM and also the resulting PMSPICE PRM.
- **Development of the PMSPICE PAM.** It will expand the PMSPICE PRM by including a set of performance indicators, base practices, for each process. The PAM will also define a second set of indicators of process performance

by associating work products with each process in the PRM. This second stage will be initiated very soon.

- **Development of the PMSPICE OMM.** The model will identify the process sets associated with each of the levels in the scale of Organizational Maturity. It will follow the guidelines provided by ISO/IEC TR 15504-7 to perform assessments of project management organizational maturity and on the application of Organizational Maturity ratings for process improvement and capability determination. This last stage will start once the results of the other two have been analysed and validated.

3   ISO Requirements for Process Reference Model Design and Associated Constraints

For the last decade, Process Reference Models have been developed for being used for process assessment, therefore based on a Process Assessment Model(s). These PRMs were fulfilling requirements of the ISO/IEC 15504-2 standard. This latter defines *"the basis for process assessment"*. It *"sets out the minimum requirements for performing an assessment;"* it *"identifies the measurement framework for process capability and the requirements for a) performing an assessment; b) Process Reference Models; c) Process Assessment Models and d) verifying conformity of assessments"*. *"An assessment is carried out against a defined assessment input utilizing conformant Process Assessment Model(s) related to one or more conformant or compliant Process Reference Models."*

In the context of this paper, only PRM development is considered. So only the requirements for PRM development are detailed here. ISO/IEC 15504-2 specifies that:
"A Process Reference Model shall contain:

  a)   *a declaration of the domain of the Process Reference Model;*
  b)   *a description, meeting the requirements of 6.2.4 [process description] of this International Standard, of the processes within the scope of the Process Reference Model;*
  c)   *a description of the relationship between the Process Reference Model and its intended context of use;*
  d)   *a description of the relationship between the processes defined within the Process Reference Model."*

The PRM shall also *"document the community of interest of the model and the actions taken to achieve consensus within that community of interest."*

About the process description, the processes have to be *"described in terms of purpose and outcomes"*. The outcomes have to be *"necessary and sufficient to achieve the purpose of the process"*, and *"process descriptions shall be such that no aspects of the measurement framework ... beyond level 1 are contained or implied."*

An outcome statement describes one of the following: "production of an artefact; a significant change of state; meeting of specified constraints, e.g. requirements, goals etc."

For the last years, PRMs have been developed according to these requirements, and in the same time, the revision of the ISO/IEC 15504 series has been performed. The ISO 33000 series on process assessment emerged for replacing the ISO/IEC 15504 one. The first documents have been published in 2015: ISO/IEC 33001 Concepts and terminology, ISO/IEC 33002 Requirements for performing process assessment, ISO/IEC 33003 Requirements for measurement framework, ISO/IEC 33004 Requirements for process reference, process assessment and maturity models, and ISO/IEC 33020 Process measurement framework for assessment of process capability (The ISO/IEC 33014 Guide for process improvement was the first document of the series to be published in advance).

The recently published ISO/IEC 33004 [23] is from now on dedicated to the modelling of PRMs, PAMs and maturity models. The corresponding clause of ISO/IEC 15504-2 for Process reference models (clause 6.2) is now clause 5 within ISO/IEC 33004.

It is important to notice that there were no changes between releases for PRMs development. As recommended by Notes within ISO/IEC 33004, the *"ISO/IEC TR 24774 presents guidelines for the elements used most frequently in describing a process: the title, purpose statement, outcomes, activities and tasks. The primary purpose of ISO/IEC TR 24774 is to encourage uniformity in the description of processes, and following these guidelines allows the combination of processes from different process reference models."* Furthermore, as defined in ISO/IEC TR 24774, *"an outcome is an observable result of the successful achievement of the process purpose, and thus it is assessable."*

Finally, after developing a PRM, a statement of conformity has to be formulated in order to demonstrate how requirements for modelling a PRM have been met.

For the PMSPICE PRM development, ISO/IEC 15504-2 (therefore ISO/IEC 33004) requirements were fulfilled as well as ISO/IEC TR 24774 guidelines were considered; it is detailed in section 4 throughout the TIPA transformation process.

4   Development of the PMSPICE PRM

This section firstly introduces the transformation process which was followed in order to develop the PMSPICE PRM. Then, it details the main results obtained after the application of each of the steps it defines to develop a PRM. Finally, the resulting PMSPICE PRM is presented.

4.1   The TIPA Transformation Process

The TIPA transformation process is a goal oriented requirements engineering technique which was developed by the Luxembourg Institute of Science and Technology to provide clear guidance on how to transform a set of domain requirements into PRMs and PAMs which are compliant with the requirements of ISO/IEC 33004 and ISO/IEC TR 24774.

The TIPA transformation process advocates identifying elementary requirements and organising these requirements into requirement trees. These requirement trees are then oriented around the business goals to which they are related to form goal trees. More details about this transformation process can be found in [17].

The TIPA transformation process is composed of nine steps. Steps 1, 2, 3, 4 and 7 were selected for the development of the PRM. The remaining steps of the transformation process are associated with the development of the PAM and will be applied during a future stage of this research. These steps are:

1. Identify elementary requirements in a collection of requirements.
2. Organise and structure the requirements.
3. Identify common purposes upon those requirements and organise them towards domain goals.
4. Identify and factorise outcomes from the common purposes and attach them to the related goals.
5. Group activities together under a practice and attach it to the related outcomes.
6. Allocate each practice to a specific capability level.
7. Phrase outcomes and process purpose.
8. Phrase the Base Practices attached to the Outcomes.
9. Determine Work Products among the inputs and outputs of the practices.

4.2   Application of the TIPA Transformation Process

Based on the transformation process mentioned above, steps 1, 2, 3, 4 and 7 were applied in order to develop the PMSPICE PRM. For most of the processes of this PRM, several iterations and interactions between previous steps were required in order to refine and check consistency of the PRM elements (semantic and structural aspects).

It is important to mention that PMSPICE PRM developers had made the decision to strictly align with the processes described in the ISO 21500 standard, without changing any process name neither attempting to grouping several processes nor splitting a process into several ones. This is required by the PMSPICE community of interest and ISO 21500 users. This implies that the considered collection of requirements for each process corresponds to a unique clause of ISO 21500. The PMSPICE PRM development has repeated the TIPA transformation process 39 times.

With the aim of facilitating the understanding of the work performed, this section shows the application of the transformation process steps to one exemplar ISO 21500 process, the *Develop schedule* process. This process belongs to the Planning process group in the Time subject group. Table 1 shows the description for this process in ISO 21500.

Step 1: Identify elementary requirements in a collection of requirements

The first step consists in identifying all of the requirements under the form of a collection of elementary requirements. As mentioned before, ISO 21500 provides, for each process, a process description which details together both the purpose of the process, the actions to be taken in order to implement the process and the expected results of its implementation. During this first step, each of the sentences describing a process was analysed, conveniently separating the clarification of the process purpose from the actions to be taken to implement the process.

Table 1. Extract of the ISO 21500 *Develop schedule* process

The purpose of **Develop schedule** *is to calculate the start and end times of the project activities and to establish the overall project schedule baseline.*
Activities are scheduled in a logical sequence that identifies durations, milestones and interdependencies to provide a network.
The activity level provides sufficient resolution for management control throughout the project life cycle. The schedule provides a vehicle for evaluating actual progress in time against a predefined objective measurement of achievement.
The schedule is established at the activity level, which provides the basis for assigning resources and developing the time-based budget. Schedule development should continue throughout the project as work progresses, as the project plans change, as anticipated risk events occur or disappear and as new risks are identified. If necessary, duration and resource estimates should be reviewed and revised to develop an approved project schedule that can serve as the baseline against which progress may be tracked.

In our case, the "verbs in passive voice statements" (revealing requirements) were easily identified and split into elementary requirements. Other sentences with a verb in present tense, clearly indicating an action to perform or a condition to be satisfied, were also considered elementary requirements. When a sentence was composed of two parts separated by the coordination conjunction "and", it was divided into two elementary requirements. If there was an enumeration, each element of the list was identified as an elementary requirement.

For the particular case of the *Develop schedule* process, nine elementary requirements were identified.

Step 2: Organize, and structure the requirements

During the second step, the elementary requirements were organized and gathered around the objects they are about in order to build a "requirement tree" by applying mind mapping techniques. A requirement tree offers a graphical view of the connections between the components of each elementary requirement.

Figure 1 shows the requirement tree obtained for the *Develop schedule* process.

Step 3: Identify common purposes upon those requirements and organize them towards domain goals

From the requirements tree, some common purposes were identified and the elementary requirements were organized accordingly, taking the original meaning of the ISO 21500 process descriptions into account. Furthermore, as this international standard defines the main purpose of each process, the authors were able to use this field to identify the domain goals. A goal tree was then built for each process, in which the inter-related activities were properly grouped.

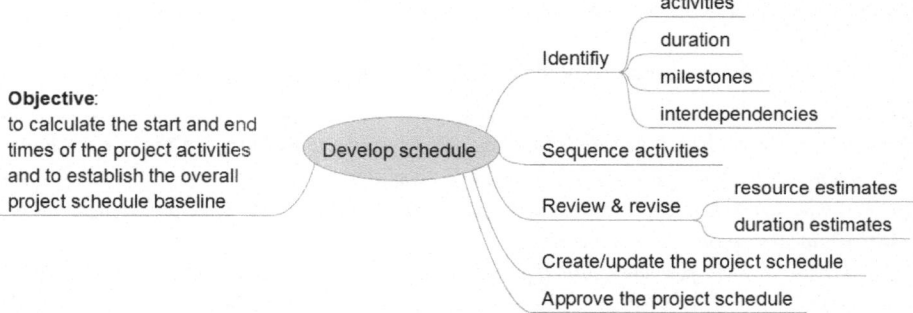

Fig. 1. Requirement tree for *Develop schedule* process

For the example of the *Develop schedule* process, two domain goals were identified:

- To calculate the start and end times of the project activities, and
- To establish the overall project schedule baseline.

Step 4: Identify and factorize outcomes from the common purposes and attach them to the related goals

The common purposes identified during step 3 were considered as the process outcomes and were attached to the related domain goals. An outcome is an observable result of 1) the production of an artefact, 2) a significant change of state, or 3) the meeting of specified constraints. The outcomes of each process had to be factorized or merged, according to convenience and expert judgement, in order to define from 3 to 7 outcomes per process, and thus to follow the recommendations of ISO/IEC TR 24774.

The goal tree for the *Develop schedule* process (Figure 2) shows the resulting six process outcomes. The first four outcomes are related to the first main domain goal (identified during step 3): the calculation of the start and end times of the project activities. Outcomes 5 and 6 are linked to the second domain goal: the establishment of the project schedule baseline.

Step 7: Phrase outcomes and process purpose

During the execution of this step, each outcome was phrased as a declarative sentence using verbs at the present tense. As an example, the *Develop schedule* process outcomes 1 and 5 were phrased as follows:

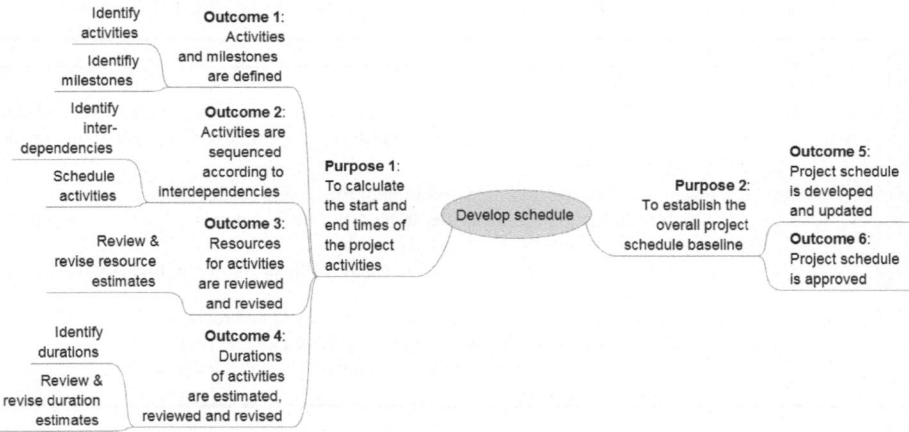

Fig. 2. Goal tree for *Develop schedule* process

- *Outcome 1: Activities and milestones are defined at a sufficient resolution for management control throughout the project life cycle.*
- *Outcome 5: Project schedule is developed according to the schedule constraints.*

Then, the purpose was phrased to state a high-level goal for performing the process and provide measurable and tangible benefits to the stakeholders through the expected outcomes (process assessment concern). The *Develop schedule* process purpose was phrased as follows:

- *To develop a project schedule based on sized and sequenced activities where the start and end times are calculated and a baseline of the schedule is established.*

4.3   Result: The PMSPICE PRM

The application of the five steps of the TIPA transformation process described in the former section resulted in the creation of the PMSPICE PRM. This model is composed of the 39 ISO 21500 project management processes, distributed in the ten subject groups and the five process groups proposed by this international standard.

As ISO 21500 does not provide process IDs, an identifier (composed of three capital letters summarizing the subject group name, a dot and a consecutive number) was added to each process. Associating this identifier to the process name, together with its purpose and outcomes enabled to build the PMSPICE PRM.

Table 2 shows the example of the description of the *TIM.3 Develop schedule* process defined in the PRM, which is the third process in the Time subject group.

Table 2. Extract of the *TIM.3 Develop schedule* process in the PMSPICE PRM.

Process ID	TIM.3
Process Name	Develop schedule
Process Purpose	The purpose of *Develop schedule* is to develop a project schedule based on sized and sequenced activities where the start and end times are calculated and a baseline of the schedule is established.
Process comes	Out-As a result of the successful implementation of the Develop schedule process:

    1.   Activities and milestones are defined at a sufficient resolution for management control throughout the project life cycle.

    2.   Activities are sequenced in a logical schedule according to the identified inter-dependencies.

    3.   Resources for activities are estimated, reviewed and revised.

    4.   Durations of activities are estimated, reviewed and revised.

    5.   Project schedule is developed according to the schedule constraints.

    6.   Project schedule is approved.

The resulting PMSPICE PRM is suitable for use in process assessment performed in accordance with the requirements for a PRM described in Clause 6.2 of ISO/IEC 15504-2 (now in Clause 5 of ISO/IEC 33004).

a) The declaration of the domain is Project Management.

b) The description of the processes is provided in the PMSPICE PRM.

c) The PMSPICE PRM describe at an abstract level the processes implied by ISO 21500. The purpose of the PMSPICE PRM is to facilitate the development of a process assessment model for project management.

d) A description of the relationship between the processes defined within the PMSPICE PRM is supported by a figure collecting all the processes by process groups and by subject groups.

The process descriptions are unique. The identification is provided by unique names and by the identifier of each process of the PMSPICE PRM. Processes are described in terms of its purpose and outcomes. For all processes, the set of process outcomes are necessary and sufficient to achieve the purpose of the process. No aspects of the ISO/IEC 15504 Measurement Framework beyond level 1 are contained in process descriptions.

5   Discussion

From the application of the TIPA transformation process for the creation of the PMSPICE PRM some concerns are worth noting. Firstly, it has been validated that this transformation process enables to build PRMs based on a collection of requirements in a systematic way. According to [17], it should be mentioned that having an accurate understanding of the requirements identified by the domain (in our case, Project Management) is a prerequisite to get good results from the transformation activities. Secondly, it is also strongly recommended having experience in using mind-mapping techniques to develop the requirement and goal trees required by steps 2, 3 and 4.

Another important point to be considered is the brevity of the process descriptions in the ISO 21500 standard. This can be seen as an advantage when identifying the elementary requirements. In most process descriptions, elementary requirements can be clearly extracted and no confusing elements or attributes are provided. However, the lack of additional information for each requirement can be also seen as a weakness. In the case of the ISO 21500 standard, primary inputs and outputs are nevertheless an additional support in the determination of outcomes. We believe that this conciseness will make difficult the application of the remaining steps of the TIPA transformation process (steps 5, 6, 8 and 9), mainly contributing to the development of the PAM. The project management good practices collected in other project management frameworks should be considered when creating the base practices for each process in the PMSPICE PAM, since additional knowledge will be needed in order to widen the explanation on how to perform the proposed base practices.

6   Conclusions and Future Work

This paper has presented the work performed in order to develop an ISO/IEC 15504-2 compliant project management PRM by applying the TIPA transformation process. The resulting PMSPICE PRM is covering the project management guidance recommended by the ISO 21500 International Standard. In the second stage of our research, a PAM based upon the developed PMSPICE PRM will be constructed and then an organizational maturity model. This will allow companies to assess the capability of their project management processes and their organizational maturity and then, to use the results as a basis for process improvement.

The PMSPICE PRM, PAM and OMM will be validated through expert opinion by collecting feedback from the developers of the TIPA® framework. Other R&D experts working in process models for other domains are planned to be consulted. Moreover, validation will also be carried out from the industry perspective. Different Heads of Project Management Offices will be consulted about the suitability of the structure and contents of the PMSPICE PRM and PAM and then, they will be asked to use these models in order to evaluate their effectiveness. Requirement and goal trees could be used as a tool supporting validation of the models. All changes requested and comments obtained from the validation process will be incorporated into the final version of the PMSPICE Framework. Moreover, the final version of the PMSPICE models will need to be updated to be aligned to the new ISO/IEC 33000 series superseding the ISO/IEC 15504 series.

Another future work will consist in developing a software tool to support companies to perform a self-assessment to determine which ISO 21500 processes have already been implemented and at what capability level.

Acknowledgments. This work has been partially supported by the Spanish Ministry of Science and Technology with ERDF funds under grant TIN2013-46928-C3-2-R.

References

1. ISO 21500:2012 (2012). Guidance on project management
2. Clarke, P., Lepmets, M., McCaffery, F., Finnegan, A., Dorling, A., Flood, D.: MDevS-PICE - a comprehensive solution for manufacturers and assessors of safety-critical medical device software. In: Mitasiunas, A., Rout, T., O'Connor, R.V., Dorling, A. (eds.) SPICE 2014. CCIS, vol. 477, pp. 274–278. Springer, Heidelberg (2014)
3. Clarke, P., Lepmets, M., Dorling, A., McCaffery, F.: Safety critical software process assessment: how MDevSPICE® addresses the challenge of integrating compliance and capability. In: Rout, T., O'Connor, R.V., Dorling, A. (eds.) SPICE 2015. CCIS, vol. 526, pp. 13–18. Springer, Heidelberg (2015)
4. Renault, A., Barafort, B.: TIPA for ITIL - from genesis to maturity of SPICE applied to ITIL 2011. In: Proceedings of the International Conference EuroSPI 2014, Luxembourg (2014)
5. Renault, A., Cortina, S., Barafort, B.: Towards a maturity model for ISO/IEC 20000-1 based on the TIPA for ITIL process capability assessment model. In: Rout, T., O'Connor, R.V., Dorling, A. (eds.) SPICE 2015. CCIS, vol. 526, pp. 188–200. Springer, Heidelberg (2015)
6. Mangin, O., Barafort, B., Heymans, P., Dubois, E.: Designing a Process Reference Model for Information Security Management Systems. In: Mas, A., Mesquida, A., Rout, T., O'Connor, R.V., Dorling, A. (eds.) SPICE 2012. CCIS, vol. 290, pp. 129–140. Springer, Heidelberg (2012)
7. Mesquida, A.L., Mas, A.: Integrating IT service management requirements into the organizational management system. Computer Standards & Interfaces **37**, 80–91 (2015)
8. Mesquida, A.L., Mas, A.: Implementing information security best practices on software lifecycle processes: The ISO/IEC 15504 Security Extension. Computers & Security **48**, 19–34 (2015)
9. Stallinger, F., Plösch, R.: Towards methodological support for the engineering of process reference models for product software. In: Mitasiunas, A., Rout, T., O'Connor, R.V., Dorling, A. (eds.) SPICE 2014. CCIS, vol. 477, pp. 24–35. Springer, Heidelberg (2014)
10. ISO/IEC 15504-5:2012. Information technology - Process assessment - Part 5: An exemplar software life cycle process assessment model (2012)
11. ISO/IEC 15504-6:2013. Information technology - Process assessment - Part 6: An exemplar system life cycle process assessment model (2013)
12. ISO/IEC TS 15504-8:2012. Information technology - Process assessment - Part 8: An exemplar process assessment model for IT service management (2012)
13. Mesquida, A.-L., Mas, A., Lepmets, M., Renault, A.: Development of the project management SPICE (PMSPICE) framework. In: Mitasiunas, A., Rout, T., O'Connor, R.V., Dorling, A. (eds.) SPICE 2014. CCIS, vol. 477, pp. 60–71. Springer, Heidelberg (2014)
14. ISO/IEC 15504-2:2003. Information Technology - Process assessment - Performing an assessment (2003)
15. ISO/IEC TR 15504-7:2008. Information technology - Process assessment - Process assessment - Part 7: Assessment of organizational maturity (2008)
16. Cortina, S., Mayer, N., Renault, A., Barafort, B.: Towards a process assessment model for management system standards. In: Mitasiunas, A., Rout, T., O'Connor, R.V., Dorling, A. (eds.) SPICE 2014. CCIS, vol. 477, pp. 36–47. Springer, Heidelberg (2014)
17. Barafort B., Renault A., Picard M., Cortina S.: A transformation process for building PRMs and PAMs based on a collection of requirements – Example with ISO/IEC 20000. In: Proceedings of the International Conference SPICE 2008, Nuremberg, Germany (2008)

18. MacMahon, S.T., McCaffery, F., Eagles, S., Keenan, F., Lepmets, M., Renault, A.: Development of a process assessment model for assessing medical IT networks against IEC 80001-1. In: Mas, A., Mesquida, A., Rout, T., O'Connor, R.V., Dorling, A. (eds.) SPICE 2012. CCIS, vol. 290, pp. 148–160. Springer, Heidelberg (2012)
19. MacMahon, S.T., McCaffery, Keenan, F.: Transforming requirements of IEC 80001-1 into an ISO/IEC 15504-2 compliant process reference model and process assessment model. In: Proceedings of the International Conference EUROSPI 2013, Dundalk, Ireland (2013)
20. Picard, M., Renault, A., Cortina, S.: How to improve process models for better ISO/IEC 15504 process assessment. In: Riel, A., O'Connor, R., Tichkiewitch, S., Messnarz, R. (eds.) EuroSPI 2010. CCIS, vol. 99, pp. 130–141. Springer, Heidelberg (2010)
21. Mangin, O., Mayer, N., Barafort, B., Heymans, P., Dubois, E.: An Improvement of Process Reference Model Design and Validation Using Business Process Management. In: Woronowicz, T., Rout, T., O'Connor, R.V., Dorling, A. (eds.) SPICE 2013. CCIS, vol. 349, pp. 73–83. Springer, Heidelberg (2013)
22. ISO/IEC TR 24774:2010. Systems and software engineering - Life cycle management - Guidelines for process description (2010)
23. ISO/IEC 33004:2015. Information Technology - Process assessment - Requirements for process reference, process assessment and maturity models (2015)

Blending Process Assessment and Employees Competencies Assessment in Very Small Entities

Vincent Ribaud[1] and Rory V. O'Connor[2(✉)]

[1] Lab-STICC, Université de Brest, Brest, France
ribaud@univ-brest.fr
[2] Dublin City University, Dublin, Ireland
roconnor@computing.dcu.ie

Abstract. The ISO/IEC 29110 series aims to provide Very Small Entities (VSEs) with a set of standards based on subsets of existing standards. Process capability determination does not seem suitable for a VSE in terms of return on investment. Our approach moves the viewpoint away from process and to the human resources. We propose a blended assessment model using the ISO/IEC 15504 for the level 1, but based on competency assessment for higher levels.

Keywords: Small entities · Process assessment · Competency framework

1   Introduction

Since 2011 the ISO/IEC 29110 [1] series provides Very Small Entities – VSE (up to 25 people) with a set of standards establishing a framework for software life cycle processes and helping VSEs in achieving capability recognition of their processes. A requirement for the Working Group 24 (of which the authors are members) mandated to develop the 29110 series was that processes should be assessed using ISO/IEC 15504 [2] approach. A meta-analysis [3] about case studies reporting process improvement approaches for 122 SMEs states that the ISO/IEC15504 model was used only in 9% of the reported improvement efforts, which would tend to support that a 15504-based approach for VSE process assessment may not be the most appropriate approach. Accordingly, the first research question addressed in this paper is: How small organizations or projects can use the ISO/IEC 29110 standard to effectively monitor their progress and to evaluate their performance?

Competency frameworks, such as the e-Competences Framework [4] focus on professional skills rather than organizational and technical processes. We propose that such information will be found more relevant by VSEs staff and furthermore that competency assessment helps ICT professionals by developing the right skills and by deploying them to best effect, it will, in time, improve understanding and performing software processes. Thus we define a second research question: How can we relate VSE process performance with employees' competencies proficiency?

Section 2 overviews background work and section 3 Process Assessment Models. In section 4, we present a Competency Assessment Model for VSEs, and then we conclude the paper.

© Springer International Publishing Switzerland 2015
R.V. O'Connor et al. (Eds.): EuroSPI 2015, CCIS 543, pp. 206–219, 2015.
DOI: 10.1007/978-3-319-24647-5_17

2   Background and Related Work

2.1   Standard Background

The documents in the ISO/IEC 29110 series are referred to as VSE profiles (organized within Groups) [5] and are based on subsets of appropriate standards elements, which are relevant to the VSE context such as processes and outcomes of ISO/IEC 12207 [6] and products of ISO/IEC 15289 [7]. The Basic Profile describes software development of a single application by a single project team with no special risk or situations factors [1]. The Basic Profile yields a comprehensive set of life cycle processes, activities and tasks, with input and output work products. The starting point for a VSE aiming to establish conformance to a profile is the use a Process Assessment Model, suitable for the purpose of assessing process capability, based on the targeted profile. One result presented in this paper is to formally exhibit the underlying Process Reference Model (PRM) contained into the ISO/IEC 29110 Basic Profile documents, and to propose a Process Assessment Model for the capability level 1.

A competency framework is intended to foster the development of skills, either by individuals or organizations. The European e-Competence Framework (www. ecompetences.eu/) is a reference framework of 40 ICT competences that can be used and understood by ICT stakeholders [4]. A competence is *"a demonstrated ability to apply knowledge, skills and attitudes to achieving observable results [8]."*

Following the recommended ISO/IEC 15504 approach, a Process Assessment Model (PAM) will expand the Basic Profile PRM by adding the definition and use of assessment indicators, either process performance indicators or process capability indicators. The latter are, in our opinion, too complex and too far from day-to-day VSE concerns. Our approach proposes to move the viewpoint from process perspective to human resource (i.e. the VSE staff). Job profiles contain many components describing the essential elements of a job and how it should be performed. Jobs profiles provide a bridge between enterprises and individuals, and establish the link between an organization processes and employees' competencies. It is our proposition that VSE employees should be motivated by competencies assessment related to their job profiles. It is also considered that assessing employees' competencies provide a correct indication of the VSE maturity as long as process and competency framework are correctly aligned.

2.2   Related Work

A lot of research has been performed on software process assessment for small companies based either on ISO/IEC 15504 [10, 11, 12, 13] or CMMI [14, 15, 16]. Almost all approaches aims to minimize the assessment time or are reducing the number of assessed processes or the number of resources involved. Several approaches are using process-area interviews (or questionnaires) as the central stage to collect evidences of process achievement. In [17], the authors propose the development of a novel process assessment model for VSEs using the ISO/IEC 29110. The proposed PRM is similar to ours, expected that base practices are extracted from ISO/IEC 15504-5 and based on the mapping to ISO/IEC 12207 outcomes. They limit the assessment model to process performance indicators, excluding capability levels higher than level 1. We are not aware of other research performed on software process assessment based on ISO 29110.

3   Process Assessment Model

3.1   A Process Reference Model for VSEs

ISO/IEC 12207 and 15504. ISO/IEC 12207:2008 Clause 7 describes software-specific processes in terms of Title, Purpose, Outcomes, Activities and Tasks. ISO/IEC 15504:2004 separates process and capability levels in two dimensions [2]. In the process dimension, individual processes are described in terms of Process Title, Process Purpose, and Process Outcomes as defined in ISO/IEC 12207. In addition to this PRM, the 15504 process dimension provides a set of Base Practices (BP); a number of input and output Work Products (WP); and characteristics associated with each work product [2].

ISO/IEC 29110 Basic Profile Processes. The Basic Profile [5] is made of 2 processes: Project Management (PM) and Software Implementation (SI). Processes are described with: Name; Purpose; Objectives; Input, output, and internal products; Roles involved; Activities list and activities description. Clause 7 contains the specification of the standardized profiles and its conceptual model is represented in Figure 1. Clause 8 establishes the reference between the 29110 elements and the source standards [18] and its conceptual model is also represented in Figure 1.

As pointed out in [17], ISO/IEC 29110-4-1 cannot be considered as a Process Reference Model (PRM) per se, but the ISO/IEC 29110 set of documents is containing all materials required to build a PRM for the Basic Profile. A PRM is *a model comprising definitions of processes in a life cycle described in terms of process purpose and outcomes, together with an architecture describing the relationships between the processes* [2]." ISO/IEC 29110-4-1 provides the architecture and processes purposes. We only lack of outcomes and we created process outcomes using 12207 process outcomes referenced by each 29110 objective. This appears in Figure 1 with a dotted dependence link between 29110 and 12207 outcomes. The PRM we built is available at http://29110.univ-brest.fr/en.nexus.

3.2   A Process Assessment Model for VSEs

ISO/IEC 15504. The capability dimension consists of six capability levels and nine Process Attributes (PA) for levels 1 to 5. A process attribute is *a measurable characteristic of process capability applicable to any process* [2].". The ISO/IEC 15504 approach indicates that a Process Reference Model lacks of level of detail for conducting consistent and reliable assessments. Therefore, a) the PRM needs to be supported with a comprehensive set of indicators of process performance; and b) the capability levels and process attributes need to be supported with a set of indicators of process capability.

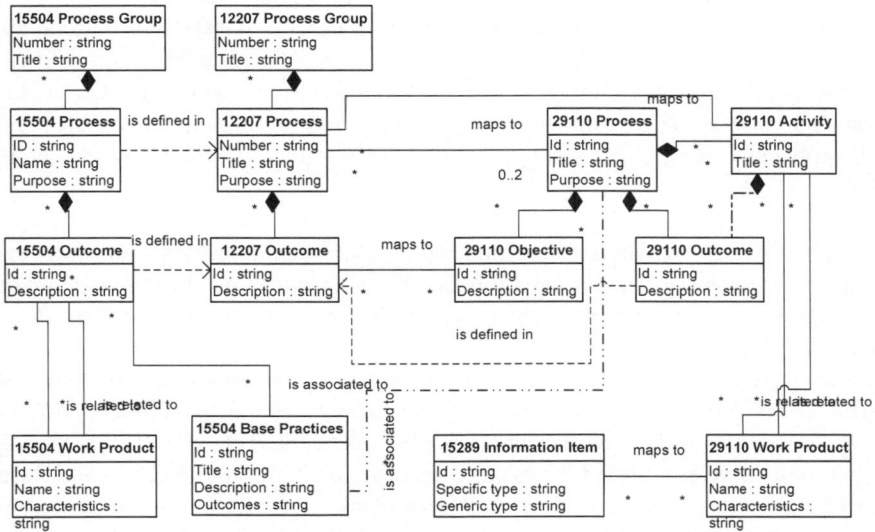

Fig. 1. Structure of 15504, 12207, 29110 standards and of their relationships.

A Deployment Package (DP) is a set of artifacts developed to facilitate the implementation of the ISO/IEC 29110 series. DPs are provided, at no cost, by a network of centers to support VSEs. Our research results use the set of available Deployment Packages to provide the set of indicators of process performance. In order to prepare our contribution to an Assessment Model for VSEs (see next section), we present in the left part of Figure 1, the conceptual model of the ISO/IEC 15504 Process assessment, mainly 15504 processes, outcomes, base practices and work products. The ISO/IEC 15504-5 provides an exemplar model for performing process assessments that is based upon and directly compatible with the Process Reference Model in ISO/IEC 12207. References appear in Figure 1 with a dotted dependence link between 15504 and 12207 elements.

ISO/IEC 15504 Performance Indicators. ISO/IEC 15504 states the result of successful implementation of process assessment: information and data that characterize the processes assessed is determined; the extent to which the processes achieve the process purpose is determined [2, Part 2]. This extent is derived from the process attributes ratings for an assessed process. The extent of achievement of a process attribute is measured on a scale using values: N Not achieved, 0 to 15 % achievement; P Partially achieved, > 15 % to 50 % achievement; L Largely achieved, > 50 % to 85% achievement; F Fully achieved, > 85 % to 100 % achievement.

Capability Level 0 denotes an incomplete process. Capability Level 1 denotes a performed process. Higher levels denote higher process maturity: the process is managed (Level 2), established (Level 3), predictable (Level 4), optimizing (Level 5).

Performing its business processes is the main concern of a VSE. That means that a VSE's main (and may be the unique one) goal in a Process Assessment is to be assessed at Capability Level 1 for each selected process. Therefore helping a VSE to perform process through a Capability Level 1 assessment will probably retain its attention and raise some investment. The rating of process performance indicators, which apply exclusively to capability level 1, should motivate VSEs. These indicators are BPs and WPs.

ISO 29110 Process Attributes. Our first research question is asking how small organizations or projects can use the ISO/IEC 29110 standard to effectively monitor their progress and to evaluate their performance. Our answer is to focus on Base Practices and Work Products indicators.

Specifying BPs and WPs for the Basic Profile is submitted to the problem that ISO/IEC 29110 process granularity is too broad and we will specify BPs and WPs at the 29110 activity level. In an earlier work [19] about ISO/IEC 29110 Process Assessment Issues, we established the reduced set of ISO/IEC 15504 Processes and Base Practices that are related to 29110 Processes and Objectives thanks to a mapping between ISO 15504 BPs and 29110 processes. The merge of this earlier work and the work presented should be the basis to build an exemplar process assessment model for VSEs. This model shifts the viewpoint from process assessment to activity. Following this point of view, our contribution is to propose in the next section a set of BPs for each ISO/IEC 29110 activities.

ISO 29110 Performances Indicators. In Part 5-1-2 [18], each activity is associated with a set of constitutive tasks that shall be considered as Base Practices. 6 Deployment Packages are provided with the Basic Profile. DP 1 [21] covers the whole Project Management Process; DPs 2 to 6 [22] cover all of the activities of Software Implementation Process. We carefully examined DPs 1 to 6, which cover the majority of the Basic Profile activities. Almost none excepted DP Software Design is using the standardized tasks decomposition and almost all – DP Software Design excepted - are providing alternative activity decomposition with input and output WPs. The analysis is available at http://29110.univ-brest.fr/en.nexus/index.php/AAB

Each corresponding DP provides a task decomposition – although not standardized – and for each task, a step-by-step guideline to perform the task. Formally, the term 'task' should not be used in DPs and we will call 'sub-activity' the elements of the alternative activity decomposition provided in DPs.

Once the 4-level decomposition is established for the Basic Profile, we can map this decomposition with the 15504 Exemplar Process Assessment Model. Thus, sub-activities play an equivalent role than 15504 Base Practices. Hence, within PM and SI processes, each activity will be assessed at Capability Level 1 on the basis of two Process Performance Indicators: Sub-activities and Work Product. This is an answer element to research question 1 - regarding using ISO 29110 for progress monitoring and performance evaluation - because evidence of performance of the sub-activities, and the presence of work products with their expected work product characteristics, provide objective evidence of the achievement of the purpose of the activities.

Performing a Basic Profile Assessment. The ISO/IEC 15504 distinguishes between two different classes of indicators: indicators of process performance - related to the Base Practices and Work Products, and indicators of process capability - related to the management practices. BPs and WPs are the heart and the soul of a software lifecycle and the minimal maturity level of a VSE imply to perform a suitable set of BPs and WPs. Management practices relate to the process attributes grouped into capability levels 2-5. Process capability determination seem not suitable from a VSE point of view: the return on investment is too long, the recommendations are highly complex, and process improvement projects require a large investments in terms of budget, timeframe and resources.

A lot of work has been done in relation to tailoring process assessment for VSEs, mainly by reducing the number of processes assessed [23], the number of conceivable capability levels [24], or the burden of the assessment task [16]. A base practice is a work performance that addresses the purpose of a particular process (an activity). Base practices are described at an abstract level, identifying "what" should be done without specifying "how". Consistently performing base practices associated with a process / activity will help the consistent achievement of its purpose. While DPs are providing a step-by-step guide for each DP, we can use it as a guide to "how" implement the activity. That is another answer element to research question 1 because it provides VSEs with a way of doing activities, motivating them to achieve activities at Capability Level 1.

4   Competency Assessment Model

4.1   Overview

This section is intended to examine research question 2 and presents some potential resolving issues. This work proposes an alternative way of assessing capability, profiled from the ISO/IEC 15504 for the capability level 1, but based on competency assessment for higher capability levels. In our opinion, frontier between the VSE – as an organization – maturity and VSE employees' proficiency is thin and porous. VSE strength and weakness are closely related to its staff performance and it may be reasonable to suggest that assessing employees' proficiency will give a good indication of VSE performance so long as the competency assessment framework is closely related to VSE business and needs. Therefore, this is the proposal we put forward for answering to research question 2 and the results proposed in the rest of this paper need to be validated through several studies.

4.2   Reference Models

Models Architecture. The European e-Competence Framework is based on a four-dimensional approach, based on competence areas (dimension 1) and competences (dimension 2). Dimension 3 provides level assignments that are appropriate to each competence. Dimension 4 provides short sample of knowledge and skills. Dimension 1 is composed of 5 e-Competence areas that reflect the ICT Business process and its main sub-processes, from a broad perspective. Dimension 1 is mapped to 12207 Process Group, to 15504 Process Group and to 29110 Processes (because they have a very broad scope). Dimension 2 identifies and describes a set of key e-Competences for each area. We established the mapping between e-Competences and Life Cycle Processes by comparing the e-Competences titles, generic descriptions and skill examples with the Processes titles, purposes and activities and tasks (12207) or Base Practices (15504). We reduced the e-CF to the software perspective because it is the scope of the ISO/IEC 12207 standard. Dimension 4 is populated with samples of knowledge and skills related to e-Competences in dimension 2. They are provided to add value and context and are not intended to be exhaustive. Conversely, Base Practices are supporting the process and are exhaustive. Accordingly Base Practices and sub-activities cannot be mapped with skills but all these concepts form the third level of the reference models. In next sections, we will see that an exhaustive list of skills within a role is essential to competency assessment.

Activities and e-Competences. There are different views of what the ICT profession is and no common agreement regarding a shared body of knowledge, especially for VSEs. The purpose of the ISO/IEC 29110 Basic Profile is to provide the minimal subset of ISO/IEC 12207 processes, thus we may use this to obtain a minimal subset of e-Competences for a VSE. The complete mapping between e-Competences and ISO/IEC 12207 processes provides us with a starting point upon we established a mapping between ISO/IEC 29110 activities and e-Competences. We produced the mapping between e-Competences and ISO/IEC 29110 activities by carefully comparing the e-Competences titles and generic descriptions with the activities descriptions. To clarify ambiguities, it was necessary to compare the scope of skills examples in Dimension 4 with tasks lists of activities and the corresponding DP materials. The mapping is at http://29110.univ-brest.fr/en.nexus/index.php/E-C_Mapping.

4.3   Using the e-CF for ISO/IEC 29110

Rationale. In section 2.1, we stated that process capability indicators are too far from day-to-day VSE concerns and we proposed to focus on job profiles. Job profiles or roles "*add to job descriptions by including additional job related components such as mission, main tasks, accountability, requested deliverables, Key Performance Indicator's etc. In this context a job profile provides a comprehensive description written and formal of a job* [9]". Job profiles establish the link between an organization processes and employees' competencies. Our proposition is that VSE employees should be motivated by competencies assessment and will accept the long return of investment, the high complexity and the required commitment and effort because they will be the main beneficiaries of this assessment.

Roles and Job Profiles. Roles are defined inside ISO/IEC 29110 activities description [18], as function to be performed by project team members. Different roles are: PM Project Manager, TL Technical Leader, AN Analyst, DES Designer, and PR Programmer. A single person may play several roles and several persons may assume one role. Roles competencies are drafted [18]. Thus, it was straightforward to establish the pivotal place of roles between software activities and competences, http://29110.univ-brest.fr/en.nexus/index.php/Roles_and_e-C. As a response to the huge number of ICT profile frameworks and profile descriptions, the CEN Workshop Agreement "European ICT Profile" defines a number of representative ICT profiles covering the full ICT business. Each profile defines a mission statement, a list of required e-competences to carry the mission, a list of deliverables, a list of tasks and some Key Performance Indicators (KPI). There are four ICT profiles that correspond to the five 29110 roles. The associated e-competences with the required proficiency level are presented in Table 1.

Proficiency Level. Proficiency can be defined as a level of being capable or proficient in a specific knowledge, skill domain expertise or competence [8] and is related to job performance. Proficiency indicates a degree of mastery that allows an individual to function independently in her/his job. In the e-CF, proficiency levels are described along three facets [8]: Autonomy ranging between "Responding to instructions" and "Making personal choices"; Context complexity ranging between "Structured-Predictable situations" and "Unpredictable-Unstructured situations"; Behavior ranging between "Ability to apply" and "Ability to conceive".

Completing the e-CF Dimension 4. Roles competencies shall be completed with their required proficiency level. Once an e-Competence required within a role, it is possible to establish an exhaustive list of knowledge and skills. However, a detailed description of required skills is missing in the e-CF but is needed to be able to assess the proficiency level. Establishing Basic Profile roles and specializing required e-Competences knowledge and skills is an exhaustive work that will be proposed to the WG24, and may provide a new part of ISO/IEC 29110 for each profile, dedicated to roles and competencies.

Our pragmatic approach is to define e-Competences skills within a role, but a useful synthesis will be to gather all knowledge and skills related to the same e-Competence through the different Basic Profile roles, in order to have at one's disposal a centralized definition of each e-Competence related to the Basic Profile.

Table 1. Profiles based on e-CF 3.0

ICT Profile Title	e-Competences 3.0	Level
Project Manager (PM)	A.4. Product / Service Planning	4
	E.2. Project and Portfolio Management	4
	E.3. Risk Management	4
	E.4. Relationship Management	3
	E.7 Business Change Management	3
System Architect (TL)	A.5. Architecture Design	4
	A.7. Technology Watching	4-5
	B.1. Design and Development	4-5
	B.2. System Integration	4
System Analyst (AN / DES)	A.6. Application Design	3
	E.5. Process Improvement	3-4
	B.1. Design and Development	3-4
Developer (PR)	B.1. Design and Development	3
	B.2. System Integration	2
	B.3. Testing	2
	B.5. Documentation production	3
	C.4. Problem Management	3

4.4   Performing a Proficiency Level Assessment

Rationale. While proficiency assessment is performed within a role, it allows the VSE to select the adequate skills from the whole framework. For instance, if programmers do not hold the test process, B.3 Testing will be reduced to skills B.3.6 and B.3.7. Proficiency levels are related to job performance and as mentioned in previous section proficiency levels are described along three facets: Autonomy, Context complexity, and Behavior. Despite the detailed skills added to e-competences, the scope is still very broad and we need to go further in details to understand the proficiency level and our proposal is to add outcomes to each skill of each e-competences. Outcomes are worded in operational terms.

Competence Reference Framework. Table 2 presents excerpts of the framework for the skills of e-Competence B.1. Design and Development. Each skill has a purpose and a set of outcomes, expressed in term of "be able to know" or "to be able to do".

Rating Outcomes. Each skill is described as a set of cohesive outcomes. Our rating scheme is based on the assessment of each VSE employee about her/his achievement of outcomes. We use the N-P-L-F scale of ISO/IEC 15504. When an employee states that an outcome is Largely and Fully achieved, he/she is supposed to accompany the rating by objective evidence, generally a product that he/she produced or contributed to. When all outcomes of a general goal are rated at L or F, the skill should be rated at the same rating.

Table 2. e-Competence B.1 outcomes

B.1. Design and development
B.1.3. Establish a detailed design, including a database schema
• To detail SW components and interfaces • To detail and update the SW design document • To normalize a database schema and to understand the normalization impact on queries performances • To perform human-centred design activities
B.1.5. Develop batch modules interacting with the database
• To understand the difference between the SQL set model and a procedural language model • To grasp procedural constructs and their execution conditions • To master the development of procedural constructs and the exception handling mechanism • To develop and perform unit testing, including a regression test strategy • To manage the backup, storage, archiving, handling and delivery of configured items

Rating Proficiency Level. When all skills of an e-competence are rated at L or F, the e-competence is considered to be achieved, but the proficiency level needs to be established. The e-CF uses a 5-point ordinal scale from e-1 to e-5 (e-5 is rarely used). Due to an alignment with European Community directives, level 2 is divided in 2 sublevels: 2-A and 2-B. The hypothesis is made that VSE employees will commit in a self-assessment. As mentioned in this section overview, the hypothesis is also made that assessing employees' competencies provide a correct indication of the VSE maturity as long as process and competency framework are correctly aligned. Challenges of this approach are related to provide a straightforward competency framework with a lightweight competency assessment approach and a precise and correct alignment between process models and competency framework.

4.5   A Case Study

We trialed this approach through the PR role mobilizing 7 skills: B.1.2 Preliminary design, B.1.3 Detailed design, B.1.4 Develop SQL scripts, B.1.5 Develop batch modules, B.3.6 Conduct tests, B.3.7 Report tests, B.5.4 Documentation. A 4-week vocational education training session on information system development under the ISO/IEC 29110 Basic Profile has been used to measure the attendees' proficiency level and to relate it to 29110 processes used in teamwork. A total 21 students in the 2nd year of an MSc programme in Information Technology participated in a 4 week training exercise building small an information system. 36 hours of lectures and practical labs were performed along the skills: B.1.2, B.1.3, B.1.4, B.1.5, B.3.6, B.3.7, and B.5.4. The remaining time is devoted to a capstone project performed by teams of 3-4 attendees. There were 14 female students and 7 male students, all coming from different Moroccan universities. The mean age is 23 years with a low standard deviation.

For each skill, each attendee self-assessed their achievement of outcomes on the N-P-L-F scale. In order to get averages, numerical values are associated with N-P-L-F values - don't know: 0%, N: 15%, P: 50%, L: 85%, F: 100%. A skill is valued with the average of its outcomes values. We gathered values for each team, where each team's general goal value is the average of its members' values. Table 3 presents the assessment for the 6 teams and the whole set of attendees; the last line is the overall average, and represents teams' self-esteem. Team average is roughly the same, except for team B that is probably over-estimating itself.

Table 3. Teams' self-assessment of PR role.

Skill	A	B	C	D	E	F	All
B.1.2 Preliminary design	0,68	0,69	0,78	0,81	0,85	0,69	0,75
B.1.3 Detailed design	0,51	0,69	0,72	0,56	0,43	0,63	0,58
B.1.4 Develop SQL scripts	0,37	0,63	0,42	0,48	0,42	0,46	0,47
B.1.5 Develop batch modules	0,39	0,68	0,20	0,29	0,41	0,34	0,40
B.3.6 Conduct tests	0,22	0,59	0,15	0,15	0,24	0,24	0,28
B.3.7 Report tests	0,22	0,29	0,38	0,27	0,33	0,33	0,30
B.5.4 Documentation	0,33	0,29	0,15	0,62	0,20	0,24	0,30
Team avg.	0,31	0,49	0,32	0,34	0,32	0,36	0,36

During the training session, we collected individual observations from attendees regarding autonomy, context complexity and behavior. The autonomy of each attendee was the easiest thing to observe. Behavior observations were mostly performed while reviewing the work products issued by teams; hence it was more difficult to assign it individually. Context complexity was not relevant in this case, because all teams are developing the same software from the same requirements specification. Nevertheless, using the self-assessment, and our observations, we assessed each attendee's skill at a proficiency level 1, 2-A or 2-B. Table 4 presents this proficiency assessment with (x,y,z) where x is the number of team members at level 1; y at level 2-A and z at level 2-B.

Table 4. Teams' proficiency assessment.

Skill	A	B	C	D	E	F
B.1.2 Preliminary design	(0,3,0)	(0,4,0)	(0,2,1)	(0,1,2)	(0,2,2)	(0,1,3)
B.1.3 Detailed design	(2,1,0)	(2,2,0)	(0,2,1)	(0,3,0)	(3,1,0)	(1,2,1)
B.1.4 Develop SQL scripts	(3,0,0)	(1,2,1)	(2,1,0)	(1,2,0)	(3,1,0)	(2,2,0)
B.1.5 Develop batch modules	(3,0,0)	(1,2,1)	(3,0,0)	(2,1,0)	(3,1,0)	(1,2,1)
B.3.6 Conduct tests	(3,0,0)	(4,0,0)	(0,3,0)	(0,3,0)	(1,3,0)	(1,3,0)
B.3.7 Report tests	(2,1,0)	(2,2,0)	(0,3,0)	(0,3,0)	(0,3,1)	(0,3,1)
B.5.4 Documentation	(3,0,0)	(4,0,0)	(2,1,0)	(0,2,1)	(2,1,1)	(2,2,0)

In relation to the capstone project, the life cycle processes were extracted from ISO/IEC 29110. The schedule is roughly: one week for architectural design (including the problem understanding), one week for detailed design, two weeks of development (including end-user documentation), and one day for qualifying the software. Hence, teams are concerned with three ISO/IEC 29110 activities: Design, Construction, Integration and Tests. We assessed each team's activity capability level using the standard ISO/IEC 15504 scheme. Capability level 1 is measured with the PA 1.1 Process performance attribute. Capability level 2 is measured with the PA 2.1 Performance management attribute and the PA 2.2 Work product management attribute. Table 5 presents the assessment results.

Table 5. Teams' processes assessment.

	A	B	C	D	E	F
SI.3 SW Architectural and Detailed Design						
PA 2.1	N	N	N	P	P	L
PA 2.2	P	P	P	L	L	L
PA 1.1	P	P	L	L	F	L
SI.4 SW Construction						
PA 2.1	N	N	N	P	P	P
PA 2.2	P	P	P	P	P	P
PA 1.1	P	L	L	L	F	F
SI.5 SW Integration and Tests						
PA 2.1	N	N	N	P	P	L
PA 2.2	P	P	L	L	L	L
PA 1.1	P	L	L	L	F	F

We may correlate the capability level achieved by a team (Table 4) with the team proficiency level (Table 5). The correlation is working well for the SI.3 Design activity, except for team B. The correlation is not working for all teams with the SI.4 Construction activity that is not surprising because development is probably the most unpredictable activity. The correlation is working roughly for the SI.5 Integration activity, but we suspect that B.3.6 and B.3.7 form only a part of the set of skills required to perform the Integration tasks.

This case study is still encouraging; however three issues require further work. To reduce the complexity, we worked within a unique role but the association between activities and skills should work through the different Basic Profile roles. The second issue is related to the proficiency level assessment that has to be more objectively defined. The third issue is concerned with the graduation of different skills that are not of equal importance for a given activity and we should probably weight the skills with a coefficient. Resolving these issues requires us to build the complete model and to validate it through several pilot studies in VSEs.

5   Perspectives and Conclusion

The next major step will be to develop the approach for all ISO/IEC 29110 roles and validate each role through a series of pilot projects in VSEs. The aim of our research was to contribute to an exemplar Process Assessment Model (PAM) suitable for VSEs, related to a Process Reference Model (PRM) of the Basic Profile. The exemplar PAM expands the Basic Profile PRM by adding the definition and use of assessment indicators. We proposed to add an additional level to the ISO/IEC 29110 by dividing each activity in sub-activity playing a role similar to ISO/IEC 15504 Base Practices. These sub-activities were extracted of the different Deployment Package provided by a network of VSE support centers. Sub-activities and Work Products will be used as process performance indicators and permit a VSE to be assessed at Capability Level 1. For higher capability levels, we proposed to replace process capability determination with competency proficiency level assessment. Proficiency indicates a degree of mastery that allows an individual to function independently in the performance of a specific knowledge application, skill domain, expertise or competence.

We proposed to add to the ISO/IEC 29110 roles definition a set of e-Competences mobilized with their required proficiency level. Then we established an exhaustive list of skills for each e-Competence and we associated a set of outcomes to each skill of each e-Competence. Self-rating is devoted to VSE employees and proficiency level determination will be performed by external assessors. We made the proposal that as main beneficiaries of competency assessment, they will accept to self-assess each outcome on a classical N-P-L-F scale, conducting to rate each skill. Through an external assessment, VSE employees will contribute to establish a proficiency level for each e-Competence that will replace process capability determination. It is assumed that it provides an indication of the VSE organizational maturity, but this has to be proven through several case studies.

References

1. ISO/IEC 29110-1:2011. Software Engineering – Lifecycle profiles for Very Small Entities – Part 1: Overview. ISO, Geneva (2011)
2. ISO/IEC 15504:2004. Information technology – Process assessment – Part 1: Concepts and vocabulary. ISO, Geneva (2004)
3. Pino, F.J., Piattini, M.: Software process improvement in small and medium software enterprises: a systematic review. Software Quality Control **16**(2), 237–261 (2008)
4. CEN. CWA 16234-1:2014. European e-Competence Framework 3.0- Part 1: A Common European Framework for ICT Professionals in All Industry Sectors. CEN (2014)
5. ISO/IEC 29110-4-1:2011. SE – Lifecycle profiles for VSE – Part 4-1: Generic profile group. ISO, Geneva (2011)
6. ISO/IEC 12207:2008. IT – Software life cycle processes. ISO, Geneva (2008)
7. ISO/IEC 15289:2006. Systems and SE – Content of life cycle process information products. ISO, Geneva (2006)
8. CEN. CWA 16234-2:2014 - Part 2: User guidelines for the application of the European e-CF 3.0. CEN (2014)

9. CEN. CWA 16458:2012. European ICT Professional Profiles. CEN, Bruxelles (2012)
10. von Wangenheim, C.G., Anacleto, A., Salviano, C.F.: Helping Small Companies Assess Software Processes. IEEE Software **23**(1), 91–98 (2006)
11. Cater-Steel, A.P.: Process improvement in four small software companies. In: Proc. of the 13th Australian Conf. on Soft. Engineering, p. 262 (2001)
12. Rout, T.P., Tuffley, A., Cahill, B., Hodgen B.: The rapid assessment of software process capability. In: Proceedings of SPICE 2000. pp. 47–55 (2000)
13. Oktaba, H., Garcia, F., Piattini, M., Ruiz, F., Pino, F.J., Alquicira, C.: Software Process Improvement: The Competisoft Project. Computer **40**(10), 21–28 (2007)
14. Grunbacher, P.: A software assessment process for small software enterprises. In: Proc. of the 23rd EUROMICRO Conference, pp. 123–128 (1997)
15. Mc Caffery, F., Taylor, P.S., Coleman, G.: Adept: A Unified Assessment Method for Small Software Companies. IEEE Soft. **24**(1), 24–31 (2007)
16. Habra, N., Alexandre, S., Desharnais, J.M., Laporte, C.Y., Renault, A.: Initiating software process improvement in very small enterprises Experience with a light assessment tool. Information and Software Technology **50**, 763–771 (2008)
17. Varkoi, T.: Process Assessment In Very Small Entities - An ISO/IEC 29110 Based Method. Quality of Information and Communications Technology, 436–440 (2010)
18. ISO/IEC TR 29110-5-1-2:2011. SE – Lifecycle profiles for VSEs – Part 5-1-2: Management and engineering guide: Basic profile. ISO, Geneva (2011)
19. Ribaud, V., Saliou, P.: Process Assessment Issues of the ISO-IEC 29110 emerging standard. In: Proc. of the Profes Conf. ACM Press, NY (2010)
20. Alexandre, S., Laporte, C.Y.: Deployment Package - SW Requirement Analysis. CETIC, Charleroi. http://profs.etsmtl.ca/claporte/VSE (last accessed July 13, 2010)
21. O'Connor, Rory V., Laporte, Claude Y.: Deploying Lifecycle Profiles for Very Small Entities: An Early Stage Industry View. In: O'Connor, Rory V., Rout, Terry, McCaffery, Fergal, Dorling, Alec (eds.) SPICE 2011. CCIS, vol. 155, pp. 227–230. Springer, Heidelberg (2011)
22. Deployment packages. http://profs.etsmtl.ca/claporte/VSE (last accessed July 2015)
23. Kuvaja, P., Palo, J., Bicego, A.: TAPISTRY—A Software Process Improvement Approach Tailored for Small Enterprises. Software Quality Journal **8**, 149–156 (1999)
24. Pino, F.J., Pardo, C., Gracia, F., Piattini, M.: Assessment methodology for software process improvement in small organizations. Information and Software Technology **50**, 1044–1061 (2010)

Extending SPICE for Safety Focused Systems Engineering Process Assessment

Timo Varkoi[1(✉)] and Risto Nevalainen[2]

[1] Finnish Software Measurement Association – FiSMA ry, Espoo, Finland
timo.varkoi@fisma.fi
[2] Spinet Oy, Espoo, Finland
risto.nevalainen@spinet.fi

Abstract. Issues in systems engineering will increasingly affect our everyday life. One approach to address the increasing concerns in systems and software engineering are process assessments. Systems engineering approach is more relevant because it covers both software and systems viewpoints. This paper discusses systems and software engineering related process assessments in safety-critical domains, including nuclear, automotive and medical devices. We analyse the key stakeholder requirements related to a safety-critical domain, using nuclear domain as an example. We propose that the SPICE framework should be extended to take into account also safety demonstration and conformity with requirements use cases. Balance with product evaluation is essential to achieve this.

Keywords: Systems engineering · Process assessment · Safety · SPICE

1 Introduction

As systems grow in size and complexity, also concerns of their safety increases. Effect of future development, especially Internet of Things, will most likely mean that computer-based systems, including their software elements, are the key in creating and maintaining a safe environment for human life. Issues in systems engineering will easily affect our everyday life.

One approach to address the increasing concerns in systems and software engineering are process assessments. Standards for software process assessment date back to 1990's. Based on those ideas, process assessments have spread to other disciplines like systems engineering, services and governance.

The existing SPICE framework [1] is based on two main purposes and use cases: process improvement and process capability determination. There is a strong focus in process capability, which means the ability of processes to meet business goals. It works well for generic software engineering, when applied in parallel with quality management standards like ISO9001. Complex systems engineering and development of safety-critical systems might require consideration of other process aspects.

We propose that the SPICE framework should be extended to include also use cases for safety demonstration and conformity with requirements. Also the focus

© Springer International Publishing Switzerland 2015
R.V. O'Connor et al. (Eds.): EuroSPI 2015, CCIS 543, pp. 220–229, 2015.
DOI: 10.1007/978-3-319-24647-5_18

should be systems engineering instead of software engineering, when dealing with safety issues.

Next, in chapter 2 we clarify safety in systems and software engineering. Chapter 3 shortly describes process assessments in some safety-critical domains, including nuclear, automotive and medical devices. In chapter 4 we discuss safety-critical domain requirements for a process assessment model, using nuclear domain as an example. Chapter 5 presents the extended use cases for process assessment. Finally, chapter 6 summarizes our findings and conclusions.

2 Engineering Approach for Systems and Safety

Safety can be considered as a system or software property. We can apply safety requirements in engineering of both systems and software. However, in safety-critical domains, safety systems ensure safe operation and shutdown of an operational system e.g. a plant, reactor, vehicle or equipment. In safety systems, safety is regularly considered in relation to the system as a whole. Therefore, dealing with highest safety-criticality demands systems engineering approach.

Software process assessment covers insufficiently systems engineering perspective. A software system can be seen as a system element of a larger system. Typically, all safety-critical systems have also other than software elements. A software-intensive system (Fig. 1) could be considered as a system, in which most of the requirements are satisfied with software.

Software-intensive system

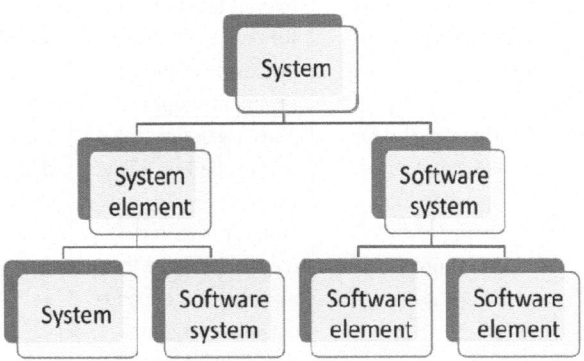

Fig. 1. Concept of a software-intensive system

However, part of the requirements are system specific and therefore systems engineering approach is more relevant and can cover both software and systems viewpoints.

3   Process Assessments in Safety-Critical Domains

3.1   Generic Assessment Requirements

Generally, process assessment is utilized for two purposes: to determine the capability of the processes for particular requirements or to gain understanding of an organization's own processes for process improvement. Determination of process capability aims to objectively resolve the state of the processes against a given set of requirements. These requirements express the necessary attributes of the processes and are typically documented in a Process Assessment Model (PAM). Often capability determination is carried out by a party external to the assessed organization and the result can be used for supplier selection or organization's recognition. Capability determination can also be used as an input for process improvement (Figure 3).

Formal process assessments are well documented and guidance is available for lead assessors to apply specific Process Assessment Models. Assessor competency requirements include education, training and experience. This is one way to ensure that assessment results are comparable. One major benefit of the assessment approach is that it leads to a systematic walk-through of organization's processes.

A process assessment shall be performed according to a class of assessment, as specified in ISO/IEC 33002 standard [2]. Typical factors that determine the selection of the assessment class include rigour, confidence, repeatability and costs. Three classes of assessment and their characteristics are identified in Table 1.

Table 1. Characteristics of Classes of Assessment [2]

Aspect	Class 1	Class 2	Class 3
Purpose	Results are suited for comparisons across different organizations.	Results indicate the overall level of performance of the key processes in the assessment scope.	Results provide a general indication of process rating.
Requirements for lead assessor	Two assessors who are independent of the organizational unit being assessed, one of whom shall be a lead assessor.	Two assessors, one of whom shall be a lead assessor. Note: It is recommended that the lead assessor is independent of the organizational unit being assessed.	One assessor who shall be a lead assessor.
Minimum number of process instances	A minimum of four process instances for each process within the scope of the assessment.	A minimum of two process instances shall be identified for each process within the scope of the assessment.	No minimum of process instances.

Table 1. (*Continued*)

Evidence required	For each process attribute of each process in the scope of the assessment, across the set of process instances, objective evidence drawn both from evaluation of work products and from testimony of performers of the process shall be collected.	For each process instance, objective evidence drawn both from evaluation of work products and from testimony of performers of the process shall be collected for each Process within the scope of the assessment.	Objective evidence required for evaluating the processes within the scope of the assessment shall be collected in a systematic manner.
Data sources (assessment instruments, interviews and documents)	Requires all three data sources.	Requires only two data sources (one must be interviews).	Requires only one data source.
Type of independence	The type of independence shall be recorded.	The type of independence shall be recorded.	The type of independence shall be recorded.

To demonstrate compliance with relevant safety standards, we have to satisfy classification criteria and requirements. A typical case to verify and validate a safety requirement is to check compliance with relevant standards and regulatory requirements. Based on our experience mainly from the nuclear power domain: the list of relevant nuclear safety standards and regulatory guides is long!

Safety-critical standards have typically some classification scheme. In the generic functional safety standard IEC 61508 [3] it is Safety Integrity Level (SIL), in range 1 – 4. SIL 1 is lowest and SIL 4 the highest integrity level. In higher SIL levels, requirements to use more formal methods and techniques increase.

3.2   Nuclear SPICE Assessment Model

The current Nuclear SPICE® method consists of a process assessment model (PAM) and a supporting assessment process. The method has been developed for nuclear power domain that is one of the strictest in safety-criticality. The method is based on ISO/IEC 15504 and the first version was created in 2011 as a result of the Finnish national nuclear safety program SAFIR2014 [4].

Nuclear SPICE assessments are typically performed to evaluate candidate system suppliers for nuclear industry. The core of the assessment is to assess capability of systems and software development processes.

Safety systems in nuclear power plants are classified according to their importance for safety. Safety classes in descending order are 1, 2 and not important for safety. Safety systems are independent from operational systems. Qualification process and required rigor in development/manufacturing is significantly higher in safety class 1 than in others.

To cover rigour in a systematic manner we need to extend Nuclear SPICE assessment process to include methods and techniques as evidences. In lower safety classes also a capability determination is an important part of qualification evidence.

3.3   Assessment Models in Other Domains

Automotive SPICE® is one of the first domain specific assessment models based on ISO/IEC 15504. First version was published in 2005 by Automotive Special Interest Group [5]. The model is a subset of SPICE processes, but contains also some additional processes for acquisition. Automotive SPICE has its own Process Reference Model (PRM) and Process Assessment Model (PAM). Especially within the German car industry, the model is considered mandatory, providing objective process evaluation and findings for process improvement both on project and organizational level.

Automotive SPICE does not specifically consider safety-related issues. In the car industry there are specific standards for functional safety, i.e. the ISO 26262 series [6]. Recently, in the development of a new version, there have been discussions to include functional safety requirements to the assessment model.

MDevSPICE® is a framework for medical device software process assessment [7]. MDevSPICE can be used to determine the capability level of medical device software development processes. MDevSPICE has been developed in cooperation with the international working groups for IEC 62304 and ISO/IEC 15504. Its focus is mainly on processes and risks. It was published in 2015 by an Irish research group.

Also, medical devices are often safety-critical, and safety is addressed by the MDevSPICE assessment model by providing a reference point to relevant standards. Medical device software safety is addressed with the risk management process of IEC 62304 Medical device software -- Software life cycle processes. Device level safety risks are addressed in system lifecycle processes of ISO 14971 Medical devices -- Application of risk management to medical devices, and its software specific guidance in IEC TR 80002-1 Medical device software -- Part 1: Guidance on the application of ISO 14971 to medical device software.

4   Stakeholder Requirements for a Process Assessment Model in Nuclear Domain

4.1   The Current Approach

The required assessment in nuclear domain is often related to a specific product or system that is developed within a single organizational unit and by a limited team of experts.

Our ultimate goal has been to cover most of the relevant requirements in the nuclear domain safety standards and regulatory guides by Nuclear SPICE. In this chapter we explain, to what extent we have achieved this goal.

The current Nuclear SPICE scope covers systems including software, at least to some extent (digital systems, system elements and software systems). So, it is quite near to the current SPICE standard approach, including also ISO/IEC 15504-5 PAM as a starting point. The main application has been pre-qualification with a limited set of processes.

Validation of Nuclear SPICE has been done by performing pilot assessments and getting feedback from assessment sponsors and from regulators. The main elements of Nuclear SPICE approach are depicted in Figure 2.

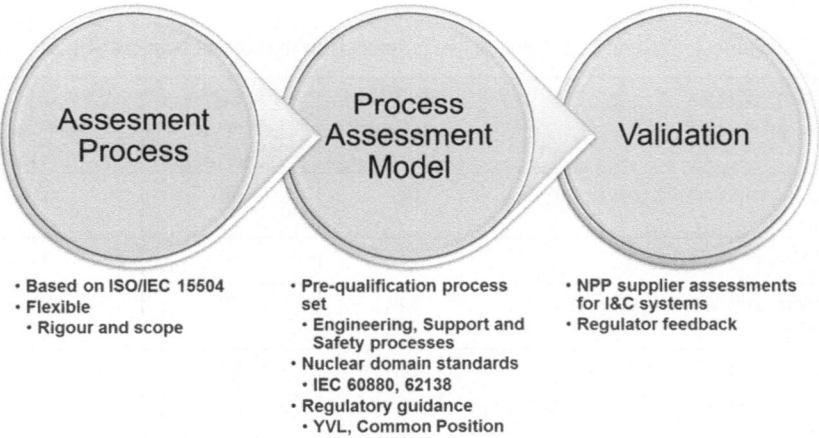

Fig. 2. Main elements in current Nuclear SPICE assessment method

4.2   Coverage of Regulatory Requirements

Nuclear domain is highly regulated. Legislation is well established at EU and national level. Also nuclear safety standardization is quite active, even it varies a lot between continents and countries.

All countries have also their own regulatory requirements. In Finland the regulatory body is STUK (Radiation and Nuclear Safety Authority). It has a large number of regulatory guides, called YVL [8]. Whole YVL set has approximately 10000 individual requirements. Each requirement is well identified by an individual ID and a short text. Only a small amount of them is relevant for digital systems, because most YVL requirements are at plant level or are otherwise at higher abstraction level.

Regulatory requirements YVL B.1 (Safety design of a nuclear power plant) and YVL E.7 (Electrical and I&C equipment of a nuclear facility) are most relevant for Nuclear SPICE. However, all of those requirements cannot be directly mapped with Nuclear SPICE assessment model.

Another highly relevant set is Common Position 2013 [9], a set of requirements for licensing of safety critical software for nuclear reactors. It has been developed by WENRA (Western European Nuclear Regulators Association).

To evaluate the overall "goodness" of the current Nuclear SPICE to cover regulatory requirements, we mapped it at detailed level with YVL B.1 and E.7 and with Common Position 2013 (later CP2013). Result of the mapping is in Table 2.

The term "relevant requirement" in Table 2 is needed, because YVL and CP2013 contain also a lot of other kind requirements. Most of these are related with administrative guidance (for example documentation for STUK) or licensing process (for example differences between safety classes in licensing I&C systems). Many requirements, especially in the YVL sets, are only at system or hardware level and therefore not directly relevant for Nuclear SPICE. Examples of such requirement areas are control room designs, ventilation and air conditioning, and electric cables.

Table 2. Coverage of regulatory requirements in the current Nuclear SPICE

Nuclear SPICE topic/ process	CP2013, # of relevant requirements	YVL E.7, # of relevant requirements	YVL B.1, # of relevant requirements
Systems engineering (excl. software)	68	30	63
Software engineering	51	30	1
Software support, e.g. CM, QA, VER, VAL[1]	34	29	5
Safety management and engineering, e.g. qualification and cybersecurity	70	58	26
Project management, e.g. risk management and measurement	0	5	15
Agreements and acquisitions	0	1	6
Organisational processes, e.g. quality management	0	6	23
Sum of relevant requirements to be validated by Nuclear SPICE	223	159	139
Total number of relevant requirements for digital systems	337	182	434
Coverage %, max in ideal case	**66**	**87**	**32**

[1] Configuration Management (CM); Quality Assurance (QA); Verification (VER); Validation (VAL)

Table 2 shows clearly that system or plant level regulatory requirements are not well covered. They are presented mainly in YVL B.1. Coverage is 32 % in an ideal case, when all YVL B.1 requirements are relevant and required. The real coverage of all requirement sets (CP2013, YVL E.7 and YVL B.1) is always much lower than in the ideal case. In real life, assessments are performed mainly for supplier organisations and only a small fraction of the requirements is relevant for them.

In practice, it is even more challenging to meet the regulatory requirements, because they can be interpreted differently. Safety systems in nuclear power plants can be technically very different. Also their software intensity varies. In some cases also new technologies can be applied, for example FPGA based hardware at least in some secondary systems. The practical qualification is a mix of analytical approaches and engineering judgement.

One important scaling factor is the applicable safety class. Nuclear domain is using different standards for different safety class. In the highest safety class 1 the most relevant standards are IEC 61513 for systems [10] and IEC 60880 for software systems [11]. In safety class 2 the main software standard is IEC 62138 [12]. Our experience is that it is easier to apply Nuclear SPICE in lower safety classes, in which the major part of requirements is in quality assurance and management topics.

One way to get higher coverage is to perform combined assessments, in which both nuclear utility and the selected system supplier/manufacturer are assessed together as a value chain. That is difficult in real life mainly for practical reasons. Assessment is most useful when it is done early in the system engineering lifecycle, and then main technical and commercial details are still open. Pre-qualification assessment is most useful in supplier selection, and is quite far from the system delivery and commissioning phase.

5   Nuclear SPICE Extended Use Cases

The existing SPICE framework is based on two main purposes and use cases: process improvement and process capability determination. Our experience is that these original ideas are inadequate for current systems engineering needs, especially in safety-critical systems.

The other major limitation in current SPICE framework (especially when based in ISO/IEC 15504) is the very strong focus in process capability. It has been a good innovation for less critical software engineering, to be applied in parallel with quality management standards like ISO9001.

In the nuclear domain the situation is much more challenging. Main references are based on regulatory requirements and relevant nuclear safety standards. Their granularity is more detailed and covers more than quality management and basic engineering.

Our current thinking for Nuclear SPICE development is that the whole SPICE framework should be extended to include also safety demonstration and conformity with requirements use cases. The old framework and main purposes are still valid and maybe quite adequate in some cases. But in most cases the framework needs to be extended also to cover these new use cases. Our proposed new framework is visualized in Figure 3.

Process assessment is not adequate and effective alone to realize the new use cases. Product evaluation has been used for a long time to analyse specific and highly important safety topics, for example the estimated reliability of system. In our opinion, these calculations and analyses are important evidences also for process assessment. In fact, most product evaluation topics can be converted to be process assessment topics as well. For example, system qualification process in safety class 1 systems should include the main product evidences, but can be seen also as a process. It works also vice versa; a high-quality system/software development process can be a strong evidence for product evaluation.

Process assessment and product evaluation have established application areas and provide partly different benefits for stakeholders. So, our solution is to integrate them, but also keep their specific strengths. In Figure 3 this is illustrated with arrows between these approaches and use cases. Arrows mean primarily "contributes to", "is evidence for" or "supports to perform" relationships. For readability, even important details are not included in Figure 3.

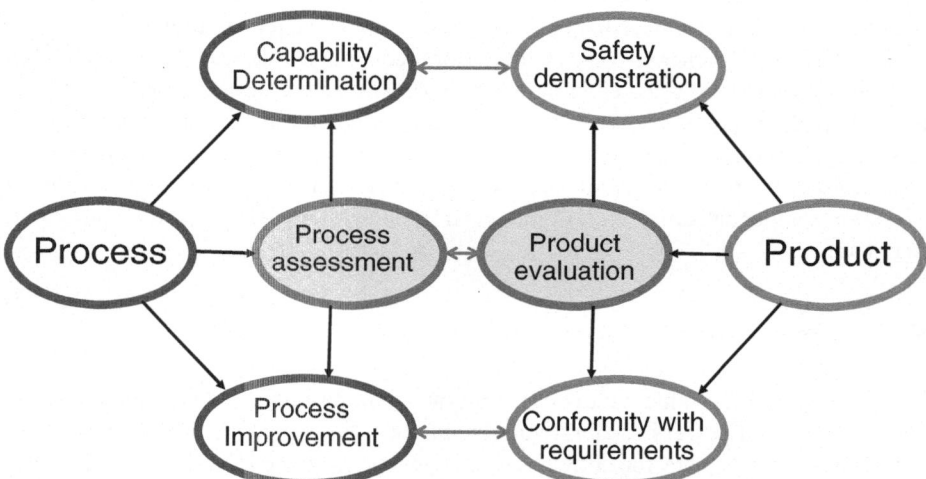

Fig. 3. Use cases in the extended Nuclear SPICE, balanced with product evaluation

In our latest pilot assessments we have covered conformity with requirements already to some extent. Our experience is that it is quite difficult because of the need to interpret requirements and to get adequate evidence in the early phase of systems engineering lifecycle. There is also an obvious need to get more specific product and analysis evidences as a part of process assessments or in some other parallel evaluation activities.

New national four years nuclear safety research program SAFIR2018 is starting in Finland. As a part of that program we will refine Nuclear SPICE further to cover also the extensions and new use cases.

6   Conclusions

Process assessment can be used in safety critical domains to demonstrate high quality process. The main focus in present process assessment approaches is process capability and to some extent organisational maturity. This is very useful and effective in process improvement and in demonstrating high process capability. It is also relevant to safety critical domains.

Safety critical domains must meet also regulatory and standard based requirements. They are mostly at system level, to support licensing and commissioning. Present process assessment approaches, like SPICE, are inadequate in meeting these stakeholder requirements.

We propose that process assessments are extended to include also safety demonstration and conformity with requirements use cases. There is also a need to get more specific product analysis evidences as a part of process assessments or in some other parallel evaluation activities. Better integration with product evaluation is needed.

Also other models in safety-critical domains, like Automotive SPICE and MDevSPICE, might benefit of similar approach for safety demonstration. Future cooperation between the model developers could lead to more generic evaluation methods for safety.

Acknowledgements. This work has been partially funded by the Finnish national nuclear safety program SAFIR2018.

References

1. ISO/IEC 15504-5:2012, Information technology – Process assessment – Part 5: An exemplar Process Assessment Model (2012)
2. ISO/IEC 33002, Information technology – Process assessment – Requirements for performing process assessments (2015)
3. IEC 61508-3 Ed. 2.0, Functional safety of electrical/electronic/programmable electronic safety-related systems – Part 3: Software requirements (2010)
4. Varkoi, T., Nevalainen, R., Mäkinen, T.: Toward Nuclear SPICE – integrating IEC 61508, IEC 60880 and SPICE. J. Softw. Evol. and Proc. **26**, 357–365 (2014)
5. Automotive SPICE®. http://www.automotivespice.com/ (accessed July 11, 2015)
6. ISO 26262, Road vehicles – Functional safety, ISO (2011)
7. MDevSPICE®. http://www.mdevspice.com/ (accessed July 11, 2015)
8. STUK: New YVL guides. https://ohjeisto.stuk.fi/YVL/?en=on (accessed July 11, 2015)
9. Common Position revision 2013. Licensing of safety critical software for nuclear reactors. Common position of seven European nuclear regulators and authorised technical support organisations (2013)
10. IEC 61513 FDIS, Nuclear power plants – Instrumentation and control for systems important to safety – General requirements for system (2011)
11. IEC 60880, Nuclear power plants – Instrumentation and control systems important to safety – Software aspects for computer-based systems performing category A functions (2006)
12. IEC 62138, Nuclear Power Plants – I&C Systems Important to Safety – Software Aspects for Computer Based Systems Performing Category B and C Functions (2004)

Creating Environments Supporting
Innovation and Improvement

The 10 Must Haves for Global Innovation and Networking. A New Strategic Approach

Gabriele Sauberer[1(✉)], Aliyou Mana Hamadou[2], Jolanta Maj[3], and Valery Senichev[4]

[1] European Certification and Qualification Association (ECQA),
Piaristengasse 1 3500, Krems, Austria
ECQA_vicepresident2@ecqa.org
[2] Forum European Diversity Management, Vienna, Austria
[3] Opole University of Technology, Poznań, Poland
[4] Charles University, Prague, Czech Republic

Abstract. We all know and agree that innovation has become a critical success factor in any kind of business, in particular in saturated markets. Increasingly, we also agree that innovation, efficiency, effectiveness, quality and continuous improvement are not enough – that companies, organisations, networks, nations and societies need to excel, to reach excellence and leadership in their fields. But HOW to do that? What do we really need t? In the past, we were talking about the ``Ten Good Reasons for … (Innovation, Design Thinking, Sustainability, etc.)", addressing safety and security issues together with rational and economic thinking. In other words, we addressed our oldest part of the brain (the amygdala, i.e. our reptile brain) which identifies and re-acts to threats, fear and bad news. The paper introduces a new approach to global innovation and a new, thought-provoking way of thinking: It addresses those powerful "positive" emotions which are crucial to make people and organisations flourish – and which enable global innovation and networking in the 21st Century. The paper is based on and inspired by the research of Barbara L. Fredrickson [1], a renowned Professor of Psychology and principal investigator of the Positive Emotions and Psychophysiology Laboratory at the University of North Carolina at Chapel Hill.

Keywords: Innovation · Ex-novation · Diversity · ECQA certified diversity manager · ECQA certified innovation manager · Positive leadership · Positive psychology

1 Introduction

In her ground-breaking "broaden-and-build-theory" [2], Barbara Fredrickson analyses and describes the "10 key positive emotions" of human beings, which are experienced frequently in our daily life: joy, gratitude, serenity, interest, hope, pride, amusement, inspiration, awe and love. All of these emotions are strongly related to and success factors of global innovation and networking. This is the theory and assumption of the given paper, to be elaborated and discussed. The order in which we describe the 10 positive emotions follows their relative frequency according to Barbara Fredrickson´s findings [2].

© Springer International Publishing Switzerland 2015
R.V. O'Connor et al. (Eds.): EuroSPI 2015, CCIS 543, pp. 233–246, 2015.
DOI: 10.1007/978-3-319-24647-5_19

2 Joy and Playfulness: Drivers of Innovation

Why joy is crucial for global innovation and networking? "Joy creates the urge to play and get involved" and: "The durable resources created through play are the skills acquired through the experiential learning it prompts." [3]. This is what Barbara Fredrickson´s research showed, and this is exactly what we need for global innovation and networking: People who are keen on learning and getting involved with new things and other people. Why? Because only such people will be drivers of global innovation and networking. Not because it is their job to make a living, but because they are rewarded and motivated by joy and playfulness.

How do we bring joy to innovation managers and global networks? "Joy emerges when one's current circumstances present unexpected good fortune. People feel joy, for instance, when receiving good news or a pleasant surprise." [3]. This means, organisations need to provide a framework, culture and working conditions where joy can emerge, where "unexpected good fortune, good news or pleasant surprises" are cultivated.

Let us compare this new approach and requirement with the current attitude and state-of-the-art in innovation management. Joy and playfulness in a working and learning environment are still considered as "dubious", not serious, childish and unprofessional. When it is fun and joyful, it can not be hard work or real learning. Example: When German children begin school, for them literary starts "the serious side of life" ("der Ernst des Lebens"). And the mind-set of many engineers and managers reflects this common attitude: Engineering and managing is hard work and therefore can not be joyful. This mind-set definitely has to be changed – and now we know how to do that, thanks to new insights of neuro-plasticity and the magic of how our brains work (see chapter 8 below ("Inspiration").

To enjoy ideation, innovation and innovation management in a professional environment, we also need tools. Unfortunately, the joy they bring usually is limited. There is definitely room for improvement. Examples: Interfaces and interoperability are still a challenge. But they are key issues of real user-friendliness and competitive advantage: The better an innovation or networking tool is embedded in and interoperable with the client´s software architecture (e.g. Microsoft Office, Enterprise Resource Planning Systems, Social Media, etc.) the easier it is to use, the more it will be used (and bought), because users will enjoy it more than other tools.

Concerning playfulness, what is really "cool" in innovation management? Not much, to be honest with you. Innovation increasingly has the image of a boring buzzword more than an exciting thing to excel in global markets and industries. We have to change that, we have to make innovation "sweet and sexy". Let us create "cool stuff", InnoApps, Games, whatever works. Your current customers may not be playful – your future customers will be, as those you did not address or convince yet.

You may not be playful yourself – but even decent engineers need some fun. Please note the irony in this sentence. Even decent researchers need some fun, too.

So bring in joy and playfulness to find ideas for new products and solutions. Sources of playfulness are everywhere, we just need to use different resources. Talking to people, trying out something new and playing around with different aspects of playful approaches might lead to exciting new things. Remember: Innovate or die.

3   Gratitude: Treat your Customers and Stakeholders Well

Why gratitude is important for global innovation and networking? Because gratitude makes us aware of and appreciate that we have customers, peers and communities where innovation takes place. "Gratitude creates the urge to creatively consider new ways to be kind and generous oneself. The durable resources accrued when people act on this urge are new skills for expressing kindness and care to others." [3].

Being an innovation expert, manager or tool provider, we should be grateful that we have customers after all. Our products and services might not be that convincing or different from our competitors that our customers come back to us all the time – so:

To show our gratitude and create a sound and beneficial customer relationship basis, we must know our customers well and treat them well, or at least in an appropriate way (see below, Table 1, Stakeholder management interest grid).

Why "new skills for expressing kindness and care to others" are important? Because we need to understand and learn a lot from our customers, peers and networks in order to improve our products and services or create something new.

The same is true for our suppliers, our service and tool providers. Let us be grateful that there are "crazy" people out there caring for our innovation nightmares and our organisational hell. If we know them, talk to them, and show them our gratitude, they might solve our problems even if we didn´t know that we had those particular ones.

"Gratitude emerges when people acknowledge another person as the source of their unexpected good fortune." To better understand who are our customers, peers, communities, and other (potential) "sources of unexpected good fortune", let us introduce a useful tool for Stakeholder Analysis: the Power Grid we use in the ECQA Certified Terminology Manager_advanced courses.

ISO 29383 Annex A: Tools for stakeholder analyses

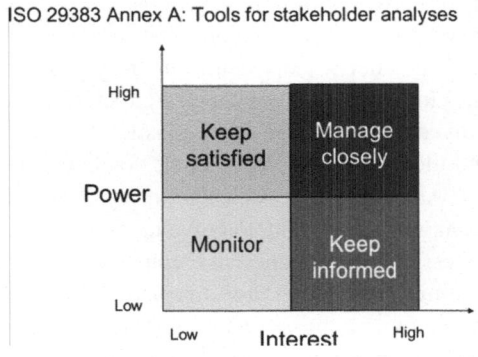

Fig. 1. ISO 29383 Annex A: Tools for stakeholder analyses [4]

The power/interest grid shown in Figure 1 is designed to identify groups and individuals who have varying levels of influence (power) and interest in our products, services, networks, projects, policies, etc. It´s a useful tool to identify and manage stakeholders according to their "power" and "interest":

- High power, high interest (red –top right): offer information to these people on an ongoing and extensive basis, in order to facilitate their full engagement
- High power, low interest (orange – top left): Offer information on a regular basis although not excessively
- Low power, high interest (dark green – on the bottom right): Need to be adequately informed and offered opportunity for feedback to ensure that no major issues are arising.
- Low power, low interest (light green – on the bottom left): Offer information occasionally and not intensively.

4   Serenity: Embrace Diversity and Change

Why serenity is crucial for global innovation and networking? "Also called contentment, serenity emerges when people interpret their current circumstances as utterly cherished, right, or satisfying. People feel serenity, for instance, when they feel comfortable, at ease in, or at one with their situation. Serenity creates the urge to savor those current circumstances and integrate them into new priorities or values. The durable resources created through savoring and integrating include a more refined and complex sense of oneself and of one's priorities." [3].

No doubt, we all live in circumstances completely or mainly opposite to these circumstances. Living in turbulent times, product and innovation circles are changing as fast as everything else (customers, suppliers, habits, values, trends). This makes us nervous, hectic, nuts. That is not a good pre-condition to navigate organisations in challenging times, that is not good at all for innovation, prosperity and positive, sustainable developments of networks and organisations.

So, how to obtain serenity and get a "more refined and complex sense of oneself and of one's priorities" in order to cope with our busy professional lives with little room for creativity and innovation? Recent research suggests, that it is important to embrace change and diversity [5], to use neuro-plasticity of our brains [6], [7] instead of fighting change and globalisation. Why? First, you can not change it anyhow, so make the best out of it. Also nasty things change, nasty clients, nasty trends, etc. And second, you can use change and diversity to come up with innovations.

How? Surf the waves of change, otherwise you will risk to drown. Use diverse teams to invent new things (Question: How many female software programmers do you have?). Tell your customers, bosses and yourself, that change and diversity are wonderful resources to design new solutions. Bio diversity, Human diversity, diversity of design to make things safer, etc., are all resources we can use for innovation. That is why Diversity Management has become a success factor for organisations that want to excel and meet the needs and requirements of global innovation and networking.

How much positive leadership and diversity management is related to successful change management is shown in the ground-breaking theories and publications of the leading expert and scholar in leadership, Kim S. Cameron. [14] To be able to embrace change and diversity in order to innovate and survive, you need serenity. When we do practice serenity and embrace change and diversity, we will make our products and services (and our people) more resilient in turbulent times of crisis, break-downs, budget cuts, sales decreases, etc.

5   Interest: A Conditio Sine Qua Non

The relevance of interest, which is considered by Barbara L. Fredrickson as positive emotion, for global innovation and networking is obvious:

If we – both suppliers (including researchers) and customers – are really interested in the needs of our customers and our suppliers, we will find extraordinary new solutions together. If we are really interested in trends and global developments, we will get new ideas on how to improve or innovate, in general and in particular.

No doubt, that is common knowledge – but is it also common practice?

Inter-disciplinary thinking, exploring other fields and industries definitely is our strength and competitive advantage in ECQA and in the EuroSPI and EuroAsiaSPI communities.

Why? Software is like terminology, i.e. it is like weed which is everywhere. And global innovation and networking which is boosting globalisation, is everywhere, too.

There might be applications for software process improvement and for terminology solutions where you would not expect them.

What does that mean with respect to interest? It means that our interest must be real and honest, not a buzzword or empty talk. It means that we need to:

- Listen carefully and with interest in order to come up with solutions who are really interesting for our customers, peers and communities
- Enlarge our views, think out of the box, co-operate and join networks and communities of interest and trust

According to Barbara Frederickson, "Interest arises in circumstances appraised as safe but offering novelty. People feel interest, for instance, when they encounter something that is mysterious or challenging, yet not overwhelming." [3] To feel "challenged, yet not overwhelmed" is exactly the mental state which Mihaly Csikszentmihalyi was calling "flow" in his famous book, 25 years ago [15]. Whenever people are absorbed and totally interested in what they are doing, they are in the "flow mode". Professionals who love their profession know very well how this flow mode feels like and how essential it is to excel and innovate in their profession.

"Interest creates the urge to explore, to learn, to immerse oneself in the novelty and thereby expand the self (...). The knowledge so gained becomes a durable resource." [3]. How the essence of innovation could be described better?

The notion of knowledge sharing is crucial here: If we use our knowledge for competition, we will get specialisation. Those who practice co-operation and knowledge sharing instead of competition get real innovation. Why?

Fascinating new research suggests that competition always lead only to specialisation in our evolutionary history. To create something new, cells, organisms, animals, human beings and human societies need co-operation and communication, not competition. [16]

6   Hope: There is also Post-Traumatic Growth

Hope is, maybe, the positive emotion we need most in times of harsh competition, failure, innovation pressure, threatening political and social developments, etc. Why?

"Hope creates the urge to draw on one's own capabilities and inventiveness to turn things around. The durable resources it builds include optimism and resilience to adversity." [3]

Inventiveness surely is crucial and a core component of innovation. Resilience is considered as a key success factor of organisations – and a key competence of individuals, as well. Resilience is a new, highly inter-disciplinary subject field and strongly related to diversity (of systems, human resources and organisations). [17]

Hope is the only positive emotion growing under *bad* conditions. "Whereas most positive emotions arise in circumstances appraised as safe, hope is the exception. Hope arises in dire circumstances in which people fear the worst yet yearn for better (…). People feel hope, for instance, in grim situations in which they can envision at least a chance that things might change for the better." [3]

So, if you are about to start with an innovation (or any other) project: Fear the worst, yearn for the better. If, at the end of the project, your (positive) expectations are not only met, but exceeded, you and your supplier (or: you and your customer) did a real good job.

Example: If you are introducing a terminology policy in your organisation, keep hoping in difficult times and project phases. Remember the terminology pain curve: When you do not care at all about terminology management, you will go away with it for a certain time, but then pain will explode and you will get a perfect terminology emergency. On the other hand, if you are brave and do tackle terminology issues, it might terribly hurt in the beginning, but gets better soon.

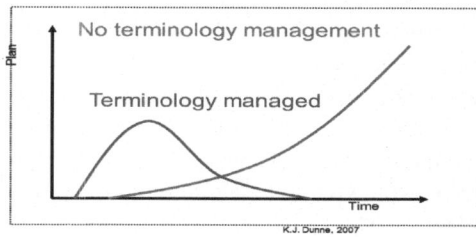

Fig. 2. The "Terminology Pain Curve" based on Keiran J. Dunne, 2007 [18]

"Necessity is the mother of invention" is a common saying in our western cultures.

Let us hope that the necessity of time pressure, delivery costs and product liability will be the mother of great inventions and innovations.

If you are disappointed by your innovation, your project, client or supplier, let us hope together that next time it will be different, and give them, him or her and yourself a second chance. After budget cuts, project failure, crisis and nightmares, there is not only post-traumatic stress but also post-traumatic growth, a term coined by Martin Seligman [19]. If we are ready to learn from our mistakes, to analyse and discuss why our product or service is not sold, not used or not maintained, we will do a better job next time. And let us hope that there will be a next time…

7   Pride: Share your Success Story with your Community

"Pride emerges when people take appropriate credit from some socially valued good outcome. Pride creates the urge to fantasize about even bigger accomplishments in similar arenas. The big dreams sparked by pride contribute to the durable resource of achievement motivation (…)." [20]

Share your pride with us: You did it, so tell us your success story! It is important for us to learn from your good or best practice example. And maybe you will get an award from ECQA – or EuroSPI? It is also important to share your good vibes with the community. Why? Because you could make a difference – you could inspire us and we will come back to you, with new ideas, new brains and new business.

Positive emotions raise your chances to innovate and survive. When you are proud, you will dream BIG and you will go for further achievements, which is good for innovation and business.

Why? Because it motivates us again and again. We are keen following our big dream and doing a lot of good work again to make you – and all of us – proud again.

Pride can be a powerful positive emotion. In the German speaking world, we learned to distrust national pride. In the Christian world, pride is more a sin than a virtue. Now it is time to learn (from *proud* Canadians, Americans and South Africans) to be proud again – not because we belong to a certain nationality, but because we did a real good job – ideally in global innovation and networking.

8   Amusement: Share Laughter, Knowledge and Ideas

Innovation creation and management is hard work, as we all know. And innovation experts are most serious people. So, do not take both too serious. Laughter in your team will increase creativity (that you need to innovate and survive). And laughter will guide you through a chaotic and dangerous life with poor innovation management.

"Amusement creates urges to share a laugh and find creative ways to continue the joviality. As people follow these urges, they build and solidify enduring social bonds (…)" and: "Amusement occurs when people appraise their current circumstances as involving some sort on nonserious social incongruity. It can erupt, for instance, in the wake of a harmless speech error or physical blunder." [20]

Fig. 3. Cartoon "Communication: … and that is why we lift on three …" copyright: www.dolighan.com

The fun part in this cartoon is the „Nonserious social incongruity" that amuses us.

Amusement should be the basis of our team work in any kind of projects and innovation. Why? Because:

1) When we share our laughter, we share your insights. Sharing knowledge is not the favourite sports of many experts, colleagues or leaders in our teams. There is definitely room for improvement – as for communication. Amusement might help here to get the message through in a nice and easy way.

2) Even the Nobel Price increasingly is awarded to teams, not to outstanding individuals any longer. Thus, if you want to excel and deliver outstanding results in your groups and projects, you better care for excellent team work, where amusement plays a crucial role.

We might laugh or mock at Google´s company culture or other Silicon Valley playgrounds. But it is a fact that they are successful and creative.

9   Inspiration: Create the Urge to Excel

There is no innovation without inspiration: "Inspiration creates the urge to excel oneself, to reach one's own higher ground or personal best. The durable resource it builds is the motivation for personal growth (...)." [20]. Thus, inspiration is an extremely important emotion to innovate and flourish in our knowledge rich industries. If we manage to create a „WOW effect" with our innovation, tools and projects, we will win.

Business as usual is not an option any longer. We saw so many giants fail and vanish, just think of Nokia as world market leader for so many years. And now? The markets are saturated, even in booming industries we will see even more competition and price fight. We know from our competitors and many company failures such as Nokia that we can not oversleep innovations and can not win price fights for too long. We can only win and survive with outstanding quality, excellent customer relationship management and cool new products people *love* to buy and to use.

So let us get inspired by the excellence of products, by the "craziness" and braveness of successful people and businesses. There are so many examples out there – and in the ECQA and EuroSPI communities. ECQA started as a small project co-financed by

European Union. ECQA today is the leading and fast growing certification network and continuously improving and enlarging its product portfolio. [26]

"Inspiration arises when people witness human excellence in some manner. People feel inspired, for instance, when they see someone else do a good deed or perform at an unparalleled level." [20]. "It always seems impossible until it is done" –a famous quote from Nelson Mandela.

Example: When TermNet initiated an international certificate for terminology professionals 5 years ago, people were sceptical, doubting whether there would be a market for such a niche product. Immediately after the launch of this certificate with a first exam in 2010, we got a phone call from European Central Bank asking if we could also do in-house trainings to guide their experts to become "ECQA Certified Terminology Managers". Since then, EU institutions, companies and organisations from all over the world sent their people to our online courses and face-to-face Terminology Summer Schools to qualify for that certificate.

Many success stories are like that: if you get inspired by others, if you are committed and if you really believe in your project, you are irresistible and will succeed with your endeavour.

Let us get inspired by innovation and by exnovation – another inspiring trend: "Exnovation is the process of eliminating the unsustainable, irrelevant or unsuitable to constantly improve and renew the innovation process." [21]

What does that mean? How can we eliminate the unsustainable, irrelevant or unsuitable – how can we learn to unlearn? I'll give you an example of a "crazy" Austrian entrepreneur: "At Zotter, everything is possible: cheese chocolate, fish chocolate, mass wine and incense chocolate and now the sweet variation of hummus. 20 years of chocolate history Mr Zotter filled with a tremendous amount of creations, crazy ideas and the rebellion against the mainstream." [22]

So what is one crazy thing he did for innovation? It is his "cemetery of ideas" where he buries bad ideas – where he eliminates the unsustainable, irrelevant or unsuitable to constantly improve and renew the innovation process. Plenty of varieties are annually added to the assortment whilst others disappear and end up on the Cemetery of Ideas. The Cemetery of Ideas exists in reality: In the Edible Zoo (another provocative innovation), Sepp Zotter has set gravestones for past chocolate varieties and ideas. And if some visitors grieve over the variety, Zotter resurrects the most popular former varieties for a short while, such as the wonderful combinations "Pink Coconut and Fish Marshmallow" or "Penuts and Ketchup" Chocolate. [23]

10   Awe: Be Part of the Bigger Picture and the Greater Good

"The durable resources awe creates are new worldviews (…)." [20] New worldviews definitely are key issues of global innovation and networking. New worldviews help us to develop or find something new or to connect with people who are (very) different from us.

How to bring awe to innovation managers and networkers? "Awe emerges when people encounter goodness on a grand scale. People feel awe, for instance, when overwhelmed by something (or someone) beautiful or powerful that seems larger than life." [20]

We can learn (again) to be overwhelmed not only by work loads or bureaucracy, but by the beauty of innovation and communication, by the precision of technology and terminology, by the complexity of software processes, human nature, brains, etc.

Do not unlearn to *marvel* about all the wonderful things you are surrounded by and where innovation should be the underlying quality and success factor. The world is awesome – and not enough. When Professor Budin, the first Full Professor in Terminology and Language Technology was asked in an interview about the future of translation, he answered without hesitating a second: The Universal translator like in Star Trek.

So remember: You are part of something *much* bigger than you and your innovation challenge or your innovative solution. You are part of Star Trek's Universal Translator, you are part of the smartest smart phone feature, you are part of the cutest search engine for web contents in hundreds of languages. You are contributing to the greater good, you are part of the bigger picture. *Awesome.*

11   Love: Love It or Leave It

Love is the best and most complex positive emotion we have, and comprises all the previous 9 Must Haves in global innovation and networking we were talking about.

"Love, which appears to be the positive emotion people feel most frequently, arises when any other of the positive emotions is felt in the context of a safe, interpersonal connection or relationship. (…) as an amalgam of other positive emotions, love broadens thought–action repertoires both in an "all of the above" manner and by creating momentary perceptions of social connection and self-expansion. Likewise, love builds a wide range of enduring resources, especially social bonds and community." [20]

Table 1. Ten Representative Positive Emotions according to Barbara Fredrickson [24]

Emotion label	Appraisal theme	Thought-action tendency	Resources accrued
Joy	Safe, familiar, unexpectedly good	Play, get involved	Skills gained via experiential learning
Gratitude	Receive a gift or benefit	Creative urge to be prosocial	Skills for showing care, loyalty, social bonds
Serenity (also known as contentment)	Safe, familiar, low effort	Savor and integrate	New priorities, new views of self
Interest	Safe, novel	Explore, learn	Knowledge
Hope	Fearing the worst, yearning for better	Plan for a better future	Resilience, optimism

Table 2. (*Continue*)

Pride	Socially valued achievement	Dream big	Achievement motivation
Amusement	Nonserious social incongruity	Share joviality, laugh	Social bonds
Inspiration	Witness human excellence	Strive toward own higher ground	Motivation for personal growth
Awe	Encounter beauty or goodness on a grand scale	Absorb and accommodate	New worldviews
Love	Any/all of the above in an interpersonal connection	Any/all of the above, with mutual care	Any/all of the above, especially social bonds

12   Conclusions

So these are the "Top 10 Must Haves" in global innovation and networking: Ten positive emotions explored by Barbara Fredrickson and connected with innovation and networking by Gabriele Sauberer and the co-authors of this paper.

All you need to innovate, connect and flourish is:

✓ to create joy with your products and use playfulness to innovate,
✓ to show your customers your gratitude and learn from them,
✓ to practice serenity and embrace change & diversity,
✓ to keep your interest in clients, trends, and inter-disciplinary thinking,
✓ to hope for the better in difficult times and rely on post-traumatic growth after failures,
✓ to continue your success story – and dream big,
✓ to share your laughter with innovation experts,
✓ to get inspired by other "crazy" people who innovate and exnovate (it is who learn to unlearn the useless),
✓ to be overwhelmed with positive emotions & the blessings of innovation and networking for the greater good.

Yes, this is what we are saying: Love it or leave it. We do need to capitalise on these positive emotions to survive and flourish in our industries, businesses, networks and communities.

13   Outlook: Future Innovation and Diversity Manager Certifications

In her master thesis, Gabriele Sauberer examined the required knowledge, skills and competences of successful diversity managers compared with those of innovation managers. [8] The correlation between diversity and innovation is obvious and clear: The majority of managers in the Forbs Insights Survey considered diversity at the workplace at "Key Driver" of innovation:

"The business case for diversity and inclusion is intrinsically linked to a company´s innovation strategy. Multiple and varied voices have a wide range of experiences, and this can help generate new ideas about products and services. Survey respondents overwhelmingly agreed that a divers and inclusive workforce brings the different perspectives that a company needs to power its innovation strategy." [9]

The list of publications about the business case and benefit of diversity management is huge and continuously growing [10]. However, research results about the correlation between diversity management and innovation are less frequent, but case studies about how diverse teams and work force are fostering innovation are published widely, e.g. Forbes insights studies [9].

So, how the skills of innovation managers are correlating with diversity management skills? From 38 performance criteria (PC) of the "ECQA Certified Innovation Manager 2.0" certificate, there are 8 overlapping criteria in ECQA Certified Diversity Manager certificate. Four criteria are in Skill Unit 1: Innovation Domains and four in Skill Unit 2: Architecture of a Dynamic Learning Organization. In particular, these overlapping skills are found in Learning Element 3, "Ideation and Entrepreneurship" (U1.E3).

Examples [11]:

- S/he knows the Key Success Factors for a successful Ideation Process (InnoMan2.0.U1.E3.PC1)
- S/he knows how to develop and assess personal skills, such as empathy, self-reflection, ability to work in a team, to negotiate, handle conflicts, etc. (DiMMan.U5.E1.PC3)

The correlation between innovation and diversity management is even more obvious when it comes to managing (diverse/innovation) teams and key competences of (innovation) managers [12]:

- S/he knows how to compose Innovative (Ideation) Teams (InnoMan2.0. U1.E3.PC3)
- S/he knows how to manage and train diverse teams (DiMMan.U2.E2.PC4 + PC5 = InnoMan.U2.E3.PC1 + PC2)
- S/he knows how to identify a core competence (InnoMan2.0.U2.E1.PC1)
- S/he is able to identify and measure potentials and diversity in the work place (DiMMan.U2.E1.PC1)
- Last but not least, the ability to identify and measure potentials is a prerequisite of our ability to create learning organisations [13]:
- S/he knows how to establish a learning organisation architecture model (InnoMan2.0.U2.E1.PC2)
- S/he is able to identify and measure potentials and diversity in the work place (DiMMan.U2.E1.PC1)

In a rapidly changing complex world, we need new skills and competences to enjoy innovation and to make global innovation and networking "flourish", i.e. successful and sustainable.

Which new skills do we need as innovation managers?
1.   We need terminology skills to communicate precisely in and with global networks and to coin new concepts and terms for new things.
2.   We need diversity management skills to make use of the existing potential we already have (in our "human resources") and of new potentials and resources we need to create innovation and sustainable networks
3.   We need story telling skills to bring the message through, to tell a convincing story, to "sell" global innovation and networking.

These skills shall and will be represented in the new "ontology of skills and competences" [25] of ECQA, the European Certification and Qualification Association. They are or will be included also in the skills and competence portfolios of "ECQA Certified Innovation Manager", "ECQA Certified Applied Sustainability and CSR Professional" and "ECQA Certified Diversity Manager".

References

1. Fredrickson, B.: Professor of Psychology and principal investigator of the Positive Emotions and Psychophysiology Laboratory at the University of North Carolina at Chapel Hill. (http://en.wikipedia.org/wiki/Barbara_Fredrickson)
2. Fredrickson, B.L.: Positive emotions broaden and build. In: Devine, P., Plant, A. (eds.) Advances in Experimental Social Psychology, vol. 47, pp. 1–53. Academic Press, Burlington (2013). © Copyright 2013 Elsevier Inc., Academic Press. ISBN 978-0-12-407236-7
3. Fredrickson, B.L.: Positive Emotions Broaden and Build, p. 4. Elsevier Inc., Academic Press (2013)
4. ISO 29383:2010, Terminology policies – Development and implementation, Annex A: Tools for stakeholder analyses. The International Organization for Standardization (ISO) (2010)
5. Cameron, K., Lavine, M.: Making the Impossible Possible: Leading Extraordinary Performance. The Rock Flats Story San. Barrett-Koehler, Francisco (2006)
6. Hanson, R. http://www.rickhanson.net/writings/articles/positive-neuroplasticity/, http://www.wisebrain.org/science/key-scientific-papers
7. Hüther, G.: Etwas mehr Hirn, bitte. Eine Einladung zur Wiederentdeckung der Freude am eigenen Denken und der Lust am gemeinsamen Gestalten. Vandenhoeck & Ruprecht (2015)
8. Sauberer, G.: Der Europäische Diversity Führerschein: Neue Fähigkeiten und Strategien für Diversitäts- und Innovationsmanagement in Europa und weltweit, Masterarbeit zur Erlangung des akademischen Grades Master of Business Administration an der Fachhochschule Burgenland (Austrian Institute of Management) (2014)
9. Forbes insights, Global Diversity and Inclusion: Fostering Innovation Through a Diverse Workforce, Forbes Study, p. 5, July 2011. http://www.forbes.com/forbesinsights/innovation_diversity/index.html
10. Sauberer, G.: Der Europäische Diversity Führerschein: Neue Fähigkeiten und Strategien für Diversitäts- und Innovationsmanagement in Europa und weltweit, Masterarbeit, Austrian Institute of Management, pp. LXXXV (2014). Literaturverzeichnis
11. Sauberer, G.: Der Europäische Diversity Führerschein, p. LXIX (2014)
12. Sauberer, G.: Der Europäische Diversity Führerschein, p. LXX (2014)
13. Sauberer, G.: Der Europäische Diversity Führerschein, p. LXXIf (2014)

14. Cameron, K.S.: Selected articles and books about organisational culture and change. http://webuser.bus.umich.edu/cameronk/Organizational_Culture.htm
15. Csikszentmihaly, M.: FLOW – The Psychology of Optimal Experience. Harper & Row, New York (1990)
16. Hüther, G.: Etwas mehr Hirn, bitte. Eine Einladung zur Wiederentdeckung der Freude am eigenen Denken und der Lust am gemeinsamen Gestalten, Vandenhoeck & Ruprecht, p. 67 (2015)
17. Seidler, S.: Linked diversity & resilienz. In: Andrlik, M., Pauser, N. (eds.) Realisierung Von Diversity & Inclusion, p. 147. Facultas, Wien (2015)
18. Keiran, J.D.: Terminology: ignore it at your peril. In: Multilingual, p. 32f, April/May 2007
19. Seligman, M.: Learned Optimism: How to Change Your Mind and Your Life. Knopf, New York (1991)
20. Fredrickson, B.L.: Positive Emotions Broaden and Build, p. 6. Elsevier Inc., Academic Press (2013)
21. Kimberly, J.R., Evanisko, M.J.: Organizational innovation: The influence of individual, organizational and contextual factors on hospital adoption of technological and administrative innovation (1981)
22. About Zotter, Creativity. http://www.zotter.at/en/about-zotter.html
23. Sepp Zotter´s Cemetery of Ideas. http://www.zotter.at/en/choco-shop/new-products-and-sale/cemetery-of-ideas-exhumed.html
24. Fredrickson, B.L.: Positive Emotions Broaden and Build, Table 1.1 Ten Representative Positive Emotions, p. 5. Elsevier Inc., Academic Press (2013)
25. Nájera, B.: ECQA Term. Terminology on European Certification and Qualification Association (ECQA), Master in Terminology, Final Master Project, Barcelona, Universidad Pompeu Fabra (2013)
26. Reiner, M., Sauberer, G., Messnarz, R.: European certification and qualification association – developments in europe and world wide. In: EuroSPI 2014 Industrial Proceedings. DELTA-Verlag, Denmark (2014)

Achieving Sustainable Development by Integrating It into the Business Process Management System

Tomislav Rozman[1(✉)], Anca Draghici[2], and Andreas Riel[3]

[1] DOBA Faculty Maribor/BICERO Ltd., Maribor, Slovenia
tomislav.rozman@bicero.com
[2] Politehnica University of Timisoara, Timisoara, Romania
anca.draghici@upt.ro
[3] Grenoble Alpes University/EMIRAcle AISBL, Saint-Martin-D'Heres, France
andreas.riel@emiracle.eu

Abstract. The purpose of the article is to present an approach how to integrate sustainability related topics into an organization's management system. As a starting point and connecting tissue, we use a process-oriented approach (BPM) for managing companies and then apply sustainability dimensions (economic, ecologic, and social) to it. Using this approach we do not change existing or already established management systems of companies, but we adapt it by modifying company vision, strategy and most importantly, management and core processes. Integrating sustainability related processes into organization management system prevents "fire-fighting" and ad-hoc activities, which are performed by companies to comply with the increasing number of sustainability related standards. In addition, we present two managerial trainings (business process management and sustainability management), which when combined, will enable managers to adapt to today's highly competitive business environment. The concept presented here is a novel approach under the ECQA (European Certification and Qualification Organization), which will allow on-demand clustering of managerial skills and trainings (BPM and sustainability management). The results presented are particularly useful for process analysts, quality managers, sustainability managers, social responsibility managers and similar professional profiles in order to improve their companies' activities and processes with respect to the sustainable development values.

Keywords: Leadership · Business process management · Sustainability · Life-long learning · Certification · Business analysts

1 Introduction

We all strive for sustainability, in every aspect of our lives. We want to sustain our lives, our families, our companies and the whole society. We are very good at sustaining ourselves (as a person) and what directly affects us (our social, technical or eco-environment). This kind of sustainability related knowledge we have 'built-in' (some) and we learn it in our families through generations (as knowledge base experiences

© Springer International Publishing Switzerland 2015
R.V. O'Connor et al. (Eds.): EuroSPI 2015, CCIS 543, pp. 247–259, 2015.
DOI: 10.1007/978-3-319-24647-5_20

transmitted in order to survive and develop ourselves). Despite this individual behavior, we are not so good (and we have proved this many times) at sustaining larger scale subjects, for example companies, countries, and natural resources. Therefore, learning from good practices of subjects (individuals and groups), who already have success in this area could be a solution for this kind of group behavior and knowledge acquirement (acquisition).

At the organizational level (seen as multilayer of functional groups or cross-functional groups), the problem of behavior and knowledge acquirement is more complex.

Process oriented organizations have traditionally focused on the following aspects: time, cost and the quality. The key performance indicators for the development expenses were time and costs, where other resources and impact on the environment and the society was usually neglected.

But what is sustainability in the business and development context? The authors of (Fistis, Rozman, Riel, & Messnarz, 2014) define it as "an integrated approach to ecological, social and economic impact issues (both internal and external), which leads to long term, sustainable survival of the organization and its environment, which also includes profit growth (but not at any cost)."

In addition to these three dimensions, and upon all of them management and leadership skills are a "must", if we want to achieve the behavior and knowledge in order to develop a sustainable business of a company. It became obvious that to build a sustainable society, we need sustainable companies. To make a company sustainable, we firstly need leaders and managers, well educated in all mentioned aspects.

Sustainability aware leaders define a sustainable vision, strategy and tactics that will determine sustainable activities and processes in a company's internal environment and these will generate sustainable products and services. Business and process analysts define processes for a company. Middle managers and process owners ensure that processes are performed. Processes are executed by employees. This is how it should be in ideal organization. But where do we start? How do we integrate sustainability aspects into company's management system?

In previous years, there was a focus on an incremental process change and improvement. While this approach results in optimized processes, it may not take into account social and environmental sustainable business processes. To address these issues, companies need to adopt a radical approach (sometime) by introducing completely new processes into their practices simultaneously with the reshaping the existing ones with respect to the sustainable development values, norms and standards. Therefore, this article tries to answer the following research questions:

RQ 1: *Are business process management and sustainability management complementary and can they be integrated?*
RQ 2: *Which existing BPM related standards could be used to integrate sustainability into organization?*

2   Business Process Management and Sustainability

Business Process Management (BPM) is a structured way of understanding, documenting, modeling, analyzing, simulating, executing, measuring and improving end-to-end business processes and resources. The aim of BPM is to improve business in all aspects (transparency, efficiency, resource usage). While many organizations follow functional management (departments as islands), a process-oriented management promises to deliver value or better experience to customers. In real life, strict separation of functional and process oriented management is difficult to achieve, therefore a mix of those two is more realistic and common.

The usual approach to BPM follows the PDCA process. In reality, when a company and/or consultant starts with implementing BPM in an organization, some BPM principles are already in place. Many companies to which we provide our BPM consulting services have already some form of process descriptions in place. For example, the majority of them have already established an ISO 9001 compliant quality management system. On the other hand, the quality management system is rarely fully in use. Many times, we get the comment: "Yes, we do have our processes described, but we perform our work differently as described." This is a clear sign that the respective company's efforts to establish BPM were not successful and are thus not sustainable. Others are reluctant to model AS-IS processes (because they are broken) and want to model ideal (TO-BE) processes. The lesson learned from the real world consulting is, the process thinking implementation is not as straightforward as usually presented in the literature. Some companies see BPM as a purely information technology related initiative, but it is actually not. It is true that BPM is an enabler for process automation, however information technology is not the core of the approach. The key message is 'Integrate work, not (only) applications'.

In this article, we distinguish between sustainable BPM and a sustainable organization, which is not the same. Sustainable BPM means that we take a process-oriented approach to an organization's primary way of management and we continuously refine, measure and optimize processes. Implementing sustainability aspects in BPM means that we reengineer existing processes or introduce new ones in our organizations, which cover all the sustainability dimensions (economic, social, environment).

2.1   Similar Work from BPM and Sustainability Field

Sustainability and BPM topics started to appear in combination in the literature several years ago, for example with (Jeston & Nelis, 2008) or (zur Muehlen & Su, 2010), just to mention some of them.

A literature review of sustainability in BPM research has been published in 2012 (Stolze, Semmler, & Thomas, 2012) and there were findings "if the BPM research provides the right tools and methods to green the underlying business activities or if it is rather embracing sustainability only on a descriptive/argumentative level without true incorporation into its methodological foundations".

The CAiSE'11 Panel on Green and Sustainable Information Systems (Pernici, Aiello, Donnellan, Gelenbe, & Kretsis, 2012) has underlined aspects that are more specific and practically oriented. It has been recognized that BPM and the associated optimization actions that are developed in companies have not been specifically explained for some important sustainable aspects such as energy savings and business process environmental impact in general. "With the notion of *green BPM*, it has been argued that *green information technology* may be too limited to allow for a full exploration of the role of information systems". Therefore, studying the mechanisms of innovating and transforming business processes toward more environmentally sustainability work practices seems to be a promising field of information systems research (vom Brocke, Seidel, & Recker, 2012).

In order to understand the link between sustainability and BPM, six essential research directions for green BPM have been identified, which are related to six factors or core elements of BPM (vom Brocke et al., 2012). The associated questions for each factor try to explain the motivation, meaning and the importance of sustainability association with BPM:

1. *Strategic Alignment*: How can we operationalize sustainability? What are the relevant value dimensions? Should they be measured?
2. *Governance*: How can we organize sustainability? What roles are needed? What procedures can be applied in specific organizational contexts?
3. *Methods*: How can we identify the sustainability impact of processes? What extensions to modelling languages are needed?
4. *Information technology*: How can we find technology that supports process change? What is sustainability-enabling technology? What are best-practice use cases?
5. *People (Human resources)*: How can we educate people to adopt sustainability practices? What is the Curriculum of Sustainability Training?
6. *Organizational culture*: How can we identify, operationalize, and communicate values relevant to sustainable processes? How can we transform people's attitudes?

More recently, the Green BPM concept was defined (from an information system researcher's perspective) as "the sum of all information systems-supported management activities that help to monitor and reduce the environmental impact of business processes in their design, improvement, implementation, or operation stages, as well as lead to cultural change within the process life cycle" (Opitz, Krüp, & Kolbe, 2014). As a general conclusion, of the more recent published works in the field, researchers provide good ideas about sustainability and business process management (most on green information systems and green BPM), but they provide only little or no guidance how to integrate sustainability in the concrete organization business processes.

2.2   Sustainable Business Process Management

According to (Tregear, 2009), sustainable BPM in an organization should have: process architecture, continuous measurement and a consistent framework.

Process architecture is a top-level view on an organization's key process areas [Fig. 1]. Continuous measurement is a system of key-performance indicators established and monitored. Consistent framework means all levels of the organization should be involved in BPM:

1. *Enterprise level*: top management and members of the process office manage enterprise processes. This means they identify, model, measure, govern and align high-level processes with corporate strategy.
2. *Process level*: analysts should understand, analyze, redesign, implement and roll out operational processes and deal with day-to-day management.
3. *Implementation level*: IT professionals transform process models and rules into applications; manage changes, while middle managers manage people and projects.

According to these perspectives on business process management, we are proposing a model to integrate sustainability aspects into organization using existing BPM related standards and frameworks.

3   Integrating Sustainability into an Organization

3.1   How to Achieve Sustainability of an Enterprise?

If the enterprise wants to sustain its business, it should (Reeves, Zeng, & Venjara, 2015) : keep resetting the vision, experiment with business models, focus on seizing and shaping strategic opportunities, not on executing plans and get good at adapting the organization. This is the so called "self-tuning" and the main pre-requirement for it is a system which allows fluidity and feedback. In addition, this means that the top management tasks like setting the vision, strategy and tactics is not a one-time job, but rather have to be continuously performed based on the client and market feedback. To put it simply: an enterprise without an established and integrated feedback loop is not sustainable from its existence point of view. To be more concrete, an organization should integrate a process called "Re-planning" in its process landscape [Fig. 2, KPA 1.2]. Leading companies (from business sustainability perspective) operating globally through the Internet as Google, Netflix, Amazon, Alibaba use this approach. But there's more to sustainability than leadership in income, pervasiveness and number of users. People usually see only economic dimension of the sustainability, while having a blind spot on the environmental and social. If the organization has a BPM system in place and working, a good starting point is to integrate sustainability into it related processes (following this order): 1. update the organization's vision, strategy, tactics (corporate level); 2. update its process architecture; 3. update management, core and supporting processes.

In the following chapters, some guidance how to implement sustainability aspects in those three levels is provided.

3.2   Implementing Sustainability Aspects: At a Corporate Level

For managing or better structuring organization vision, strategy and tactics, a BMM can be used ("Business Motivation Model, Version 1.3," 2015).

To integrate sustainability into organization, we have to start with top level concepts, which are according to BMM:

- Ends: What (as opposed to how) the business wants to accomplish.
- Means: How the business intends to accomplish its ends.
- Directives: The rules and policies that constrain or govern the available means.
- Influencers: Can cause changes that affect the organization in its employment of its means or achievement of its ends. Influencers are neutral by definition.
- Assessment: A judgment of an Influencer that affects the organization's ability to achieve its ends or use its means.

The BMM defines both the structure of the strategic concepts as well as the semantics of the terms used. It not only covers the traditional components of strategic planning, but also includes the concepts of Influencers (e.g. stakeholders) and Assessments. An important feature of this model is the perspective offered on its components by Reference Elements. The ones of most interest from the point of view of BPM are Organizational Units and Process. The message is that every level of the organization and also the processes of the organization should have a model with a consistent structure as depicted by the BMM framework (vom Brocke & Rosemann, 2010).

The BMM helps us to clarify and structure corporate-level concepts such as vision, mission, tactics, influencers etc. To demonstrate the practical usage of this model, we will show how the company's top-level quality manual can be improved and updated with sustainability aspects. The example shown in Tables 1 to 4 is related to a company that produces electrical tools and wants to be more sustainable (this is only an example to demonstrate the usability of the BMM model in the field of sustainability).

Table 1. BMM *means* (an example including some sustainability aspects)

Summary: Using MEANS, we achieve business goals.
Mission: "Designing and producing electrical tools".
Sustainable mission: *"Designing, producing electrical tools and providing renting services"*.
Course of action:

- Strategy: "Producing of electrical tools for professionals, who can order personalized package of attachments"
- ***Sustainable strategy:*** Same as above + *"providing a service where professionals can borrow tool attachments"*
- Tactic: "Selling them as many tool attachments as possible".
- ***Sustainable tactic:*** Same as above + *"Providing tool attachment exchange service and battery renting service"*

Directive:

- Business policy: (usually unstructured): "If the tool is broken, buy a new one",
- ***Sustainable business policy:*** *"If the tool is broken, rent a new one"*
- Business rule: (usually structured): "Return policy of tools: within warranty period"
- ***Sustainable business rule:*** same as above + *"return old tool (if it still works) or battery anytime and rent a new tool or battery"*

Table 2. BMM **ends** (an example including some sustainability aspects)

Ends:
Vision: "To become the best electrical tools maker in the European Union".
Sustainable vision:
   "To become the best electrical tools maker in the European Union with lowest quantity of electronic waste and most natural resources preserved".
Desired result:
   Goals: Qualitative description, for example: "New tool model launched every year, bigger number of units sold".
Sustainable goals:
   Same as above + *"less resources used, lower water and carbon footprint, less units on the junkyard, more serviced units"*
Objective (quantitative description): "To increase sales of tool units by 10% by 2016".
Sustainable objective: *"To reduce the amount of energy spent for production for 5% by 2016 while maintaining sales volume"*

Table 3. BMM **influencers** (an example including some sustainability aspects)

Internal influencers:
   Assumptions, habits, (un)written rules, relations among employees, management power and actions, (dis)satisfaction. For example: *"Professionals want to buy, not borrow tools* OR *by lowering the production and providing services I will lose my job as production worker"*
External influencers:
   Customers, environment, regulations, delivery, technology etc. For example: *"Information Technology services for mobile phones, which allows professionals to borrow tools from each other"*

• Influencing other organizations. Example: *"Play a role model for a competition."*

Table 4. BMM **assessments** (an example including some sustainability aspects)

Potential impacts:
   Risks: *"Convincing professionals to borrow instead of buy tools is difficult"*,
   Potential reward (**sustainability related**): *"Lower number of tools produced, more units borrowed, cleaner environment and maintaining high profit because of new sustainability related services"*.

By starting integrating sustainability aspects into highest levels of corporate management we ensure that lower levels follow the guidance easier as when using a bottom-up approach. This is called *leadership* (show the way, not enforce it). *"A sustainability leader is someone who inspires and supports action toward a better world"* (Visser & Courtice, 2011).

3.3   Implementing Sustainability Aspects: Process Landscape Level

After redefining vision and other corporate concepts, we can continue by re-engineering process architecture. Similar approach was used by (Rozman & Geder, 2012), when defining key process areas for higher education institutions.

An example of process architecture showing some sustainability aspects already integrated is shown on [Fig. 1]. Key process areas (KPAs marked bold) are those where sustainability aspects were considered:

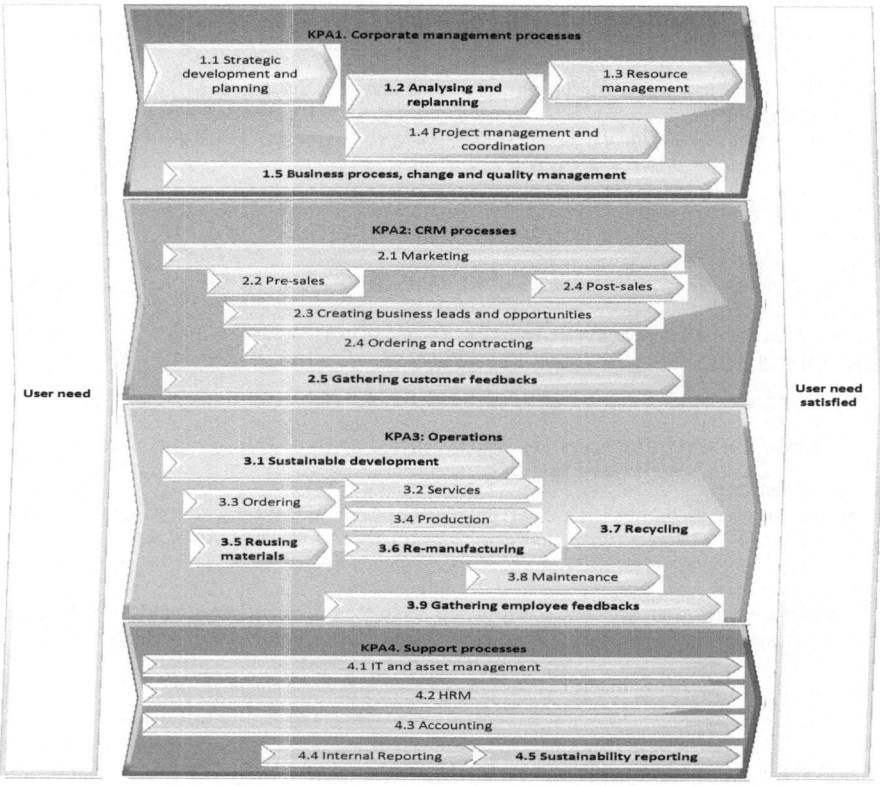

Fig. 1. Process architecture with some sustainability related processes covered

KPA1: Corporate Management Processes

1.2 *Analyzing and re-planning* - As mentioned earlier, constant observation of the environment and continuous re-planning is one of most important management tasks to ensure business will survive. Re-planning action means adapting to the environment, building better services with sustainability in mind.

1.5 *Business Processes, Change and Quality management* - A company without established processes, which make sure processes are constantly updated and improved, cannot be sustainable on the long-term. This includes process, change and quality management. Process management approach means that company has defined well all its processes, place and running them as they have established. In addition, a prerequisite for this is *change management*: gathering suggestions for changes from employees, customers and the environment and implementing it into management system and better processes.

KPA 2: CRM Processes

2.5 *Gathering customer feedbacks* – this is a typical CRM process, which could be modified to gather sustainability related feedbacks from customers. Without a closed loop (feedback-improvement), sustainability cannot be achieved.

KPA3: Operations

3.1. Development – This process is one of the most important processes to achieve sustainable products. Sustainability aspects should be built-in to products already in the product development phase. For example, the development process should incorporate end-of-product-life aspects into new products. This means we should think ahead how our old products can be reused/recycled/remanufactured.

3.5 Reusing materials, 3.6 Re-manufacturing and 3.7 Recycling should be specified as processes too. The example of reusing process is presented in [Fig. 3].

3.9 Gathering employee feedback – this is another process which is necessary for closed-loop development. Without standardized gathering and managing employee's ideas and innovations, the company will have hard time achieving sustainability.

KPA4: Support Processes

4.5 Sustainability reporting – This process serves as a main contact point with the external stakeholders. The main purpose is to communicate to stakeholders in accordance with GRI[1]. The input to this process is constant measuring of operational processes resource usage per product. This information can be also used as a competitive marketing information (e.g. *During the development of a product X, only Y liters of water was used*).

For the above description because of the big number of processes and related activities, not all sustainability aspects can be shown on a big picture (as a process landscape diagram). Many of the operating processes or activities should be introduced in lower process levels (depends of each company's specifics).

3.4   Implementing Sustainability Aspects: Process and Operations Level

To demonstrate how the sustainability related processes can be added to process structure, let us refine key process area "3.5 Reusing materials" from [Fig. 2]. This is an alternative process of the "3.3 Ordering process". This way we are changing a supply chain for the "3.4 Production processes", which previously included only "3.3. Ordering (of new materials)". On the first and second levels of details, we used 'process map' technique from Aris Express tool, which shows only the rough sequence of the processes or process groups. We have refined the 'Reusing materials' process area with 3 sub-processes: "3.5.1. Accepting used batteries", "3.5.2 Disassembling and sorting" and "3.5.3 Warehousing of sorted materials" [Fig. 2].

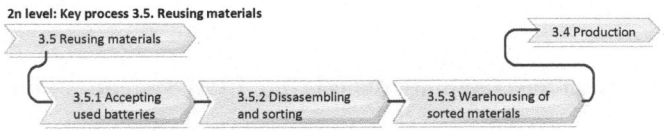

Fig. 2. Excerpt from 2nd level of process architecture

---

[1] Global Reporting Initiative.

The next step is to define the process in even greater details. For this purpose, BPMN (Business Process Modelling Notation) is appropriate. For the demonstration purposes, we show the details of the sub-process "3.5.1 Accepting used batteries only". This process [Fig. 3] is performed by three roles: User of the product, Customer service department, Return center and Disassembly unit. The process starts with two triggers: 1. Customer service department informs customers about battery return policy on yearly basis or 2. When it receives user registration form of his electrical tool.

Then, the return center accepts used batteries from customers. After accepting the used battery, they check for type, weigh it and send it to the disassembly unit. At the same time, they calculate the bonus for the user and send them a bonus in the form of discount for the next purchase or lease of the battery. The Disassembly unit sorts the received batteries, disassembles them and sorts the raw materials.

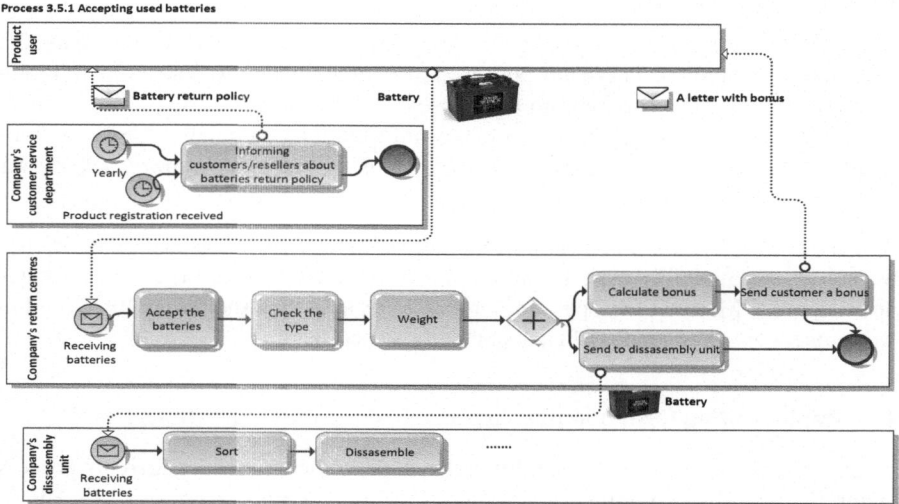

Fig. 3. Excerpt from 3rd level of processes

We have shown only the small excerpt of integrating a new process into organization using BPM approach and notations (Aris process landscaping and BPMN), but the idea should be clear. Integrating sustainability into organization should not be an isolated initiative. It should be integrated right into the entire management system; otherwise it is likely to fail at least in the long run.

3.5   Implementing Sustainability Aspects into BPM System: A Summary

The following table summarizes the recommended usage of BPM related standards and approaches for better sustainability management of organizations. With this summary table we directly address RQ 2: *Which existing BPM related standards could be used to integrate sustainability into organization?*

Table 5. Summary of BPM related approaches with sustainability management

Sustainability related action/task	BPM related standard / approach	Usefulness
Redefining vision, mission, strategy, tactics of an organization	BMM (Business Motivation Model)	Strategic concepts can be defined in the form of clear structure and related to processes
Redefinition of processes – high level	Process maps (ARIS process landscaping)	High level sustainability related processes can be presented
Redefinition of processes – low level	BPMN (Business Process Modelling Notation)	Sustainability related activities can be clearly defined and incorporated in business processes (operations level)
Maintaining sustainable organization	PDCA (Plan-Do-Check-Act) cycle	Continuous monitoring and improvement of sustainability related processes
Automating sustainability related processes	BPMS (Business Process Management Systems)	Less complex automation of sustainability related processes (in comparison with traditional software development)

As we see, there is a strong relation between BPM and sustainability management. A very good example of such integration (although not directly related to BPM standards), is presented in (O'Hare, C. McAloone, Pigosso, & Howard, 2014).

4   Conclusion

Within this article, different perspectives of the relation between BPM and sustainability have been discussed. The main objective was to propose an approach on how to integrate sustainability related topics (values and principles) into an organization's management system. We focused most on practically oriented solutions of this approach. Starting with a brief overview of BPM concept and some explanations of different links, aspects and implications with sustainability (part 1 and 2 of the article) we have created the knowledge base for the proposed model of integrated sustainability aspects into organization using existing BPM related standards and frameworks (part 3).

The references analysis in this article has proved that the sustainability concept and its implementation is a major challenge and different successful approaches in organization's practice have proofed that solutions required out-of-the-box thinking. For the BPM discipline, such thinking means increasingly thinking in terms of innovative/creative solutions, services and processes (rather than disciplines) in order to support organizations' sustainable development.

Vice versa, considering the vital role of information in all areas of the modern world, this development can embody a great opportunity for the BPM discipline since it can prove its usefulness. The notion of process and the knowledge of process management can prove particularly helpful since processes are the nucleus of socio-technical work systems, and BPM has proven particularly successful at integrating the perspective of various disciplines (vom Brocke et al., 2012).

The proposed model of integrated sustainability aspects into organization using existing BPM related standards and frameworks could support practitioners (analysts and managers of different levels) to re-engineer, re-design their corporate and operations' level processes having in mind both BPM and sustainability principles (way of actions). However, a coherent training program in the field of sustainability should support these new ways of people thinking and behavior and there have been briefly demonstrated that LeadSUS training program is a feasible solution to this problem.

Through the ideas discussed we can conclude that contributions to theory and innovative solutions will both be needed in order to leverage BPM for sustainability leadership and management. Building on the BPM body of knowledge, research should focus on the specific challenges imposed by the phenomenon of greenness, or sustainability in a wider sense (recognized also by (Pernici et al., 20112)). In addition, finding the right answers on how sustainability approach could be supported by BPM and how it can be better operationalized (in detail) in the case of different type of organizations (small, medium, big, public or private etc.) leads to another major challenge for our future researches.

According to our research, the market of the BPM training (Draghici, Olariu, & Rozman, 2012; Draghici, Prostean, Mocan, & Draghici, 2011) and sustainability training (Draghici, Fistis, Albulescu, & Draghici, 2015) have been developed, but there is a lack of a combination of such training. Therefore, we address this issue by clustering the following ECQA trainings: ECQA Certified Business Process Manager, ECQA Sustainability Manager, ECQA Social Responsibility Manager, ECQA Certified Applied Sustainability and CSR Professional, ECQA Certified Diversity Manager and ECQA Innovation Manager 2.0. This initiative could satisfy better the news of information technology specialists in order to support the sustainable development initiatives in their organizations and also, the analysts in different sustainable development areas to better define, develop and realize (implement) their business processes.

Acknowledgements. The paper is related to the project: "Leadership in Sustainability – Sustainable Manager" (LeadSUS, LLP-LdV/TOI/2013/RO/022), which has been funded with the support of the European Commission. This paper and the communication reflect the views only of the authors, and the Commission cannot be held responsible for any use, which may be made of the information contained therein.

References

1. Business Motivation Model, Version 1.3. Object Management Group (2015). Retrieved from http://www.omg.org/spec/BMM/
2. Draghici, A., Fistis, G., Albulescu, C., Draghici, G.: Research on training needs identification. leadership in sustainability. In: Proceedings of the MakeLearn and TIIM Joint International Conference: Managing Intellectual capital and innovation for sustainable and inclusive society, Bari, Italy (2015). Retrieved from http://www.toknowpress.net/ISBN/978-961-6914-13-0/MakeLearn2015.pdf

3. Draghici, A., Olariu, C., Rozman, T. Business process management training and certification program: a slovenian-romanian collaboration experience. In: Knowledge and Learning: Global Empowerment; Proceedings of the Management, Knowledge and Learning International Conference 2012, pp. 651–663. International School for Social and Business Studies, Celje (2012). Retrieved from http://ideas.repec.org/h/isv/mklp12/651-663.html

4. Draghici, A., Prostean, G., Mocan, M., Draghici, G.: State of business process management in companies from romania west region. In: Proceedings of Management of Technological Changes (MTC 2011), Alexandoupolis, Greece (2011)

5. Fistis, G., Rozman, T., Riel, A., Messnarz, R.: Leadership in sustainability. In: Barafort, B., O'Connor, R.V., Poth, A., Messnarz, R. (eds.) EuroSPI 2014. CCIS, vol. 425, pp. 231–245. Springer, Heidelberg (2014)

6. Jeston, J., Nelis, J.: Management by Process: A roadmap to sustainable Business Process Management. Elsevier (2008)

7. O'Hare, J., McAloone, T.C., Pigosso, D.C.A., Howard, T.J.: Eco-Innovation Manual. United Nations Environment Programme (2014)

8. Opitz, N., Krüp, H., Kolbe, L.M.: Green business process management - a definition and research framework. In: Proceedings of the Annual Hawaii International Conference on System Sciences, pp. 3808–3817 (2014). http://doi.org/10.1109/HICSS.2014.473

9. Pernici, B., Aiello, M., Donnellan, B., Gelenbe, E., Kretsis, M.: What IS can do for Environmental Sustainability: A Report from the CAiSE´11 Panel on Green and Sustainable IS. Communications of the Association for Information Systems **30**(18), 275–292 (2012)

10. Reeves, M., Zeng, M., Venjara, A.: The Self-Tuning Enterprise – HBR (2015). Retrieved May 29, 2015. https://hbr.org/2015/06/the-self-tuning-enterprise

11. Rozman, T., Geder, M.: Procesno usmerjeno vodenje visokošolskih ustanov (Process-oriented management of higher educational institutions). DOBA Journal **4**(2) (2012). Retrieved from http://journal.doba.si/letnik_4_(2012)_st__2?aid=453&m=1

12. Stolze, C., Semmler, G., Thomas, O.: Sustainability in business process management research – a literature review. In: Proceedings of AMCIS 2012, p. 10 (2012)

13. Tregear, R.: Business Process Management: Is - Is Not - Must Have - Must Not (2009). Retrieved June 8, 2015. http://www.slideshare.net/rtregear/business-process-management-is-is-not-must-have-must-not?utm_source=slideshow&utm_medium=ssemail&utm_campaign=download_notification

14. Visser, W., Courtice, P.: Sustainability Leadership: Linking Theory and Practice. Leadership, 14 (2011)

15. Vom Brocke, J., Rosemann, M. Handbook on Business Process Management 2: Strategic Alignment, Governance, People and Culture. International Handbooks on Information Systems (2010). http://doi.org/10.1007/978-3-642-01982-1

16. Vom Brocke, J., Seidel, S., Recker, J.: Green Business Process Management - Towards the Sustainable Enterprise | Springer. Springer, New York (2012). http://www.springer.com/us/book/9783642274879

17. Zur Muehlen, M., Su, J. (eds.): Business process management workshops. In: BPM 2010 International Workshops and Education Track. Springer, Hoboken (2010). Retrieved from http://www.springer.com/gp/book/9783642205101

ECQA Governance Capability Assessor Skills for Managing Strategic Directions

János Ivanyos[1(✉)], Éva Sándor-Kriszt[2], and Richard Messnarz[3]

[1] Trusted Business Partners Ltd., Katica u. 12, Nagykovácsi 2094, Hungary
ivanyos@trusted.hu
[2] Budapest Business School, Buzogány u. 11-13, Budapest 1149, Hungary
kriszt.eva@bgf.hu
[3] ISCN LTD/GesmbH, Schieszstattgasse 4 8010, Graz, Austria
rmess@iscn.com

Abstract. ISO/IEC 15504 process capability assessments (or similar audit approaches) are widely used in specific industries and sectors, like automotive, medical, space, finance, etc. Most of these assessments are performed only at operational levels aiming up to level 2 (Managed) capability targets. The coverage of the governance objectives referred by the enabling processes of the Governance Model for Trusted Businesses helps to use the industry and sector specific process assessment models by establishing the applicable organizational contexts of level 3 (Established) and level 4 (Predictable) process attributes concerning to the operational and supporting business processes. The Managing Strategic Directions scenario - by adapting skills and processes from ECQA certified Governance Capability Assessor job role - helps the management to select and apply those governance practices which are relevant for improving and ensuring the better market recognition, the transparency and accountability of enterprise management, and the commitment to business excellence. This approach is also applicable for the key goals of future global innovation and networking aimed by the ECQA.

Keywords: Enterprise governance · ISO/IEC 15504 (SPICE) · ISO 31000 risk management · Enterprise risk management (ERM) · Internal control · Governance capability assessment · Assurance management · Global innovation and networking · Business trust and transparency

1 Strengthening Business Trust and Transparency

It is important to all economic and social partners, that the enterprise governance milieu - by keeping in mind all the needs and requirements of the markets' demand and supply relations, the regulatory environment enforcing public societal interests, and the stakeholders' expectations together - supports the optimal framework of risk taking in establishing and maintaining long term and fruitful business relationships necessary for the sustainable development. Therefore it is desirable for the achievement of a standard level of business trust that those governance principles and enabling practices which

© Springer International Publishing Switzerland 2015
R.V. O'Connor et al. (Eds.): EuroSPI 2015, CCIS 543, pp. 260–275, 2015.
DOI: 10.1007/978-3-319-24647-5_21

are commonly interpretable and observable by all types of economic entities will be as widely as possible acquainted and also applied according to the specific business conditions. Implicitly the enterprise has the more and the more types of business relationships and stakeholders, the more important is the control and transparency of its governance system supporting business trust. Nevertheless, the successful conformity to governance requirements and the credible presentation of the achieved results are equally important to the entities either in start-up, growing or matured phases - independently from size, industry sector or ownership types.

For publicly listed companies, the regulators or supervision authorities request compliance to the local corporate governance codes or recommendations. In Europe the *"comply or explain"* type disclosures are generally accepted, however stakeholders would be more happy with wider transparency of how the fulfilled compliance objectives are achieved instead of just receiving short explanations of why some compliance requirements are missed or managed in different than the recommended way.

Other organizations, like Small or Medium sized Enterprises or Innovation Network Organizations are typically not requested to disclose conformity statements. However if their products or services are embedded into their customers' production lines, the necessary technical, quality and financial indemnity insurance requirements and the validation processes are established and maintained within formal supply chain management. For example even the small entities might be asked to provide independent audit reports on *Service Organization's Control* in outsourcing business or small training organizations are also requested for providing validation reports for compliance with international standards or local regulatory requirements. Funding agencies, investors and financial institutions can rate their potential SME clients not only based on the historical financial figures, in optimal business environment the "soft" organizational management factors and company goodwill are also evaluated and important for decision making. For these reasons, even the SMEs and network organizations can benefit from presenting their governance capability conforming to international standards without exaggerated implementation and assurance costs by adapting the **Governance Model for Trusted Businesses** [1] aligned with their own business goals and environment. Most of the given governance processes and necessary practices don't need to be implemented in different or new way from existing company/organization management practices by linking existing - already proofed - management practices to generic governance objectives for better achieving transparency to external stakeholders.

All organizational and operational levels have specific enterprise goals and related governance objectives. Criteria for tolerable level of risks should be established based on those business and enabling governance processes and their capability level targets, which are closely related to these enterprise goals. (For simplicity reason any type of business organization or entity will be referred as "enterprise" in this paper).

For implementing Enterprise Governance the executive management and - if it exists - the supervisory board should follow *scenarios* to design, implement, direct, monitor and improve business operation in alignment with the adapted governance objectives. In this term the *"Enterprise Governance"* is driven by the organization's specific business goals and enabling governance objectives instead of generic control or regulatory framework based "checklists".

The term of "scenario" is also used for systematically considering integrated risk management aspects of enterprise/entity governance practices implemented at operational and organizational levels. These considerations are focusing on the customized design of governance objectives, processes and practices enabling the better achievement of the concerning enterprise goals, and the presentation of related risk criteria as management assertions or risk appetite statements. Based on the evaluation of how these risk criteria are fulfilled, the next improvement or correcting actions (risk treatments) are planned and performed. The **ISO 31000 Risk Management standard** [2] sets applicable requirements for these risk management activities at organizational and process levels.

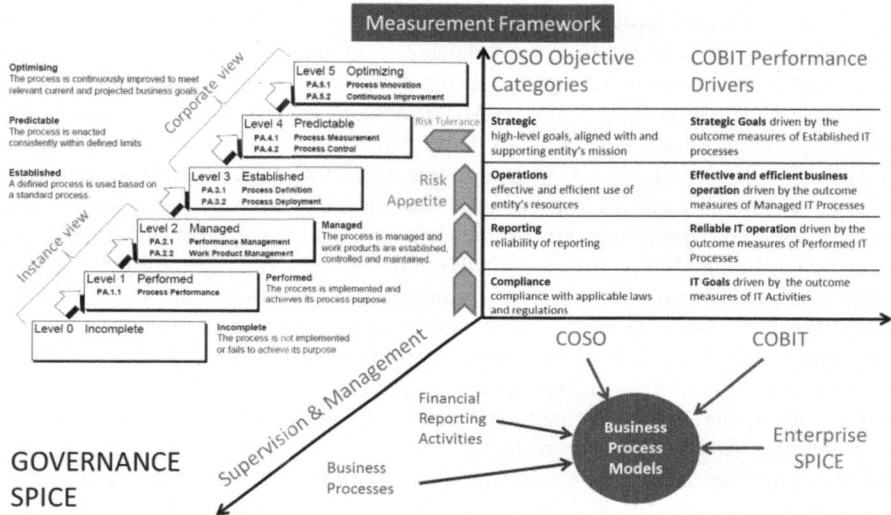

Fig. 1. Governance Capability Assessment Model

When **ISO/IEC 15504 standard (SPICE)** [3] based **Governance Capability Assessment** [4] concept is applied, the evaluation of compliance will focus on how the capability profiles of the implemented core business and governance processes are aligned with the governance objectives customized for the specific enterprise goals.

The governance processes defined by the Governance Model for Trusted Businesses are supported by application practices selected from the **COSO** [5], **COBIT** [6] and **Enterprise SPICE** [7] reference models. The governance processes associated with the process attributes defined by ISO/IEC 15504 provide a common basis for performing assessments of governance capability regarding Enterprise Governance and reporting of results by using a common rating scale. ISO/IEC 15504 standard (SPICE) offers not only transparent method for assessing performance of relevant governance processes, but also tools for assessing related risk areas based on the gaps between target and assessed capability profiles.

2   Enterprise Goals Driven Integrated Risk and Assurance Management Scenarios

The **Integrated Risk and Assurance Management Scenarios** [8], [9] should be established by mapping already implemented or newly developed management practices to governance objectives - through specific enterprise goals. By this way also the compliance and assurance works are aligned with the enterprise specific business objectives and might keep the less meaningful elements of general governance or control frameworks out of scope. By comparing existing practices to those offered by these frameworks, the management and - if requested due to enterprise size or corporate laws - the board might benefit from getting wider professional knowledge and best practice suggestions for improving enterprise governance.

The Integrated Risk and Assurance Management scenarios are distinguishing different operational and organizational levels having specific targets and time-horizons. Each level defines **"Usefulness" and "Efficiency" goals and measures** [10] allowing management to see recognized professional framework practices as enablers instead of just compliance requirements. The following Integrated Risk and Assurance Management scenarios were developed and maintained by the **BPM-GOSPEL** - Business Process Modelling for Governance SPICE and Internal Financial Control - project (2010-2013) and the **HARBIF** - Holistic Approach to Risk – Based and Continuous Internal Financial Control for SMEs project (2013-2015) co-funded by the European Commission under the Leonardo da Vinci Lifelong Learning Programme:

- Managing Operational Performance
- Managing Performance Reliability
- Managing Operational Effectiveness
- Managing Strategic Directions
- Managing Operational Risks

The Integrated Risk and Assurance Management scenarios can help even local small business organizations to implement compliant governance/control frameworks efficiently with respect of its real business needs and risks, and to exhibit the implementation results for external evaluation or audit in a cost effective way.

By changing from the traditional *model based compliance* to *enterprise goals driven integrated assurance*, the management assertions (the links between business activities and governance practices) are implemented by applying significantly different scoping approach. The key business processes are viewed as instances of business performance at different operational and organizational levels, so the Integrated Risk and Assurance Management scenarios are enhancing the meaning of "compliance" as *in what extent the model based governance/control practices are relevant for supporting the achievement of enterprise goals within their acceptable tolerance levels*. The proposed Integrated Risk and Assurance Management scenarios help to select and apply model based governance/control practices by considering the operational and organizational performance levels and their adequate time-horizons for setting enterprise objectives. The term of *"Assurance Management"* also refers to how the governance capability assessment model is adapted, understood and used by the assurance providers of all organizational and operational levels, including the oversight board, the executive and line management, the internal and external auditors, and other roles relevant in governance, risk management, control system and compliance related works.

Capability profiles of the business processes together with the enabling governance and control processes are representing "reverse", but well understandable measures of **management's risk appetite** [11] as the higher capability levels indicate the more robust risk treatment for achieving relevant business objectives.

At the **Managing Operational Performance** scenario, the capability profiles of the baseline business processes will show how the management keeps under control of these processes. Normally the *Performance Management* and *Work Product Management* process attributes of the **Managed (level 2)** capability are sufficient to provide reasonable assurance to achieve the performance objectives of the business operation - like fulfilling service or product specification and delivery time requirements. Targeting higher capability levels for a business process is also reasonable when its performance objectives are directly linked to customer satisfaction, operational effectiveness or even to strategic objectives. For example a *Monthly Payroll Calculation* process related performance metrics (e.g. number of calculations, resource usage, error rates, missed deadlines, etc.) are also applicable indicators of business reliability, operational effectiveness and market recognition within the different time horizons of the specific enterprise goals. The higher process capability of the *Monthly Payroll Calculation* process means the more extended management and risk treatment practices concerning to the objectives of customer satisfaction, pay-off and order renewal in shorter periods, and of economical sustainability in longer terms. Quantitative measures of key product or service deliveries at recognized quality level are applicable to establish risk tolerance indicators. For example increasing error rates should indicate management actions to improve integrity of the calculation process, technology support and human skills. Unsatisfactory volume (or growth) of monthly transactions should force management to implement changes not only in resource allocation, but also to reorganize business processes and human capacity, or even reconsider business scope, strategy and enterprise structures.

At the **Managing Performance Reliability** scenario the **Satisfaction**, **Accuracy** and **Data Protection** objectives related governance practices - referred by the Governance Model for Trusted Businesses - are selected for implementation and improvement in order to enable achievement of pay-off cycle related business objectives, like customer retention and capacity utilization. These practices are also supporting the achievement of *Performance Management* and *Work Product Management* process attributes of the **Managed (level 2)** capability for the baseline business processes. For example Accuracy and Data Protection objectives are helping to identify Work Products related requirements in specific IT-enabled business environments, as of the payroll processing.

The *risk appetite* at this operational level can be identified as the coverage of business processes by the Satisfaction, Accuracy and Data Protection objectives related governance processes. This means that not all, but the relevant set of the business activities should be covered and there is an interrelation between the capability profiles. The wider coverage of business processes has been achieved, the more reasons appear to investigate capability profiles of the related governance processes. The achievement of the - level 2 - *Performance Management* and *Work Product Management* attributes for the business processes will be evidenced by the outcomes of the

Satisfaction, Accuracy and Data Protection objectives related governance processes. And vice versa, for example the performance of the "Ensure Systems Security" IT governance/control process (from COBIT) is better evidenced by the coverage of payroll operational processes, than by simple checking the related IT projects or functions. The *base practices* and *work products* of the governance processes should be evidenced by the underlying business operation. E.g. avoiding system security incidents has to be proved by the payroll operation. A payroll calculation process at Managed capability level will provide more systematic evidences for the Process Performance attribute of the "Ensure Systems Security" IT control process by setting the relevant performance objectives and work product requirements for payroll calculation.

At the **Managing Operational Effectiveness** scenario the **Exploitability**, **Process Integrity** and **Competency** objectives related governance practices - referred by the Governance Model for Trusted Businesses - are selected for implementation and improvement in order to enable achievement of (quarterly or yearly) reporting period specific business objectives, like profitability and agile resource allocation. As these practices provide business unit level framework for effective development and deployment of resources, process control and competency, the achievement of *Process Definition* and *Process Deployment* attributes of the **Established (level 3)** capability profiles for the business processes can be evidenced by them. It is also important to avoid unnecessary or over regulation of business processes: the business unit (or entity) level controls should be implemented not just in compliance with generic control models, but by keeping in mind the business unit level "Usefulness" and "Efficiency" objectives. It is not reasonable to maintain business unit level documentation of those procedures which are not aligned with the business objectives. Documenting, implementing and auditing those procedures which are in conflict either with operational efficiency or simply with process performance objectives, have no value for the organization. Most of those model based compliance works which are not driven by the business unit's specific objectives are just waste of time and efforts. For example scope of business or quality procedures (manuals) should be determined by keeping the impact on business unit goals in mind, otherwise management and staff will continuously override these internal rules. Internal rules and guidelines such as for investment or procurement procedures should also have deployment or tailoring guidance allowing customization based on business conditions.

The *risk appetite* at this organizational level can be identified as the coverage of business processes by the Exploitability, Process Integrity and Competency objectives related governance processes. For example the internal rules and tailoring guidance for managing business unit level resources, quality procedures, process descriptions and human skills are kept by the payroll operational manager in supervising how payroll staff follows them in individual service projects. Therefore the **Managed (level 2)** capability profiles for the Satisfaction, Accuracy, Data Protection, Exploitability, Process Integrity and Competency objectives related governance/control processes will enable the payroll business processes to achieve **Established capability (level 3)**, when the lower risk level is reasonable for achieving profitability and agile resource allocation targets. The Managed level of the referred governance processes emphasizes the management's awareness of performance objectives and documentation criteria for implementing business unit (or entity) level operational rules. In smaller organizations or in case of less rule-sensitive services (like reacting to ad hoc advisory requests), there is no need to overregulate all business activities. **Performed (level 1)** profiles of the governance processes related to key business activities might be also sufficient, when management considers the higher risk exposure with control cost savings adequately.

Management's attitude towards control risk taking should be validated by the **Managing Operational Risks** scenario, where the **Risk Awareness** and **Control Efficiency** objectives related governance practices - referred by the Governance Model for Trusted Businesses - are selected for implementation and improvement. **Quantitative Performance Measurement** is necessary at each operational and organizational level by considering specific time-horizons of the business objectives. The **Predictable (level 4)** profiles of the relevant business processes are enabled by the **Managed (level 2)** capability profiles for the Satisfaction, Accuracy, Data Protection, Exploitability, Process Integrity, Competency, Risk Awareness and Control Efficiency objectives related governance/control processes. The Predictable process capability ensures that the performance of the business process (e.g. Monthly Payroll Calculation) supports the achievement of the related business goals within tolerable limits. For example, if the reasonable business revenue, cash flow, operating margin and unit cost targets were achievable by performing ca. 10.000 calculations per month with a tolerable limit of 500 less or unpaid, then the Predictable level of operational processes will provide high level of assurance, that in case of the forthcoming customer orders, the business unit will provide the business performance in alignment with the stakeholders' needs.

Measurable Risk Management performance objectives can be established by the *capability targets* of the business and governance processes, and by the *tolerance levels* (control limits around Enterprise Goals) used by the risk treatment cycles. However, the consulting, improvement and assurance efforts and costs might differ e.g. at Managing Operational Performance or at Managing Operational Effectiveness scenarios. Where the risk treatment cycle is more frequent, then the less consulting or assurance cost would gain faster benefit return. For example a simple improvement - like better technology support - in payroll calculation will cause immediate and repeatable benefits. Implementing, assessing and improving processes at **Established** capability level might take more effort and slower, but potentially higher return on investment. Automating an activity level control within payroll calculation (e.g. evaluating differences from previous calculation results) might have relatively low costs, but immediate benefits of less personal effort, while changing client's data takeover rules and procedures definitely requests more implementation time and effort with slower return, but will evidently improve data processing integrity, client satisfaction, resource utilization and profitability.

At the **Managing Strategic Directions** scenario the **Competitiveness, Accountability** and **Commitment** objectives related governance practices - referred by the Governance Model for Trusted Businesses - are selected for implementation and improvement in order to enable achievement of strategic planning period specific business objectives, like revenues and cash flow. As these practices provide the enterprise level framework for setting business strategy and market positioning, management's accountability and commitment towards internal and external stakeholders, they also support the achievement of *Process Definition* and *Process Deployment* attributes of the **Established (level 3)** capability profiles for all relevant governance processes.

Theoretically above the achieved level 3 profiles the Risk Management practices with applicable **Quantitative Performance Measurement** - like process capability gaps based risk assessment - would enable the achievement of **Predictable (level 4)** attributes of governance processes; however this would be reasonable only when measurable links between the capability level of governance processes and the achievement of business goals were evident. As Risk Management and Internal Control systems do not provide absolute assurance for achieving business goals due to their inherent limitations (like management's bad decisions or override of controls), setting Predictable capability level target for governance processes is generally not reasonable.

In case of public or listed companies, the high level information about Competitiveness, Accountability and Commitment objectives related governance practices are available in enterprise institutional documents, governance reports and other disclosure statements; however their format and content are typically less informative than would be needed by the external stakeholders. Furthermore the prevalent "*comply or explain*" format of governance reports doesn't help to understand what is really going on. There are explanations of why criteria are missing, but no information available how and in what extent the "compliant" items work, which is more or less in conflict with the transparency requirements.

3   Implementing the Managing Strategic Directions Scenario

The following figure presents role of the Managing Strategic Directions scenario in supporting of Enterprise Governance and improving transparency:

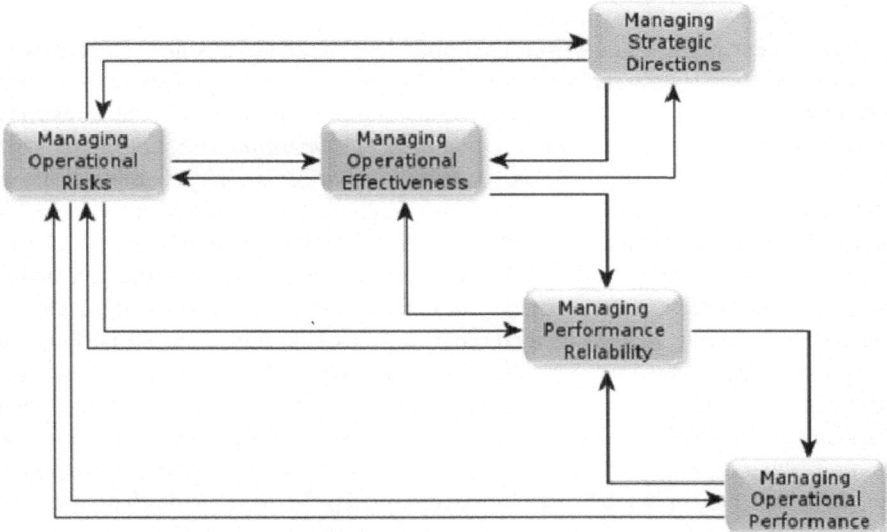

Fig. 2. Role of the Managing Strategic Directions scenario in Enterprise Governance

In the context of **Managing Strategic Directions**, Enterprise Governance should focus on those issues which are considered as relevant for the following sample management problems:

1. The enterprise runs successful business operation(s) with expected profitability; however the organization is not proactive enough to react well to the rapidly changing business environment and market demands.
2. Due to changing or new client requirements and growing competition the business offers and proposals are not received as well as in the past.
3. New business operation (service or product) start-up is in progress which requests new organizational structures and procedures.
4. Increasing volume of business operation request more robust business continuity planning.
5. Changes in business volume need to explore new funding solutions by extensive communications with external parties.
6. New shareholders, investors request more transparency and management accountability over running business operation(s).
7. Stakeholders request attestation and public disclosures of business excellence.

Normally these issues are occurring and being managed in different time-scale than of the other Integrated Risk and Assurance Management scenarios. **Managing Operational Performance** is limited to the individual instances of the business processes and activities by considering service or product delivery requirements and schedule. **Managing Performance Reliability** considers contractual pay-off cycles with parallel or reoccurring business operational cycles, while **Managing Operational Effectiveness** typically has the time-horizon of the budgeting or reporting periods. **Managing Strategic Directions** is focusing on longer perspectives. **Operational Risk Management** takes each governance objective into its specific time-horizon when setting risk criteria and measurable risk levels for selecting treatment options and evaluating their effectiveness.

Any reoccurring deviation from enterprise level strategic business objectives like achieving *business goals* and availability of *funding resources* (indicators for strategic planning periods) will call the management's attention to check whether lower level *Operational Performance*, *Reliable Operation* and *Operational Effectiveness* objectives are adequately fulfilled as operational performance, reliability and entity/business unit level effectiveness failures might also cause problems in achieving strategic objectives. Furthermore some operational performance, reliability and effectiveness metrics - like more than planned resource usage, frequent corrective actions, customer dissatisfaction, low capacity utilization within operational life-cycles and decreasing operating margin or increasing unit costs during reporting periods - are going to be early indicators of problems in achieving strategic business objectives at enterprise level. Most of the strategic issues are coming to surface only by reviewing or closing strategic planning periods, so early indicators of *Operational Performance, Reliable Operation* and *Operational Effectiveness* will help management and the boards (where they exist) to be more proactively prepared to strategic challenges.

In case of no root cause having been found at Managing Operational Performance, Managing Performance Reliability and Managing Operational Effectiveness, then **Competitiveness**, **Accountability** and **Commitment** objectives and related governance practices should be assessed whether the selection of practices and their capability targets are aligned with the enterprise level strategic goals or the implemented practices are achieving their target capability levels.

Reoccurring deviations e.g. from profitability and agile resource allocation goals are early indicators of those *Strategic Direction* issues which might be identical only by reviewing strategic planning periods. Assessment and improvement of Competitiveness, Accountability and Commitment objectives related process capability profiles are necessary risk management actions enabling better alignment to *Strategic Directions*.

Management actions taken during strategic planning period to achieve Competitiveness, Accountability and Commitment objectives - together with the other governance objectives - should be monitored by the board or other supervisory bodies (or by equivalent functions of the entity), and adequate level of transparency to all of the stakeholders should be provided by management disclosures.

By the support of Managing Strategic Directions scenario, the organization is enabled:

- to ensure market recognition of the business operation;
- to ensure that the management of the organization is able to control business processes in a way which is adequate to the objectives of trusted business operation including internal control over financial reporting;
- to ensure that the organization and its staff are committed to comply with ethical and integrity requirements relevant to the objectives of trusted business operation, financial controls, and the availability principle.

A consistent risk assessment should be performed as the first step to establish management assertions by linking business activities to applicable governance practices and capability profiles for supporting the relevant governance objectives.

By using the ISO 31000 definition of risk as *"effect of uncertainties on objectives"*, during the **Managing Strategic Directions** scenario we have to identify the *risk criteria (tolerances and appetite)* for governance objectives which are related to the enterprise level *Strategic Directions*. In terms of strategic directions we use the "Usefulness" and "Efficiency" measures for setting metrics in time-horizon of strategic planning periods, for example:

- Business goals measured by revenues
- Funding resources measured by cash flow

For ensuring risk optimisation we need targets and tolerances e.g. measured by:

- Percentage of achieving revenue targets for strategic planning periods and
- Variance from planned cash flow.

The strategic directions related **Competitiveness**, **Accountability** and **Commitment** governance objectives should have such risk criteria which are applicable to measure effective risk treatment for achieving business goals and funding resources by applying governance practices. Applicable governance practices should be selected and implemented by considering their relevance to the above "Usefulness" and "Efficiency" measures.

If a lower level governance practice offered by the Governance Model has no significant relevance for the established enterprise level *Strategic Directions*, then there will be no need to apply that. If management specifies a governance practice as relevant for managing strategic directions within the context of stakeholders' needs, then the target capability profile for implementing the governance process will include it and will be used *as risk criteria (risk appetite)*. Capability level target should be set aligned with the relevant Enterprise Goals, as in this case in accordance with enterprise level Strategic Business goals.

Settings of *Strategic Directions* (Strategic Business Goals) are similar in each type of business organization. However related governance practices and their capability levels might differ in wide range. Effective small enterprises might run their business operation without extensive implementation of strategic planning, control management or integrity assurance practices. When business volume is growing with facing to new customer requirements and organizational changes, then the need for more formal strategic thinking, higher level of transparency and accountability together with commitment to business integrity and availability principles will emerge. Managing these needs according to expectations of the business environment and the stakeholders is a challenge even for the more matured enterprises. By using of the **Managing Strategic Directions** scenario, the management will be able to select and apply those governance practices which are relevant for improving or ensuring better market recognition, transparency and accountability of enterprise management and commitment to business excellence.

Either well running management practices are used to define policies and procedures or designing new management processes can help to improve governance at enterprise level. **Competitiveness**, **Accountability** and **Commitment** objectives related governance practices contribute to develop **- level 3 - Established** capability of those management processes which constitute governance of business operation by establishing their organizational contexts.

Selection and implementation of those governance practices which are offered by the **Governance Model for Trusted Businesses** for Competitiveness, Accountability and Commitment objectives should be driven by the *management's usefulness and efficiency considerations*. Therefore the optimal (meaningful) coverage of offered governance practices, together with a capability profile aiming higher (e.g. Level 2 - Managed or Level 3 - Established) requirements should be concluded and implemented by performing mature risk management practices.

Loosing market during strategic time-horizon means danger for business sustainability. A short term impact is the decreasing value of the enterprise (stock) jeopardizing working conditions of the management and the employees. For longer term the ownership structure of the enterprise or the legal entity owning the business operation might be dramatically changed, or at worst case the business operation might be terminated.

The implemented governance practices are tools for improving ability of the enterprise to refine its strategy and aligned business goals according to the changeable business environment and clients' needs and to maintain successful proposal preparation practices to achieve sales targets. The selected governance practices for **Competitiveness** should enable the achievement of the following outcomes:

- Business goals and targets are systematically maintained.
- Customers and other stakeholder needs and expectations are considered for improvement of product or service features.
- Effective proposal preparation practices are maintained.

Accountability of the management is evidently important for all stakeholders of the enterprise. Normally the legal documents and the company law extended with the internal policies and procedures constitute the static environment for management accountability, however this should be also dynamic to effectively respond to the current needs or changes of the running business operation. Therefore the governance practices enabling effective management control of business operation should be selected and implemented not just according to legal requirements, but also in alignment with the strategic business objectives, the stakeholders' needs and the expectations of the business environment. The selected governance practices for **Accountability** should enable the achievement of the following outcomes:

- Policies and procedures relevant for the governance objectives of trusted business operation including internal controls are consistently implemented and communicated.
- Management structure is adequate to trusted business operation including internal controls.
- Management takes stimulating behaviour for supporting trusted business operation and internal controls.

Commitment to business ethics, integrity and availability (business continuity) principles is an important message to the market that the enterprise management is aware of and manage reputation risks. The implementation of these principles are embedded in the effectively managed, reliable business operations, however enterprise level attestation and communication of business excellence have additional value for the stakeholders. Companies might get advantages from not only mitigating reputation risks, but even increase their competitiveness by qualifying and presenting their strengths in governance and high capability profiles for trusted business operation. The selected governance practices for **Commitment** should enable the achievement of the following outcomes:

- Ethical values are articulated and kept.
- Active policies and procedures are in place to ensure business continuity.
- Information from external parties are collected and reviewed systematically.

The set of applied governance practices and the target Process Capability Attributes comprise those risk criteria against the business performance should be assessed. Evaluation of Process Attribute Gaps (between target and assessed capability) provides measurement of residual risk status.

4   Applying Governance Capability Assessor Skills to Integrate ECQA Knowledge Elements for Global Innovation and Networking

Using the **Governance Model for Trusted Businesses** provides ready to use structure for implementing selected or all elements of the recognized governance/control frameworks and generic enterprise models. Regulatory or voluntary compliance requirements could be looked through clear business driven governance objectives helping better understanding and meaningful design and operation by enterprise management. Besides the less implementation efforts, this structure unburdens the internal and external audit activities in concluding opinion about the fulfilment of compliance requirements.

The Governance Model for Trusted Businesses offers sufficient set of practices to determine the enterprise specific governance and control objectives. The management can easily select and communicate those minimum requirements which are considered as crucial for running business on the specific market (composing the risk appetite). This decision is a **clear message to all stakeholders**, including potential partners, customers and suppliers, that which operational risks are planned to be mitigated by the enterprise management, and which risks remain unattended.

ISO/IEC 15504 process capability assessments (or similar audit approaches) are widely used in specific industries and sectors, like automotive, medical, space, finance, etc. Most of these assessments are performed only at operational levels aiming up to level 2 (Managed) capability targets by using domain specific process assessment models adapting generic standards or recommendations, like ISO 12207, ITIL, COBIT, etc. The coverage of the governance objectives referred by the enabling processes of the Governance Model for Trusted Businesses helps to use the industry and sector specific process assessment models by **establishing the applicable organizational contexts** of level 3 (Established) and level 4 (Predictable) process attributes concerning to the operational and supporting business processes.

As presented in the previous chapter, the **Managing Strategic Directions** scenario helps the management to select and apply those governance practices which are relevant for improving or ensuring the better market recognition, the transparency and accountability of enterprise management, and the commitment to business excellence. The **Competitiveness, Accountability and Commitment** objectives related governance practices - as referred by the Governance Model of Trusted Businesses - contribute to target and achieve the level 3 (Established) capability of the governance processes relevant for better transparency of rules and business needed by all internal and external stakeholders. However the same approach might be followed by the management of innovation networking organizations such as the ECQA.

The **European Certification and Qualification Association (ECQA)** [12] is the result of a series of EU funded projects from 2005–2015. ECQA operates as an organization that is independent from funding. The members of ECQA are widely spread all over Europe and vary from universities, companies and NPOs as well as individuals. ECQA has recently defined the key goals for future networking and global innovation. The essential objective is to integrate all ECQA knowledge elements in form of a portfolio of necessary competencies to cover global innovation in a holistic way and to provide answers to key questions:

1) How to create a VISION and a Dynamic Network
2) How to create a GLOBAL Community of TRUST
3) How to be prepared for Constant Change and being able to (UN)LEARN
4) How to provide TRANSPARENCY of Rules and Business

By using the terminology outlined in the **ECQA skills definition model** [13], the skills hierarchy for the job role **"Governance SPICE Assessor"** [14] has been designed and maintained. The skill units and elements cover the relevant "Governance" domain specific knowledge (Governance, Risk and Controls), the principles of the Governance Model for Trusted Businesses (Governance Objectives), the basics of SPICE (Process Assessment) and the mapping of capability levels with Compliance, Reporting, Operations and Strategic objectives (Governance Capability). Next figure shows how the referred **Governance Objectives** can be applied for future networking and global innovation goals aimed by the ECQA:

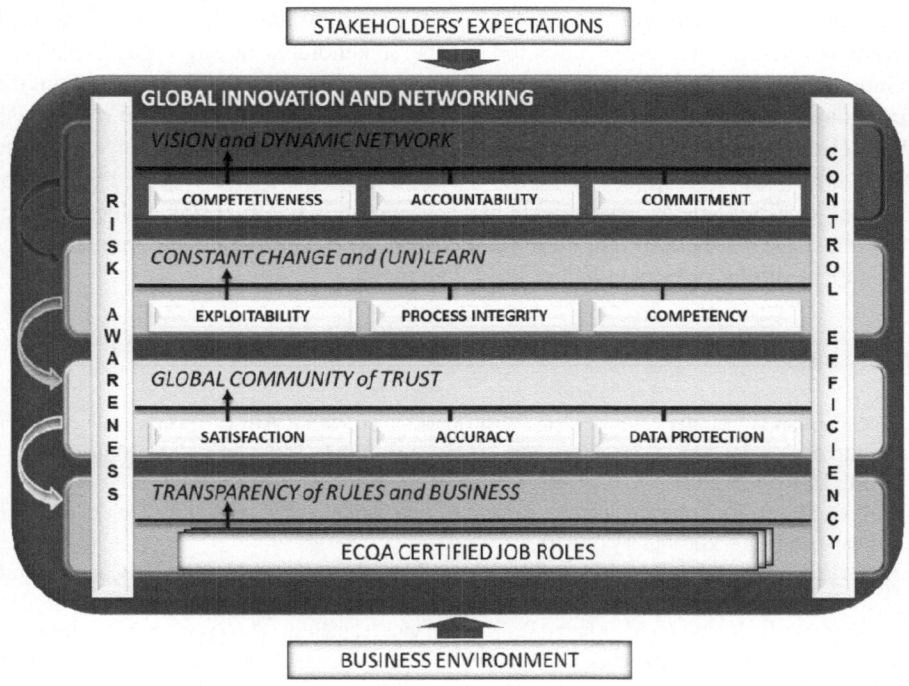

Fig. 3. Mapping Governance Objectives to Global Innovation and Networking Goals of ECQA

By applying the mapping above, all the integrated risk and assurance management scenarios might be followed by the management of the ECQA. *Operational Performance* means the works of the ECQA Job Role Committees for providing transparency of rules and business in each specific (or combined) domain. *Performance Reliability* is interpreted as running a global network community of trust. *Organizational Effectiveness* is based on ECQA goals of enabling constant change and (un)learn for its members and external stakeholders. *Strategic Directions* are those, which are relevant to ensure the vision and the dynamic network organizational goals.

Governance capability issues have come into the view of the management as the huge cost of regulatory compliance activities request consideration of sustainability and added business value of such efforts. This challenge has been answered by utilizing the ISO/IEC 15504 standard based **Governance Capability Assessment** (Governance SPICE) concept applicable for the executive managers, the boards of directors, the audit committees, the internal and external auditors and the supervisory bodies for assessing the effectiveness of internal controls even in different business units and activities, IT management and financial reporting processes. As pictured above, the same concept is applicable for supporting the governance of innovation network organizations.

Major governance scandals, independently from the recent global financial and economic crisis, call the attention that the assessments and audits of core business operations (production, sales, supply chain, etc.) and certifications of business units to the conformance with specific standards are not really convincing in terms of avoiding serious business failures or frauds. In these circumstances the term of **"trusted business"** has got additional attention by the stakeholders in any type of business relationship – including innovation network organizations like the ECQA. Beyond the traditional marketing methods, the product and service providers need to distinguish themselves from their market competitors not just with higher quality or excellence level, faster market response or better pricing, but they are also enforced to present themselves as reliable and sustainable business partners. External stakeholders respect those business partners in long term relationship, whose corporate culture and objectives are at similar or even at higher level than theirs.

References

1. Governance Model for Trusted Businesses, BPM-GOSPEL Deliverable (2011). http://www.governancecapability.com/attachments/article/54/Governance%20SPICE%20Model%20v24.pdf
2. ISO 31000, Risk management – Principles and guidelines (2009). ISO Guide 73, Risk management – Vocabulary (2009)
3. ISO/IEC 15504-1 Information technology – Process assessment – Part 1: Concepts and vocabulary (2004)
4. Ivanyos, J., Roóz, J., Messnarz, R.: Governance capability assessment: using ISO/IEC 15504 for internal financial controls and IT management. In: The MONTIFIC Book, MONTIFIC-ECQA Joint Conference Proceedings (2010). http://training.ia-manager.org/file.php/1/The_MONTIFIC_Book.pdf
5. The Committee of Sponsoring Organizations of the Treadway Commission (COSO). http://coso.org/guidance.htm
6. COBIT - Control Objectives for Information and related Technology. http://www.isaca.org/cobit/pages/default.aspx
7. Enterprise SPICE® - An Integrated Model for Enterprise-wide Assessment and Improvement. Technical Report – Issue 1 September 2010. Copyright © The SPICE User Group 2010. http://enterprisespice.com/page/publication-1
8. Ivanyos, J., Messnarz, R., Roóz, J., Hammrich, O.: EU project BPM-GOSPEL – applying compliance management scenarios in business process modelling for trusted business coaching programs. In: Winkler, D., O'Connor, R.V., Messnarz, R. (eds.) EuroSPI 2012. CCIS, vol. 301, pp. 288–299. Springer, Heidelberg (2012). http://link.springer.com/chapter/10.1007%2F978-3-642-31199-4_25
9. Ivanyos, J., Sándor-Kriszt, E., Kurt, G., Uçma, T.: Applying integrated risk management scenarios. In: HARBIF (Holistic Aproach to Risk-based Internal Financial Control for SMEs) project Deliverable (2014). http://training.ia-manager.org/file.php/1/HARBIF_Integrated_Risk_Management_Scenarios_v2.pdf

10. Wells, C., Ibrahim, L., LaBruyere, L.: New Approach to Generic Attributes. Systems Engineering **6**(4) (2003). © 2003 Wiley Periodicals, Inc. http://onlinelibrary.wiley.com/doi/10.1002/sys.10050/pdf

11. The Committee of Sponsoring Organizations of the Treadway Commission COSO. Enterprise Risk Management - Understanding and Communicating Risk Appetite (2012). http://coso.org/guidance.htm

12. Reiner, M., Sauberer, G., Messnarz, R.: European Certification and Qualification Association - Developments in Europe and World Wide, EuroSPI technical proceedings, June 2014. http://www.ecqa.org/fileadmin/documents/EuroSPI-paper-ECQA-2014.pdf

13. Rules and Process Steps for Certification of ECQA Job Role, Version: Approved. European Certification and Qualification Association (2011). http://ecqa.org/index.php?id=221

14. Governance SPICE Assessor and Internal Financial Control Assessor Skill Cards, ECQA Committees (2011). http://ecqa.org/index.php?id=8

Innovation and Project Management in International Distributed Teams. A Description of an Current Project Work

Christian Reimann[1($\boxtimes$)], Elena Vitkauskaite[2($\boxtimes$)],
Thiemo Kastel[3($\boxtimes$)], and Michael Reiner[4]

[1] FH Dortmund, Dortmund, Germany
christian.reimann@fh-dortmund.de
[2] KTU, Kaunas, Lithuania
elena.vitkauskaite@ktu.edu
[3] Fh St. Pölten, St. Pölten, Austria
Thiemo.Kastel@fhstp.ac.at
[4] IMC FH Krems, Krems a.d. Donau, Austria
michael.reiner@fh-krems.ac.at

Abstract. This project tried to combine students from different degree programmes together in workgroups to get the best learning in communication within project teams with dirstributed teams. Students were given tasks weekly and reports were made continuously. Learning were made not only by programming for the companies, but also in information exchange of business-, media- and programming studentns.

1 Introduction

In the modern world, communication and marketing are very strong parts within projects of companies. These project teams more and more are not located within the same location, but, due to the fact of internationalisation, have their experts spread all over Europe (or worldwide). The question is now, how to teach students to work in distributed project teams and to communicate (online) in multicultural environments? The project tried to connect students of different degree programmes (IT, Multimedia, Marketing, Business) within one project to have hands on experience. The focus here clearly lies on the learning of the students to increase the awareness of the problems within the tasks and to increase the employability for participating students.

2 Theoretic Approach

According to businessdictionary.com innovation is "The process of translating an idea or invention into a good or service that creates value or for which customers will pay." By this definition innovations requires skills from a wide variety of areas, which can be grouped into "Technology" (to create the product), "Business & Marketing"

R.V. O'Connor et al. (Eds.): EuroSPI 2015, CCIS 543, pp. 276–283, 2015.
DOI: 10.1007/978-3-319-24647-5_22

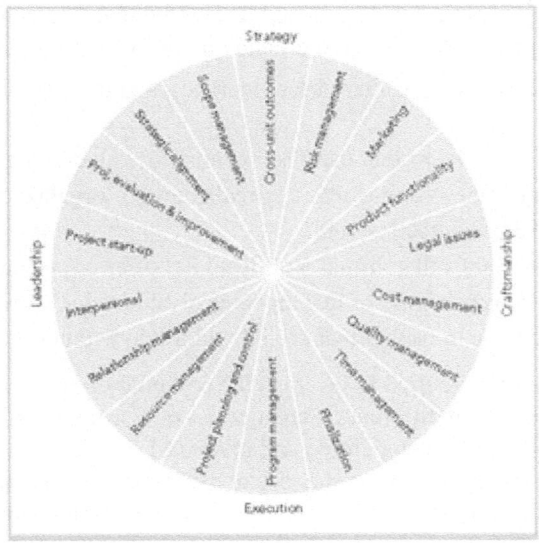

Fig. 1. Categories of project management, Crawford, Pollack, England, 2006

(to understand value creation) and "Project Management" (for the execution of the process itself).

Crawford, Pollack and England [1] suggested 18 categories (see Figure 1) within modern project management that can be grouped into several main groups.

In the review of several journals from 2003-2008 he identifies the most important categories as Interpersonal Skills, Relationship management, Resource management, project planning & control, product functionality and strategic alignment. The outcome of a questionnaire, distributed to several project managers (all with experience and master's degree) is nearly the same as the previous data. [5].

Experiential learning is important to provide "real world contexts" to the students. These help the students to develop rhetorical skills while also connecting academia to communities. Additionally to improve relationships with their fellow students [8]. If this is to be connected with international aspects, students appreciate it most. Interaction skills, communicating and collaborating with others as well as leadership and broadening perspective were some of the highlights, mentioned in the questionnaire given by Craig and Piskur [2].

From an organizational management perspective, individual abilities, experiences, competencies, and qualifications of human resources build a success factor in organizations, which enable entrepreneurial strategies of increasing flexibility and continuous learning [9]. Creating a deeper understanding and interest for cross-cultural issues may further improve the effectiveness of project management practices [10].

Many organizational actors are tempted by the new phenomenon of virtual worlds, but still they desire guidance on the possible applications, business value, and implications of use that accompany these environments [6].

Brente et.al. analysed their data data and it revealed that claims about the organizational value of virtual worlds clustered around one of four general value categories:

- current value—claims that virtual worlds are currently valuable to organizations;
- future value—claims that there is potential for value to organizations;
- contingent value—claims that any realization of organizational value is contingent on certain factors; and
- no value—claims that virtual worlds do not offer organizational value, either due to their very nature or that any conceivable value would never be able to be realized due to factors that prohibit adoption within organizations.[3]

Several companies have tried to leverage the potential of virtual worlds and invited avatars in SL to engage in different co-creation tasks. For instance, the light manufacturer Osram started an idea competition and invited SL residents to contribute lighting ideas. Toyota's Scion brand launched a virtual car model and encouraged participants to modify and customize their cars. Before building the physical hotel, Aloft created a virtual prototype that was discussed and evaluated by consumers in SL [11]. The critical challenge for co-creation in virtual worlds is not so much in devising the technological infrastructure, but in creating and maintaining an experience for participants. Hence, companies have to think about how they find and attract qualified participants, what events they want to organize during the co-creation project, and how to establish and nurture a community characterized by a shared consciousness of kind and mutual support. The key to becoming successful in virtually collaborating with consumers will depend on the ability to aggregate participants, retain them, and encourage them to make contributions [4].

However, a branded virtual good – even for a high-status good like avatar hair – did not guarantee desire. Garnier hair in limited quantity, with a stylised look, may have been successful in getting clicks and name recognition. However, higher-status users associated the hair with newer users so it became less desirable. Further, relying on users as crew members to promote brands brings expectations to represent the brand meaningfully in social roles, and adhere to brand guidelines. With Garnier hair, and broader crew promotions, findings reflect how marketers must factor co-creation into how tactics will play out virtually in uncontrolled ways. Though marketers and platform are of influence, ultimately co-creation of value or meaning happens with the user. Marketers and platform can manipulate values of the virtual world. This issue calls into question related ethics and expectations, the revenue model for the virtual economy, and reinforcements of consumer culture. Some virtual worlds are free to use, others require subscriptions for particular features. As such, marketers and platform must be mindful of the motivations for the user, whilst not overstepping the relationship, threatening the user experience, and distorting values of potential impact on impressionable young users. Brands supporting co-creation activities – related or unrelated to the brand itself – improved activities and fun for users. Further, co-creation seen in the virtual world, and spilling into the real world, may buoy feelings of realism. In turn, what is virtual becomes related, and potentially impactful, in the real world. Anecdotally, among interviewees, brand interactions supported some purchase intentions [7].

Based upon these theoretical aspects, the group of lecturers were planning how to best include those topics into a project.

3   Practical Work

The basic idea of this project was to bring together international students and to make them work as a distributed team, going through different phases of innovation, communication redesign and planning of marketing and business strategies. For this topic, lecturers of several universities agreed to work out this project. Together university of applied sciences Dortmund, KTU Lithuania, University of applied sciences St. Pölten and IMC university of applied sciences Krems decided to go for this task. The lecturers Christian Reimann, Elena Vitkauskaite, Timo Kastel and Michael Reiner decided to use the new idea of virtual reality as a technical tool that the students should generate usage for some SME´s.

The approach was to allocate the amount of students in the different universities and after that include the students into an online system that they could share documents, communicate and be guided by the lecturers. For this task, the Ilias Online Learning Platform[1] was chosen. This platform provides a large toolbox including document management, group management, option for grading as well as a video conferencing account that the students could use. Lecturers planned the details of the different working weeks, including the fact that semesters are starting on different weeks in the different countries. KTU in Lithuania starts its semester beginning of February, where IMC and St. Pölten start at the end of February/beginning of March with Dortmund beginning their lectures end of March/beginning of April.

The project was kicked off with some lectures at KTU, to inform the students about the project and on the basic timeline. Additionally students were introduced in Ilias system and in the basics of virtual reality.

The plan was to start with the teambuilding by adding students from Krems to Lithuania into 22 teams with 3-4 students per team. After the first online kick-off, students were asked to check online for the two given companies and to generate a use case analysis. Krems students had to prepare a short presentation per company that had to be distributed to all of the students. (Weingut Stadt Krems & Brantner Abfall Wirtschaft Krems). The students then had one week to decide to go either for Brantner or Weingut Krems (limitation was set in the list of Ilias, that an equal number of groups per company was generated). After the decision, the groups went into the rounds of innovation, where they had to analyse the companies and their competitors. Next to create ideas on how to use a virtual reality tool (like the given Oculus rift) for a SME, what will be the target group, what should be the scenario, what are the benefits of VR and what should be the game objectives. This was discussed in several online meetings by students with feedback loops of other students and

---

[1] www.ilias.de

lecturers. Students were given an online lecture on how to generate a Video pitch and what are the main tasks for such a video. In the week 5 the one video per idea (2 ideas per group) had to be uploaded to a YouTube channel and at the same time the videos of the other groups had to be watched and graded (online voting tool). This also was the week when the students of Dortmund joined the project and were also asked to grade the different videos. Out of the grading of the students, the lecturers and the companies a ranking was produced and per company one project idea was selected to be programmed and two additional ideas were chosen to be worked on theoretical (Marketing plan, business plan,…). The students then were informed about the choice and partly regrouped into those remaining teams or grouped into other projects of the university. After the Easter holidays groups were introduced into SCRUM and it was agreed to have weekly feedback by a wiki to see what has happened and how the groups were performing. The students were working online, communicating with either video conferencing tools (skype, GoToMeeting, Ilias) or within social media platforms, (closed groups were generated). Documents and files were distributed by using different platforms (mainly ilias). So besides actually very few restrictions, the students were free to choose which of the supplied tools (or even additional ones) they would use for the different purposes of their respective project. For example both teams, who developed a prototype, choose an online tool to support cooperation in SCRUM driven projects. Although the participation in SCRUM was possible for (and recommended to) all team members, mainly the developers choose to participate in the daily stand-up-meetings (which were held every second day).   As the weekly SCRUM meetings were extended into general team meetings at least one student of each university participated. For the last week of the semester in Lithuania (from 20th until 27th of May) a workshop was planned to bring all participants in person together. Students and lecturers travelled to Kaunas differently. This was done, because in the different degree programmes still exams were to be done. Dortmund students arrived in Kaunas Wednesday and started working with Lithuanian students already on Thursday and Friday, where Austrian students joined the groups on Friday afternoon. Saturday was the main working day, with working on the prototype until the evening (including a nice social event in the evening) and some finalizing on Sunday (students were asking for permission to work on, as they wanted to improve their work). Monday $25^{th,}$ some more workshops (e.g. Augmented reality) took place and some lectures and in the evening starting at 5p.m., the official presentations in front of an audience took place. Groups presented their projects and the two main groups showed their marketing plans and ideas as well as their prototypes (that could be tested afterwards, see Figure 2 & Figure 3).

Due to the fact that the semester in Lithuania ended by the end of May and so did their official (and mandatory) time for classes, the students of Lithuania were invited to continue working in their teams, if they liked to, for the rest of the time (but didn´t have to). Students of Dortmund, St. Pölten and Krems continued to improve on the prototypes and the marketing plans as well as the business plans for their projects.

The lecturers monitored the online meetings and the information given by the students in Ilias. Finally, the projects were be presented to the companies end of June and the final feedback and grading was given to the students of Dortmund, St. Pölten and Krems.

After the final presentation students were interviewed to check what were the learnings, the main obstacles, the benefits and impressions they got during this project. In addition to this the organizing lecturers had a project wrap-up meeting to discuss the project.

Fig. 2. Picture of game

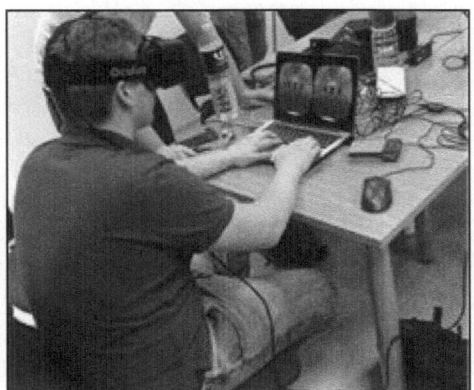

Fig. 3. Tester in game mode

4   Results, Lessons Learned and Next Steps

The student feedback on the course was in general very positive, with the in person meeting end of may being one of the highlights. The main points for criticism being the mostly unknow set of tools and communications difficulties. On the other hand most students perceived those communication problems (especially with students from other faculties) and overcoming them as an interesting and enriching learning experience.

In the wrap-up meeting of the lecturers the feedback was also in general very positive. The most positive aspect being the high quality results achieved by the teams, especially the huge progress for the communication within the teams during the in person meeting. Main point for criticism being here the unexpected high effort for coordinating the course, most of which was due to doing it for the first time. Also the influence of different teaching styles on the communication with student teams was underestimated. Students were communicating mainly with their local lecturer (as intended) and usually used email or the local e-Learning system and their native language. This resulted in slightly different understandings of assignments for the team, which caused some irritation for the students. To minimize such misunderstandings during the project (it was too late to totally change communication structures and habits) an unusually high amount of coordination between the lecturers was needed.

Besides a multitude of small findings the main lessons learned were more upfront planning, clear, centralized and public communication between lecturers and students, monitor and ensure team building and defined processes for escalation (like dropouts). Although the participating lecturers had experience with larger groups of students, distributed teams and teaching within a team of lecturers, this kind of course setup turned out to be very resisting to change during the course. Due to this such a course has to be **planned** in quite finely **detailed** granularity **before** the start, as adapting things during the course is either not possible or results in signifcantly higher coordination efforts. A **clear, centralized and public communication** between students and lecturers has to be established and rigidly applied. This includes a central repository, where students and lecturers can check old communications and which is open to all members of the course. To allow this accessibility it is absolutely crucial to keep this in the language of the course (usually english). As one of the main reasons for lower team productivity in the beginning was the difficult communication within the teams, some kind of **organized team building** activity is of high importance. When the teams change during the project, as in the chosen setup, it is highly recommend to establish a specific role within the students teams to take care of the (re-)building of the team. On the other hand if possible changes in the teams should be avoided in general to reduce the difficulty (and potential for frustration) for the students. Last but not least it should be decided beforehand how to deal with students who drop out of the project (due to whatever reasons). While it is not an unusual thing in academic teaching that students leave a chosen course during the semester, in team projects and even more if they have the additional challenge of being interdisciplinary, international and distributed, this behaviour creates a lot of problems for the respective team. Therefore at the beginning of the project there has to defined (and of course clearly communicated to the students) a **process how to escalate problems** if a team is not able to deal with them on its own.

The next step on a short term basis is to plan the course with the lessons learned in mind for the next spring/summer semester. This might also include dividing the participating universities and lecturers into different roles or groups to be more clear and efficient in coordination.

On a more strategic perspective the goal is to adapt the involved study programs in a way that similar formats are easier to implement and become a regular part of the curriculum, as they have proven to be good opportunity to combine teaching of specialized knowledge with soft skills and interdisciplinary competences.

References

1. Crawford, L., Pollack, J., England, D.: Uncovering the trends in project management: Journal emphases over the last 10 years. International Journal of Project Management (Elsevier Science, Netherlands) **24**(2), 175–184 (2006). ISSN 0263-7863
2. Craig, C., Piskur, B.: Students perspectives on the development and evaluation of a joint international education to promote employability in Europe. Work (IOS Press, Netherlands) **41**(4), 439–446 (2012). ISSN 1051-9815
3. Berente, N., et al.: Arguing the value of virtual worlds: patterns of discursive sensemaking of an innovative technology. MIS Quarterly (MIS Research Center, Minnesota) **35**(3), 685–709 (2011). ISSN 0276-7783
4. Kohler, T., Fueller, J., Matzler, J., Stieger, D.: Co-Creation in Virtual Worlds: The design of the user experience. MIS Quarterly (MIS Research Center, Minnesota) **35**(3), 773–788 (2011). ISSN 0276-7783
5. Ingason, T.H., Jónasson, H.I.: Contemporary knowledge and skill requirements in project management. Project Management Journals (Wiley) **40**(2), p59–69 (2009). ISSN 8756-9728
6. Ives, B., Junglas, I.: APC Forum: Business Implications of Virtual Worlds and Serious Gaming. MIS Quarterly Executive **7**(3), 151–156 (2008)
7. Hansen, S.: Exploring real-brand meanings and goods in virtual-world social interaction: enhance rewards, rarity and realism. Journal of marketing management (Routledge, UK) **29**(13/14), 1443–1461 (2013). ISSN 0267-257x
8. Mahin, L., Kruggel, T.: Facilitation and assessment of student learning in business communication. Business Commuication Quarterly (Association for business communication, Blacksburg USA) **69**(3), 323–327. ISSN 1080-5699
9. Aretz, H.J., Hansen, K.: Erfolgreiches Management von Diversity. Die multikulturelle Organisation als Strategie zur Verbesserung einer nachhaltigen Wettbewerbsfähigkeit. Zeitschrift für Personalforschung **17**(1), 9–36 (2003)
10. Narayanaswamy, R., Henry, R.M.: Effects of culture on control mechanisms in offshore outsourced IT projects. In: Moore, J.E., Yager, S.E. (eds.) Proceedings of the 2005 ACM SIGMIS CPR 2005, ACM SIGMIS CPR Conference on Computer Personnel Research, pp. 139–145. ACM Press, New York (2005)
11. Kohler, T., Matzler, K., Füller, J.: Avatar-Based Innovation: Using Virtual Worlds for Real-World Innovation. Technovation (Pergamon Press, UK) **29**(6/7), 395–407 (2009). ISSN 0166-4972

Social Aspects of SPI: Conflicts, Games, Gamification and Other Social Approaches

Process Improvement with Retrospective Gaming in Agile Software Development

Milos Jovanovic, Antoni-Lluís Mesquida$^{(\boxtimes)}$, and Antònia Mas

Department of Mathematics and Computer Science, University of the Balearic Islands,
Cra. De Valldemossa, Km 7.5, Palma de Mallorca, Spain
{milos.jovanovic,antoni.mesquida,antonia.mas}@uib.es

Abstract. Agile software development methods have changed nature of cooperation, collaboration and communication in software development. Retrospective is a regular part of Scrum framework and it is devoted to software process improvement. In this paper different games for improving agile software development processes are presented. These games can be applied during the retrospective meetings and they are grouped in five sections: data gathering, ongoing activities, timeline, and team cohesion and risk management.

Keywords: Agile · Software process improvement · Scrum · Retrospective · Games

1 Introduction

Agile methods came as a respond to traditional software development and project management, which are primarily focused on identifying and documenting numerous requests that project should fulfil at the sole beginning of the project [1]. Adaptability is the main characteristic that would describe the agile approach (also called lean, adaptive and extreme). It is the new approach differing from traditional methods where predictability would be the key word [2]. Agility is the ability to balance between flexibility and stability. Agile software development changes the nature of collaboration, coordination and communication [3].

First Agile principles were introduced in the 1930 in Automobile industry [4] but nowadays agile framework may be found in many other fields such as software development, project management, agile enterprises or service management. One of the key points was the publishing of the Agile Manifesto in the year 2001[5] which joints all the Agile practices in the market to the group of Agile methodologies [6].

In [7] a systematic review on agile software development summarizes the main agile development methods: crystal methodologies, DSDM, feature-driven development, lean software development, Scrum and eXtreme Programming (XP). Results from survey performed in 2011 by VersionOne [8] show that Scrum is the most used Agile method in more than 50% of surveyed participants. One quarter of surveyed users use custom or Scrum/XP hybrid which shows the importance and significant trends of hybrid methods.

© Springer International Publishing Switzerland 2015
R.V. O'Connor et al. (Eds.): EuroSPI 2015, CCIS 543, pp. 287–294, 2015.
DOI: 10.1007/978-3-319-24647-5_23

Use of Agile methods does not necessarily mean exclusion of traditional methods [9], and they can be used together. Hybrid approach means combining features of plan-driven and agile process designs [10]. Creating a hybrid methodology (mix of already existing methodology in the company with agile method) is a complex endeavour but often a necessity in current markets. Implementing Scrum or a hybrid method may not be an easy task. In highly changing business environments, initial requirements may be found inappropriate and obsolete [11][12] because requirements are changing after initiation of the project and not at only the beginning. Plan driven standards for project management (such as the PMBOK Guide, PRINCE2, IPMA, etc.) have certain limitations regarding change management, and other agile frameworks could be used instead. In [13] the authors discuss about difficulties in merging lightweight agile processes with existing standard industrial processes. Moreover, they present a potential problem of mature organisations regarding their rating of CMMI or ISO/IEC 15504 (SPICE) when incorporating agile processes. In [14] an example of unsuccessful transition of multi project environment from waterfall towards Scrum is presented. They conclude that transition and resources have to be planned properly in order to make a successful implementation.

Agile approach is not pure process following but more about effective communication and collaboration between team members and client [15]. Therefore, significant change in traditional methodologies can be noticed, and agile principles have been integrated in some way. For instance, in the latest (fifth) edition of the PMBOK Guide, Stakeholder knowledge area was added thus improving engagement of project stakeholders which definitely leads toward better collaboration between client and project team.

Communication and collaboration issues between the members of an agile team and also the engagement of the main stakeholders involved in the project can be assessed and improved during joint meetings. Scrum recommends performing these meetings with the main goal of improving both the software development and the project management processes followed by the team. There are lots of games such as: timeline driven by feelings or data, known issues problems and actions and 360 degree appreciation game, to be deployed during joint meetings to foster different features of a highly effective agile team.

In this paper different games for improving agile software development processes are presented. The selected games can be used by an agile team applying Scrum. Scrum has been taken as a reference in this work since it is the mostly used agile method and it reflects very well all the agile principles. The paper is structured as follows. The workflow of Scrum is addressed in section 2. Section 3 considers how software process improvement issues are treated in Scrum. Section 4 presents the selection of games that can be used in agile retrospective meetings to improve software process. Finally, Section 5 concludes the paper and opens discussion about the results obtained.

2   Agile Software Development with Scrum

The nature of agile is mostly defined by its set of core values, principles and practices. Agile is not a standardized process with clearly defined steps that should be pursued.

The agility definition highlighted the five fundamental agile *characteristics*: responsiveness, flexibility, speed, leanness, and learning. In the same way, agile *values* propose fundamental statements in agile development: individual and interactions over process and tools, working software over comprehensive documentation, responding to change over following plan, keeping the process agile and keeping the process cost effective [16]. Similarly, Agile strongly relies on 12 *principles* stated in Agile manifesto [5]. Agile practices provide concrete actions and a set of guidelines based on agile characteristics, values and principles. One of the most recognized and used practice in the world is Scrum. Elements of Scrum practice are next described.

2.1 Scrum Roles

Scrum framework defines only the roles that have to exist in a project setup, but in the organisation there will be many more organisational roles. When companies are using hybrid methods (custom mix of agile and traditional methods), standard role of the project manager is expected if we are observing medium and big enterprises. In this organisational setup it would be expected to have both project manager and standard Scrum roles.

In the Scrum framework following roles are defined: *product owner, Scrum master* and *development team.*

- *Product owner* (client) maintains and communicates to all other participants a clear vision of what the Scrum team is trying to achieve.
- *Scrum master* helps everyone involved to understand and acquire all the values, principles and practices in Scrum. Also, as a mediator and enabler Scrum master resolves issues and makes improvements in the process.
- *Development team* self-organizes and is typically composed of five to nine diverse and cross-functional members.

2.2 Scrum Activities and Artefacts

The Scrum process starts from the vision of the client (product owner) about the final product. This deliverable is broken down in smaller parts through activity called grooming, resulting in an artefact called *product backlog* (consisting of more Product Backlog Items - PBI). Each item in the product backlog is prioritised, respecting one of most important principles of agile to focus on activities making highest value. Grooming process of product backlog includes creating, refining, estimating and prioritizing activities. Size and duration of activities is directly connected to costs and usually relative size measure is used such as story points or ideal days.

Lifecycle of software development project is performed in iteration cycles of up to calendar month called *sprints*. Sprint is time boxed and no changes of resources or time frame is allowed during the sprint implementation. As a first activity in sprint, planning is conducted and PBI are divided in *sprint backlog* which is a set of tasks grouped in a manner of deliverable feature, to create upon successful execution. During one sprint, daily Scrum (also called daily stand up) meeting are held each day and they last up to 15 minutes. During daily Scrum meetings, team members have opportunity to update others about work done, choose some of the pending tasks and to identify problems but not to resolve them at this point of time.

Two additional inspect and adapt activities are performed during one sprint, usually at the end of the sprint. First one is *sprint review* where all the stakeholders are involved and focus of this activity is to inspect and adapt the product that is being built. The other one is *sprint retrospective* and focus of this activity is to inspect and adapt the process.

It would be important to mention that at the end of each sprint potentially shippable *product increment* should be delivered to product owner. This fact is one fundamental principle of agile development: to perform feedback through each sprint and add value through each iteration.

3   Software Process Improvement in Scrum

As mentioned in the previous section, sprint retrospective is an activity devoted to software process improvement and to inspect and adapt processes in the Scrum framework. Anything that affects how the team creates the product is to be discussed in the retrospective meeting. During the retrospective meeting the following topics should be assessed: what worked well, what did not work and innovative ideas that should be introduced or improved.

Sprint retrospective would involve Scrum master and development team. Product owner should be also present if needed and has gained trust from the development team. If that is not the case it should be resolved in near future since involvement, constant feedback and prioritisation is one of key agile principles.

In order to prepare an effective retrospective, the following points should be established before the beginning of a meeting:

- Focus: each sprint retrospective should have well defined focus.
- Exercises: once focus and participants are defined games that would help participants to engage, think, explore and think collectively should be chosen.
- Data collection: data should be gathered objectively and in time manner.
- Structure: retrospective meeting has to be structured in order to be effective. Day, time, venue and participant dynamics should be defined.

4   Games for Software Process Improvement in Scrum

In this section different groups of game exercises and other techniques for process improvement in agile framework are presented. The games that can be used in retrospective meetings gathered in Table 1 have been grouped according to the criteria of different authors [17, 18]. Rows of Table 1 shows names of the games, which are categorized in two parts, corresponding to games for retrospectives that examine and collect data: about previous events (*looking back*) and games to predict and gather data about potential problems and solutions (*looking ahead*).

Furthermore, columns show the focus (outcome) of the games. Five main outcomes of games, in looking back and ahead, have been identified: *data gathering*, *ongoing activities*, *timeline*, *team cohesion* and *risk management*. Some games enable more than one outcome and different games may be chosen for retrospective meeting depending on the aim of the current sprint.

Table 1. Retrospective games and their focus.

Activity type	Name of the game	Data gathering	Ongoing activities	Time-line	Team cohesion	Risk man-agement
Looking back	Peaks and valleys Timeline (Cliffs and valleys or emotional seismograph)			Emotions		
	Empathy snap (Big hotter moments)	Team			Ice breaker	
	Repeat/avoid	Practices				
	Speed car	Enablers / disablers				
	Hot air balloon	Enablers / disablers				
	Anchors and engine	Enablers / disablers				
	WWW: Worked well, kind of worked, did not work	Practices				
	KALM: Keep, add, more, less		Review, value			
	Open the box		Innovation, challenges			
	Following up on action items		Review			
	Known issues	Issues				
	Problems & actions	Problems / solutions				
	360 degrees appreciation				Moral, relations	
	Thumbs up and down, new ideas				Acknowledgment, innovation	

Table 1. (*Continued*)

Activity type	Name of the game	Data gathering	Ongoing activities	Time-line	Team cohesion	Risk man-agement
	Timeline driven by feelings			Feelings		
	Timeline driven by data			People, process, tools, other		
	PMI: plus, minus, interesting	Practices				
	FMEA	Failure				
	DAKI: drop, add, keep, remove	Practices				
	3L (or 4L)– liked, learned, lacked and (longed for)	Practices				
	Starfish (and small starfish)	Practices, value				
	CAPT	Anxiety and confidence				
	Lessons learned: planned vs. success	Lessons learned				
Looking ahead	Defining path to Nirvana				Team building	
	Pre-mortem activity					Planning and mitigation
	Speed car - Abys					Identification
	Hot air balloon - bad weather					Identification
	Risk brainstorming and mitigation					Planning
	Pre-mortem activity					Mitigation
	Letters to the future				Expecta-tions	
	RAID: risks, assump-tions, issues, depend-encies					Planning
	Hopes and concerns				Ice breaker	

Data gathering may be done with the aim of collecting different practices which are good or bad, and may identify how their value is perceived among the team members. Also, different enablers and disablers may be identified through the games of data acquisition. Finally, data about team feelings, issues, failures and lessons learned may be collected with different games. Assembling all the data is very important for process improvement, and the more often it is performed, it is less likely that some information will be lost due to the time elapsed from the occurrence of the events [18].

Ongoing activities primarily focus on review of current situation but can also impose process innovation and improvement during ongoing iterations.

Timeline games always have important events (milestones) on horizontal axis. Data in rows shows different information such as: team member emotions, feeling, tools and processes. Aim of these games is to interlink different parameters in some points of time and draw conclusions from identified dependencies.

Team cohesion games focus on different aspects of team building and motivation. Conclusions from these games may improve the following aspects of the team: ice braking, moral, relationship, team building, innovation and expectations.

Risk management games focus on future problems in practice, communication with client, among team members and general problems that could influence project results. These games help in risk identification, planning and mitigation.

5   Conclusions and Future Work

This paper presents a set of games to analyse, discuss and enhance both the software development and the project management processes and activities followed by an effective agile team. Keeping all the project stakeholders engaged and providing a space where they can discuss and, at the same time, have fun is fundamental to continuously improve the processes established.

It is wide accepted that one of the most important factors for a successful deployment, and also for the improvement of a process is to have the commitment of the people that should apply it. Agile methods let the development team members to decide which activities to perform that best fit to their particular needs. As each team is different, there is no single recipe for organising work and joint meetings. Moreover, it takes time to create bonds between colleagues. We truly believe that this time can be shortened by using some of the games we have collected in this work.

The games presented can be used in Scrum retrospectives on the one hand, to reflect and analyse the past and on the other hand, to imagine and prepare for the future.

Future work will consist in widening the set of games presented in this paper with specific games for other process improvement areas, such as communication and innovation.

Acknowledgments. This work has been partially supported by the Spanish Ministry of Science and Technology with ERDF funds under grant TIN2013-46928-C3-2-R.

References

1. Wiliams, L., Cockburn, A.: Agile Software Development: It's about Feedback and change. IEEE Comput. Soc. **36**, 39–43 (2003)
2. Špundak, M.: Mixed Agile/Traditional Project Management Methodology – Reality or Illusion? Procedia - Soc. Behav. Sci. **119**, 939–948 (2014)
3. Moe, N.B., Aurum, A., Dybå, T.: Challenges of shared decision-making: A multiple case study of agile software development. Inf. Softw. Technol. **54**, 853–865 (2012)
4. Von Rosing, M., von Scheel, J., Gill, A.Q.: Applying Agile Principles to BPM. Elsevier Inc. (2015)
5. Authors, group of: Agile manifesto. http://agilemanifesto.org/
6. Dingsoyr, T., Nerur, S., Balijepally, V., Moe, N.B.: A decade of agile methodologies: Towards explaining agile software development. J. Syst. Softw. **85**, 1213–1221 (2012)
7. Dybå, T., Dingsøyr, T.: Empirical studies of agile software development: A systematic review. Inf. Softw. Technol. **50**, 833–859 (2008)
8. VersionOne inc.: Survey on Agile methods (2011)
9. Fernandez, D.J., Fernandez, J.D.: Agile project management : Agilism versus traditional approaches. J. Comput. Inf. Syst. **49**, 10–17 (2008)
10. Sheffield, J., Lemétayer, J.: Factors associated with the software development agility of successful projects. Int. J. Proj. Manag. **31**, 459–472 (2013)
11. Highsmith, J.: Agile Software Development Ecosystem. Addison Wesley (2002)
12. Fernandez, D.J., Fernandez, J.D.: Agile project management : Agilism versus traditional approaches. J. Comput. Inf. Syst. **49**, 10–17 (2008)
13. Boehm, B., Turner, R.: Management Challenges to implementing agile processes in traditional software development organizations. IEEE Softw. **22**, 30–39 (2005)
14. Hajjdiab, H., Taleb, A.S., Ali, J.: An industrial case study for Scrum adoption. J. Softw. **7**, 237–242 (2012)
15. Špundak, M.: Mixed Agile/Traditional Project Management Methodology – Reality or Illusion? Procedia - Soc. Behav. Sci. **119**, 939–948 (2014)
16. Von Rosing, M., von Scheel, J., Gill, A.Q.: Applying Agile Principles to BPM. Elsevier Inc. (2015)
17. Caroli, P., Caetano, T.: Fun Retrospectives - Activities and ideas for making agile retrospectives more engaging. Leanpub (2015)
18. Esther, D., Larsen, D.: Agile retrospectives - Making Good Teams Great. The pragmatic bookshelf, Dallas (2007)

Relating ICT Competencies with Personality Types

Vincent Ribaud[✉] and Philippe Saliou

Lab-STICC, Université de Brest, Brest, France
{ribaud,psaliou}@univ-brest.fr

Abstract. ICT competency frameworks establish the definition of competences required and deployed by ICT professionals. Job profiles articulate competencies together with an organization needs, objectives and constraints. The evolution of the software industry impacts personality trends in the profession. This work-in-progress studies the relationship between competencies, profiles and personality types.

Keywords: Personality type · Competency framework

1   Introduction

Competency frameworks, such as the e-Competences Framework [1] provides a reference of competences as required and applied at the Information and Communication Technology (ICT) workplace. The application of the European e-Competence Framework is centered upon workplace competence articulation, profiling, assessment and measurement [2]. A person's inclination towards a specific way of acquiring information or making decisions influences their preference for certain tasks and jobs [3]. Because certain jobs require certain competences, we may think that personality types and traits of software engineers are related to engineers' competences and performance. Thus we define a first research question: How can we relate personality types with employees' competencies proficiency?

Competences are sufficiently comprehensive to represent complexity and to fit variable organization structures. Customization is generally performed through the definition of various job profiles reflecting organization needs and objectives. The European ICT Professional Profiles [4] was created to define a number of representative ICT Profiles covering, at their level of granularity, the full ICT Business process. The European ICT Profiles build a consistent bridge between existing competence and profile approaches because profiles are worded in terms of capabilities needed to successfully perform a role and related to the required e-competences. Our interest is focused on four major roles involved in the development of software products: project manager, system architect, system analyst and developer. Through the study of a small set of software engineers graduated 10 years ago, we aim to empirically verify that the set of e-competences related to a role is suitable to their job occupation.

In section 2, we overview the background and related work. In section 3, we present the selected job profiles and the sample set. In section 4, we discuss the questionnaire results, and then we conclude the paper.

© Springer International Publishing Switzerland 2015
R.V. O'Connor et al. (Eds.): EuroSPI 2015, CCIS 543, pp. 295–302, 2015.
DOI: 10.1007/978-3-319-24647-5_24

2   Background and Related Work

2.1   Background

The Myers-Briggs Type Indicator (MBTI) is based on Jung's theory that people are predisposed to different alternatives in their behavior. Jung's work introduced a sequence of four cognitive functions (thinking, feeling, sensation, and intuition), each having one of two orientations (extraversion or introversion). This leads to a typology of 8 personality types. Cook Briggs and her daughter Briggs Meyer added a fourth dimension related to the way people interact with the outside world (judging or perceiving).

A competency framework is intended to foster the development of skills, either by individuals or organizations. The European e-Competence Framework (www.ecompet ences.eu/) is a reference framework of 40 ICT competences that can be used and understood by ICT stakeholders [1]. A competence is *"a demonstrated ability to apply knowledge, skills and attitudes to achieving observable results* [2]." Competences can be aggregated, as required, to represent the essential content of a job role or profile. On the other hand, one single competence may be assigned to a number of different job profiles [2].

Job profiles contain many components describing the essential elements of a job and how it should be performed. Jobs profiles provide a bridge between enterprises and individuals, and establish the link between an organization processes and employees' competencies. A CEN Workshop Agreement (CWA) has been established to provide a set of European ICT Professional Profiles [4]. The profiles may be used for reference, or for the basis to develop further profile generations. Profiles are structured from six main ICT Profile families: Business Management, Technical Management, Design, Devolvement, Service & Operation, and Support.

2.2   Related Work

A lot of research has been performed to relate personality type with team performance, employee assignment or learning styles.

Bradley and Hebert [5] propose a model of the impact of the personality-type composition of a team on overall team performance. The model applies personality-type theory to the team-building process and then illustrates the importance of this theory by evaluating a case example of two software development teams.

Capretz [6] uses the MBTI to understand differences in learning styles and to develop teaching methods that cater for the various personality styles.

Gorla and Wah Lam [7] aims to find the relationship between personality composition of teams and the team performance in small IS teams.

Karn and Cowling [8] use the MBTI as a basis for studying how individuals interacted within the teams, and the effects of disruptive issues on the quality of work produced by the team.

Varona and al. [3] reviewed sixteen studies that explore various dimensions of human factors in software engineering. They conclude that the changes in the complexity of software processes and products have created new roles and demanded new skills for software engineers.

Alboaie, Vaida and Pojar [9] argue that agile software methodologies, psychology and spirituality elements, information technology developments offer possibilities to create dynamic and efficient groups.

Ylmaz, O'Connor and Clarke [10] analyzes the validity and reliability of a personality-profiling questionnaire particularly developed to assess personality types of software practitioners.

Farhangian and al. [11] investigate the effects that player personality can have on team performance in serious games.

We are not aware of research work relating competencies with MBTI types.

3   Competencies and Profiles

This section is intended to set up a small study for exploring research questions. Therefore this proposal needs to be validated through several studies.

3.1   Reference Models

e-Competence Framework
The European e-Competence Framework is based on a four-dimensional approach, based on competence areas (dimension 1) and competences (dimension 2). Dimension 3 provides level assignments that are appropriate to each competence. Dimension 4 provides short sample of knowledge and skills.

Dimension 1 is composed of 5 e-Competence areas that reflect the ICT Business process and its main sub-processes, from a broad perspective. Dimension 2 identifies and describes a set of key e-Competences for each area. We reduced the e-CF to the software development perspective because it is the scope of our study. Furthermore, descriptions in Dimension 2 provide general and comprehensive explanations of the reference e-Competences. These explanations are detailed in Dimension 3 through e-Competence proficiency level specifications. Dimension 4 is populated with samples of knowledge and skills related to e-Competences in dimension 2. They are provided to add value and context and are not intended to be exhaustive.

Proficiency Level
Proficiency can be defined as a level of being capable or proficient in a specific knowledge, skill domain expertise or competence and is related to job performance. Proficiency indicates a degree of mastery that allows an individual to function independently in her/his job. In the e-CF, proficiency levels are described along three facets [2]: *Autonomy* ranging between "Responding to instructions" and "Making personal choices"; *Context complexity* ranging between "Structured-Predictable situations" and "Unpredictable-Unstructured situations"; *Behavior* ranging between "Ability to apply" and "Ability to conceive".

European ICT Professional Profiles

Job profiles or roles *"provide a comprehensive description written and formal of a job* [4]". Job profiles establish the link between an organization processes and employees' competencies. As a response to the huge number of ICT profile frameworks and profile descriptions, the CEN Workshop Agreement "European ICT Profile" defines a number of representative ICT profiles covering the full ICT business. Each profile defines a mission statement, a list of required e-competences to carry the mission, a list of deliverables, a list of tasks and some Key Performance Indicators (KPI). There are four ICT profiles that are mobilized in a software development project. The associated e-competences with the required proficiency level are presented in Table 1.

Table 1. Software development profiles based on e-CF 3.0

ICT Profile Title	e-Competences 3.0	Level
Project Manager	A.4. Product / Service Planning	4
	E.2. Project and Portfolio Management	4
	E.3. Risk Management	4
	E.4. Relationship Management	3
	E.7 Business Change Management	3
System Architect	A.5. Architecture Design	4
	A.7. Technology Watching	4-5
	B.1. Design and Development	4-5
	B.2. System Integration	4
System Analyst	A.5. Architecture Design	3
	B.1. Design and Development	3-4
	E.5. Process Improvement	3-4
Developer	A.6. Application Design[1]	3
	B.1. Design and Development	2
	B.2. System Integration	2
	B.3. Testing	3
	B.5. Documentation Production	3
	C.4. Problem Management	

3.2   A Case Study

A Software Engineering Master Degree

The Master program called "Software Engineering by Immersion" provided software engineering learning by doing, with a long-term project as the foundation of all apprenticeships. Young engineers made up teams of 6; each team was led by one associate professor acting as project manager. The field of the study is to observe two teams graduated in 2006 and 2007 and led by one of the authors. We choose this sample set because graduates had completed a free MBTI test at Master studies time that was used to help to define teams' composition. Participants were aware of MBTI

---

[1]   This e-Competence is missing in the Developer profile definition and was added by authors.

usage and we asked their willingness to participate to this study. Participants completed their IT bachelor 10 years ago and this period of time seems suitable to see the job paths that they followed.

A questionnaire was send to the participants concerning her/his current occupation, how job profile related e-competences are mobilized with a self-assessment of the proficiency level. Participants were asked to run a free MBTI test to ensure that their personality type was accurate.

Participants' Personal Data
Table 2 and 3 present participants' information: gender, age, job profile, MBTI type.

Table 2. Information on Team 1 (graduated in 2004 and 2006)

ID	Gender	Age	Current occupation	MBTI Type
1A	Male	32	System Architect	ISTJ
1B	Male	41	System Analyst	ESFJ
1C	Female	33	Project Manager	INTP
1D	Male	34	Developer	INFP
1E	Male	33	System Analyst	ISTP
1F	Male	35	System Architect	INTJ

Table 3. Information on Team 2 (graduated in 2005 and 2007)

ID	Gender	Age	Current occupation	MBTI Type
2A	Male	32	Developer	ESTP
2B	Male	32	Developer	ISFJ
2C	Female	32	Project Manager	INFP
2D	Male	31	System Architect	ISTP
2E	Male	32	Project Manager	INFJ
2F	Female	31	System Analyst	ISFP

The sample set distribution is compatible with a study conducted by Lyons [12] that included 1229 computer professionals employed by 100 companies. In our set, 75% were men and 25% were women (vs. 83% and 17%); 75% were introverts (vs. 57.8%); 58.3% were sensors (vs. 63.8%). We have only 50% thinkers (vs. 85.4%) and 41.8% judgers (vs. 79.4%) but the study is 30-years old and our set is composed from Y generation individuals.

Participants' Questionnaire Results
We proposed to participants to assess if a general set of e-competences was useful for the jobs they occupied until now and also to assess if the dedicated set related to her/his current occupation. For each e-competence, participants selected a value ranging from Totally Useful, Largely Useful, Partially Useful, Not Useful. When a competence was considered as being Totally or Largely Useful, participants had to self-assess the proficiency level using the definition given in the e-CF document [1].

The general set comprises main e-competences related to the A. PLAN and B. BUILD areas. Software development is less concerned with the areas C. RUN and D. ENABLE. Only the Project Manager profile is concerned with the E. MANAGE area. The general set is made of: A.4 Product / Service Planning, A.5 Architecture Design, A.6 Application Design, A.7 Technology Trend Monitoring, B.1 Design and Development, B.2 System Integration. Dedicated sets are those given in Table 1.

Table 4. Competencies' proficiency.

ID	MBTI	Job	A.4	A.5	A.6	A.7	B.1	B.2	B.3	B.5	C.4	E.2	E.3	E.4	E.5	E.7
1A	ISTJ	Arc.	2-3	4	3	3	3	3	-	-	-	-	-	-	-	-
1B	ESFJ	Ana.	2	3	2	4	3	2	-	-	-	-	-	-	-	-
1C	INTP	Man.	4	3	2	-	3	2	3	3	3	3	2	3	-	3
1D	INFP	Dev.	-	3	3	3	3	3	3	3	3	-	-	-	-	-
1E	ISTP	Ana.	2	3	3	3	3	3	-	-	-	-	-	-	3	-
1F	INTJ	Arc.	2	3	2	3	3	2	-	-	-	-	-	-	-	-
2A	ESTP	Dev.	-	4	3	3	3	3	2	2	2	-	-	-	-	-
2B	ISFJ	Dev.	-	3	3	3	3	3	3	3	3	-	-	-	-	-
2C	INFP	Man.	3	3	2	-	2	2	3	3	2	3	2	3	-	4
2D	ISTP	Arc.	3	5	3	5	3	3	-	-	-	-	-	-	-	-
2E	INFJ	Man.	4	4	3	3	3	3	4	4	3	3	3	3	3	3
2F	ISFP	Ana.	2	3	3	-	2	2	-	-	-	-	-	-	-	-

4 Aggregation of Results

Table 5 presents a comparison between the average of the whole set with the average of subsets grouped on MBTI trends. Values that differs significantly are bolded.

Table 5. Proficiency self-assessment grouped by MBTI type

MBTI	Nb	A.4	A.5	A.6	A.7	B.1	B.2	B.3	B.5	C.4	E.2	E.3	E.4	E.5	E.7
Whole	12	2,67	3,42	2,67	3,44	2,83	2,58	2,73	2,64	2,55	3,00	2,33	3,00	3,00	3,33
E	3	**2,00**	3,33	2,67	3,50	2,67	2,33	**2,00**	**2,00**	**2,00**					
I	9	2,86	3,44	2,67	3,43	2,89	2,67	3,00	2,88	2,75	3,00	2,33	3,00	3,00	3,33
N	5	**3,25**	3,20	2,40	3,00	2,80	2,40	**3,25**	**3,25**	2,75	3,00	2,33	3,00	3,00	3,33
S	7	2,20	3,57	2,86	3,67	2,86	2,71	2,43	2,29	2,43				3,00	
T	6	2,60	3,67	2,67	3,60	3,00	2,67	2,60	2,40	2,60	3,00	2,00	3,00	3,00	3,00
F	6	2,75	3,17	2,67	3,25	2,67	2,50	2,83	2,83	2,50	3,00	2,50	3,00	3,00	3,50
J	5	2,50	3,40	2,60	3,40	3,00	2,60	3,00	2,75	2,75	3,00	3,00	3,00	3,00	3,00
P	7	2,80	3,43	2,71	3,50	2,71	2,57	2,57	2,57	2,43	3,00	2,00	3,00	3,00	3,50

Extraverts (E) have a proficiency self-assessment significantly lower than Introverts (I) for competences A.4 Product / service Planning, B.3. Testing, B.5. Documentation Production, C.4 Problem Management. A possible explanation is that these competences involve methodic and routinely tasks that Extraverts tend to avoid.

Intuitive individuals (N) have a proficiency self-assessment significantly higher than Sensing individuals (F) for competences A.4 Product / service Planning, B.3. Testing, B.5. Documentation Production. A possible explanation is that these competences also involve abstract, methodic and precise tasks that Intuitives like.

There are no significant differences neither between Thinkers (T) and Feelers (F) nor between Judgers(J) and Perceivers (P).

Since only few individuals were queried, it is difficult to discuss about classical MBTI grouping such as intuitive-thinkers (NT), intuitive-feelers (NF), sensing-thinkers (ST), and sensing-feelers (SF). We need a larger set to draw observations.

Table 6 presents a comparison between the average of the whole set with the average of subsets grouped on job profiles. Values that differs significantly are bolded.

Table 6. Proficiency self-assessment grouped by job profiles

Role	Nb	A.4	A.5	A.6	A.7	B.1	B.2	B.3	B.5	C.4	E.2	E.3	E.4	E.5	E.7
Whole	12	2,67	3,42	2,67	3,44	2,83	2,58	2,73	2,64	2,55	3,00	2,33	3,00	3,00	3,33
Man.	3	**3,67**	3,33	2,33	3,00	2,67	2,33	3,33	3,33	2,67	3,00	2,33	3,00	3,00	3,33
Ana.	3	2,00	3,00	2,67	3,50	2,67	2,33							3,00	
Arc.	3	2,33	**4,00**	2,67	**4,00**	3,00	2,67								
Dev.	3		3,33	3,00	3,00	3,00	3,00	2,67	2,67	2,67					

Recall that the general set comprises main e-competences related to the A. PLAN and B. BUILD areas. Managers are obviously more concerned with competence A.4 Product / Service Planning while Architects are more involved with competences A.5. Architecture Design and A.7. Technology Watching. There are no others significant differences.

5   Conclusion

We made the hypothesis that personality types and traits of software engineers are related to engineers' competences. For the first research question that tries to relate personality types with employees' competencies proficiency, we did not observe significant results apart those that are relatively obvious and predictable. Since the sample set is small, we may expect better observations from a larger set.

Regarding the second question related to the suitability of job profiles' definition, participants agreed on the required competencies whatever their MBTI types.

References

1. CEN. CWA 16234-1:2014. European e-Competence Framework 3.0- Part 1: A Common European Framework for ICT Professionals in All Industry Sectors. CEN, Bruxelles (2014)
2. CEN. CWA 16234-2:2014 - Part 2: User guidelines for the application of the European e-CF 3.0. CEN, Bruxelles (2014)

3. Varona, D., Capretz, L.F., Piñero, Y., Raza, A.: Evolution of software engineers' personality profile. ACM SIGSOFT Software Engineering Notes **37**(1), 1–5 (2012)
4. CEN. CWA 16458:2012. European ICT Professional Profiles. CEN, Bruxelles (2012)
5. Bradley, J.H., Hebert, F.J.: The effect of personality type on team performance. Journal of Management Development **16**(5), 337–353 (1997)
6. Capretz, L.F.: Implications of MBTI in software engineering education. ACM SIGCSE Bulletin **34**(4), 134–137 (2002)
7. Gorla, N., Lam, Y.W.: Who should work with whom?: building effective software project teams. Communications of the ACM **47**(6), 79–82 (2004)
8. Karn, J., Cowling, T.: A follow up study of the effect of personality on the performance of software engineering teams. In Proceedings of the 2006 ACM/IEEE International Symposium on Empirical Software Engineering, pp. 232–241 (2006)
9. Alboaie, L., Vaida, M.F., Pojar, D.: Alternative methodologies for automated grouping in education and research. In: Proceedings of the CUBE International Information Technology Conference, pp. 508–513 (2012)
10. Yilmaz, M., O'Connor, R.V., Clarke, P.: An exploration of individual personality types in software development. In: Barafort, B., O'Connor, R.V., Poth, A., Messnarz, R. (eds.) EuroSPI 2014. CCIS, vol. 425, pp. 111–122. Springer, Heidelberg (2014)
11. Farhangian, M., Purvis, M.K., Purvis, M., Savarimuthu, B.T.R.: Modelling the effects of personality and temperament in small teams. In: Balke, T., Dignum, F., van Riemsdijk, M., Chopra, A.K. (eds.) COIN 2013. LNCS, vol. 8386, pp. 25–41. Springer, Heidelberg (2014)
12. Lyons, M.L.: The DP psyche. Datamation **31**(16), 103–110 (1985)

Designing Games for Improving the Software Development Process

Mehmet Kosa[1](✉) and Murat Yilmaz[2]

[1] Middle East Technical University, Ankara, Turkey
mehmet.kosa@metu.edu.tr
[2] Çankaya University, Ankara, Turkey
myilmaz@cankaya.edu.tr

Abstract. With the proliferation of relevant technologies that enables interactive social engagements, games became a strong driving power for next generation social environments. One of the reason for this is that there is an engaging nature in both digital and non-digital games, which is also suitable for creating serious kind of interactions such as teaching, training, learning, etc. Recently, researchers have started developing games or game-like applications in particular domains such as education, management, medicine. Although there are loads of empirical studies about game-based learning in general, scholars from information systems, computer science and software engineering domains have only a few attempts to develop and use the specific properties of games in their context-dependent environments. This workshop paper takes a look at some of these efforts and discusses about the pros and cons of such approaches. It is also argued that using well-designed, validated and pertinent non-digital games could be beneficial for improving the software development process. In particular, such approaches can be transformed into useful tools for teaching information systems and software engineering undergraduate or post-graduate students the fundamentals of information systems and software engineering.

Keywords: Software development process · Games · Interactive approaches · Game-based learning · Game-based training

1 Introduction

The software process improvement (SPI) is a continuous effort to improve the software development process over a scheduled time-frame. The aim is to ensure that a software development organization can tailor, implement and maintain a software development process for managing the development activities to meet their planned goals on budget and time. The customized process should address organizational strengths, highlight organizational weaknesses, and ultimately an enabler to reflect the organizational culture.

However, unlike a mechanical or manufacturing process software development involves the element of creativity, which has a human and social side that makes

© Springer International Publishing Switzerland 2015
R.V. O'Connor et al. (Eds.): EuroSPI 2015, CCIS 543, pp. 303–310, 2015.
DOI: 10.1007/978-3-319-24647-5_25

it hard to preplan [1]. Therefore, several researchers suggest that software development is a social activity [2–4] where a software development process should consider the requirements of participants' interactions. In fact, a software process encompasses the participants who must work in an interactive and collaborative way. Such social engagements are also visible in several interactive approaches that are planned for software development. For example, agile methodologies are highly based on customer interactions and even accept them as a key factor to improve the software development process [5]. Cockburn [6] defines agile development as a group of tasks which may be performed similar to a cooperative game.

Games are a set of interactions based on the rules that constraint the way that participants behave. They create a self-sustaining culture, which are one of the oldest from of interactions that thrives with humans. However, defining games is somewhat elusive and lots of attempts have been made to form a basic definition. One of the well-known, widely accepted definitions comes from Salen and Zimmerman [7]: *A game is a system in which players engage in an artificial conflict, defined by rules, that results in a quantifiable outcome.*

A famous framework (MDA) towards understanding games is developed by Hunicke et al. [8], which consists of three facades that are Mechanics, Dynamics and Aesthetics. Mechanics are mainly the rules that govern the game worlds and the ingredients of game design, dynamics describe the run-time behaviors emerged according to players interaction with the mechanics and aesthetics is the emotions evoked in the player. Braithwaite and Schreiber [9] state that, there are various patterns comprises the core of the game that show up over and over again: *territorial acquisition* (controlling a piece of territory), *prediction* (guessing what will happen and be awarded if true), *spatial reasoning* (requiring spatial reasoning as in Tetris-like games), *survival* (protecting oneself till the end which is a secondary pattern in most of the games), *destruction* (wrecking everything on sight as the primary goal), *building* (developing resources, cities, civilizations), *collection* (gathering up resources, points, coins or matching patterns), *chasing or evading* (contact sport games or Pac-man-like games), *trading* (cooperation of players where they trade resources that each of them wins) or *race-to-the-end* (being the first to finish the line).

2   Background

When briefly having looked at the literature, there are studies that focus mainly on software engineering along with information systems education. For instance, an experimental study was carried out to teach software engineering processes [10]. A card game that simulates the software engineering process is developed for students to merge the disconnection between theory and practice. Players take the role of a project manager individually and try to deliver the project to the client in time with pre-specified budget and with quality work while competing with each other.

Connolly et al. [11] administered a study focusing on software engineering concepts, which puts the students in the project manager's, system analyst's, system designer's and team leader's shoes. Players work together in those roles to deliver the project in time with a limited budget like the previously mentioned study.

To teach risk management concepts and to enhance decision-making skills of individuals, Taran [12] conducted a card game on students. The idea of the project is to play the card game before providing any risk management concept so that they experience the situations first hand which is generally called problem-based learning. There are different cards which are project cards (projects to be completed), surprise cards (positive or negative external events), oops cards (project problems), risk cards and mitigation cards (what the potential risks are and how to avoid them).

Brown et al. [13] developed a game to simulate the software development cycle and to communicate concepts of uncertainty, risks, options and technical debt. In this study, a board game is developed for 2 to 4 players, where the core dynamic is race-to-the-end that the players compete with each other to come first in a track or path. The players try to get to the finish line first, however at the same time they need to get the most points among other players. There are shortcuts provided that seems to shorten the way to finish line but sacrificing points along the way. The aim of the game is to show that using shortcuts each and every time generally ends up getting limited points (which corresponds to the quality of work in real life project).

Hamey [14] developed a highly visual and interactive non-digital game to teach a particular subject: Secure Data Communication Protocol in computer networking domain. The game is said to be emphasizing the three key issues that are encountered in secure data communication protocol that are: Confidentiality, integrity and authentication. In the game, as some players tries to *securely communicate* with each other by writing messages on sheets of papers, putting them in required envelopes and paper clipping additional sheets that defines destination and source, other players tries to intrude and simulate well-known attacks such as man-in-the-middle attack or replay attack.

Connolly [15] carried out a study to develop a game-based environment that aims to teach the database analysis and design. In the digital game, instead of getting a written document, players interact with characters (clients) to get the requirements for a database project which is actually akin to real-world settings. There are also studies that are mostly focusing on teaching coding skills [16] where the students engage in coding duels, earning medals and competing in leaderboards. A study by Ye et al. [17] reported that a virtual environment is used to enhance communication and collaboration outside the class providing two multi-player online software engineering educational games and also using the system as an enabler of office hours where students meet with instructors. After playing the games and using the system, students were interviewed and ultimately pros and cons of the system were recorded. All in all, it was stated in the paper that the system helped improve students' learning. In addition, Claypool and Claypool [18] utilized video games for software engineering class projects. Their empirical study showed that the students that are participating in a game-centric project in software engineering classes show better performance and lower drop-out percentages.

Leemkuil et al. [22] developed a simulation game where the game is played by three players that each of them has the same role of a knowledge manager trying to improve the companys knowledge accumulation. Sharp and Hall [23] describes an open course for post graduate education for software professional. The novelty about the program is that, students join the system as an employee and take actions as the member of a company. Dantas et al. [24] propose a game, Incredible Manager, to provide experiential learning to project managers where the players are required to act as a software project manager and try to plan and control the software project with success.

Navarro and Hoek [25] developed SIMSE that is an educational, interactive and graphical computer game which aims to train students on software engineering processes. In this single player game, players take role of a project manager to complete a software engineering project. Martin [26] designed two simulation/games for teaching information systems development where one of them was a board game and the other one is the computerized version of the board game with some modifications. It has been reported that the digital version was a better one with the richness and possibilities it provides in terms of using a greater number of scenarios with greater level of detail.

Shifroni and Ginat [27] designed a non-digital game to teach the commination protocols where twelve grade high school players/students take role of protocol components. The game is played with five groups: Network Sender, Data-Link Sender, Physical Layer, Data-Link Sender and Network Receiver. The goal of the game is to process and transfer the plain message given by the instructor to the Network Sender Group all the way to the Network Receiver Group passing through the other groups. This way, students are able to experience the internal workings of protocols first hand, and all the problems and their solutions become clearer than if it would have been explained by traditional methods.

Other than the games developed for information systems and software engineering students, there are also attempts being made across many other disciplines that were mentioned in a review paper [19]. It was stated that the simulation games in engineering education could be used for improving students ability to transfer their academic knowledge to practical use. Civil engineering, electrical engineering, chemical engineering, mechanical engineering, industrial engineering, environmental engineering are some of the fields that these studies were carried out. As for the non-engineering domains, architecture, medical, physics and mathematics were also given as examples among others.

All of the selected studies on software engineering and information systems are summarized in Table 1.

Table 1. Summary of Educational Simulation Games and Educational Game Approaches in IT and Software Engineering Domains

Study	Subject/Area	Year	Type
3-D online virtual worlds for software engineering education [17]	Software Specification and Development Processes	2007	Digital
Software engineering education using game design [18]	Software Engineering Studio	2005	Digital
Software engineering educational gaming [16]	Software Engineering and Programming	2013	Digital
Database design education through online games [15]	Database Analysis and Design	2006	Digital
Improving decision-making skills [13]	Software Development Cycle	2010	Non-Digital
A game to teach secure networking protocols [14]	Security Protocols	2003	Non-Digital
Risk management in software engineering [12]	Risk Management	2007	Non-Digital
Game-based learning to software engineering [11]	Software Engineering Fundamentals	2007	Digital
Card game for software engineering education [10]	Software Development Process	2005	Non-Digital
Computer security education [20]	Computer Security Principles	2003	Digital
Software engineering training simulation [21]	Software Engineering	2000	Digital
Collaborative simulation game [22]	Knowledge Management	2003	Digital
Interactive software house simulation[23]	Software Engineering	2000	Digital
Software management simulation [24]	Software Project Management	2004	Digital
Software engineering simulation [25]	Software Development Process	2004	Digital
Information system education [29]	Software Specifications	2006	Digital
Information system education [26]	Information System Development	2000	Both
Simulation game for communication protocols [27]	Communication Protocols	1997	Non-Digital
A video game for cyber security training and awareness [28]	Cyber Security Training and Awareness	2007	Digital

3   Summary and Discussion

In this paper, we briefly summarize the games that are designed to improve some aspects of software development and education. Software engineering is a challenging endeavor which requires a good combination of theoretical and practical knowledge. In general, software practitioners have hard time to understand the software engineering issues that have no simple, well-known or correct solution. This requires lots of practices which should certainly in the field. Games are well-structured interactive environments that shall be defined by rules with several benefits for motivating the participants. Therefore, a non digital game-based environment can be turned into a powerful tool for teaching or even training software practitioners. However, as mentioned in the literature review, there are only a few attempts to address such issues.

Taken together, these studies suggest a visible advantage to design for games in improving the software development process. SPI can be envisioned as a engineering management approach that can benefit from a multidisciplinary perspective where games has already accommodated such a viewpoint. To this end, designing card games or board games as a class activity (even instead of a computerized version) for software engineering and management courses are vitally important. To improve the social aspects of software development, such activities can also be used as collaboration enhancer.

Tailoring a process for a software development organization has several challenges. The designer should be equipped with theoretical information and its practical implications with high level concepts and details about the target domain. It is also preferable if the subject that is intended to be taught requires communication among people such as software development processes or software management. Designing digital games can also be utilized as it can be found more convenient according to the topics being taught. Designing both the digital and the non-digital versions may be also beneficial and complementary to support all aspects.

While playing certain non-digital games in a classroom (or in a work environment), the teacher (or manager) is just like a game master to direct the game but not participating actively. Instead, students interact with each other and the game. Couple of play sessions may be held to see different strategies ad outcome to grasp the subject fully. After the play sessions, students draw their own conclusions about the subject and the teacher (manager) actually just provides support mechanisms and follows an instructional scaffolding attitude. These activities provide a participant engagement loop (i.e. the flow [30]), which helps player to learn and participate more frequently and ultimately a well-balanced game offers a enjoyable game play and create planned participant behavior.

Studies being published on simulation games for learning should provide the specifics and formal elements of the games developed for others to test if possible. If not, concepts, the exact subject that is being taught and how the game aims to do that should be stated clearly for readers to get the idea. While designing games for learning, domain experts, game designers and instructional designers should be incorporated in the process.

References

1. Conradi, R., Fuggetta, A.: Improving software process improvement. IEEE Software **19**, 92–99 (2002)
2. Dittrich, Y., Floyd, C., Klischewski, R.: Social thinking-software practice. The MIT Press (2002)
3. Acuna, S.T., Juristo, N., Moreno, A.M., Mon, A.: A Software Process Model Handbook for Incorporating People's Capabilities. Springer-Verlag (2005)
4. Yilmaz, M.: A software process engineering approach to understanding software productivity and team personality characteristics: an empirical investigation. PhD thesis, Dublin City University (2013)
5. Fowler, M., Highsmith, J.: The agile manifesto. Software Development Magazine **9**, 28–35 (2001)
6. Cockburn, A.: Agile software development: the cooperative game. Addison-Wesley (2007)
7. Salen, K., Zimmerman, E.: Rules of play: Game design fundamentals. MIT press (2003)
8. Hunicke, R., LeBlanc, M., Zubek, R.: Mda: a formal approach to game design and game research. In: Proceedings of the AAAI Workshop on Challenges in Game AI, vol. 4 (2004)
9. Brathwaite, B., Schreiber, I.: Challenges for game designers. Cengage Learning (2009)
10. Baker, A., Navarro, E.O., Van Der Hoek, A.: An experimental card game for teaching software engineering processes. Journal of Systems and Software **75**, 3–16 (2005)
11. Connolly, T.M., Stansfield, M., Hainey, T.: An application of games-based learning within software engineering. British Journal of Educational Technology **38**, 416–428 (2007)
12. Taran, G.: Using games in software engineering education to teach risk management. In: 20th Conference on Software Engineering Education & Training, CSEET 2007, pp. 211–220. IEEE (2007)
13. Brown, N., Nord, R., Ozkaya, I., Kruchten, P., Lim, E.: Hard choice: a game for balancing strategy for agility. In: Proceedings of the 2011 24th IEEE-CS Conference on Software Engineering Education and Training, CSEET 2011, Washington, DC, p. 553. IEEE Computer Society (2011)
14. Hamey, L.G.: Teaching secure communication protocols using a game representation. In: Proceedings of the fifth Australasian conference on Computing education-Volume 20, pp. 187–196. Australian Computer Society, Inc. (2003)
15. Connolly, T., Stansfield, M., McLellan, E.: Using an online games-based learning approach to teach database design concepts. The Electronic Journal of e-Learning **4**, 103–110 (2006)
16. Xie, T., Tillmann, N., De Halleux, J.: Educational software engineering: where software engineering, education, and gaming meet. In: Proceedings of the 3rd International Workshop on Games and Software Engineering: Engineering Computer Games to Enable Positive, Progressive Change, pp. 36–39. IEEE Press (2013)

17. Ye, E., Liu, C., Polack-Wahl, J., et al.: Enhancing software engineering education using teaching aids in 3-d online virtual worlds. In: 37th Annual Frontiers In Education Conference-Global Engineering: Knowledge Without Borders, Opportunities Without Passports, FIE 2007, pp. T1E–8. IEEE (2007)

18. Claypool, K., Claypool, M.: Teaching software engineering through game design. In: ACM SIGCSE Bulletin, vol. 37, pp. 123–127. ACM (2005)

19. Deshpande, A.A., Huang, S.H.: Simulation games in engineering education: A state-of-the-art review. Computer Applications in Engineering Education **19**, 399–410 (2011)

20. Irvine, C.E., Thompson, M.: Teaching objectives of a simulation game for computer security. Technical report, DTIC Document (2003)

21. Drappa, A., Ludewig, J.: Simulation in software engineering training. In: Proceedings of the 22nd international conference on Software engineering, pp. 199–208. ACM (2000)

22. Leemkuil, H., De Jong, T., De Hoog, R., Christoph, N.: Km quest: A collaborative internet-based simulation game. Simulation & Gaming **34**, 89–111 (2003)

23. Sharp, H., Hall, P.: An interactive multimedia software house simulation for postgraduate software engineers. In: Proceedings of the 22nd international conference on Software engineering, pp. 688–691. ACM (2000)

24. Dantas, A.R., de Oliveira Barros, M., Werner, C.M.L.: A simulation-based game for project management experiential learning. In: SEKE, vol. 19, p. 24 (2004)

25. Navarro, E.O., van der Hoek, A.: Simse: an interactive simulation game for software engineering education. In: CATE, pp. 12–17 (2004)

26. Martin, A.: The design and evolution of a simulation/game for teaching information systems development. Simulation & Gaming **31**, 445–463 (2000)

27. Shifroni, E., Ginat, D.: Simulation game for teaching communications protocols. ACM SIGCSE Bulletin **29**, 184–188 (1997)

28. Cone, B.D., Irvine, C.E., Thompson, M.F., Nguyen, T.D.: A video game for cyber security training and awareness. Computers & Security **26**, 63–72 (2007)

29. Awasthi, P.: The groupthink specification exercise. In: Inverardi, P., Jazayeri, M. (eds.) ICSE 2005. LNCS, vol. 4309, pp. 89–107. Springer, Heidelberg (2006)

30. Abuhamdeh, S., Csikszentmihalyi, M.: The importance of challenge for the enjoyment of intrinsically motivated, goal-directed activities. Personality and Social Psychology Bulletin **38**, 317–330 (2012)

Risk Management and Functional Safety Management

Controllability in ISO 26262 and Driver Model

Masao Ito[⊠]

Nil Software Corp., Tokyo, Japan
nil@nil.co.jp

Abstract. The standard, ISO 26262[1], aims for functional safety of automobile E/E systems, and it provides "a framework within which safety-related systems based on other technologies can be considered." We focus on the hazard analysis and risk assessment (clause seven) in the concept phase of ISO 26262 part3. Usually, the risk is calculated from the probability of exposure and severity of harm, but in this standard we also have to consider the controllability of the driver for avoiding the harm. First of all, we'll present the DESH-G (driver, environment, software, hardware and goal) model as a framework. Then we show the driver model in detail, and it gives us the capability of the driver. We calculate the task demand from the situation-scenario matrix (SSM). If the task demand exceeds the driver capability or is in the neighbourhood, we regard it as the hazardous situation. Easiness of avoiding a dangerous condition is the controllability. The way to judge the degree of controllability is proposed using the driver capability and the task demand. In the system, such as the advanced driver assistance system (ADAS)[2], the part of the driver's task is done by the system. It is harder to the design system to decide the behaviour at the border between computer and driver. Our idea is also effective in the development under such situations.

Keywords: Controllability · ISO 26262 · DESH-G · Driver model · Driver capability · Task demand · D-zone

1 Introduction

The ISO 26262 standard requires the ASIL (Automotive Safety Integrity Levels) is given to an item (i.e. an abstract system). We calculate it from the three elements: the probability of exposure (E), the severity of harm (S) and the controllability of a driver (C). In general, E and S are used in the calculation of risk of a system. The controllability is specific to the automobile. When we are in the high-risk state (and we called it D-zone, 5.4), it shows the probability that we can go back to a safe state.

But, it is hard to define the class of controllability. In [3], authors say that "It was more problematic to establish a reliable metric for the controllability parameter". In this paper, we propose the model including the driver and environment to calculate the controllability.

The key point is the model of a driver. We already have various methods to analyse the "machine", but it goes without saying that human is not a machine. We define a

© Springer International Publishing Switzerland 2015
R.V. O'Connor et al. (Eds.): EuroSPI 2015, CCIS 543, pp. 313–321, 2015.
DOI: 10.1007/978-3-319-24647-5_26

simple model of the driver who has several characteristics, and we will show how to use the model in defining a class of controllability.

In the next chapter, we introduce the DESH-G model to clarify the position of the driver in our analysis. In chapter three, we check the hazard analysis and risk assessment (HARA) process of ISO 26262 part 3 because it is the baseline on which our approach works. And, we briefly explain our approach for the hazard identification (chapter four) we've already introduced in [4]. In chapter five (it is the main topic in our paper), we show how to express the driver capability and the environment. We also give the idea of D-Zone and controllability. Finally, we conclude them in chapter six.

2   A DESH-G Model

We, first of all, introduce the DESH-G (driver, environment, software, hardware and goal) model as a framework to solve the general driving problem (Fig. 1).

The car includes two components, hardware (H) and software (S). The environment (E) has various categories such as, "road type", "road condition" and so on. We explain again in section 4.3. The driver recognizes various environmental attributes and controls the car.

We assume that the capability of the driver (D) consists of the skill and the state of the driver.

Here, we mean that the goal (G) is the driver's one. When we drive a car, we usually have a goal. For instance, "I have to go and pick up my daughter at the elementary school by my car". And a goal is divided into several activities (Fig. 1, tables on the right side). For example, going out the car from the garage is an activity. And more, an activity consists of several actions, like getting into a car, starting the engine, moving out slowly from the garage, etc. When we rethink the activity of "starting engine", we let out the clutch by step on the clutch pedal and rotate the engine key ... We take various complicated actions unconsciously. We call those lowest level work operations.

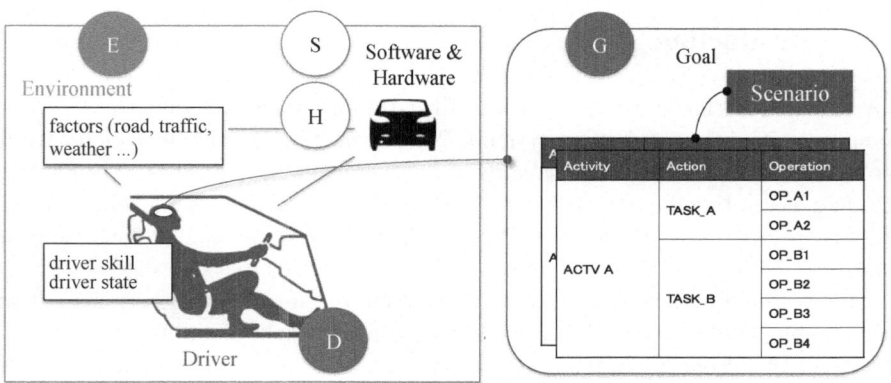

Fig. 1. DESH-G model

3   HARA Process

In the concept phase, we have to do the hazard analysis and risk assessment (HARA) based on the process showing in ISO 26262 standard. That process is in clause seven of part three:

(1)   Initiation of the hazard analysis and risk assessment (7.4.1)
(2)   Situation analysis and hazard identification (7.4.2)
(3)   Classification of hazardous events (7.4.3)
(4)   Determination of Automotive Safety Integrity Level (ASIL) and safety goals (7.4.4)
(5)   Verification (7.4.5)

As for (1) and (2) steps, we've already proposed a method in [4]. First we describe the *item sketch* and describe the goal model based on KAOS approach[5]. Using the guidewords of the hazard and operability studies (HAZOP studies)[6], we can find the hazards.

In this process, we use the situation-scenario matrix (SSM). This matrix expresses the environment around a car. We again explain this approach in the next chapter. We also use this matrix to calculate the controllability in the next step.

In the classification of hazardous events (3), we decide each class of the probability of exposure (E), the severity of harm (S) and controllability of driver (C).

We mainly focus on the controllability in this paper and we explain it in chapter five. As for E, we can calculate it, "based on traffic statistic for the target market of the vehicle"[1]. And we can estimate the severity from the factors such as type of collision, relative speed between collision participants, relative size, health and age of vehicle and so on [7]. The SSM gives the base information of those factors.

After defining the class of E/S/C, we get the ASIL value from the table 4 of ISO 26262 part 3. After that, we check the output of (1)-(4) mutually for verification purpose.

4   The Approach of Hazard Identification

4.1   Goal Model

We use the goal model of the KAOS approach [5]. It supports stepwise refinement of the goal[2]. KAOS is a method for requirement engineering. And in the concept phase of ISO 26262 we analyze and specify the (safety) requirement of an item. So, we can easily use the KAOS approach in this phase.

At the beginning of the concept phase, an item has just a goal of it. As the development proceeds, we refine the goal repeatedly into the sub-goals. Finally, we get a goal tree as a directed graph. In this process, we just make refinement for development, later we find the hazard as an "obstacle node" by using the item sketch (4.2) and guidewords (4.4).

---

[1] ISO 26262 part 10, 6.2.2, p.11.
[2] And this goal is of an item. Later we see the goal of the driver, but two objects are different.

4.2   Item Sketch

The standard requires us to make HARA in the concept phase of the system development. In this stage, the structure of a system does not fix yet. We can only have an abstract object of a system (i.e. an item, the term of ISO 26262).

As the standard does not mention the way of describing an item, in our approach we use the item sketch to express it. There are two forms of the item sketch: the dynamic and the static one.

As the goal is refined (4.1), the item sketch is also refined. The item sketch reinforces the description of the goal. We show a simple example. We have a description of a goal in the goal model; "a driver can switch on the adaptive cruise control system (ACC) [8]". In this case, the static version of the item sketch has an object "switch". And the dynamic item sketch has the two states "on" and "off" and the transition from the "off" state to the "on" state, and vice versa.

This item sketch is useful for us to find hazards in the later phase (4.4).

4.3   Situation-Scenario Matrix (SSM)

In this section, we briefly explain situation-scenario matrix (SSM) to define an environmental condition (Fig. 2).

When we think about the moving system such as the automobile, it is important to cover the environment in which it could move around. A situation consists of the combination of elements in the environment, and one can write different situations with different values in those elements.

The situation helps us to identify hazards and threats that a system might have.

Considering the ACC system, we can find the several categories in a situation; "subject car," "target car," "perimeter," "road type," "road condition," "regulation," "climate," "radio wave condition," and so on.

Furthermore, each category has several elements. For example, the category "subject car" has elements like "speed," "acceleration," "jerk," "engine state," etc.

When considering control of an embedded system, it is often modelled using only the controller and the control targets ("plants"). But we have to consider the environment, especially when analysing a moving object like the automobile.

Of course, we consider the influence of the environment. When designing the ACC system that keeps the distance with target car, we reflect a slope on a road and the friction drag that changes by weather condition. The SSM describe this effect from the environment explicitly.

The scenario is the collection of situations and it expresses the environment that changes as car moves. To achieve a goal of a driver, we can describe an SSM as a scenario that has detailed environmental information.

Attrib.	Road				Structure		Neighboring Car			meter (automobile)		Regulations			RW cond.
	situation category														
Time (HM:S)	Type*	State*	Lane#	Curve (m)	Light-ing	Guard Rail	Front Dist. (m)	Rear Dist. (m)	F	pedes trian	obsta cle	Signal	Speed Limit KMH	other	Reach able (m)
	situation attribute														
1010:00	RT_SB	GR(0), GG(0), MU(0.8)	2	-	Y	Y	30	20		0	0	G	M60	N/A	200
1012:00	↑	↑	↑	-	↑	↑	30	20		↑	0	↑	↑	↑	↑
...															
1030:00	RR_CL	GR(0), GG(0), MU(0.6)	1	-	N	N	150	200		0	0	-	M40	N/A	200

*: appendix   segment

Fig. 2. An example scenario of SSM

4.4   Hazard Identification

We can find the simple hazard by the unusual behaviour of elements described in the item sketch (4.2). It looks like the FMEA[9] approach except for the difficulty in defining the failure mode. The more complicated hazards will be found by manipulating the information on the item sketching (for example, multiplicity).

In this task, we also use the SSM (4.3), because to understand the situation of driving helps us to find the hazards.

The hazard becomes "obstacle" node in the goal model (4.1), and we add it to the goal model. Finally, we fill in all the hazards on a hazard list. We also write the possible measures to avoid the hazard (5.4). Those are "solution" nodes, and we also add them to the goal model.

5   Driver Model and Evasion from the Harm

The driver capability is defined from the driver model (5.2). The driver capability is the ability of a driver to operate a car. The task demand is the load to accomplish a task in a situation.

In Figure 3, we show the relationship between them. If a driver capability is lower than a task demand, the possibility to meet harm is high.

In this chapter, first we explain the structure of driver's goal (section 5.1 and chapter 2). Then we show our driver model (section 5.2). Next in 5.3, we will give the definition of our task demand, which is calculated using the SSM (4.3). And we define the D-zone and show the steps for calculating the controllability, which is the possibility of evading from D-zone.

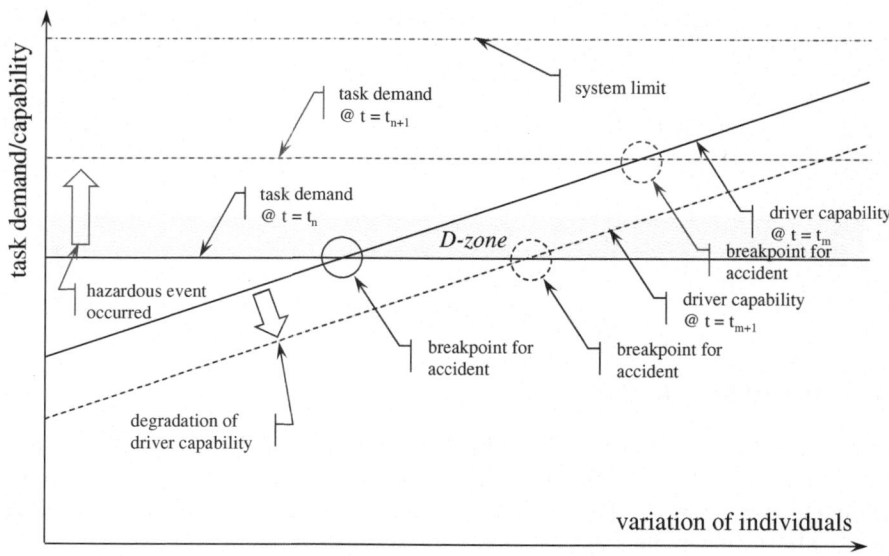

Fig. 3. Driver capability and task demand

5.1   Structure of Driver's Goal

First of all, we think about the structure of the driver's goal (it is not the goal of an item, which we already see in section 4.1). Usually, the driver has a goal for driving: for example, "we have to go and pick up our child at the school (goal_1)".

This goal is divided in the hierarchy manner like the activity theory[10] of the Human-Machine Interface (HMI) field: i.e. *activity*, *action* and *operation*. There are several hierarchical models. In [11], the author uses the three levels: i.e. strategic behaviour, tactical behaviour and operational behaviour.   These levels can correspond to our level respectively.

The activities are tasks to achieve a goal. In the goal_1 case, those are activities: "moving a car from garage to a front road (activity_1)", "driving a car on the arterial road (activity_2)" and "parking the car near the school (activity_3)".

An activity consists of several actions. For example, in the activity_1, we can identify these actions: "getting into the car (action_1)", "starting the engine (action_2)" and "slowly moving the car into the road (action_3)".

Moreover an action is divided into the operations: in case of the action_2, "footing down the clutch pedal (operation_1)", "checking the gear (operation_2)", "turning the engine key (operation_3)" and so on. Those operations are the unconscious task; usually the driver is not conscious of the details of the operation.

The difference between the action and operation is important, and this distinction is not static. If we repeat same task many times, it becomes operation. That means we do the detail steps unconsciously. Vice versa, if some trouble occurs, the operation becomes the action: aka the cognitive breakdown (e.g. [12, 13], "loss of situation awareness, critical performance decrements"[14]) . We will check the each operation carefully.

When we are forced to enter the D-Zone because of failure of a system, an operation changes to an activity. We will check each task with caution, so it takes longer time than normal operation.

5.2   Driver Model

We will define the *driver model*. It has two attributes: the driver state and the driver skill. The driver state also has two facets: the physical state and the psychological state. For example, if the driver is tired, his physical state is low. If she is depressed, her psychological state is low.

There are various factors that affect the driver's state. The goal of the driver (5.1) is one of them.   Going back to the goal_1 (the previous section), she might hurries if it is too late to go to the school. It affects her psychological state.

Driver skill is individually different, but it does not vary dynamically.

We define the performance of driver as driver capability, and we can formulate like this:

$$dc = h_{dc}(c_{state}, c_{skill}) \approx c_{state} \cdot c_{skill} - \varphi_{inattention} \tag{1}$$

The driver capability dc is calculated from the function h_{dc} with parameters; driver's state c_{state} and drivers experience c_{exp}. $\varphi_{inattention}$ shows the influence of the second task. It is not the primary task (i.e. driving) like tuning the radio or speaking other people with a mobile phone. It decreases the driver's capability for driving.

$$c_{state} = h_{state}(state_{physical}, state_{psychological}) \tag{2}$$

$$c_{skill} = h_{skill}(skill_{experience}, skill_{knowledge}) \tag{3}$$

The driver state c_{state} comes from driver's physical state $state_{physical}$ and psychological state $state_{sychological}$. The skill of driver c_{skill} defines by his experience $skill_{experience}$ and his knowledge $skill_{knowledge}$.

5.3   Task Demand

The *task demand* is the required efforts for the driver in a situation. Various situations surrounding a car need the different task demand. For example, if we drive on a rainy night, the value of task demand is high compared with taking a drive in the shiny daytime.

First, we calculate the task demand of the route segment. The road segment is the section where we can assume that the environment is almost same. On the highway, the road segment is long. In the city it is short. Total task demand is given as the summation of every route segments that are needed to achieve a goal (i.e. in case of goal_1, total means a path from home to school).

In SSM, each row in the matrix indicates a situation, and the situation consists of various components. As we've already seen in 4.3, those are road type, road condition, weather, traffic regulations like the speed limit, current self-car speed and so on.

If we can give the value of each component of a route segment, we can get the value of task demand.

We can formulate like this:

$$td \in TD = (st_1, st_2, st_3, ...) \tag{4}$$

The task demand td is a sum of task demands of each segment st_s.

$$st_s = \frac{\sum_{i=1}^{n} w_i s_i}{\sum_{i=1}^{n} w_i} - \phi_{GOAL} \tag{5}$$

The task demand of each segment st_s is calculated by the weighted average of each value of elements (e.g. road type, visibility and so on) in a situation. The weight w and value of the element s are given the real number from zero to one.

5.4   D-Zone and Steps for Classifying the Controllability

The D-Zone is the zone where we are in danger. And if we don't get the measures to cope with a hazard, the probability for us to become in harm is high.

Here, there are two ways to evade D-Zone. First is increasing the level of the driver's capability, especially the driver state. It is useful to send an alarm to the driver, whose attention is distracted or who could decide promptly. For example, if the driver is sleepy and he needs the long time to judge the situation, sending an alarm to the driver is effective. But this might not work well with a driver whose state is a normal condition.

Second is decreasing the task demand level. To this, we have to change the car behaviour, such as braking, turning a steering wheel and so on. The controllability is relating to the latter. ISO 26262 says that it "is assumed that the driver is in an appropriate condition to drive (e.g. he/she is not tired)". So, as for controllability, we have to decide whether the driver skill (5.2) can take measures in D-Zone.

We add the tasks to the HARA process:

- Decide the operation-level (5.1) measures to avoid harm, and add them to a hazard list (4.4).
- Select a situation and check it.   Do this repeatedly for every situation
  - ➤ Check whether a driver might be in D-Zone or not
  - ➤ Calculate the possibility to evade the D-Zone state for each measure in the hazard list
    - ✧ Possibility is defined from the viewpoint of driver's skill and current task demand
- Decide the class of controllability, the worst case is applied

6   Conclusion

We introduced the DESH-G model to support the functional safety in the automobile field. Also, we defined the driver model (D) and expressed the environment (E) by SSM.

The term "controllability" is the word that means "the ability to avoid a specified harm (1.56) or damage through the timely reactions of the persons involved". And it is very important because the controllability is essential to define the ASIL of an "item".

But it is hard to classify this value because it is relating to human, not machine. We believe that driver model and our proposed process is helpful to define the controllability.

Recently advanced automobile system checks the drivers' physiological features in real time and estimates the physical and psychological state to more appropriate personalized control for the driver (e.g. [15, 16]). The idea of driver model also can use the system design such an advanced driver assistance system (ADAS).

Reference

1. ISO, ISO 26262. Road vehicles - Functional safety, ISO (2011)
2. Thalen, J.P.: ADAS for the Car of the Future (2006)
3. Spanfelner, B., et al.: Challenges in applying the ISO 26262 for driver assistance systems, 5, vol. 15(16), p. 2012. Tagung Fahrerassistenz, München (2012)
4. Ito, M.: Finding threats with hazards in the concept phase of product development. In: Barafort, B., O'Connor, R.V., Poth, A., Messnarz, R. (eds.) EuroSPI 2014. CCIS, vol. 425, pp. 277–284. Springer, Heidelberg (2014)
5. Lamsweerde, A.v.: Requirements engineering : from system goals to UML models to software specifications, pp. xxix–682. John Wiley, Hoboken (2009). Chichester, England
6. CEI/IEC, Hazard and operability studies (HAZOP studies) - Application guide, CEI/IEC 61882:2001, IEC (2001)
7. SAE, J2980: Considerations for ISO 26262 ASIL Hazard Classification, SAE (2015)
8. SAEInternational, Adaptive Cruise Control (ACC) Operating Characteristics and User Interface (J2399), SAEInternational (2003)
9. Goddard, P.L.: Software FMEA techniques. In: Proceedings.of the Annual Reliability and Maintainability Symposium, 2000 (2000)
10. Nardi, B.A.: Context and consciousness: activity theory and human-computer interaction. Mit Press (1996)
11. Shinar, D.: Traffic safety and human behavior, vol. 5620. Elsevier (2007)
12. Reason, J.: The Contribution of Latent Human Failures to the Breakdown of Complex Systems **327**, 475–484 (1990)
13. Norman, D.A.: The design of everyday things: Revised and expanded edition. Basic books (2013)
14. Salvendy, G.: Handbook of human factors and ergonomics. John Wiley & Sons.(2012)
15. Heide, A., Henning, K.: The "cognitive car": A roadmap for research issues in the automotive sector. Annual Reviews in Control **30**(2), 197–203 (2006)
16. Li, L., et al.: Cognitive Cars: A New Frontier for ADAS Research. IEEE Transactions on Intelligent Transportation Systems **13**(1), 395–407 (2012)

KTM Functional Safety Environment – Break Silos, Ensure Full Traceability, Modularity and Automate Reporting

Matthieu Aubron(✉)

KTM AG, Mattighofen, Austria
matthieu.aubron@ktm.at

Abstract. This paper discusses how KTM AG company addresses ISO26262 functional safety challenges internally and with its partners. KTM has identified four key resolutions to success. 1st - breaking the silos between safety and other departments, 2nd - ensuring traceability between development items to cover the norms, 3rd - accessing the modularity and reusability organisation to make the most of legacy knowledge, 4th - automating the reporting to ensure engineers focus on design (not on document generation). KTM targets an environment embracing Model Based Engineering and a repository of crosswise (work fields) design items. With a strong fo-cus on system engineering, KTM's ambition is not to provide an ideal environment but to intro-duce one solving its current issues for its present maturity. The environment is implemented and operational on a major KTM project as a proof of concept for future KTM projects.

Keywords: Functional safety · ISO26262 · Model-based engineering · Model-based safety assessed · Sys-tem engineering · KTM

1   Introduction

According to a paper "Intelligence Transport System for Motorcycle Safety and Issues" [12]: *Intelligent Transport Systems (ITS) have significant potential to enhance traffic safety. [...] ITS appli-cations have been developed with car safety in mind, but the potential for developments for motorcycle is great. Very few ITS have been developed specially for motorcycles, and all of those that do exist are in-vehicle systems. Many ITS exist or are emerging for other classes of vehicle that have potential to enhance motorcycle safety directly or indirectly. There several ITS technologies in-vehicle system to be introduced and adapted to motorcycles; advanced driver assistance system, intelligent speed adaptation, driver monitoring system, collision warning and avoidance system, lane keeping and lane-change warning system, visibility enhancing system, seat belt/helmet reminder system.*

These safety systems have slightly increase the complexity of cars. With an acknowledged [3] exponential increase of complexity in the automotive over the last few years, the question is, according to KTM, not "WHETHER" but "WHEN" the breakthrough for motorbikes will occur in E/E embedded sys-tems complexity (If it has not already started).

© Springer International Publishing Switzerland 2015
R.V. O'Connor et al. (Eds.): EuroSPI 2015, CCIS 543, pp. 322–336, 2015.
DOI: 10.1007/978-3-319-24647-5_27

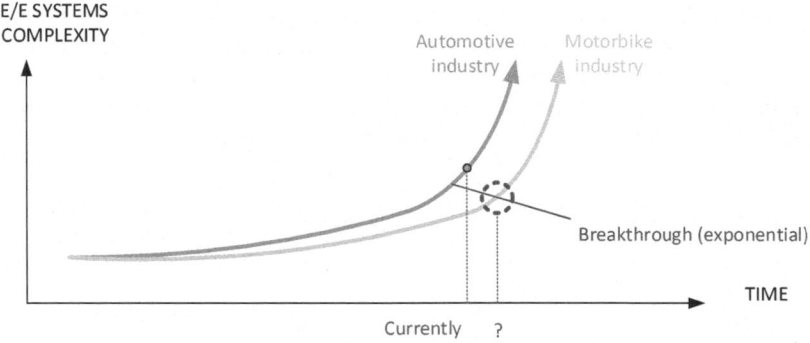

Fig. 1. EE Systems complexity - Automotive versus Motorbike industries (Source: KTM internal study)

This complexity is a challenge for the motorbike industry. The industry has to structure organization, knowledge and resources with the automotive state-of-the-art in mind. The KTM AG company, an Austrian manufacturer of high-quality and efficient motorbikes, acts as a leader and brings the best standards to its industry. To address the oncoming highly complexity challenge, KTM has selected a major internal project as the candidate for best practices implementation. This project is a completely new vehicle, with complex and safety-critical features. The project has been considered from a systemic point of view according to the state-of-the-art [1,2 with a focus on Electrical and Electronic systems. The size of the project remains relatively small (6 ECUs) compared to most modern cars (with up to 80 ECUs [3 but is currently among the most complex of the motorbike industry. The process & tools to be implemented in this project is referring to an internal KTM specification which aims at solving general issues. Among those specified problematic, we have prioritized five characteristics this environment shall handle:

1.1 Central Repository for Traceability, Workflows, Configuration and Change Management

We want a central repository of design to ensure full traceability[1] over the product lifecycle. We also want this repository to provide workflows, configuration and change management capacities to support all the lifecycle processes requested by Automotive SPICE [11] process reference model or similar.

Rationale: Our engineers and functional safety managers are losing too much time checking consistency between the different sources of information (usually hosted in different tools. This prevents from having traceability. Risk management requires

---

[1] Full traceability is understood here as a capability to trace any item required during the entire lifecycle of a product. Traceable items can be a design item (function, interface, etc.), a requirement, a failure or any project management items (milestone, actions, activity, etc.). This traceability feature, in combination with configuration and change management, tracks evolution of linked items and provides strong impact analysis capabilities.

traceability between risks, requirements and design. So we are in search for a repository covering most of development items and maximizing traceability. This repository shall be automatically updated when the de-sign changes in the environment (whatever the tool where the change occurs). Objective is to fully cover the ISO26262 (design, safety, production, project management items, etc.).

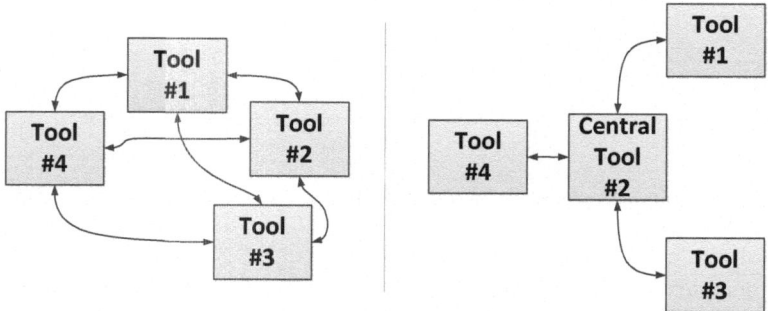

Fig. 2. From a dispatched environment (left side: "no master") to a centralized environment (right side: "one to rule them all")

1.2   Model Based Engineering

We want to introduce the Model Based System Engineering [5,6] and the safety analysis by the models in a fluent and integrated manner. The goal is to execute the safety analysis activity based on described and updated model by the architects (not based on more or less equivalent side architectures because of tools constraints).

__Rationale__: contribute to break silos in a manner which avoids unproductive and error prone processes due to multiple interface tools exchanging information. Safety teams are always running after the current baseline. Safety analysis and requirements shall be available for all and integrated in the architecture baseline.

1.3   Joint Activities Management

We want to cover the functional safety management scope in the same environment R&D and other departments operate in. This includes Model Based Engineering but also project management, specifications, planning, etc. As for Model Based Engineering, we want the stakeholders to share the same working content.

__Rationale:__ to break the silos between functional safety and R&D (and any other department).

1.4   Automatic Reporting

We want an automatic documentation generation to avoid errors and maximize productivity; the underlying content shall still be validated and reviewed; but the formatting and the generation of the document shall be executed automatically based on iterative patterned representation of structured data.

Rationale: *our engineers would focus more on their core objective (safety, design, etc.) instead of the formatting of documents or the consistency of its content. Another argument is that the ISO26262 required safety case is basically only a good report. What if the safety case was automatically generated out of a consistent database (notwithstanding the need for a review afterwards)? Expected automated documents are: Item definitions, Safety plan, V&V plans, Functional safety specifications, test reports and various project progress reports.*

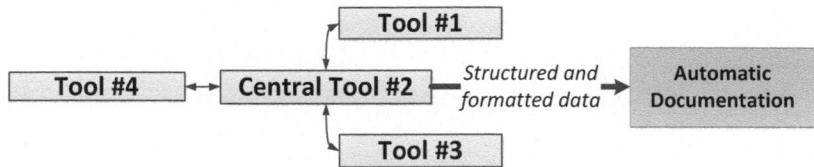

Fig. 3. Produce documentation based on a consistent and centralized content

1.5   Modularity and Reuse

We want to access the modularity knowledge and skills [6]. We want to populate our new projects with existing and validated items (functions, products, requirements, risks, etc.). We want to be able to "branch" design items (copy an item in another project and make it evolve independently from the original instance). We want to create platforms of products reusable on various bikes for modularity.

Rationale: *we do not reuse enough legacy developments which is the core knowledge of the company. Doing so could save significant time, money and risks.*

2   ISO26262 Coverage

KTM aims at getting the largest coverage possible for these identified artefacts and activities. The KTM environment keeps this objective as a requirement.

For a better readiness of what is covered by the KTM development process, every ISO26262 chapter and its coverage status are listed. Most of the system and concept phase is covered because, as an OEM, KTM does not have hardware / software developments. Though, KTM expects a low effort to ensure this environment complies with the hardware / software requirements (part 5 / 6 of the ISO26262).

Legend of the following table:

(1): support through documentation, storage and configuration management
(2): covered but not implemented because out of the OEM scope
(3): possible but to be further investigated and implemented
(4): not possible
N/A: Not Applicable - this is information or guidelines but not requirements

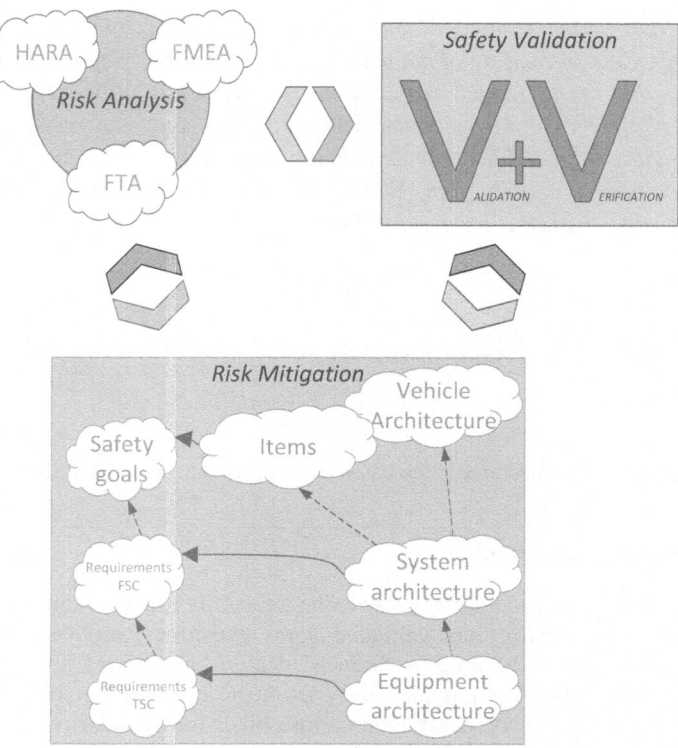

Fig. 4. KTM understanding of major ISO26262 artefacts and activities

Item	Description	Coverage
Part 1	**Vocabulary**	**N/A**
Part 2	**Management of functional safety**	
	Overall safety management	**Covered**
	Safety management during the concept phase and the product development	**Covered**
	Safety management after the item's release for production	**Covered**
Part 3	**Concept phase**	
	Item Definition	**Covered**
	Initiation of safety lifecycle	**Covered**
	Hazard analysis and risk assessment	**Covered**
	Functional safety concept	**Covered**
Part 4	**Product development at system level**	
	Initiation of product development at the system level	**Covered**
	Specification of the technical safety requirements	**Covered**
	System design	**Covered**
	Item integration and testing	**Support (1)**
	Safety validation	**Support (1)**
	Functional safety assessment	**Support (1)**
	Release for production	**Available (3)**

Item	Description	Coverage
Part 5	**Product development at hardware level**	
	Initiation of product development at hardware level	**Out of scope (2)**
	Specification of hardware safety requirements	**Out of scope (2)**
	Hardware design	**Available (3)**
	Evaluation of the hardware architectural metrics	**Available (3)**
	Evaluation of safety goal violations due to random hardware failures	**Out of scope (2)**
	Hardware integration and testing	**Available (3)**
Part 6	**Product development at software level**	
	Initiation of product development at software level	**Out of scope (2)**
	Specification of software safety requirements	**Out of scope (2)**
	Software architectural design	**Available (3)**
	Software unit design and implementation	**Available (3)**
	Software unit testing	**Available (3)**
	Software integration and testing	**Available (3)**
	Verification of software safety requirements	**Available (3)**
Part 7	**Production and operation**	
	Production	**Available (3)**
	Operation, service (maintenance and repair) and de-commissioning	**Available (3)**
Part 8	**Supporting processes**	
	Interfaces with distributed developments	**Available (3)**
	Specification and management of safety requirements	**Covered**
	Configuration Management	**Covered**
	Change Management	**Covered**
	Verification	**Covered**
	Documentation	**Covered**
	Confidence in the use of software tools	**Covered**
	Qualification of software components (possible but to be implemented)	**Available (3)**
	Qualification of hardware components (possible but to be implemented)	**Available (3)**
	Proven in use argument	**N/A**
Part 9	**Automotive Safety Integrity Level (ASIL)-oriented and safety-oriented analyses**	
	Criteria for coexistence of elements	**N/A**
	Analysis of dependent failures	**N/A**
	Safety analyses (FMEA / FTA)	**Covered**
Part 10	**Guideline on ISO26262**	**N/A**

3   Solution

3.1   Matlab Simulink(1) and Plugin Hip-Hops(2)

Description

Matlab Simulink is a wide simulation tool. According to the Matlab Simulink website: Simulink® is a block diagram environment for multidomain simulation and Model-Based De-sign. It supports simulation, automatic code generation, and continuous test and verification of embedded systems.

Simulink provides a graphical editor, customizable block libraries, and solvers for modeling and simu-lating dynamic systems. It is integrated with MATLAB®, enabling you to incorporate MATLAB algo-rithms into models and export simulation results to MATLAB for further analysis.

The HiP-HOPS tool is a Matlab Simulink plugin used to generate automatic FMEA and FTA based on the described architecture under the Matlab Simulink environment.

HiP-HOPS Important contributions of HiP-HOPS to the field of dependability so far include:

Novel algorithms for top-down semi-automatic allocation of safety requirements in the form of Safety Integrity Levels - this work automates some of the processes for ASIL allocation specified in the new automotive safety standard ISO26262.

Fast algorithms for bottom up dependability analysis via automatic synthesis of Fault Trees and Failure Models and Effects Analyses (FMEAs) where the basis of the analysis can be provided by architectural models that can be hierarchical described in a single perspective or in multiple per-spectives (e.g. HW and SW linked with allocations).

Linguistic concepts for representation and reuse of component failure patterns.

PANDORA - a new temporal logic that enables assessment of the effects of sequences of faults in Fault Tree Analysis (FTA).

A novel extension of dependability analyses with genetic algorithms that solves difficult multi-objective optimisation problems in the design of architecture and maintenance of safety critical systems.

Intended Use

KTM has used the Matlab Simulink as a physical simulator of some performance systems during the last years. After an internal trade-off decision was taken, considering the requirement to have a very integrated environment, that Matlab Simulink could fit our functional architecture needs as well. KTM has selected the HiP-HOPS plugin which can generate functional safety analysis work products based on models. KTM has consequently assumed that E/E systems could be entirely modeled under Matlab Simulink (physical, functional and safety). This is of great benefit to fulfill the requirements §1.2 - Model Based Engineering, §1.3 - Joint Activities Management, §1.4 - Automatic Reporting.

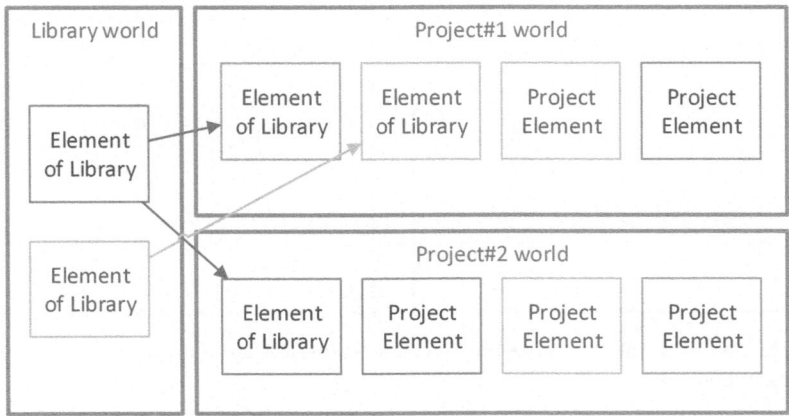

Fig. 5. Matlab Simulink data model architecture – library reuse

KTM has also considered the use of Matlab Simulink to investigate the architecture modularity topic, thus the requirement §1.5 - Modularity and Reuse. Simulink offers the use of libraries hosting reusable components. These components can embed different information such as safety.

The environment around Matlab Simulink has been set-up to fulfil requirements §1.2, §1.3, §1.4 and §1.5. The environment is made of two worlds. A world dedicated to the intended project and a library world for modularity. The project world intends to pick some modular components out of the library world. However, the project world can have its own component (non-reuse) or references to existing blocks in the library world (thus reused).

Both worlds are architected to represent physical and functional abstractions layers. The physical architecture is made of functional architecture elements (a product holds various functions). Physical elements can also be nested to create assemblies and represent abstractions (for example the ABS assembly is made of the ABS, ECU and various sensors like the pressure ones).

The functional architecture has 3 layers to represent various abstractions:

- the basic function layer – the basic function can be allocated to only one physical item– is com-posed of basic Matlab Simulink blocks,
- the vehicle function layer – a layer of abstraction to represent a set of functions which offer a vehi-cle function at rider level – it is composed of basic functions,
- the item layer – a layer to fulfill the ISO26262 and describes the border of the functional safety study - it is composed of basic functions or vehicle functions.

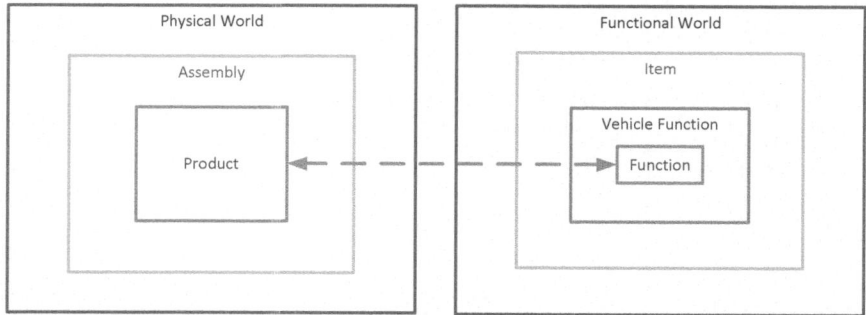

Fig. 6. Matlab Simulink data model architecture – Physical and functional worlds with arte-facts description

The developers can describe the system in terms of functions and behaviors, allo-cate the functions to the products, or describe the interfaces and expected perfor-mances. At the same time, the safety engineers can describe the safety behaviors of the system. As a consequence, we have a single content for various disciplines. We can reuse the blocks in order to take advantage of the existing knowledge and legacy projects. The prototyping at the beginning of projects is fastened and efficient. After the safety description of each safety related block under Matlab Simulink, we gener-ate a safety dependability analysis [8] with the HiP-HOPS plugin which automatically delivers a FMEA, a FTA and the minimal cut-set for each top vehicle hazard described.

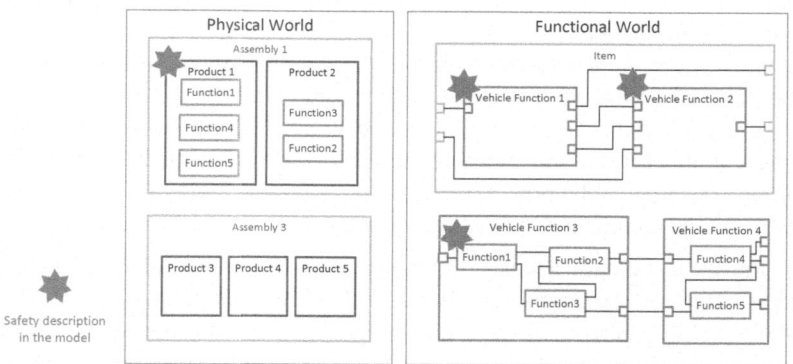

Fig. 7. Matlab Simulink data model architecture – Physical and functional worlds with arte-facts relationships and safety description

As an illustration, a top vehicle failure or hazard "Unintended Acceleration" is de-scribed under Matlab Simulink. The failed output of the system leading to the hazard (for example "Engine Torque" out of the block "Engine") is also described. Any po-tential failures of blocks/functions of the system are de-scribed with the logic of input and basic events occurrence leading to the output failure. Hence, HiP-HOPS will "follow" the flows of connections between the blocks, elucidate the potential link between the hazard and each event failure of the blocks and create a dependability analysis. At the end, the plugin offers the ability to easily identify which single failure (single point failure) or combination of failures (multiple point failures) in the system triggers the hazard. This information is of high value for the safety analysis and the ASIL allocation. Once we have this repository, with architecture, performances and safety description, we have a con-sistent and valuable content that can be transferred to Cognition Cockpit for further analysis, data management and documentation of the design.

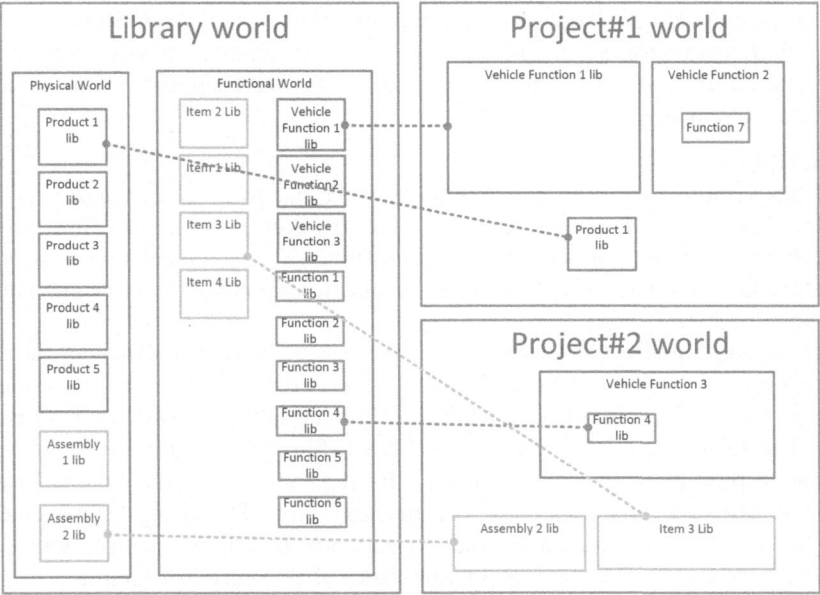

Fig. 8. Matlab Simulink data model architecture – Reuse illustration between library and projects worlds

3.2   Cognition Cockpit

Description

Cognition Cockpit is well-known as a requirement management tool, especially in medical device. According to KTM, this solution has much more to offer than this basic feature. It is also a repository with a unified data model which can host any KTM required items during a development: Requirements, Tests, Features, Products, Interfaces, Flows, Meetings, Actions, Change request, Stakeholders, Risks, Etc.

All these items can be traced, follow a defined lifecycle, be managed in configuration, be part of a change request, be documented, etc. Once configured, the tool can support the state of the art processes such as Automotive SPICE [11]. It also covers Design for Six Sigma triggering Matlab Simulink simulation to update the design values and propagate the change to the top [9].

The environment is open and very flexible. With existing features and some modifications, KTM has set up an ISO26262 environment. A connector with Matlab Simulink also offers the retrieval of any architecture items (blocks, flows, content, etc.). Choosing which Requirements Management Tool to invest time in is like surveying a house's foundation; it needs to perform well now, and be reliable and scalable later.

Cockpit's requirements management functionality is the most powerful in its class, providing the following: Infrastructure, Design Appeal, Reliability, Ease of Use, Configurability, Cost, Traceability, Speed, Integration with Design Workflows.

Cognition Cockpit is designed to help balance all of these critical elements within a single, unified architecture that keeps the product development process focused, efficient, and on-track to deliver the right product in the fastest possible time to market with total compliance.

Intended Use

KTM has identified this web-based solution as the one to fulfil the single repository of items feature, the 1st requirement of §1. The management of items is fully covered (traceability, configuration, change, documentation). The documentation is automatic and flexible. Therefore, KTM delivers documentation always consistent with the design.

The Matlab Simulink ⇔ Cognition cockpit connector allows retrieving the entire architecture (design & safety) in the repository. Each Matlab Simulink artefact is represented as a Cockpit object which has specific attributes, workflows and relationships. The relationships described under Matlab Simulink are retrieved likewise to Cockpit (a flow between two functions, a function allocation to a product, vehicle functions part of an item, a failure to a function, etc.). The change management is considered as well since each new synchronization with Matlab Simulink generates an impact analysis under Cockpit highlighting outdated elements for example.

Cockpit gives the opportunity to add attributes to the native artefacts. KTM has added a static ASIL objective to the Hazards/Failure Modes/Failures artefacts and dynamic ASIL attribute to Assembly, Product, Item, Vehicle Function, Function, Flow and Requirement artefacts. It is dynamic because it will compute the value of the ASIL based on the maximum ASIL found on its linked artefacts. Thus the allocation of the ASIL takes place at Failures level. The other artefacts like Function displays an ASIL value equal to the maximum ASIL found on its linked Requirements which itself has an ASIL value equal to the maximum ASIL found on its linked Failures. This way we have a propagation of ASIL allocation based on the single allocation done at Failures level. The allocation analysis is executed only once and the data model can automatically display the maximum ASIL located in an item whichever level it is, giving an idea of the criticality of the component.

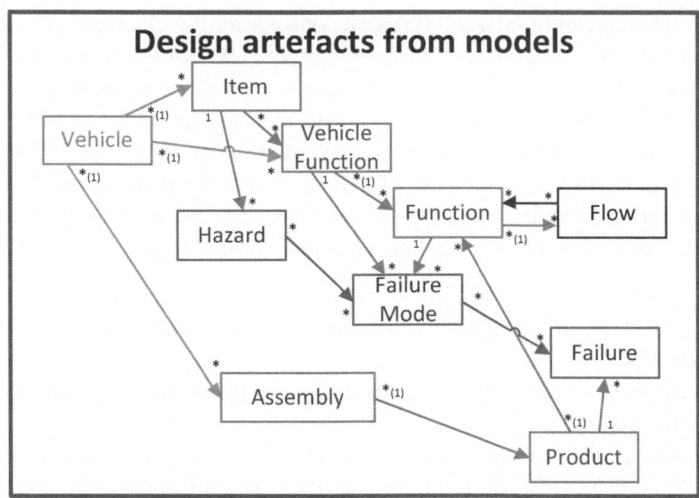

Fig. 9. Data model under Cockpit - Design artefacts

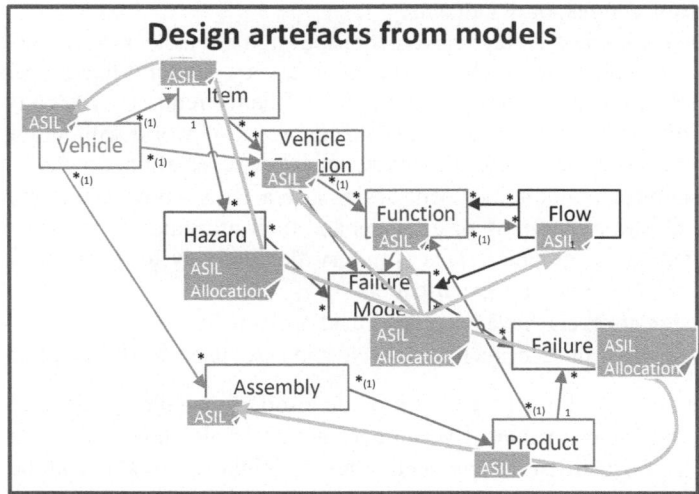

Fig. 10. Data model under Cockpit – ASIL propagation through design artefacts

The same is done for FIT rate allocation [9]. FIT rate allocation is considered by KTM as a complex activity on large systems since a function can be part of two or more hazards at the same time, it is very complex to find an optimum. Thanks to an Excel bi-directional connector provided with Cockpit, KTM exports the hazards FIT objective, the minimal cut-sets and initial function objectives out of Cockpit into an Excel template for FIT rate optimized allocation. Excel solver is launched and com-putes an optimal FIT rate allocation for each function considering the objective (to have a maximum overall FIT rate, to make sure we constraint the less our suppliers) and constraints (to remain under the hazards ISO26262 FIT rate objective for a given ASIL). Once the solver has been executed, the Excel file is saved and data are automatically retrieved to Cockpit. The value of FIT rate objectives is updated in the respective FIT rate requirements of each function. A new release of a product specifi-cation would then automatically contain FIT rate requirements in line with the overall hazard objective.

Besides the design artefacts, Cockpit provides various supporting artefacts for development:

- Processes, to describe a development process, a process is made of meetings and milestones,
- Milestones, describing the expected milestones for a given development (basically a date),
- Meetings, which have minutes and related actions, stakeholders (users), and discussed design artefacts (with the configuration at the date of the meeting),
- Actions which have a due date, related design artefacts, workflows and responsible persons (users),
- Users, which have rights and responsibilities over design artefacts, actions workflow actions, or documents,
- Change requests, which have actions, design artefacts or documents on which change is request-ed. A change request is a very powerful feature behaving as a parallel world. When an artefact en-ters a "change request", you can make modification and see the impact in the "change request" world without impacting the real repository. Thus you can see the impact an revert if unacceptable,
- Documents, which document design artefacts, is a powerful feature of Cockpit. It allows a map-ping of artefacts and their attributes to a visual representation (tabular or graphic). This is a very flexible way to document a design or create a V&V plan or a specification,
- Design artefacts, have been described previously,
- Lifecycle, can describe the lifecycle and associated workflow of any artefact.

All these artefacts, linked together provide a solid foundation to fulfil ISO26262 in an elegant and fluent manner. Every decision can be documented. Every change is traced and can be justified. Every meeting has its minutes available and the configuration of the discussed item at the time of the meeting can be traced. Documents and artefacts have a native configuration management and documents represent exactly the content of the repository.

KTM uses the Cockpit documents as the backbone for its safety activities. Thanks to the automatic documentation, KTM sets a consistent safety case with: Item definition, Functional safety specifications, Component specification, System architecture & design description (also called System Segmentation Description Document in the aerospace industry): V&V plan, V&V report, Safety analysis, Safety plan, Conclusion and Outlook.

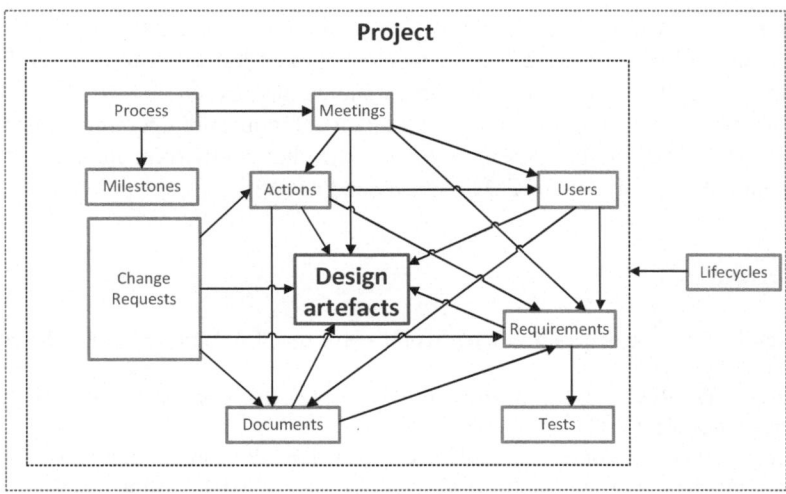

Fig. 11. Data model under Cockpit - Supporting artefacts in a Cockpit project

The process coverage of KTM environment is described below with the sharing between the "two worlds":

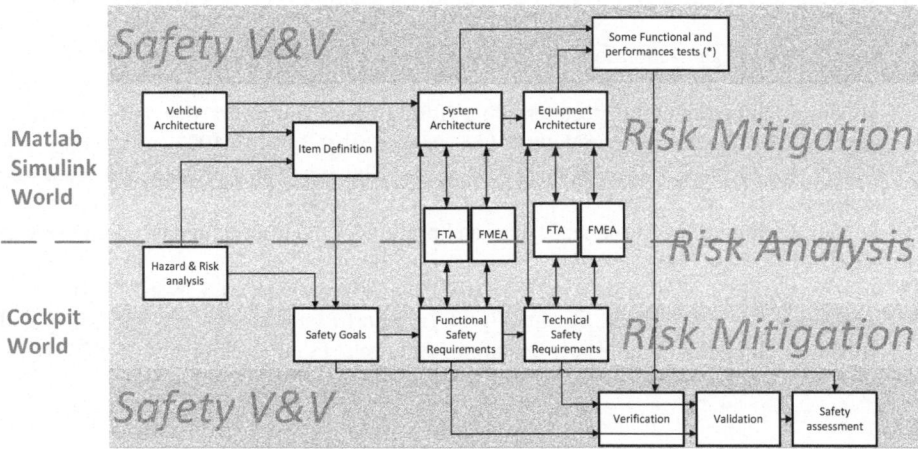

Fig. 12. Process coverage

KTM can already see benefits from this implementation. The reuse of various steps of the project like documentation template, Matlab Simulink libraries, abilities to copy a Cockpit project or "branch" it, etc. has shown evidence of productivity and quality improvement. The use of safety analysis dependability within a shared development model has also proven collaboration improvement and consistent documentation.

However, the use of the term "two worlds" still suggests segregation between two environments which, according to KTM experience, also raises useless error prone processes and remaining silos of data. KTM pursues its investigation to improve this environment and tries to make it even more integrated but the lack of flexible solutions embracing the whole process is remarkable on the market.

In the meantime, with the practical implementation and upcoming operational feedbacks, KTM will adjust the environment. The chosen environment is flexible and is open enough to evolve with KTM maturity and needs.

References

1. Leveson, N.G.: Engineering a Safer World - Systems Thinking Applied to Safety. N.p, Print (2011)
2. Luzeaux, D., Ruault, J.-R., Wippler, J.-L.: Complex Systems and Systems of Sys-tems Engineering. N.p (2011)
3. Ebert, C.,(Vector), Jones, C., (Software Productivity Research): Embedded Software: Facts, Fig-ures, and Future, IEEE Computer Science No.04 - April (vol.42), Figure 3 pp 45. N.p (2009)
4. Nicolescu G., Mosterman, P.J.: Model-based design for embedded systems: computational analysis, synthe-sis, and design of dynamic systems. Boca Raton, FL (2009)
5. Mahapatra, S., Ghidella, J., Vizinho-Coutry, A., (Mathworks): Enabling Modular Design Platforms for Complex Systems. Web (2013)
6. Baldwin, C.Y., Clark, K.B.: Modularity in the Design of Complex Engineering Systems. Web (2004)
7. International Organization for Standardization. ISO 26262 (2011)
8. Adachi, M., Papadopoulos Y., Sharvia, S., Parker, D., Tohdo, T.: An approach to optimi-zation of fault tolerant architectures using HiP-HOPS, Software Practice and Experience, pages, Wiley Interscience, ISSN: 0038-0644. Web (2010). DOI: 10.1002/spe.104436
9. Maass, E., McNair, P.D.: Applying Design for Six Sigma to Software and Hardware Systems. N.p, Print (2009)
10. Senge, P.: The Fifth Discipline: The art and practice of the learning organization: Second edition. N.p, Print (1990)
11. Automotive SIG. Automotive SPICE – Process Reference Model v4.5. Web (2010)
12. Ambak, K., Atiq, R., Ismail, R.: Intelligent Transport System for Motorcycle Safety and Issues - European Journal of Scientific Research ISSN 1450-216X Vol.28 No.4, pp.600-611 © Euro-Journals Publishing, Inc. (2009)

Author Index